SCOTT, FORESMAN AND COMPANY

EXPLORING MATHEMATICS®

AUTHORS

L. Carey Bolster
Coordinator of Mathematics
Baltimore County Public Schools
Towson, Maryland

Clem Boyer
Coordinator of Mathematics, K-12
District School Board of Seminole
County
Sanford, Florida

Thomas Butts
Associate Professor, Mathematics
Education
University of Texas at Dallas
Richardson, Texas

Mary Cavanagh
Math/Science Coordinator
Solana Beach School District
Solana Beach, California

Marea W. Channel
Mathematics Resource Teacher
Los Angeles Unified School District
Los Angeles, California

Warren D. Crown
Associate Professor of Mathematics
Education
Rutgers, The State University of
New Jersey
New Brunswick, New Jersey

Jan Fair
Mathematics Department
Allan Hancock College
Santa Maria, California

Robert Y. Hamada
District Elementary Mathematics
Specialist
Los Angeles Unified School District
Los Angeles, California

Margaret G. (Peggy) Kelly
Associate Professor
California State University, Fresno
Fresno, California

Miriam Leiva
Professor of Mathematics
University of North Carolina at
Charlotte
Charlotte, North Carolina

Mary Montgomery Lindquist
Callaway Professor of Mathematics
Education
Columbus College
Columbus, Georgia

William B. Nibbelink
Professor, Division of Early
Childhood and Elementary
Education
University of Iowa
Iowa City, Iowa

Linda Proudfit
University Professor of Mathematics
and Computer Education
Governors State University
University Park, Illinois

Cathy Rahlfs
Mathematics Coordinator
Humble Independent School District
Humble, Texas

Rosie Ramirez
Assistant Principal
Charles Rice Elementary School
Dallas, Texas

Jeanne F. Ramos
Mathematics Adviser
Los Angeles Unified School District
Los Angeles, California

Gail Robinette
Elementary Mathematics
Coordinator
Fresno Unified School District
Fresno, California

David Robitaille
Head, Department of Mathematics
and Science Education
University of British Columbia
Vancouver, British Columbia,
Canada

James E. Schultz
Associate Professor of Mathematics
The Ohio State University
Columbus, Ohio

Richard Shepardson
Professor, Division of Early
Childhood and Elementary
Education
University of Iowa
Iowa City, Iowa

Jane Swafford
Professor of Mathematics
Illinois State University
Normal, Illinois

Benny Tucker
Professor of Education; Chairman,
Education Department
Union University
Jackson, Tennessee

John Van de Walle
Associate Professor of Education
Virginia Commonwealth University
Richmond, Virginia

David E. Williams
Former Director of Mathematics
Education
School District of Philadelphia
Philadelphia, Pennsylvania

Robert J. Wisner
Professor of Mathematics
New Mexico State University
Las Cruces, New Mexico

Editorial Offices: Glenview, Illinois
Regional Offices: Sunnyvale, California • Tucker, Georgia
Glenview, Illinois • Oakland, New Jersey • Dallas, Texas

CONTRIBUTING AUTHOR

Janet K. Scheer
Director of Field Services
 for Mathematics
Scott, Foresman and Co.
Glenview, Illinois

CONSULTANTS

Reading
Robert A. Pavlik
Professor and Chairperson,
Reading/Language Arts
 Department
Cardinal Stritch College
Milwaukee, Wisconsin

At-Risk Students
Edgar G. Epps
Marshall Field
Professor of Urban Education
Department of Education
University of Chicago
Chicago, Illinois

**Limited-English-Proficient
Students**
Walter Secada
Department of Curriculum
 and Instruction
University of Wisconsin
Madison, Wisconsin

Mainstreaming
Roxie Smith
Associate Provost
Northwestern University
Evanston, Illinois

Gifted Students
Christine Kuehn Ebert
Assistant Professor of
 Education
University of South Carolina
Columbia, South Carolina

CRITIC READERS

Tony Barajas
Grace M. Nicholson School
Montgomery, Illinois

Jean (Bagley) Brennan
Johnson School
Nahant, Massachusetts

Jonathan Brinkerhoff
Shell Beach Elementary School
Pismo Beach, California

Mary P. Brown
Old Town Elementary School
Winston-Salem, North Carolina

Stanley H. Brown
Epiphany School
Coon Rapids, Minnesota

Bruce C. Burt
East Bradford Elementary
 School
West Chester, Pennsylvania

Howard Cohn
Lone Star Elementary School
Jacksonville, Florida

Rebecca Dinwiddie
Red Bluff Elementary School
Pasadena, Texas

Judith N. Fisher
Virginia Beach City Public
 Schools
Virginia Beach, Virginia

Esther M. Giacomuzzi
Public School #19
Albany, New York

Gladys N. Sanders
Lawrence Public Schools
Lawrence, Kansas

Carolyn R. Street
Merrill School
Beloit, Wisconsin

Alice Takata
Kalihi uka School
Honolulu, Hawaii

ACKNOWLEDGMENTS

Design
Cover and Special Features:
SHELDON COTLER + ASSOCIATES

Art Direction and Production/
 Core Lessons: Taurins Design
 Associates, Inc./NYC
Scott, Foresman Staff and
Rosa + Wesley Design
 Associates

Editorial Development
Scott, Foresman Staff and
 Falletta Associates

Photographs
Cover: Richard Chesnut, Fred
Schenk xi (tl): Mary Kate Denny,
PhotoEdit xi (br): Lawrence
Migdale xii (l) Grant Heilman xiv-
xv: Courtesy International
Business Machines Corporation
xvi(b): David R. Frazier xx(t):
Tony Freeman, PhotoEdit xx (b):
Richard Hutchings, InfoEdit 1 (l):
Stephen Frisch, Stock Boston
Scott, Foresman photographs by:
Richard Chestnut 2-3, 17,
36-37, 49, 59, 83, 102, 103,
118, 154, 188, 189, 252-253,
269, 292-293, 305, 322-323,
334, 335, 368, 388, 389, 407,
444, 457, 480, 481, 496-497,
508, 524-525; Arie deZanger
106-107, 155, 227, 352-353,
406, 464-465, 480, 481; Fred
Schenk 2-3, 16, 106-107,
140-141, 268, 335, 392-393;
unless otherwise acknowledged,
all photographs are the property
of Scott, Foresman and
Company. Clara Aich: 22, 26,
126, 129, 146, 147, 210, 215,
221, 294, 298, 320, 337, 364, 365,
367, 378, 486, 514 Animals
Animals: Robert Bearcy 4 Art
Resource: Tate Gallery, London
234 Woodfin Camp &
Associates, Inc.: 66-67; Dan
Budnik 176-177 Culver Pictures,
Inc.: 18, 84, 100 Duomo: David
Madison 176-177 Ellis Wildlife
Collection: Gerry Ellis 66-67
FPG: Jeffry W. Myers 428-429
Judy Gurovitz: 38 Richard
Hutchings: 34, 38, 88, 112, 116,
130, 131, 156, 157, 178, 179,
180, 190, 262, 270, 296, 310,
350, 394, 402, 414, 417,
430,432, 433, 438, 440, 455,
462, 468, 469, 472, 500 The
Image Bank: Wilfried Bauer 325;
Luis Castaneda 464-465;
Michael Melford 174; Hans
Neleman 464-465; Max Scheler
241 Ron Morecraft: 142, 200,
442, 450, 451, 454, 455 Photo
Researchers, Inc.: Van Bucher
44; Carl Frank 46; Carleton Ray
260 Photo Search Inc.: 68;
NASA, 69 Stock Boston: James
Blank 306, 374; Bob Daemmrich 186

(Continued on page 567)

Contents

Chapter 3 Addition and Subtraction

Chapter 4 Time and Measurement

Chapter 5   Multiplication Facts

Chapter 6   Division Facts

Chapter 7 Geometry

Chapter 8 Multiplication Computation

Chapter 9 — Division: One-Digit Divisors

Chapter 10 — Geometry and Measurement

Chapter 11 Fraction Concepts

Chapter 12 Decimals

Chapter 13 — Statistics, Graphing, and Probability

Chapter 14 — Exploring Addition and Subtraction of Fractions

Chapter 15 Division: Two-Digit Divisors

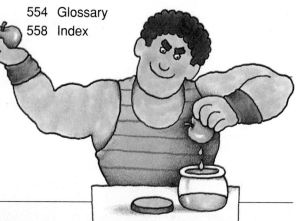

WELCOME TO
EXPLORING
MATHEMATICS

Mathematics is valuable and interesting. The next ten pages describe some of the ways your book will help you explore and discover more of the wonders of mathematics.

Your book will help you build your

Math Power

Build your math power by doing
Problem Solving and Critical Thinking

You will use math to solve problems all your life. When you solve problems in your book, you will do more than find answers. You will learn how to think mathematically.

In Chapter 1, tell the page numbers where you first find these.

1 "Problem-Solving Guide"
  • Understand
  • Plan and Solve
  • Look Back

2 "Tips for Problem Solvers"

3 An exercise called "Critical Thinking"

*Build your math power
by looking for*
Connections

Your book will help you explore connections. You will see connections between math and the real world.

Tell the page numbers where you first find these headings.

4 Social Studies Connection in Chapter 2.

5 Career Connection in Chapter 3.

6 Health Connection in Chapter 15.

7 Consumer Connection in Chapter 3.

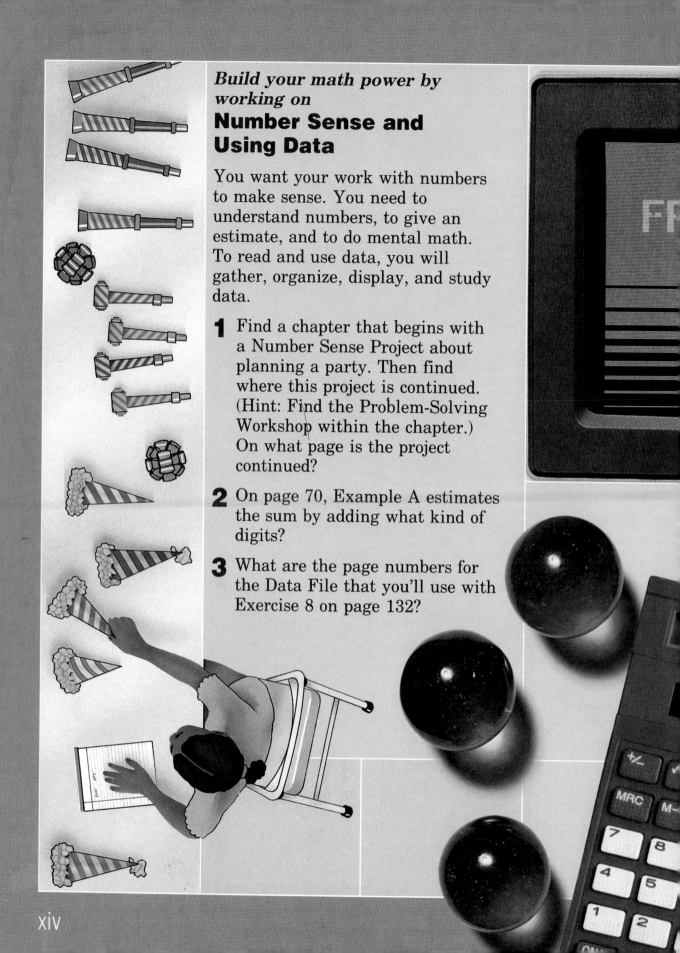

Build your math power by working on

Number Sense and Using Data

You want your work with numbers to make sense. You need to understand numbers, to give an estimate, and to do mental math. To read and use data, you will gather, organize, display, and study data.

1 Find a chapter that begins with a Number Sense Project about planning a party. Then find where this project is continued. (Hint: Find the Problem-Solving Workshop within the chapter.) On what page is the project continued?

2 On page 70, Example A estimates the sum by adding what kind of digits?

3 What are the page numbers for the Data File that you'll use with Exercise 8 on page 132?

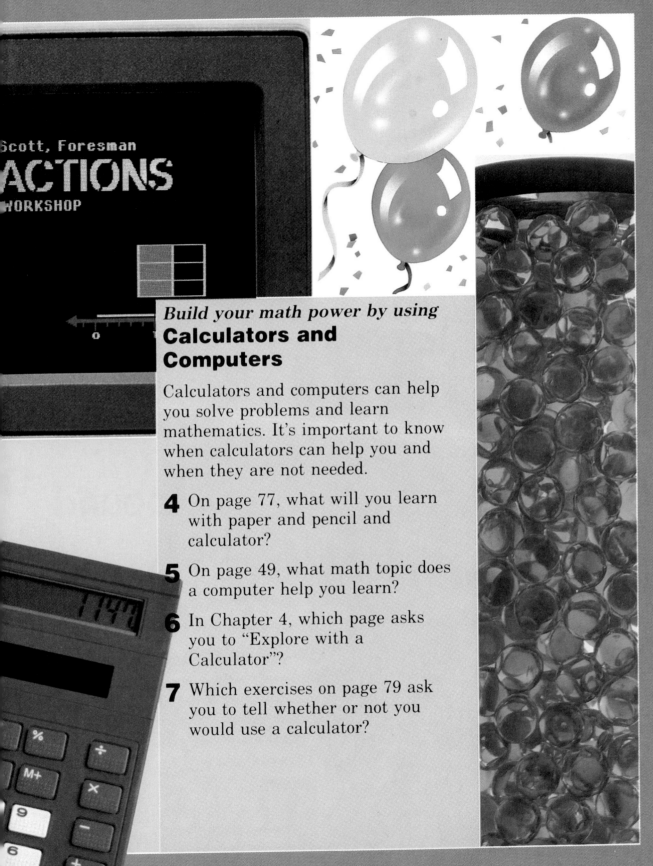

Build your math power by using
Calculators and Computers

Calculators and computers can help
you solve problems and learn
mathematics. It's important to know
when calculators can help you and
when they are not needed.

4 On page 77, what will you learn
with paper and pencil and
calculator?

5 On page 49, what math topic does
a computer help you learn?

6 In Chapter 4, which page asks
you to "Explore with a
Calculator"?

7 Which exercises on page 79 ask
you to tell whether or not you
would use a calculator?

Use your book to help you

Do Your Best

To do your best,
Expect to Succeed

When you want to learn something, it helps to believe in yourself. You will learn a sport, a musical instrument, or mathematics better with a positive attitude.

perimeter
pound
fraction

To do your best,
Build Your Understanding

When you understand what you're doing, you do it better and remember it longer. So it pays to study the "Build Understanding" part of the lessons.

1 On page 216, why is it easy to see what new math words are being taught?

To do your best, learn ways to do
Independent Study

You can learn how to study math even when a teacher is not there to help.

2 On page 4, look to the right of the words "Check Understanding." Where can you find another example for that lesson?

3 On page 5, look to the right of the word "Practice." On what pages can you find more practice for that lesson?

4 There is an Independent Study Handbook in the back of your book. On what page does the "Math Study Skills" section begin?

5 Name the first and last words defined in the glossary on page 555.

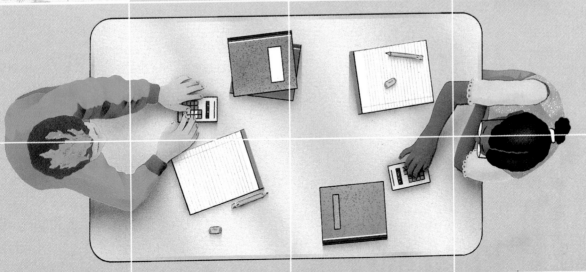

Your book will help you through
Active Learning

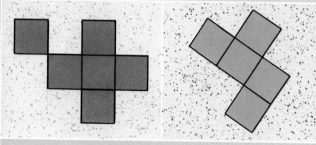

You'll learn math by doing
Math Activities

Activities help you understand math. Some activities use materials that help you show numbers, measure objects, do experiments, explore shapes, or solve problems.

1 What materials are used in the activity on page 40?

2 Use your "Math Sketcher" or a round object to draw a picture that shows four equal parts of a circle.

Doing math includes
Reading, Writing, Talking, Listening

Reading, writing, talking, and listening in math class will help you think mathematically.

3 In Chapter 1, tell the page number where these first occur.

"Talk About Math"

"Write About Math"

"Reading Math"

A good way to learn is by **Working in Groups**

In real life and in math class, people can often solve problems better by working together.

4 How many students should work together to do the "Exploring Thousands" activity on page 40?

5 In the "Explore As a Team" on page 118, what is the "Tip for Working Together"?

To have a math adventure, catch the spirit of **Exploration**

Be a Math Explorer and discover new things. Look for patterns. Check out your hunches, and try different ways to solve problems.

6 On what page in Chapter 3 do you explore using patterns to add and subtract mentally?

7 In "Explore Math" on page 129, what are you asked to do in problem 22?

A key ingredient to learning math is

Enjoying Math

Your book will help you
Enjoy Math at School

The explorations in your book will help you discover and enjoy mathematics.

1 In Chapter 1, on what page are you asked to explore patterns?

2 Draw a pattern with figures. Ask another student to draw 3 more figures to continue your pattern.

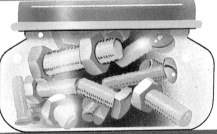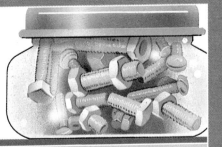

To make math a part of your life

Enjoy Math at Home

Outside of school, share math ideas with others and continue to explore math your whole life.

3 In the Math-at-Home activity on page 227, what size card will you use?

4 Play this estimation game with someone at home. Find a container of items such as paper clips, bandages, teabags, or nails. Guess how many are in the container. The player with the closest estimate scores 1 point. Repeat this with 2 other groups of items. The player with the most points wins.

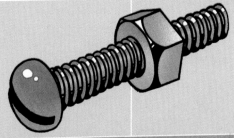

1

Basic Facts and Number Concepts

1

Did You Know:
One survey found that keeping a pet increases the work load at home by 8 hours per week.

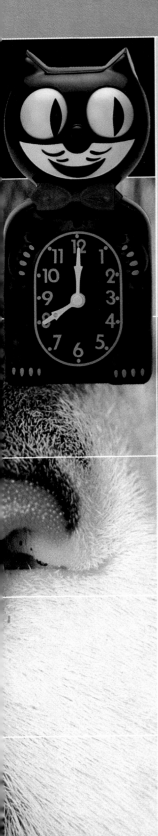

Number-Sense Project

Estimate
Estimate how many hours a week a family spends taking care of a cat as a household pet.

Gather Data
Interview someone who has a cat and also spends time cleaning the house. Have the person estimate how much extra time they spend because of the cat.

Analyze and Report
Make a chart showing the different types of activities involved. Share your findings with other students.

Using Numbers

Build Understanding

Cindy Shum is a photographer. As her entry in a photo contest shows, numbers are used in many ways.

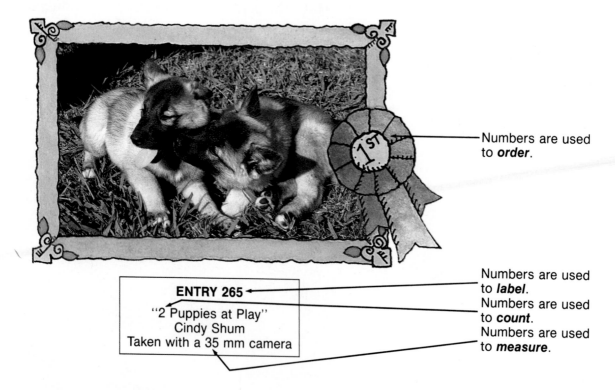

Numbers are used to **order**.

ENTRY 265

"2 Puppies at Play"
Cindy Shum
Taken with a 35 mm camera

Numbers are used to **label**.
Numbers are used to **count**.
Numbers are used to **measure**.

■ **Talk About Math** This photo was taken in 1989. Dates such as 1989 are used to show the order of years. Do you think they might also be said to label or to measure? Why?

Check Understanding

For another example, see Set A, pages 30–31.

Cindy took 24 pictures with her Polar 4 camera. She had the 6th negative developed into an 8-inch square photo. In the above sentences, which number is used

1. to count?   **2.** to label?   **3.** to measure?   **4.** to order?

For each picture, tell if the number is used to count, to measure, to order, or to label.

5.

6.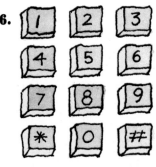

7.

8.

9.

10.

11.

12.

13.

Problem Solving

On the sign, which numbers are used

14. to count?

15. to measure?

16. to order?

17. to label?

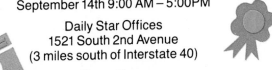

5th Annual DAILY STAR Photo Contest

Winning Photos Will Be On Display
September 14th 9:00 AM – 5:00PM

Daily Star Offices
1521 South 2nd Avenue
(3 miles south of Interstate 40)

6 Photo Classes
Over 25 Prizes!

Place Value to Hundreds

Build Understanding

The *digits* 0, 1, 2, 3, 4, 5, 6, 7, 8, and 9 are used to write numbers.

A. Sue showed 2 hundreds, 3 tens, and 7 ones.

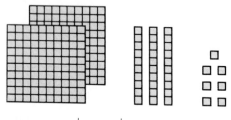

Hundreds	Tens	Ones
2	3	7

237 ← **standard form**

two hundred thirty-seven

B. Bob pictured 2 hundreds, 3 tens, and 7 ones.

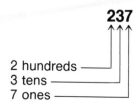

237

2 hundreds ⎯⎯⎯
3 tens ⎯⎯⎯
7 ones ⎯⎯⎯

C. What number is 10 more than 237?

Bob draws one more star in the tens column. Sue shows another ten-stick. For both, the digit in the tens place increases by one, so the number is 247.

■ **Write About Math** Draw a picture that shows the number that is 100 less than Bob's. Write the number in standard form and in words.

Check Understanding

For another example, see Set B, pages 30–31.

Find the number that is

1. 10 more than 395.   **2.** 10 less than 304.   **3.** 100 more than 98.

4. Draw a picture that shows 3 hundreds, 5 tens, and 8 ones.

6

Practice

For More Practice, see Set B, pages 32–33.

Tell what the digit 4 means in each number.

5. 145   **6.** 451   **7.** 204   **8.** 400   **9.** 64

Write each number in standard form.

10. 2 hundreds, 4 tens, 0 ones   **11.** 6 hundreds, 3 tens, 8 ones

12. 5 hundreds, 8 tens   **13.** 3 hundreds, 2 ones   **14.** fifty-eight

15. one hundred sixty   **16.** two hundred eleven   **17.** six hundred two

Write each number in words.

18. 61   **19.** 248   **20.** 305   **21.** 600   **22.** 819

What number is 10 more than the number? 10 less than the number?

23. 43   **24.** 167   **25.** 508   **26.** 694   **27.** 871

What number is 100 less than the number? 100 more than the number?

28. 105   **29.** 666   **30.** 810   **31.** 492   **32.** 378

Problem Solving

Use only the numbers from the number bin. A number in the bin can be used only once in each answer.

33. Write a 3-digit number with 4 as the ones digit.

34. Write the greatest 3-digit number with 6 as the hundreds digit.

35. Write the least 3-digit number with 8 as the tens digit.

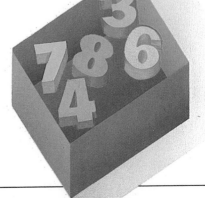

Rounding and Comparing Numbers

Build Understanding

Many trees are native to the state of California.

A. The largest Blue Paloverde tree in the United States is 53 feet tall and is found in Riverside County, California. About how tall is this Blue Paloverde tree?

Round 53 to the nearest ten. You can use a number line to round numbers. Locate 53 on the number line.

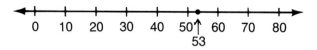

The number 53 is between 50 and 60, but it is closer to 50. Round 53 down to 50.

The largest Blue Paloverde tree is about 50 feet tall.

B. The largest Giant Sequoia tree is found in Sequoia National Park, California, and was last measured at 275 feet. About how tall is this Giant Sequoia tree?

Round 275 to the nearest hundred. Locate 275 on the number line.

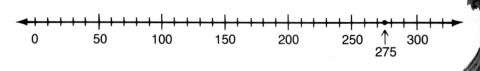

The number 275 is between 200 and 300, but it is closer to 300. Round 275 up to 300.

The largest Giant Sequoia tree is about 300 feet tall.

The General Sherman Tree has a diameter of 36.5 feet, which is wider than most city streets.

c. Compare 275 and 300.

On the number line in Example B, 275 is to the left of 300. Therefore, 275 is less than 300.

On the number line, 300 is to the right of 275. Therefore, 300 is greater than 275.

$$275 < 300$$

$$300 > 275$$

■ **Write About Math** How would you round 275 to the nearest ten?

Check Understanding

For another example, see Set C, pages 30–31.

Draw a number line. Mark and label it by tens. Locate and label each of the numbers below on your number line.

1. 250   **2.** 274   **3.** 285   **4.** 216   **5.** 205   **6.** 293

7. Write two number sentences to compare 216 and 274. Use < and >.

Practice

For More Practice, see Set C, pages 32–33.

Round each number to the nearest ten.

8. 42   **9.** 97   **10.** 658   **11.** 274   **12.** 835   **13.** 502

Round each number to the nearest hundred.

14. 146   **15.** 560   **16.** 67   **17.** 389   **18.** 450   **19.** 805

Compare the numbers. Use < or >.

20. 36 ▧ 61   **21.** 388 ▧ 279   **22.** 562 ▧ 567   **23.** 776 ▧ 767

Problem Solving

Solve each problem.

24. The largest Monterey Pine is 125 feet tall. The largest Bishop Pine is 112 feet tall. Which pine tree is taller?

25. The largest Juniper tree is 86 feet tall. Round its height to the nearest ten feet.

Basic Facts

Build Understanding

You can practice basic facts by using *families of facts*.

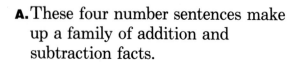

A. These four number sentences make up a family of addition and subtraction facts.

$6 + 3 = 9$

$3 + 6 = 9$

$9 - 6 = 3$

$9 - 3 = 6$

B. These four number sentences make up a family of multiplication and division facts.

$3 \times 6 = 18$

$6 \times 3 = 18$

$18 \div 3 = 6$

$18 \div 6 = 3$

C. Find the missing addend.

$7 + \text{▦} = 16$

$\text{▦} + 7 = 16$, $16 - 7 = \text{▦}$ and $16 - \text{▦} = 7$ are from the same family. Since $16 - 7 = 9$, the missing addend is 9.

D. Find the missing factor.

$4 \times \text{▦} = 36$

$\text{▦} \times 4 = 36$, $36 \div 4 = \text{▦}$, and $36 \div \text{▦} = 4$ are from the same family. Since $36 \div 4 = 9$, the missing factor is 9.

■ **Talk About Math**   Can you think of a family of facts that has only two number sentences?

Check Understanding

For another example, see Set D, pages 30–31.

Complete each pair of sentences.

1. $9 + \text{▦} = 14$
$14 - 9 = \text{▦}$

2. $4 \times \text{▦} = 12$
$12 \div 4 = \text{▦}$

3. $8 - \text{▦} = 1$
$1 + \text{▦} = 8$

4. $24 \div \text{▦} = 8$
$8 \times \text{▦} = 24$

Give the complete family of facts for each number sentence.

5. $6 + 5 = 11$ **6.** $2 \times 9 = 18$ **7.** $14 \div 2 = 7$ **8.** $8 - 4 = 4$

Practice

For More Practice, see Set D, pages 32–33.

Find each answer. **Remember** to watch the operation signs.

9. $6 + 8$ **10.** $17 - 9$ **11.** 5×7 **12.** $9 \div 1$ **13.** $8 - 5$

14. 3×6 **15.** $20 \div 4$ **16.** $9 + 2$ **17.** $6 - 0$ **18.** $0 \div 3$

19. $8 + 8$ **20.** $12 \div 2$ **21.** 6×2 **22.** $10 \div 5$ **23.** $13 - 5$

24. $3 + 4$ **25.** $4 + 3$ **26.** 3×4 **27.** 4×3 **28.** $3 + 0$

29. $7 + 0$ **30.** $0 + 8$ **31.** 4×1 **32.** 1×2 **33.** 9×1

Use a family of facts to help you find the missing number.

34. $5 + \boxed{} = 6$ **35.** $\boxed{} \div 4 = 8$ **36.** $\boxed{} - 2 = 5$ **37.** $\boxed{} \times 7 = 0$

38. $18 \div \boxed{} = 6$ **39.** $\boxed{} + 4 = 9$ **40.** $3 \times \boxed{} = 21$ **41.** $10 - \boxed{} = 8$

Problem Solving

Critical Thinking   Look at Exercises 24–33 to help you answer the questions.

42. Does the order in which you add two numbers change the sum?

43. Does the order in which you multiply two numbers change the product?

44. What is the sum when you add 0 and another number?

45. What is the product when you multiply a number by 1?

Reading ——— Math

Numbers and Symbols   Write a number sentence using the numbers and symbols given.

1. $17, 9, 8, +, =$ **2.** $0, 9, 9, -, =$ **3.** $3, 15, 5, \times, =$

4. $2, 3, 6, \div, =$ **5.** $24, 8, 3, \times, =$ **6.** $4, 9, 5, +, =$

Using a Problem-Solving Guide

Build Understanding

Solving a problem is like taking a journey. There may be more than one road that leads to an answer. Some roads are dead ends. Sometimes you need to turn back and start over. The Problem-Solving Guide is like a map that helps you find your way.

An automatic dishwasher uses 10 gallons of water and is used once a day. Washing dishes by hand three to four times uses 30 gallons a day. How many more gallons of water are used in a day to wash dishes by hand?

Understand
QUESTION
FACTS
KEY IDEA

Plan and Solve
STRATEGY
ANSWER

Look Back
SENSIBLE ANSWER
ALTERNATE APPROACH

Understand
QUESTION
What are you asked to find?

FACTS
What facts are given?

KEY IDEA
How are the facts
and question related?

Plan and Solve
STRATEGY
What can you do to solve
the problem?

ANSWER
Give the answer in a sentence.

Look Back
SENSIBLE ANSWER
Did you check your work?

ALTERNATE APPROACH
Is there another way to get
the same answer?

Understand

QUESTION   Washing dishes by hand uses how many more gallons of water than using a dishwasher?

FACTS   Washing dishes by hand uses 30 gallons of water. A dishwasher uses 10 gallons.

KEY IDEA   Washing dishes by hand uses more water than a dishwasher.

Plan and Solve

STRATEGY   Subtract to find how many more gallons of water are used.

$30 - 10 = 20$

ANSWER   In a day, washing dishes by hand uses 20 more gallons of water than a dishwasher.

Look Back

SENSIBLE ANSWER   Since $10 + 20 = 30$, the answer checks.

Talk About Math   Can you think of a different way to solve the problem?

Check Understanding

Answer each question about the problem below.

Shaving with the tap running uses 20 gallons of water. Brushing teeth uses 2 gallons of water. How much water does a man use to brush his teeth and shave in the morning?

1. What are you asked to find?

2. What facts are given?

3. How are the facts and the question related?

4. What can you do to solve the problem?

5. What is the answer to the question?

6. How can you check your work?

Practice

Solve each problem. Use the Problem-Solving Guide to help you.

7. The average bath uses 36 gallons of water. A ten-minute shower can use 14 gallons more than a bath. How many gallons of water can a shower use?

8. Washing a load of clothes in a washing machine set at top water level uses 60 gallons of water. How much water would be used to wash 2 loads of clothes?

9. Mental Math A dripping faucet can waste 30 gallons of water a day. If the faucet is not fixed, how much water would be wasted in 3 days?

10. Each day the average person in the United States uses 110 gallons of water. In one city, residents use 70 gallons of water a day. How much less water a day do these residents use?

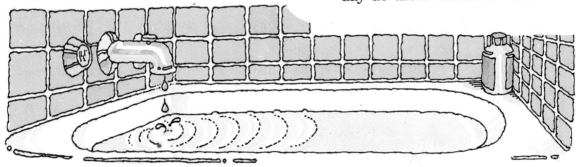

Mental Math

Build Understanding

Jane is a mental math wizard.

A. To add 30 and 50, Jane thinks:

3 tens + 5 tens = 8 tens
30 + 50 = 80

B. To subtract 20 from 60, Jane thinks:

6 tens − 2 tens = 4 tens
60 − 20 = 40

C. Jane uses patterns to multiply.

4 × 10 = 40 (4 × 1 ten = 4 tens)
4 × 20 = 80 (4 × 2 tens = 8 tens)
4 × 30 = 120 (4 × 3 tens = 12 tens)
4 × 40 = 160 (4 × 4 tens = 16 tens)

D. She uses patterns to divide:

80 ÷ 1 = 80 (8 tens ÷ 1 = 8 tens)
80 ÷ 2 = 40 (8 tens ÷ 2 = 4 tens)
80 ÷ 4 = 20 (8 tens ÷ 4 = 2 tens)
80 ÷ 8 = 10 (8 tens ÷ 8 = 1 ten)

■ **Talk About Math** Do you see any advantage in knowing many mental math shortcuts? Why?

Check Understanding

For another example, see Set E, pages 30–31.

Complete each sentence.

1. 4 tens + 5 tens = ▦ tens
   40 + 50 = ▦

2. 7 × 5 tens = ▦ tens
   7 × 50 = ▦

Practice

For More Practice, see Set E, pages 32–33.

Find each answer using mental math.

3. 20 + 40 **4.** 10 + 80 **5.** 70 + 30 **6.** 90 + 50 **7.** 70 + 60

8. 70 − 30 **9.** 90 − 20 **10.** 80 − 60 **11.** 110 − 30 **12.** 130 − 40

13. 6 × 20 **14.** 5 × 50 **15.** 4 × 80 **16.** 3 × 70 **17.** 2 × 90

18. 40 ÷ 2 **19.** 90 ÷ 3 **20.** 50 ÷ 5 **21.** 120 ÷ 3 **22.** 160 ÷ 4

Problem Solving

Each question refers to the sum 60 + 30 + 70.

23. Add the first two addends. Then add the third addend to the sum of the first two. What is the sum?

24. Add the last two addends. Then add the first addend to the sum of the last two. What is the sum?

25. Are the sums of the three addends the same in both Problems 23 and 24?

26. Which method of adding the three numbers did you find easier? Why?

Midchapter ———— Checkup

All 5 children in the 3rd row of Room 6 are 9 years old.

Tell which number in the above sentence is used

1. to measure. **2.** to order.

3. to count. **4.** to label.

Write each number in standard form.
5. nine hundred eight **6.** 3 hundreds, 2 tens **7.** 10 more than 835

Round each number to the nearest 10 and to the nearest 100.
8. 83 **9.** 879 **10.** 504 **11.** 251 **12.** 655 **13.** 312

Find each answer.
14. 17 − 8 **15.** 5 × 4 **16.** 24 ÷ 8 **17.** 6 + 7 **18.** 3 × 9

Find each answer using mental math.
19. 90 − 80 **20.** 180 ÷ 3 **21.** 60 + 40 **22.** 60 × 5 **23.** 110 − 40

Solve each problem.
24. Ed had 4 boxes of cards with 8 cards in each box. How many cards did he have?

25. Kim sold 9 of her 17 stamps. How many stamps does she have left?

Problem Solving WORKSHOP

Explore as a Team

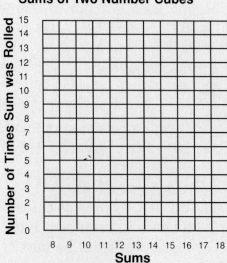

1. Make 2 number cubes, numbered 4, 5, 6, 7, 8, and 9.

2. Take turns rolling the cubes and graphing the sums.

3. After each team member has had one turn, discuss whether the sums seem more likely to be odd or even.

4. Continue rolling the cubes until one of the sums has been rolled 15 times.

5. Discuss the results. Were more odd or even sums rolled? Which sums occurred most frequently? Would the results be the same if you repeated the activity?

TIPS FOR **WORKING TOGETHER**

Involve your whole group. Help everyone to participate.

Sums of Two Number Cubes

Number of Times Sum was Rolled

15
14
13
12
11
10
9
8
7
6
5
4
3
2
1
0

8 9 10 11 12 13 14 15 16 17 18

Sums

Number-Sense Project

Look back at pages 2-3.

Sarah interviewed her grandfather and recorded the following information.

How much extra time is needed for keeping a cat as a pet?

Activity	Extra Time
Feeding cat	5 minutes per day
Cleaning cat box	10 minutes per day
Playing with cat	20 minutes per day
Buying cat food	5 minutes per week
Vacuuming cat hairs from furniture	30 minutes per week

Use information from the chart. Find the total amount of extra time that Sarah's grandfather spends per week.

Math-at-Home Activity

Greatest Phone Number Game

Play this game with someone at home. Open the telephone book to any page. Copy the first telephone number on the left page. Your opponent should copy the first telephone number on the right page.

Each player marks the greatest 3-digit number that is contained in the phone number. (For example, the phone number 3<u>72-7</u>180 contains the number 727.) The player that marks the greater number gets one point.

Open the book to a different page and play again. Continue until one player has 10 points.

Estimation

Build Understanding

Zeppelins were once used to carry passengers across the Atlantic Ocean. By the late 1930s, these huge, rigid, gas-filled airships were replaced by passenger airplanes.

A. The first zeppelin, the LZ-1, was 420 feet long. The LZ-130, one of the largest zeppelins ever built, was 384 feet longer. About how long was the LZ-130?

Estimate 420 + 384.

420 + 384
↓   ↓
400 + 400 = 800

Round 420 and 384 to the nearest hundred. Then add.

The zeppelin U.S.S. Los Angeles is at mast.

The LZ-130 was about 800 feet long.

B. Estimate 58 − 32.

58 − 32
↓   ↓
60 − 30 = 30

Round 58 and 32 to the nearest ten. Then subtract.

C. Estimate 45 × 4.

45 × 4
↓   ↓
50 × 4 = 200

Round 45 to the nearest ten. Then multiply.

■ **Talk About Math** In Example C, is the actual product greater than or less than the estimate? Why?

Check Understanding

For another example, see Set F, pages 30–31.

Complete each sentence. Estimate the sum, difference, or product. First round the two-digit numbers to the nearest ten.

1. 92 + 59
↓   ↓
▦ + ▦ = ▦

2. 74 − 26
↓   ↓
▦ − ▦ = ▦

3. 83 × 3
↓   ↓
▦ × 3 = ▦

Practice

For More Practice, see Set F, pages 32–33.

Estimate each sum, difference, or product. First round the
two-digit numbers to the nearest ten.

4. $78 + 19$ **5.** $54 + 39$ **6.** $63 + 92$ **7.** $81 + 75$

8. $67 - 38$ **9.** $93 - 29$ **10.** $88 - 12$ **11.** $57 - 49$

12. 4×59 **13.** 27×3 **14.** 73×5 **15.** 34×6

First round both numbers to the nearest hundred.

16. $123 + 187$ **17.** $288 + 498$ **18.** $209 + 179$ **19.** $334 + 548$

20. $299 - 106$ **21.** $478 - 113$ **22.** $543 - 277$ **23.** $891 - 551$

Problem Solving

Solve each problem.

24. The zeppelin R-34 was the first aircraft to make a
round trip across the Atlantic Ocean. If the airship
could travel 55 miles per hour, about how far could it
travel in 4 hours?

25. Number Sense In Exercise
17, both addends are rounded
up. Is the estimated sum less
than or greater than the actual
sum? Why?

26. Number Sense In Exercise
19, both addends are rounded
down. Is the estimated sum less
than or greater than the actual
sum? Why?

Skills _____ Review   pages 534–536

Mixed Practice Find each sum or difference.

1. $\begin{array}{r}42\\+37\end{array}$	**2.** $\begin{array}{r}85\\-31\end{array}$	**3.** $\begin{array}{r}247\\+208\end{array}$	**4.** $\begin{array}{r}805\\-388\end{array}$	**5.** $\begin{array}{r}610\\-273\end{array}$	**6.** $\begin{array}{r}200\\-\ 59\end{array}$

7. $37 + 8 + 19$ **8.** $540 + 317 + 65$ **9.** $432 + 371 + 789$

Use Data from a Graph

Build Understanding

This *pictograph* shows the number of paper art projects made by the Art Club.

It takes 50 inches of string to make a mobile. How much string was used for all the mobiles?

Number of Paper Art Projects

Papier-mâché	★★★★★★⌐
Paper folding	★★★★
Collage	★★★⌐
Paper weaving	★★★★★★★
Mobile	★★★

Each ★ means 2 projects.

PROBLEM SOLVING

GUIDE

Understand
QUESTION
FACTS
KEY IDEA

Plan and Solve
STRATEGY
ANSWER

Look Back
SENSIBLE ANSWER
ALTERNATE APPROACH

Understand   QUESTION   How much string was used in making all the mobile projects?

FACTS   Each mobile used 50 inches of string. Read the graph to find how many mobiles were made. There are 3 stars for mobiles. Each star means 2 mobiles. So there were 2 × 3, or 6, mobiles made.

KEY IDEA   Each of the 6 mobiles used 50 inches of string.

Plan and Solve   STRATEGY   Multiply to find the amount of string: 6 × 50 = 300.

ANSWER   The mobile art projects used 300 inches of string.

Look Back   ALTERNATE APPROACH   Use addition to find the number of inches of string.
50 + 50 + 50 + 50 + 50 + 50 = 300

■ **Talk About Math**   How many art projects were papier-mâché figures?

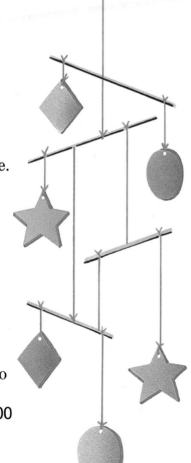

Check Understanding

Use the graph on page 20 to solve this problem.

All of the collages and paper-weaving projects were displayed on a bulletin board. How many projects were displayed on the bulletin board?

1. How many collages were displayed?

2. How many paper-weaving projects were displayed?

3. How many collages and paper-weaving projects were displayed?

Practice

The Art Club explored printmaking. The graph at the right shows the number of prints the members made.

Number of Printing Projects

Potato prints	🌼🌼🌼🌼🌼🌼🌼⚘
Leaf prints	🌼🌼🌼🌼🌼
Roller prints	🌼🌼🌼🌼🌼🌼
Glue prints	🌼🌼🌼⚘

Each 🌼 means 10 prints.

4. Red ink was used in 27 of the potato prints. The other potato prints were printed with blue ink. How many blue potato prints were there?

5. The roller prints are displayed in 3 equal rows. How many prints are in each row?

6. With each of the glue blocks designed by the club, 5 prints were made. How many glue blocks were designed?

7. To make each leaf print 2 pieces of paper were used. How many pieces of paper did the Art Club use in making leaf print projects?

8. Last year's Art Club made 8 more leaf prints than this year's club. How many leaf prints were made last year?

9. How many more leaf prints than glue prints were made?

10. How many prints were made by the Art Club in all?

Even and Odd Numbers

Build Understanding

Exploring Even
and Odd Numbers
Materials: Cubes
Groups: 2 to 4 students

A. a. Two students each take an even
number of cubes.

b. Combine the cubes.

c. Can you put the cubes into 2 equal piles?
Is the sum of these even numbers an even
or an odd number?

d. Choosing other even numbers, repeat the
activity.

Since 6 cubes can be
put into 2 equal piles,
6 is an even number.

e. Complete this sentence: "The sum of any
two even numbers is an ____?____ number."

B. a. Two students each take an even number
of cubes. Combine the cubes.

b. Another student takes away an even
number of cubes.

c. Can the remaining cubes be put into
2 equal piles? Is the number of remaining
cubes even or odd?

d. Repeat this activity choosing other
even numbers.

e. Complete this sentence: "The difference
of two even numbers is an ____?____ number."

Talk About Math   Which digits can be in the
ones place of an even number? Which digits
can be in the ones place of an odd number?

Since 7 cubes cannot be
put into 2 equal piles,
7 is an odd number.

Check Understanding

For another example, see Set G, pages 30–31.

List the numbers described. Use cubes if necessary.

1. odd numbers less than 20

2. even numbers less than 20

Complete each sentence with the words *even* or *odd*.

3. In the sentence 4 + 3 = 7 the addend 4 is an
▦ number. The addend 3 is an ▦ number.
The sum of the addends, 7, is an ▦ number.

Practice

For More Practice, see Set G, pages 32–33.

Is the sum of these numbers even or odd? Use cubes if necessary.

4. 3 + 5   **5.** 7 + 11   **6.** 9 + 13   **7.** 11 + 9   **8.** odd + odd

9. 4 + 3   **10.** 8 + 5   **11.** 14 + 7   **12.** 12 + 11   **13.** even + odd

14. 5 + 4   **15.** 9 + 6   **16.** 3 + 12   **17.** 15 + 8   **18.** odd + even

Is the difference of these numbers even or odd? Use cubes if necessary.

19. 7 − 3   **20.** 9 − 5   **21.** 13 − 7   **22.** 11 − 3   **23.** odd − odd

24. 8 − 3   **25.** 10 − 7   **26.** 16 − 9   **27.** 20 − 15   **28.** even − odd

29. 9 − 4   **30.** 13 − 6   **31.** 11 − 8   **32.** 19 − 14   **33.** odd − even

Problem Solving

Critical Thinking Answer each question.
Use cubes if necessary.

34. John stacked an odd number of cubes on
his desk. He made two more stacks with
the same number of cubes. Was the total
number of cubes even or odd?

35. Is the product of 3 and an odd number an
even number or an odd number? Why?

Compare problems
to help you relate new
problems to ones you've
solved before.

Number Patterns

Build Understanding

A. This *number pattern* uses addition. Find the next three numbers in the pattern.

3, 6, 9, 12, 15, 18, ▦, ▦, ▦

Each number is 3 more than the previous number in the pattern. The rule is "add 3."

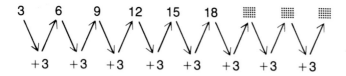

The next three numbers are 21, 24, and 27.

B. This number pattern uses addition and subtraction. Find the next three numbers in the pattern.

60, 50, 55, 45, 50, 40, 45, 35, ▦, ▦, ▦

The rule is "subtract 10 and then add 5." This continues to repeat.

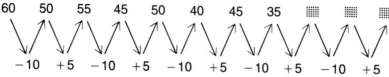

The next three numbers are 40, 30, and 35.

■ **Talk About Math** How can you tell that the pattern 40, 36, 32, 28, 24, 20 is a subtraction pattern rather than an addition pattern?

Check Understanding

For another example, see Set H, pages 30–31.

Write the first 6 numbers of the pattern.

1. Start with 50 and use the rule "subtract 9."

2. Start with 25 and use the rule "add 7 and then subtract 4."

Practice

For More Practice, see Set H, pages 32–33.

What are the next three numbers? Give the rule.

3. 5, 9, 13, 17, 21, ▦, ▦, ▦

4. 2, 4, 6, 8, 10, ▦, ▦, ▦

5. 19, 17, 15, 13, ▦, ▦, ▦

6. 59, 53, 47, 41, ▦, ▦, ▦

7. 15, 27, 39, 51, ▦, ▦, ▦

8. 88, 77, 66, 55, ▦, ▦, ▦

9. 20, 24, 23, 27, 26, 30, ▦, ▦, ▦

10. 50, 49, 149, 148, 248, 247, 347, ▦, ▦, ▦

Calculator Use a calculator to continue these patterns, which use multiplication.

11. 2, 4, 8, 16, 32, ▦, ▦, ▦

12. 1, 5, 25, 125, ▦, ▦, ▦

13. 2, 6, 4, 12, 10, 30, 28, 84, 82, ▦, ▦, ▦

Problem Solving

Explore ———— Math

Visual Thinking Continue the patterns below. Draw the next three figures.

14.

15.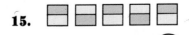

16.

17. ○ ○ ○ ○ ○

Try and Check

Build Understanding

Wayne has 7 coins. The value of the coins is 20¢. What coins does Wayne have?

Understand   QUESTION   What coins does Wayne have?

FACTS   He has 7 coins. The value of the coins is 20¢.

KEY IDEA   Find 7 coins with a value of 20¢.

PROBLEM SOLVING
GUIDE

Understand
QUESTION
FACTS
KEY IDEA

Plan and Solve
STRATEGY
ANSWER

Look Back
SENSIBLE ANSWER
ALTERNATE APPROACH

Plan and Solve   STRATEGY   Try to find a combination of coins with a value of 20¢. Do this in an organized way.

Try 2 dimes. This is only 2 coins.

Try 1 dime and 2 nickels. This is only 3 coins.

Try 1 dime, 1 nickel, and 5 pennies. This is the correct combination. There are 7 coins with a value of 20¢.

ANSWER   Wayne has 1 dime, 1 nickel, and 5 pennies.

Look Back   SENSIBLE ANSWER   The answer is sensible because the 7 coins have a value of 20¢.
10¢ + 5¢ + 1¢ + 1¢ + 1¢ + 1¢ + 1¢ = 20¢

■ **Talk About Math**   Can you think of an alternate approach to solve this problem?

26

Check Understanding

Read for the facts. Then answer each question.

1. Mary has 5 coins with a value of 40¢. Gus said, "She has 3 nickels and 2 dimes. That's 5 coins." What's wrong with Gus's answer?

2. Sue has 4 coins with a value of 25¢. Kiki said, "It's 2 dimes and a nickel. They have a value of 25¢." What's wrong with Kiki's answer?

Practice

Read for the facts. Then solve each problem.

3. Marissa has 3 coins with a value of 11¢. What are the coins?

4. Russell has 5 coins with a value of 17¢. What are the coins?

5. Tonya has 5 different coins. The value of the coins is 91¢. What are the coins?

6. Brad has a quarter and three other coins. The value of the coins is 45¢. What are the coins?

7. **Calculator** Pedro said, "I'm thinking of two numbers in a row. Their product is 306." What are Pedro's numbers?

8. Verna said, "I'm thinking of two odd numbers in a row. Their sum is 28." What are Verna's numbers?

9. **Use Data** Use the graph on page 21. The potato prints are either geometric figures or initials. There are three more geometric prints than initial prints. How many geometric prints are there? How many initial prints are there?

Choose a ————— Strategy

10. How many triangles are in this figure?

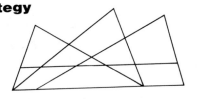

Solve each problem.

1. Which numbers on the invitation are used to count? to order? to label? to measure?

2. Write the largest and the smallest three-digit numbers you can make with the digits 1, 5, 7, 9.

3. Which is heavier, a 220-pound pig or a 202-pound pig?

4. Two numbers have a sum of 25 and a product of 156. What are the numbers?

5. Ted bought 4 packages of baseball cards with 8 cards in each package. Susan bought 3 packages of baseball cards with 9 cards in each package. Who bought more baseball cards?

6. **Data File** Use data from pages 102-103. When Cary's cat was 6 months old it weighed 6 pounds. How much weight did it gain during the next 6 months?

7. **Make a Data File** Take a survey of people who own pets and ask how much the pets weigh. Sort the information by type of animal and make a graph of the results.

Explore with a Calculator

What's Missing?

Nearly every calculator has keys labeled with signs for the four basic operations.

 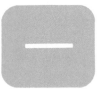  

Addition   Subtraction   Multiplication   Division

Which operation sign is missing in this key sequence?

17 ☐ 4 ⊟ 13

Since 13 is the difference of 17 and 4, the missing sign is subtraction. Check this by using your calculator.

1. Complete each key sequence with the correct operation or number.

a. 6 ☐ 4 ⊟ 10   **f.** ■ ⊞ 8 ⊟ 13

b. 8 ☐ 9 ⊟ 72   **g.** 14 ⊟ ■ ⊟ 6

c. 24 ☐ 3 ⊟ 8   **h.** ■ ⊠ 9 ⊟ 72

d. 6 ☐ 5 ☐ 8 ⊟ 19   **i.** 13 ⊞ ■ ⊟ 25

e. 36 ☐ 4 ☐ 3 ⊟ 3   **j.** 56 ⊡ ■ ⊟ 7

2. Write the key sequence to solve each problem. Then find the answers.

a. The Pirates had 6 runs, and the Indians had 7 runs. The Pirates then scored 3 more runs and won the game. By how many runs did the Pirates win?

b. There were 24 players. Each of the 2 teams had an equal number of players. How many players were on each team?

Reteaching

Set A pages 4–5

Numbers are used in many ways.

To count:
There are 3 boys and 3 girls.

To label:
We met in Room 18.

To measure:
The truck is 16 feet long.

To order:
The Mets came in second.

Remember that a number, such as a date, can be used in more than one way.

For each picture, tell if the number is used to count, to measure, to order, or to label.

1. 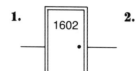   **2.**

Set B pages 6–7

How many hundreds, tens, and ones are in this number? Write the number in standard form.

four hundred ninety-seven
4 hundreds 9 tens 7 ones
   497 ← standard form

Remember that you do not use the word *and* when you write numbers like 101 in words.

Tell how many hundreds, tens, and ones. Then write the number in standard form.

1. sixty-seven   **2.** two hundred five

Set C pages 8–9

Round 133 to the nearest ten.
Locate 133 on the number line.

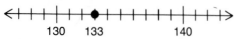
130   133   140

The number 133 is between 130 and 140, but it is closer to 130. Round 133 down to 130.

Remember that you can use a number line to help you round numbers.

Round each number to the nearest ten.

1. 54   **2.** 87   **3.** 348

4. 261   **5.** 435   **6.** 519

Set D pages 10–11

Find the missing number.

▦ − 5 = 3

▦ − 3 = 5, 5 + 3 = ▦, and 3 + 5 = ▦ are from the same family. Since 5 + 3 = 8, the missing number is 8.

Remember that if you know one basic fact, you can use it to write other facts in the family.

Use a family of facts to help you find the missing number.

1. ▦ − 2 = 7   **2.** 8 − ▦ = 3

Set E pages 14–15

Find 6 × 40.
Notice the pattern.

6 × 10 = 60   (6 × 1 ten is 6 tens.)
6 × 20 = 120   (6 × 2 tens is 12 tens.)
6 × 30 = 180   (6 × 3 tens is 18 tens.)
6 × 40 = 240   (6 × 4 tens is 24 tens.)

Remember that patterns can help you find shortcuts. Find each answer using mental math.

1. 3 × 30   **2.** 4 × 50

3. 6 × 50   **4.** 8 × 40

Set F pages 18–19

Estimate 506 − 392.
Round each number to the nearest hundred.

506 − 392
↓   ↓
500 − 400 = 100

Remember that you can use a number line to round.

Estimate each answer. First round each number to the nearest hundred.

1. 391 − 208   **2.** 412 − 189

Set G pages 22–23

Is the sum 3 + 6 even or odd? Use cubes.

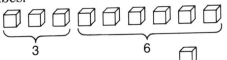

```
     3              6
```

Try to put these cubes into 2 equal piles. Since 9 cubes cannot be put into 2 equal piles, 3 + 6, or 9, is odd.

Remember that an even number has a 0, 2, 4, 6, or 8 in the ones place. An odd number has a 1, 3, 5, 7, or 9 in the ones place.

Is the sum of these numbers even or odd? Use cubes if necessary.

1. 3 + 7   **2.** 7 + 4   **3.** 10 + 12

4. 8 + 8   **5.** 12 + 6   **6.** 18 + 3

Set H pages 24–25

Find a rule and the next three numbers in this pattern: 5, 10, 9, 14, 13, ▦, ▦, ▦.

```
5    10    9    14    13
 ↘↗   ↘↗   ↘↗   ↘↗
 + 5   − 1  + 5   − 1
```

Using the rule "add 5, then subtract 1" gives the next three numbers.

```
13    18    17    22
 ↘↗   ↘↗   ↘↗
 + 5   − 1  + 5
```

Remember that the numbers decrease in a subtraction pattern and increase in an addition pattern.

What are the next three numbers? Give the rule you used.

1. 39, 36, 33, 30, 27

2. 1, 4, 2, 5, 3, 6

3. 0, 10, 20, 30, 40

More Practice

Set A   pages 4–5

For each picture, tell if the number is used to count,
to measure, to order, or to label.

1.  318

2. (clock showing about 12:00)

3.  0 0 4 1 3 1 8

Set B   pages 6–7

Tell what the digit 8 means.

1. 187   **2.** 823   **3.** 148   **4.** 84   **5.** 800

Write each number in standard form.

6. 3 hundreds, 6 tens, 2 ones   **7.** 8 hundreds, 0 tens, 9 ones

8. five hundred twelve   **9.** three hundred two   **10.** two hundred fifty

Write each number in words.

11. 33   **12.** 108   **13.** 356   **14.** 910   **15.** 400

What number is 10 more than the number? 10 less than the number?

16. 56   **17.** 144   **18.** 398   **19.** 406   **20.** 952

What number is 100 less than the number?
100 more than the number?

21. 120   **22.** 605   **23.** 888   **24.** 293   **25.** 471

Set C   pages 8–9

Round each number to the nearest ten.

1. 63   **2.** 79   **3.** 347   **4.** 432   **5.** 745

Round each number to the nearest hundred.

6. 239   **7.** 680   **8.** 58   **9.** 276   **10.** 705

Compare the numbers. Use < or >.

11. 43 ⬚ 51   **12.** 462 ⬚ 312   **13.** 376 ⬚ 372   **14.** 638 ⬚ 683

Set D pages 10–11

Find each answer.

1. $4 + 8$ **2.** $7 + 9$ **3.** 4×5 **4.** $12 - 7$ **5.** $14 \div 2$

6. 7×3 **7.** $15 \div 3$ **8.** $14 - 6$ **9.** 3×9 **10.** $8 + 3$

Use a family of facts to help you find the missing number.

11. $\blacksquare - 3 = 8$ **12.** $\blacksquare \div 4 = 9$ **13.** $8 \times \blacksquare = 0$ **14.** $8 + \blacksquare = 13$

15. $28 \div \blacksquare = 4$ **16.** $\blacksquare + 8 = 15$ **17.** $6 \times \blacksquare = 36$ **18.** $12 - \blacksquare = 7$

Set E pages 14–15

Find each answer using mental math.

1. $30 + 50$ **2.** $90 + 60$ **3.** $80 - 30$ **4.** $120 - 40$ **5.** 7×30

6. 8×20 **7.** 30×6 **8.** $320 \div 8$ **9.** $140 \div 7$ **10.** $150 \div 3$

Set F pages 18–19

Estimate each sum, difference, or product.
First round the two-digit numbers to the nearest ten.

1. $67 + 28$ **2.** $44 + 26$ **3.** $54 - 31$ **4.** $72 - 35$

5. 4×38 **6.** 22×5 **7.** 47×6 **8.** $84 - 42$

First round both numbers to the nearest hundred.

9. $144 + 126$ **10.** $377 - 189$ **11.** $320 + 264$ **12.** $491 - 126$

Set G pages 22–23

Is the answer to each exercise odd or even? Use cubes if necessary.

1. $4 + 8$ **2.** $7 + 13$ **3.** $17 + 8$ **4.** $9 + 9$ **5.** $15 + 14$

6. $9 - 6$ **7.** $20 - 11$ **8.** $18 - 9$ **9.** $16 - 8$ **10.** $20 - 12$

Set H pages 24–25

What are the next three numbers? Give the rule you used.

1. 1, 7, 13, 19, 25, $\blacksquare$, $\blacksquare$, $\blacksquare$ **2.** 44, 40, 36, 32, 28, $\blacksquare$, $\blacksquare$, $\blacksquare$

3. 56, 49, 42, 35, 28, $\blacksquare$, $\blacksquare$, $\blacksquare$ **4.** 8, 6, 10, 8, 12, 10, $\blacksquare$, $\blacksquare$, $\blacksquare$

Enrichment

Mental Math

Jane can often do addition and subtraction mentally.

This is how Jane does it.

A. 63 + 24 = ▦

Jane thinks:

60 + 20 = 80
3 + 4 = 7
80 + 7 = 87

The answer is 87.

B. 98 + 56 = ▦

Jane thinks:

98 is 2 less than 100.
100 + 56 = 156
156 − 2 = 154

The answer is 154.

C. 78 − 35 = ▦

Jane thinks:

78 − 30 = 48
48 − 5 = 43

The answer is 43.

D. 132 − 97 = ▦

Jane thinks:

97 is 3 less than 100.
Add 3 to both numbers.
135 − 100 = 35

The answer is 35.

Find each sum or difference mentally.

1. 52 + 37   **2.** 99 + 43   **3.** 86 − 45

4. 132 − 99   **5.** 47 − 19   **6.** 68 − 27

7. 28 + 44   **8.** 44 + 37   **9.** 124 − 98

10. 97 + 58   **11.** 17 + 46

12. 76 − 18   **13.** 28 + 47

14. 73 − 56   **15.** 157 − 97

16. 89 + 89   **17.** 97 − 78

Chapter 1 Review/Test

Classroom 215 on the 2nd floor has 25 students.

In the sentence above, which numbers are used to

1. count?   **2.** label?

Write each number in standard form.

3. 5 hundreds, 7 tens, 2 ones

4. six hundred fifteen

Round 319 to the nearest
5. ten.   **6.** hundred.

Compare the numbers. Use < or >.
7. 49 ▦ 94   **8.** 821 ▦ 192

Find each answer.
9. 7 + 8   **10.** 16 − 9

11. 32 ÷ 4   **12.** 8 × 1

Find each answer. Use mental math.
13. 170 − 60   **14.** 3 × 40

Estimate each sum, difference, or product. First, round the two-digit numbers to the nearest ten.

15. 58 × 6   **16.** 48 − 32

Estimate. First, round both numbers to the nearest hundred.

17. 189 + 129   **18.** 615 − 287

Is the sum even or odd?
19. 19 + 5   **20.** 6 + 15

Use the graph with the problem given below to answer Items 21 and 22.

The maple trees were planted in 5 equal rows. How many maples were there in each row?

Number of Trees Planted

Oaks	🌲 🌲 🌱
Elms	🌲 🌲 🌲 🌲 🌲
Maples	🌲 🌲 🌲 🌲
Pines	🌲 🌲 🌲 🌲 🌲 🌲 🌱

Each 🌲 stands for 10 trees.

21. Which is the key idea in this problem?

   a. More elms than maples were planted.
   b. There were 5 equal groups of maples.
   c. You can use the graph to find the number of oaks planted.

22. Solve the problem.

23. Tell a rule that would give the pattern. What are the next three numbers?

25, 24, 34, 33, 43, ▦, ▦, ▦

24. Velma has a dime and 3 other coins. The value of the coins is 21 cents. What are the coins?

25. **Write About Math**   Write a sentence in which a number is used to measure.

Place Value

2

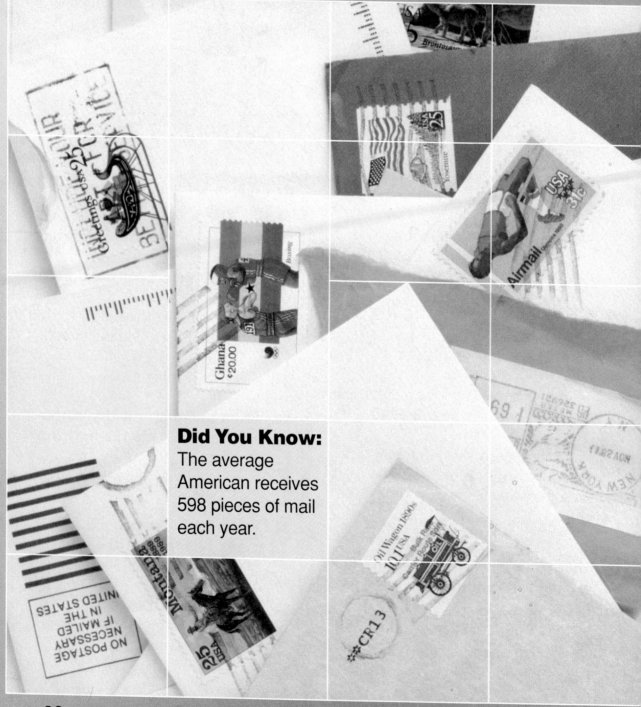

Did You Know:
The average American receives 598 pieces of mail each year.

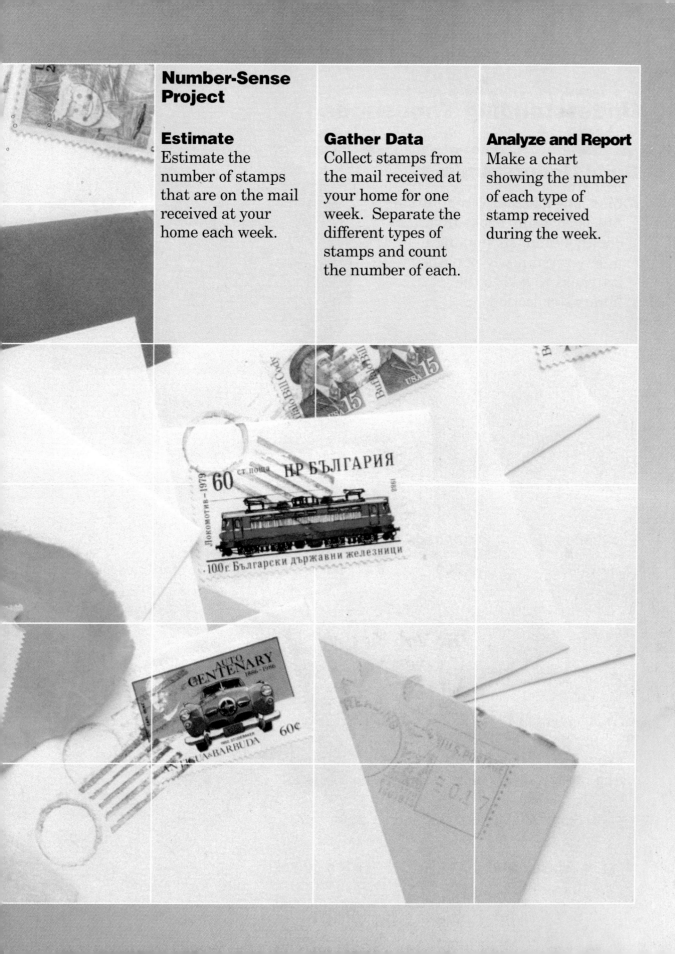

Number-Sense Project

Estimate
Estimate the number of stamps that are on the mail received at your home each week.

Gather Data
Collect stamps from the mail received at your home for one week. Separate the different types of stamps and count the number of each.

Analyze and Report
Make a chart showing the number of each type of stamp received during the week.

Understanding Thousands

Build Understanding

A. Martha Galbreath is a librarian. She is choosing books from the one thousand, six hundred ninety-seven newly published art books to add to the library's collection.

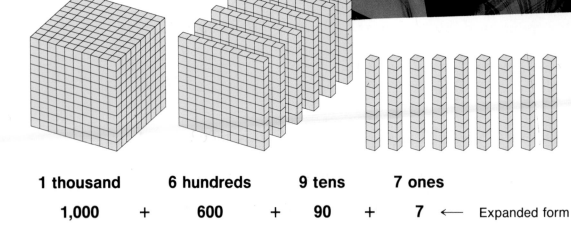

1 thousand	**6 hundreds**	**9 tens**	**7 ones**	
1,000 +	**600** +	**90** +	**7**	← Expanded form

1,697 ←———————— Standard form

thousands place ——┐ ↑ ↑ ↑ ┌—— ones place
hundreds place ————┘ └—— tens place

B. What number is 1,000 more than 1,697?

The digit in the thousands place is 1. To make the number 1,000 more, increase the 1 to a 2.

The number 2,697 is 1,000 more than 1,697.

■ **Talk About Math** What number is 1,000 less than 1,697?

Check Understanding

For another example, see Set A, pages 60–61.

For Exercises 1–4, write each number in standard form.

1. 6 thousands, 2 hundreds, 4 tens, 5 ones

2. nine thousand, sixty-two

3. 3,000 + 200 + 3

4. 1,000 more than 2,897

5. Write 5,491 in words.

6. Write 5,302 in expanded form.

Practice

For More Practice, see Set A, pages 62–63.

Write each number in standard form.

7. 7 thousands, 2 tens, 8 ones

8. 6,000 + 200 + 10 + 3

9. two thousand, one hundred fourteen

Write each number in words.

10. 405   **11.** 3,675   **12.** 7,450   **13.** 8,062   **14.** 1,008

Consider the number 4,979. Write the number that is

15. 100 more.   **16.** 100 less.   **17.** 1,000 more.   **18.** 1,000 less.

For each number, tell what digit is in the given place.

19. 6,702 (hundreds)   **20.** 5,930 (thousands)   **21.** 2,413 (tens)

Problem Solving

Read for the facts. Then write the numbers.

22. Librarians could choose from four thousand, five hundred sixteen newly published children's books. Write this number in expanded form.

23. Last week 2,948 books were checked out from the local library. Write this number in words and also in expanded form.

Thousands

Build Understanding

A. Exploring Thousands
Materials: Grid paper, scissors
Groups: 2 to 4 students

a. Each student in the group draws and cuts out a square that measures 30 squares on each side.

b. From each 30 by 30 square, cut as many 10 by 10 or hundred squares as you can.

c. Put the group's hundred squares together. How many hundred squares are there altogether? How many single squares are there altogether?

d. How many tens are in a hundred? How many tens are there altogether?

B. How many hundreds are in 3,000?

To see how many hundreds are in 3,000, cover the tens and the ones places with your hand. 3,000 is 30 hundreds.

You can name a number in different ways. Here are some other names for 3,000.

3,000 ones   300 tens   30 hundreds   3 thousands

■ **Talk About Math**   Suppose there are 35 hundreds in a number. How many tens are there in the same number?

Check Understanding

For another example, see Set B, pages 60–61.

1. How many tens are in 4,500? Explain how you got the answer.

2. How many hundreds are in 4,500?   **3.** How many ones are in 4,500?

Practice

For More Practice, see Set B, pages 62–63.

Copy and complete.

4. 520 = ▦ tens   **5.** 7,000 = ▦ tens   **6.** 6,020 = ▦ tens

7. 8,000 = ▦ hundreds   **8.** 4,100 = ▦ hundreds

9. 3,000 = ▦ ones   **10.** 5,000 = ▦ thousands

Write the standard form of the number.

11. 27 tens   **12.** 500 tens   **13.** 3 hundreds

14. 480 tens   **15.** 2 thousands   **16.** 25 hundreds

17. 3,145 ones   **18.** 60 hundreds   **19.** 850 tens + 5 ones

Problem Solving

Solve each problem.

20. A meter is 100 centimeters. How many meters are in 2,000 centimeters?

21. A kilometer is 1,000 meters. How many kilometers are in 5,000 meters?

| Skills | Review | pages 14–15 |

Mental Math Find each answer.

1. 3 × 40   **2.** 70 + 30   **3.** 80 ÷ 2   **4.** 90 − 20   **5.** 60 + 50

6. 90 ÷ 3   **7.** 4 × 50   **8.** 60 − 30   **9.** 80 + 70   **10.** 90 × 2

Give Sensible Answers

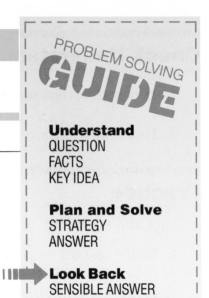

PROBLEM SOLVING GUIDE

Understand
QUESTION
FACTS
KEY IDEA

Plan and Solve
STRATEGY
ANSWER

➡ **Look Back**
SENSIBLE ANSWER
ALTERNATE APPROACH

Build Understanding

At Columbus School, 50 students are in the marching band. Many other students are not in the band. Which of these choices tells about how many students are at Columbus School?

5   50   500

Understand   Fifty students are in the band and many more are not.

Plan and Solve   Since there are more students in the school than in the band, the only choice greater than 50 is 500.

ANSWER   About 500 students are at Columbus School.

➡ **Look Back**   SENSIBLE ANSWER   There could not be fewer students in the school than in the band. So 5 is not a sensible answer. Many students are not in the band. So 50 is not a sensible answer. Therefore, about 500 students are in the school.

■ **Talk About Math**   What do you think is the smallest sensible number of students in Columbus School? Why? What do you think is the largest? Why? Do you think all sensible answers are between these two numbers?

Check Understanding

Choose the most sensible answer. Explain why the other choices are not sensible.

1. How many times does the school band practice each week?

5   50   500

2. The 50 band members sit in rows. About how many are in each row?

1   10   100

Practice

Choose the most sensible answer. Explain why the other choices are not sensible.

3. The Columbus School Band had a concert. How many people came?

2   200   200,000

4. What was the cost of a ticket to the Columbus School Band concert?

$3 $30 $300

5. How many of the 50 band members play the drums?

6   60   600

6. How many minutes does the school band practice each day?

4   45   450

7. Jamie practices her flute at home every day. How many hours does she practice at home each week?

7   17   70

8. During the school year, the band plays at least once a month at assemblies. How many times each year is this?

1   5   15

9. The band members are raising money for 50 new uniforms. How much money do they need?

$3 $30 $3,000

10. The band members had a car wash to raise money. How much did they charge to wash a car?

$2 $20 $200

Number Sense Fill in the blanks with numbers that are sensible. Then explain why each number is sensible.

11. Columbus School has an orchestra with ▦ members. There are ▦ members who play stringed instruments. There are ▦ members who play drums.

12. The orchestra made about ▦ at its last concert when each ticket cost ▦ and about ▦ people attended. The orchestra played ▦ pieces of music, which took about ▦ hours.

43

Comparing and Ordering Thousands

Build Understanding

The chart shows the lengths of seven North American rivers.

Length of North American Rivers in Miles	
Arkansas	1,459
Colorado	1,450
Columbia	1,243
Mississippi	2,348
Missouri	2,315
Ohio	1,310
Rio Grande	1,760

A. Which is longer, the Missouri River or the Mississippi River?

Over millions of years, the Colorado River formed the walls of the Grand Canyon, which shows many layers of rock.

Compare 2,315 and 2,348.

Compare the thousands digits.	Compare the hundreds digits.	Compare the tens digits.

| 2,315 | 2,315 | 2,315 |
| 2,348 | 2,348 | 2,348 |

| The digits are the same. | The digits are the same. | 4 > 1 | 2,348 > 2,315 |

The Mississippi River is longer than the Missouri River.

B. List the numbers 1,550, 1,605, and 1,459 in order from least to greatest.

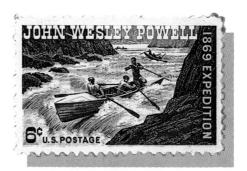

Compare 1,550 and 1,605: 1,550 < 1,605.
Compare 1,550 and 1,459: 1,459 < 1,550.

Therefore, the numbers should be listed as
1,459   1,550   1,605.

■ **Write About Math**   Suppose the number 1,495 was also in Example B. How would the four numbers be ordered?

Check Understanding

For another example, see Set C, pages 60–61.

Tell if the statements are true or false.

1. The longest river given in the chart is the Rio Grande.

2. These numbers are listed from least to greatest:
891   1,275   1,186

3. 8,310 > 8,226

4. 2,980 < 2,890

Practice

L G

For More Practice, see Set C, pages 62–63.

Compare these numbers. Use < or >.

5. 2,758 ⬚ 2,698

6. 1,430 ⬚ 1,419

7. 5,388 ⬚ 5,384

8. 4,725 ⬚ 8,120

9. 3,048 ⬚ 3,400

10. 2,440 ⬚ 1,873

11. 6,184 ⬚ 6,129

12. 7,725 ⬚ 7,825

13. 1,228 ⬚ 1,219

Write the numbers in order from least to greatest.

14. 3,547   1,388   2,490

15. 2,672   2,648   2,650

16. 5,576   5,595   5,583

17. 2,284   1,284   2,484

18. 4,705   4,570   5,704

19. 3,961   3,691   3,196

20. 483   1,072   32   1,067

21. 1,391   931   1,913   1,139

Problem Solving

Use the information in the chart on page 44 to help you solve each problem.

22. Which river in the chart has a length between the lengths of the Arkansas and the Missouri rivers?

23. The Mackenzie River is 2,635 miles long. Is this river longer or shorter than the Mississippi River? Why?

24. Is the Columbia River longer or shorter than the Ohio River? Why?

25. List the rivers in the chart in order of length from longest to shortest.

26. **Calculator** The Nile River in Africa is about 10 times as long as the 420-mile long Salmon River. About how long is the Nile River?

27. **Critical Thinking** Using all four digits, 3, 4, 7, and 9, write the largest and the smallest possible 4-digit numbers.

Reading ———— Math

Numbers and Symbols Write as many true sentences as you can by choosing one phrase from Column A, one from Column B, and one from Column C. A phrase may be used more than once.

Column A	Column B	Column C
Two thousand, forty-one	is greater than	one thousand, six hundred.
Two thousand, four hundred fourteen	is less than	two thousand, one hundred eleven.
One thousand, sixty-six	is equal to	two thousand, fourteen.

Write each number in standard form.

1. 5 thousands, 3 hundreds, 2 tens, 7 ones

2. Four thousand, seven hundred twelve

3. 5,000 + 60 + 1

4. 1,000 less than 8,500

5. 450 tens

6. 70 hundreds

Write the number in words.

7. 540   **8.** 7,980   **9.** 1,030   **10.** 6,987

Compare these numbers. Use < or >.

11. 475 ⬚ 457   **12.** 3,409 ⬚ 2,904   **13.** 6,450 ⬚ 6,540

Write the numbers in order from least to greatest.

14. 432   502   398

15. 8,756   8,140   8,324

Choose the most sensible answer.

16. The 50 band members ride in buses to concerts. About how many buses are needed?

2   5   10

17. The band was in a parade that lasted 1 hour. About how many blocks did they march?

3   30   3,000

18. The band played at a school football game. The stands were filled. About how many people were there?

8   18   800

19. The Columbus School Band attended a state band competition. How many bands were at the competition?

4   40   400

Explore as a Team

1. Estimate the number of squares or parts of squares in each drawing. You may count up to 10 of the squares in each drawing.

2. Discuss your estimates with other students on your team. What are the greatest and least numbers of squares that could be in each of the drawings? Check your estimates by counting all of the squares.

3. On grid paper, draw the outline of an object.

4. Estimate the number of squares in the drawings by the students on your team. Discuss estimation methods. Which estimates were closest?

TIPS FOR WORKING TOGETHER

When you are unsure, ask someone in your group for help or say you don't understand.

Real-Life Decision Making

1. You plan to invite 24 people to a party. Invitations are sold in packages of 10. You need to decide how many packages to buy. What reasons could you have for deciding to buy

   a. one package?

   b. two packages?

   c. three packages?

   d. zero packages?

YOU ARE INVITED
DATE:
TIME:

Explore with a Computer

Use the *Graphing and Probability Workshop Project* for this activity.

1. At the computer, type the numbers from the picture into the table. Each number is the distance that each place is from the Washington Monument. View the data as a **Bar Graph.**

2. Which place is closest to the Washington Monument? Which place is furthest from the Washington Monument? Sort the data in the table to check your answer.

3. Which two places are about the same distance from the Washington Monument? Does this mean they are near each other?

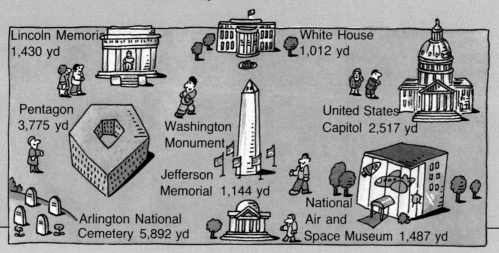

Lincoln Memorial 1,430 yd

White House 1,012 yd

Pentagon 3,775 yd

Washington Monument

United States Capitol 2,517 yd

Jefferson Memorial 1,144 yd

National Air and Space Museum 1,487 yd

Arlington National Cemetery 5,892 yd

Number-Sense Project

Look back at pages 36-37.

1. Suppose a student collects 100 stamps in a week. In how many weeks would the student be able to collect 1,000 stamps?

2. 🖩 **Calculator** About how many stamps does your home receive on mail in a week? In how many weeks would you be able to collect about 1,000 stamps? (Hint: Divide 1,000 by the number of stamps per week.)

Rounding Thousands

Build Understanding

POPULATION OF CITIES IN ALASKA IN 1980	
Barrow	2,207
Bethel	3,576
Kodiak	4,756
Nome	2,301
Valdez	3,079

A. You can use the number line to help you round the population of Nome to the nearest thousand.

This is Nome, Alaska, in 1984.

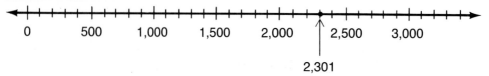

2,301

The number 2,301 is between 2,000 and 3,000, but it is closer to 2,000. The population of Nome is about 2,000.

B. Round the populations of Barrow, Kodiak, and Bethel to the nearest thousand.

To round to the nearest thousand, look at the hundreds digit.

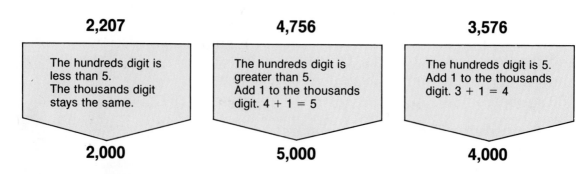

2,207

The hundreds digit is less than 5. The thousands digit stays the same.

2,000

4,756

The hundreds digit is greater than 5. Add 1 to the thousands digit. 4 + 1 = 5

5,000

3,576

The hundreds digit is 5. Add 1 to the thousands digit. 3 + 1 = 4

4,000

■ **Write About Math** Look at the rules for rounding to the nearest thousand given in Example B. Write similar rules for rounding to the nearest hundred.

Check Understanding

For another example, see Set D, pages 60–61.

Complete each statement.

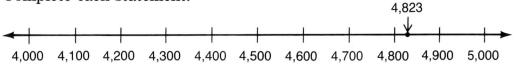

4,823

4,000 4,100 4,200 4,300 4,400 4,500 4,600 4,700 4,800 4,900 5,000

1. The number 4,823 is between ▦,000 and ▦,000 on the number line and is closer to ▦,000. So 4,823 rounded to the nearest thousand is ▦.

2. To round 4,823 to the nearest thousand, look at the digit in the ▦ place. Since it is ▦ than five, 4,823 rounded to the nearest thousand is ▦.

3. The number 4,823 is between 4,▦00 and 4,▦00 on the number line and is closer to 4,▦00. So 4,823 rounded to the nearest hundred is ▦.

4. To round 4,823 to the nearest hundred, look at the digit in the ▦ place. Since it is ▦ than five, 4,823 rounded to the nearest hundred is ▦.

Practice

For More Practice, see Set D, pages 62–63.

Round each number to the nearest hundred; to the nearest thousand.

5. 925 **6.** 5,693 **7.** 2,805 **8.** 7,341 **9.** 1,579

10. 7,998 **11.** 8,013 **12.** 3,156 **13.** 6,722 **14.** 9,289

Problem Solving

Use the chart on page 50 to solve Problems 15–16.

15. Round the population of Valdez, Alaska, to the nearest thousand.

16. Round the population of Bethel, Alaska, to the nearest hundred.

17. Critical Thinking When rounded to the nearest thousand, what is the largest number that rounds to 5,000? the smallest number that rounds to 5,000?

18. Use Data Use the chart on page 44 to solve this problem. The Yukon River in Alaska is 1,979 miles long. Is the Yukon River longer or shorter than the Rio Grande?

Ten-Thousands and Hundred-Thousands

Build Understanding

A. The Rose Bowl in Pasadena, California, can seat 106,721 football fans.

thousands period			ones period		
hundred-thousands	ten-thousands	thousands	hundreds	tens	ones
1	0	6	7	2	1

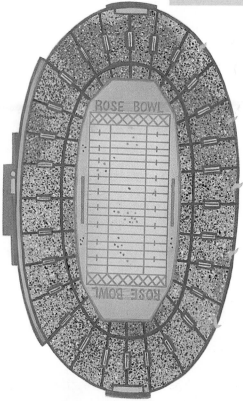

Each group of three digits forms a place-value period. The comma in the number separates the thousands period from the ones period.

The number is read: one hundred six *thousand*, seven hundred twenty-one.

B. What number is 10,000 more than 106,721?

The digit in the ten-thousands place is 0. To make the number 10,000 more, increase the 0 to 1.

116,721 is 10,000 more than 106,721.

■ **Talk About Math** What number is 1,000 less than 106,721?

Check Understanding

For another example, see Set E, pages 60–61.

Use the number 509,340 for Exercises 1–4.

1. Write the number in words.

2. What does the digit 9 mean?

3. What number is 10,000 less?

4. What number is 1,000 more?

Practice

For More Practice, see Set E, pages 62–63.

Write each number in words.

5. 60,000   **6.** 45,700   **7.** 400,033   **8.** 745,555

Write these numbers in standard form.

9. five hundred twenty-seven thousand, six hundred four

10. nine hundred five thousand, forty-seven

What number is 10,000 more? 1,000 less?

11. 52,300   **12.** 209,666   **13.** 450,220   **14.** 795,001

Mixed Practice   Write the number that is

15. 1,000 more than 4,500.

16. 100 less than 3,000.

17. 10,000 more than 34,650.

18. 10 less than 585.

Calculator   Enter the number on a calculator. Display 100,000 by adding only one number. What number did you add?

19. 99,099   **20.** 99,909

21. 99,999   **22.** 90,999

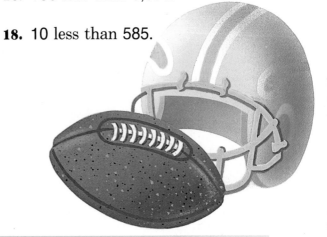

Problem Solving

Solve each problem.

23. Mile High Stadium in Denver, Colorado, can seat 76,142 football fans. What digit is in the ten-thousands place of this number?

24. **Estimation**   About 35,000 fans attended a football game at which 4,362 hamburgers were sold. Which of these numbers is exact and which is an estimate?

TIPS FOR PROBLEM SOLVERS

Visualize the problem in your mind to help you understand it better.

Millions

Average Distance From Sun	
Mercury	36,000,000 mi
Venus	67,250,000 mi
Earth	93,000,000 mi
Mars	141,750,000 mi
Jupiter	483,800,000 mi
Saturn	887,950,000 mi

Build Understanding

The chart at the right shows the average distance from the six closest planets to the sun. The average distance from Jupiter to the sun is 483,800,000 miles.

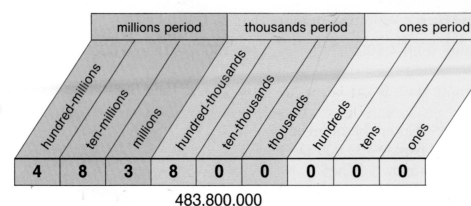

483,800,000
483 million, 800 thousand
four hundred eighty-three million, eight hundred thousand

About how far is Earth from the sun?

■ **Talk About Math**   Where else are large numbers used besides in the study of the planets?

Check Understanding

For another example, see Set F, pages 60–61.

Fill in the blanks.

1. In the number 349,778,650 the digits 3, 4, and 9 are in the ▦ period.

2. The number 300,006,012 is read: three hundred million, six ▦, twelve.

3. In large numbers, ▦ are used to separate the periods.

4. The 4 in the 483,800,000 means 4 ▦.

Practice

For More Practice, see Set F, pages 62–63.

Give the standard form. **Remember** to use zeros as placeholders.

5. four hundred sixteen million, eight hundred four thousand, nine hundred

6. thirteen million, six hundred thousand, two hundred eleven

7. 60 million, 507 thousand

8. 3 million, 17 thousand, 6

Write each number in words.

9. 957,380   **10.** 8,700,413   **11.** 63,296,174   **12.** 292,062,524

Tell what each 7 means.

13. 11,474,554   **14.** 7,800,413   **15.** 761,000,900   **16.** 272,100,425

17.  **Calculator**   What is the largest whole number that you can display on your calculator?

Problem Solving

Explore ——— Math

Billions   The average distance from the sun to Uranus is one billion, seven hundred sixty-four million, five hundred thousand miles.

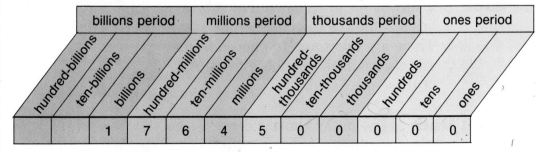

billions period			millions period			thousands period			ones period		
hundred-billions	ten-billions	billions	hundred-millions	ten-millions	millions	hundred-thousands	ten-thousands	thousands	hundreds	tens	ones
		1	7	6	4	5	0	0	0	0	0

Write each distance in words.

18. Neptune: 2,791,050,000 miles   **19.** Pluto: 3,653,900,000 miles

Draw a Diagram

Build Understanding

The Chen family is visiting the zoo. They want to take a tour of the zoo on either the train or the tram. For both the train and the tram, tours start at 10:00, 11:00, or 12:00. List the choices the Chen family has for a tour.

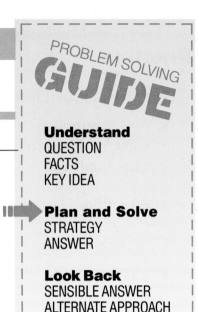

PROBLEM SOLVING GUIDE

Understand
QUESTION
FACTS
KEY IDEA

➤ **Plan and Solve**
STRATEGY
ANSWER

Look Back
SENSIBLE ANSWER
ALTERNATE APPROACH

Understand   The Chen family can choose between the train and the tram. They will also choose between the 3 different times.

➤ **Plan and Solve**   STRATEGY   Make a **tree diagram** to list the different choices.

ANSWER

Tour	Time	Choices
train	10:00	train tour at 10:00
	11:00	train tour at 11:00
	12:00	train tour at 12:00
tram	10:00	tram tour at 10:00
	11:00	tram tour at 11:00
	12:00	tram tour at 12:00

Look Back   This answer is sensible. The family has six choices to choose from. There are two tours to choose from and three times to choose from. All of these are listed.

■ **Talk About Math**   How many choices does the family have? Suppose there is also a 1:00 tour. How would this change the tree diagram? How many choices would the family have?

The earliest known zoo was established in Egypt about 1500 B.C.

56

Check Understanding

The Chens want to see either the dolphin show or the elephant show in the morning. They also want to attend the feeding of either the seals or the lions in the afternoon.

1. Copy and complete the diagram to find the possible choices that the Chens have for going to a show and to a feeding.

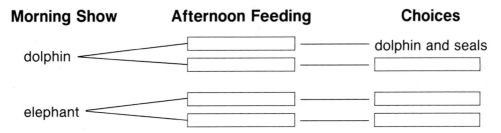

Morning Show	Afternoon Feeding		Choices

2. Suppose the Chens also want to see the small animal show. Now how many choices do they have for going to a show and a feeding?

Practice

Solve each problem by making a tree diagram.

3. The souvenir shop sells T-shirts with an animal printed on the front. You can choose between a lion and a zebra. You can choose a small, medium, large, or extra large size. List all the shirt choices.

4. The sandwich shop at the zoo offers egg salad, tuna salad, and chicken salad sandwiches. You have a choice of your salad on rye, whole wheat, or white bread. List all the sandwich choices.

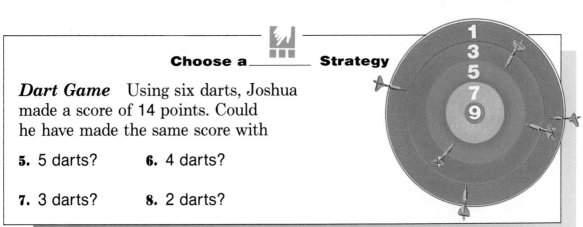

Choose a ———— Strategy

Dart Game Using six darts, Joshua made a score of 14 points. Could he have made the same score with

5. 5 darts? **6.** 4 darts?

7. 3 darts? **8.** 2 darts?

Solve each problem.

1. A kilogram is 1,000 grams. How many kilograms are in 6,000 grams?

2. Which state is larger, Vermont or New Hampshire?

State	Area (Square Miles)
Delaware	2,044
New Jersey	7,787
Hawaii	6,471
Rhode Island	1,212
Vermont	9,614
New Hampshire	9,279
Connecticut	5,018

3. Which state has an area that is between the areas of Connecticut and New Jersey?

4. Round the area of each state to the nearest hundred square miles.

5. Use the digits 9, 2, 7, and 4. Write the smallest possible 4-digit number.

6. At Jamie's Juice Bar, you can get apple, grape, orange, or pineapple juice in 8- or 12-oz sizes. How many choices are there?

7. **Data File** Use data from pages 102-103. Before what year was the population of the colonies less than one million?

8. **Make a Data File** Collect examples of large numbers from newspapers, magazines, or other references. Which numbers are rounded? Which are not rounded? Make a chart to show your data.

Explore with a Calculator

Don't go nuts!

Stanley Squirrel collected 4 nuts the first day and 4 times that many the second day. On the third day he and his friends collected 4 times as many as he had collected on the second day.

This went on for days. Every day, they collected 4 times as many nuts as the day before. If this continued, how long would it take Stanley and his friends to collect at least one million nuts in a single day?

4 ⊠ 4 ⊠ 4 ⊠ 4 ⊠ 4 ⊠ 4 ⊠ 4 ⊠ 4 ⊠ 4 ⊠ 4 ⊟ 1048576

Since 4 was multiplied by itself 10 times, it would take Stanley and his friends 10 days to collect at least one million nuts.

1. Press each key sequence. Copy the product from the display. Remember to write the commas.

a. 16 ⊠ 16 ⊠ 16 ⊠ 16 ⊠ 16 ⊟

b. 90 ⊠ 90 ⊠ 90 ⊠ 90 ⊟

c. 10 ⊠ 10 ⊠ 10 ⊠ 10 ⊠ 10 ⊠ 10 ⊠ 10 ⊟

2. Multiply each number by itself. Tell how many times it takes to reach at least one million. Write the final product.

a. 12   **c.** 7   **e.** 40

b. 5   **d.** 2   **f.** 66

Reteaching

Set A   pages 38–39

A dictionary in the library has one thousand, one hundred thirty-six pages.

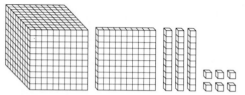

1 thousand   1 hundred   3 tens   6 ones
1,000   +   100   +   30   +   6
1,136 ← standard form

Remember that the place of each digit tells you the value of that digit.

Write each number in standard form.

1. 6 thousands, 4 tens, 5 ones

2. one thousand, two hundred six

Write each number in words.

3. 1,800   **4.** 9,467

Set B   pages 40–41

You know that 4,040 has 4 thousands. How many hundreds are in 4,040?

Cover the tens and the ones places.

4,0 4 0

4,040 has 40 hundreds.

How many tens are in 4,040? Cover the ones place.

4,0 4 0

4,040 has 404 tens.

Remember that 100 is 10 tens, and 1,000 is 10 hundreds.

Copy and complete.

1. 860 = ▦ tens

2. 5,000 = ▦ tens

3. 2,000 = ▦ hundreds

4. 6,300 = ▦ hundreds

Set C   pages 44–47

Compare 1,459 and 1,450.

Compare the thousands digits.	1,459 1,450	same
Compare the hundreds digits.	1,459 1,450	same
Compare the tens digits.	1,459 1,450	same
Compare the ones digits.	1,459 1,450	9 > 0

1,459 > 1,450

Remember that > means *greater than* and < means *less than*.

Compare the numbers. Use < or >.

1. 4,840 ▦ 4,799

2. 6,841 ▦ 6,838

3. 9,432 ▦ 9,436

4. 5,582 ▦ 3,972

5. 3,686 ▦ 2,846

Set D pages 50–51

Round 3,682 to the nearest thousand.

The digit 3 is in the thousands place. The digit to the right of 3 is 6. When the digit to the right is 5 or more, add 1 to the digit in the place to be rounded.

So, the answer is 4,000.

Remember that the digit in the place to be rounded stays the same if the digit to its right is less than 5.

Round each number to the nearest hundred; to the nearest thousand.

1. 1,946   **2.** 4,810

3. 7,252   **4.** 5,038

Set E pages 52–53

The population of Manchester is 120,835.

thousands period			ones period		
hundred-thousands	ten-thousands	thousands	hundreds	tens	ones
1	2	0	8	3	5

The number is read:
one hundred twenty thousand, eight hundred thirty-five.

Remember that counting from the right, each group of three digits forms a place-value period.

Write each number in words.

1. 70,000   **2.** 42,300

3. 800,048   **4.** 632,444

Write these numbers in standard form.

5. four hundred thirty-nine thousand, two hundred eight

6. six hundred eight thousand, forty

Set F pages 54–55

millions period			thousands period			ones period		
hundred-millions	ten-millions	millions	hundred-thousands	ten-thousands	thousands	hundreds	tens	ones
3	7	4	6	0	3	0	2	0

The number 374,603,020 is read:
three hundred seventy-four million, six hundred three thousand, twenty.

Remember that a comma separates each group of three digits, or period, beginning at the right.

Give the standard form. **Remember** to use zeros as place holders.

1. three million, six hundred fifty-one thousand, nine hundred

2. seventy-three million, forty-five thousand, seven

More Practice

Set A   pages 38–39

Write each number in standard form.

1. 4 thousands, 6 tens, 3 ones   **2.** 8,000 + 300 + 20 + 7

3. seven thousand, eight hundred nineteen

Write each number in words.

4. 706   **5.** 9,340   **6.** 4,962   **7.** 6,084   **8.** 4,003

Consider the number 6,934. Write the number that is

9. 1,000 less.   **10.** 100 less.   **11.** 1,000 more.   **12.** 100 more.

For each number, tell what digit is in the given place.

13. 4,320 (hundreds)   **14.** 9,452 (thousands)   **15.** 6,546 (tens)

Set B   pages 40–41

Copy and complete.

1. 350 = ▦ tens   **2.** 6,000 = ▦ tens   **3.** 9,050 = ▦ tens

4. 7,000 = ▦ thousands   **5.** 8,200 = ▦ hundreds   **6.** 5,700 = ▦ hundreds

Write the standard form of the number.

7. 49 tens   **8.** 800 tens   **9.** 6 hundreds   **10.** 57 tens

11. 70 hundreds   **12.** 5,249 ones   **13.** 7 thousands   **14.** 13 hundreds

Set C   pages 44–47

Compare these numbers. Use < or >.

1. 6,243 ▦ 6,481   **2.** 3,929 ▦ 3,907   **3.** 7,461 ▦ 7,460

4. 9,293 ▦ 9,162   **5.** 8,036 ▦ 8,320   **6.** 2,146 ▦ 2,139

Write the numbers in order from least to greatest.

7. 4,173   2,083   3,471   **8.** 3,826   3,854   3,830

9. 5,809   5,980   5,806   **10.** 2,619   996   2,916

Set D pages 50–51

Round each number to the nearest hundred; to the nearest thousand.

1. 736   2. 6,881   3. 4,403   4. 2,562   5. 8,222

6. 9,072   7. 3,912   8. 7,353   9. 8,644   10. 3,194

Set E pages 52–53

Write each number in words.

1. 40,000   2. 35,800   3. 700,055   4. 938,666

Write each number in standard form.

5. six hundred seventy-two thousand, two hundred one
6. eight hundred nine thousand, sixty-three

7. four hundred thousand, three hundred
8. twenty-nine thousand, one hundred eleven

For each of the following numbers, what number is 10,000 more? 1,000 less?

9. 36,800   10. 607,333   11. 840,560   12. 587,003

Mixed Practice Write the number that is

13. 1,000 more than 8,600.   14. 100 less than 4,000.

15. 10,000 more than 63,890.   16. 10 less than 864.

Set F pages 54–55

Give the standard form.

1. ninety-four million, eighty-six thousand, five
2. fourteen million, two hundred thousand, six hundred twelve

3. 40 million, 309 thousand   4. 6 million, 19 thousand, 5

Write each number in words.

5. 842,560   6. 7,400,816   7. 52,384,261   8. 494,302,182

Tell what each 6 means.

9. 12,680,142   10. 365,102,891   11. 6,800,189   12. 648,024,914

Enrichment

Roman Numerals

The Romans of long ago used numerals very different from ours. We still use Roman numerals today.

I = 1	C = 100
V = 5	D = 500
X = 10	M = 1,000
L = 50	

Most Roman numerals are written using addition.				Some numerals are written using subtraction.			
II	VI	XIII	LXX	IV	IX	XL	XC
1 + 1	5 + 1	10 + 3	50 + 20	5 − 1	10 − 1	50 − 10	100 − 10
2	6	13	70	4	9	40	90

Here are other examples.

XXV	XLIX	XCVI	MD
XX V	XL IX	XC VI	M D
20 + 5	40 + 9	90 + 6	1,000 + 500
25	49	96	1,500

Write the standard number.

1. III **2.** VII **3.** XIII **4.** XVI **5.** XXI **6.** XXXIV

7. XLV **8.** LXXX **9.** LXI **10.** CX **11.** DL **12.** MC

Write the Roman numeral.

13. 3 **14.** 8 **15.** 9 **16.** 11 **17.** 14 **18.** 20

19. 35 **20.** 41 **21.** 65 **22.** 98 **23.** 600 **24.** 1,200

Chapter 2 Review/Test

For each number, tell what digit is in the given place.

1. 3,619 (hundreds)

2. 7,254 (thousands)

Write the standard form for each number.

3. 5,000 + 200 + 30 + 5

4. two thousand, two hundred two

5. 47 tens   **6.** 85 hundreds

Compare these numbers.
Use < or >.

7. 1,691 ⬚ 1,618

8. 6,524 ⬚ 6,529

9. Write the numbers in order from least to greatest.

  7,193   7,300   3,197

Round 4,547 to the nearest

10. hundred.   **11.** thousand.

12. Write in words: 500,900.

13. What number is 10,000 more than 384,168?

Tell what each 9 means.

14. 19,361,524   **15.** 395,168

16. Choose the most sensible answer.

  Mr. Flynn bought 12 oranges. He squeezed some for juice. How many oranges did he have left?

  7   12   25

Items 17–19 refer to the following problem.

Jane bought a white sweater, a black one, and a red one. She also bought a blue skirt and a brown one. How many combinations of a new sweater and a new skirt are possible?

17. Suppose you began to solve this problem by drawing the tree diagram shown below.

Sweater	Skirt
white —	
black	

  How many choices of skirt would you show for each choice of sweater?

18. List the possible combinations of sweaters and skirts that Jane can wear.

19. Solve the problem.

20. **Write About Math** For Item 16, explain why the answers you did *not* choose are not sensible.

Addition and Subtraction

3

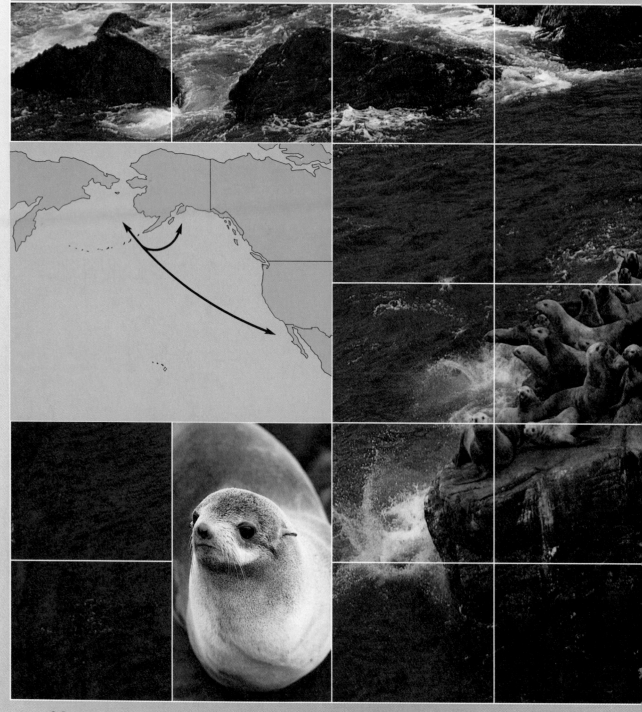

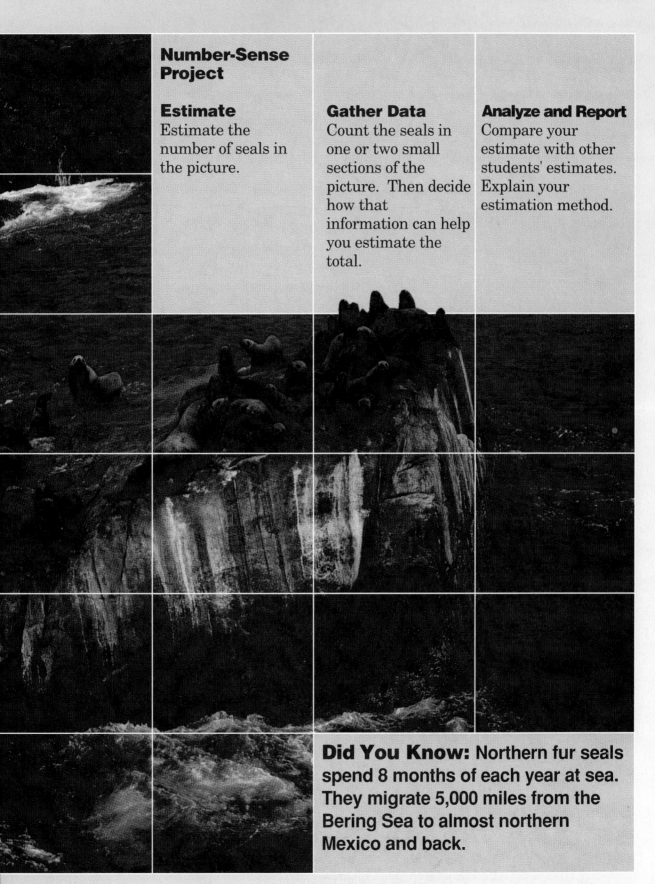

Number-Sense Project

Estimate
Estimate the number of seals in the picture.

Gather Data
Count the seals in one or two small sections of the picture. Then decide how that information can help you estimate the total.

Analyze and Report
Compare your estimate with other students' estimates. Explain your estimation method.

Did You Know: Northern fur seals spend 8 months of each year at sea. They migrate 5,000 miles from the Bering Sea to almost northern Mexico and back.

Addition and Subtraction Patterns: Mental Math

Build Understanding

The Declaration of Independence is on display in the National Archives Exhibition Hall in Washington, D.C.

A. The Declaration of Independence was adopted on July 4, 1776. A celebration of the 200th anniversary was held in 1976. In what year will the 300th anniversary be celebrated?

Count by hundreds.

1776	1876	1976	2076
↘↗	↘↗	↘↗	
+ 100	+ 100	+ 100	

The 300th anniversary will be celebrated in 2076.

B. The zipper was invented in 1891. The lawn mower was invented 60 years earlier. In what year was the lawn mower invented?

Find 1891 − 60.

Think of 60 as 6 tens and then subtract 6 from the tens digit of 1891.
1891 − 60 = 1831

The lawn mower was invented in 1831.

■ **Talk About Math** Discuss how you would add 4,000 to 23,568. Discuss how you would subtract 9,000 from 19,857.

Check Understanding

For another example, see Set A, pages 96–97.

Solve each problem.

1. Regular broadcast television in the United States was 50 years old in 1989. In what year did it begin?

2. The washing machine was invented 10 years after the zipper. What year was that? Refer to Example B on page 68.

For each exercise, start at 3,765.

3. Count by ones to 3,773.

4. Count by tens to 3,825.

5. Count backward by hundreds to 2,865.

6. Count backward by thousands to 765.

Practice

For More Practice, see Set A, pages 98–99.

Add or subtract mentally.

7. 306 + 200

8. 103 + 30

9. 828 − 600

10. 3,042 + 20

11. 2,615 + 400

12. 8,430 − 100

13. 6,895 − 3,000

14. 4,550 + 1,000

15. 9,800 − 7,000

16. 3,782
  − 200

17. 4,521
  −   60

18. 15,690
  + 2,000

19. 25,908
  − 4,000

Problem Solving

Read for the facts. Then solve each problem.

20. The first transcontinental railroad was completed in North America in 1869. One hundred years later, the first person set foot on the moon. What year was that?

21. How many years passed from 1851, when Gorrie invented an ice-making machine, to 1911, when Carrier invented air conditioning?

Estimating Sums and Differences

Build Understanding

A. Mr. Thompson is a pilot. He is flying 2,398 miles from Honolulu to San Francisco, 2,572 miles from San Francisco to New York, and 3,469 miles from New York to London. About how many miles will his trip be?

The first jet airliner service between the United States and Europe began in 1958

Estimate 2,398 + 2,572 + 3,469 by adding the *front-end digits*.

2,398 + 2,572 + 3,469

Think: 2 + 2 + 3 = 7
      7 thousands = 7,000

The trip will be about 7,000 miles.

If you need a closer estimate, you can adjust the first estimate by considering the hundreds digits.

2,398 + 2,572 + 3,469   Think: 3 + 5 + 4 = 12
                               12 hundreds = 1,200
                               There are at least 1,000
                               more miles.

A closer estimate is 8,000 miles.

B. Estimate the sum by rounding both numbers to the nearest thousand.

4,356 + 8,509
   ↓   ↓
4,000 + 9,000 = 13,000

C. Estimate the difference by rounding both numbers to the nearest ten-thousand.

76,875 − 31,821
   ↓   ↓
80,000 − 30,000 = 50,000

■ **Talk About Math** How would you use rounding to estimate the sum in Example A?

Check Understanding

For another example, see Set B, pages 96–97.

Estimate each sum or difference.

1. Round each number to the nearest thousand.

2,417 + 3,729

↓   ↓

▦ + ▦ = ▦

2. Round each number to the nearest ten-thousand.

92,630 − 29,400

↓   ↓

▦ − ▦ = ▦

3. Use only the front-end digits.

5,840 + 3,921

4. Use the hundreds digits to adjust the estimate in Exercise 3.

Practice

For More Practice, see Set B, pages 98–99.

Estimate each sum or difference.

Round each number to the nearest thousand.

5. 3,889 + 1,650	**6.** 5,324 + 9,485	**7.** 8,722 − 2,199	**8.** 7,570 − 4,935	**9.** 6,081 8,275 + 4,350

Round each number to the nearest ten-thousand.

10. 75,380 − 13,652	**11.** 42,895 + 58,534	**12.** 91,298 − 29,081	**13.** 37,150 + 34,756	**14.** 86,274 − 50,625

Use front-end digits. Adjust your estimate.

15. 5,422 + 2,950	**16.** 68,895 + 72,200	**17.** 3,325 6,842 + 7,199	**18.** 42,675 28,096 + 59,410	**19.** 3,442 2,519 + 980

Skills ——— Review   pages 44–47

Compare the following numbers. Use > or <.

1. 3,127 ▦ 3,207   **2.** 7,920 ▦ 7,902   **3.** 1,298 ▦ 1,398

4. 1,788 ▦ 1,990   **5.** 4,999 ▦ 5,000   **6.** 8,898 ▦ 8,878

Choosing a Computation Method

Build Understanding

Johanna, Willy, and Toshio were the judges for Math Contest Day. For one contest, all the students tried to guess the number of peanuts in a glass jar. One student's guess was 1,198. If 1,228 peanuts were in the jar, how close was the guess?

The three students agreed that they had to subtract to find how far the guess was from the correct number.

Pencil and Paper
Johanna used pencil and paper to write:

```
  1,2 2 8
− 1,1 9 8
─────────
     3 0
```

Mental Math
Willy thought:

1,198 is 2 less than 1,200.
1,228 − 1,200 = 28
28 + 2 = 30

Calculator
Toshio reached for his calculator and entered:

1228 $\boxed{-}$ 1198 $\boxed{=}$

Display: *30*

They agreed that 1,198 peanuts was 30 less than the correct number.

■ **Talk About Math** Which computation method do you like best? Why?

Check Understanding

For another example, see Set C, pages 96–97.

Tell whether you would use paper and pencil, mental math, or a calculator. Then find each answer.

1.	**2.**	**3.**	**4.**	**5.**
486	6,573	55	39	537
+ 199	− 1,392	− 19	+ 50	+ 286

Practice

For More Practice, see Set C, pages 98–99.

Tell whether you would use paper and pencil, mental math, or a calculator. Then find each answer.

6. 65
 + 97

7. 4,782
 − 3,226

8. 237
 + 863

9. 5,031
 + 1,000

10. 478
 − 285

11. 79
 − 36

12. 5,018
 + 3,897

13. 644
 − 111

14. 1,782
 + 4,218

15. 989
 − 199

16. 23 + 12 + 5

17. 908 + 357 + 1,356

18. 2,895 − 1,497

Problem Solving

Tell whether you would use paper and pencil, mental math, or a calculator to solve each problem and why. Then solve the problem.

19. In a contest, students tried to guess the distance around the outside of the school. Which of the guesses, 810 feet or 725 feet, is closer to the correct distance of 768 feet?

20. Students also tried to guess the distance across the baseball diamond. Which of the guesses, 150 feet or 105 feet, is closer to the correct distance of 128 feet?

Explore ———— Math

Number Sense In each exercise, fill in the boxes with the digits 1, 2, 3, 4, and 5. Use each digit once in each exercise.

21. ☐☐☐
 + ☐☐
 ‾‾‾‾‾
 1 7 7

22. ☐☐☐
 − ☐☐
 ‾‾‾‾‾
 5 2 2

23. ☐☐☐
 − ☐☐
 ‾‾‾‾‾
 2 7 6

24. ☐☐☐
 − ☐☐
 ‾‾‾‾‾
 1 1 8

25. ☐☐
 ☐☐
 + ☐
 ‾‾‾‾
 4 2

26. ☐☐☐
 − ☐☐
 ‾‾‾‾
 6 9

Renaming for Addition and Subtraction

Build Understanding

A. On Monday Jason Chang repackaged nails to be sold at his father's hardware store. Explain how he regrouped the nails. How many nails did he have in all?

Cases Thousands	Boxes Hundreds	Packs Tens	Singles Ones
3	17	4	16

Cases Thousands	Boxes Hundreds	Packs Tens	Singles Ones
3	17	5	6

Cases Thousands	Boxes Hundreds	Packs Tens	Singles Ones
4	7	5	6

He had 4,756 nails.

4,756 ← standard form

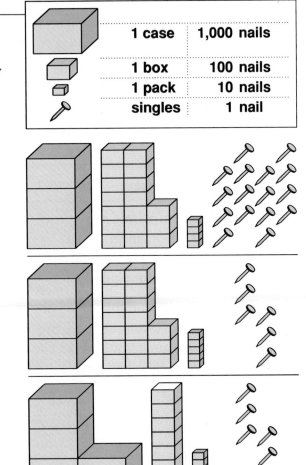

	1 case	1,000 nails
	1 box	100 nails
	1 pack	10 nails
	singles	1 nail

B. When a customer came into the store on Friday, the inventory of nails consisted of 3 cases, 1 pack, and 7 nails. The customer wanted to buy 2 packs of nails. Explain how Jason had to rearrange the inventory so that he could sell 2 packs of nails.

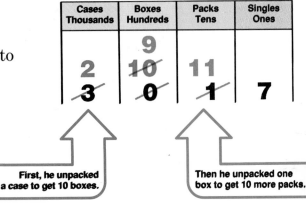

Cases Thousands	Boxes Hundreds	Packs Tens	Singles Ones
2̶3̶	9̶ 1̶0̶ 0̶	1̶1̶ 1̶	7

First, he unpacked a case to get 10 boxes.

Then he unpacked one box to get 10 more packs.

74

■**Talk About Math** What is the standard form of the number at the right?

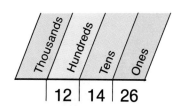

Thousands	Hundreds	Tens	Ones
12	14	26	

Check Understanding

For another example, see Set D, pages 96–97.

Write how many

1. tens can be made from 16 ones. How many ones are left?

2. thousands can be made from 23 hundreds. How many hundreds are left?

Practice

For More Practice, see Set D, pages 98–99.

Rename to show the number in standard form.

3.
6 | 2 | 17 | 3

4.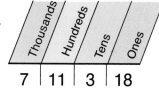
7 | 11 | 3 | 18

5.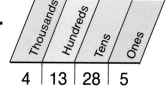
4 | 13 | 28 | 5

Copy each chart. Rename to show 10 more ones.

6.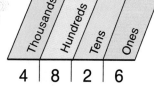
4 | 8 | 2 | 6

7.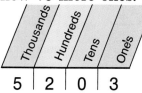
5 | 2 | 0 | 3

8.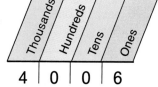
4 | 0 | 0 | 6

Copy each chart. Rename to show 10 more tens.

9.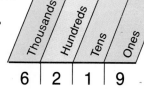
6 | 2 | 1 | 9

10.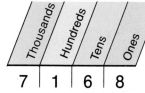
7 | 1 | 6 | 8

11.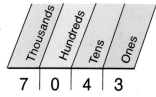
7 | 0 | 4 | 3

Problem Solving

Number Sense Find each number. Explain how you found it.

12. I am 15 ones and 6 tens greater than 3,486. Who am I?

13. I am both 15 ones less than 2,305 and 6 tens greater than 2,230. Who am I?

Adding Thousands

Build Understanding

Mr. Jackson asked his students to record the number of pages they read in library period each week. The class read a total of 2,198 pages the first week. The next week they read a total of 2,831 pages. How many pages did the class read during the two weeks?

Find 2,198 + 2,831.

Estimation Estimate the answer by rounding the addends: 2,000 + 3,000 = 5,000. The sum should be about 5,000.

Paper and Pencil

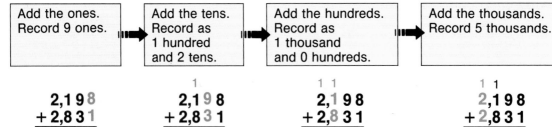

Add the ones. Record 9 ones.	Add the tens. Record as 1 hundred and 2 tens.	Add the hundreds. Record as 1 thousand and 0 hundreds.	Add the thousands. Record 5 thousands.
$\begin{array}{r} 2,198 \\ +2,831 \\ \hline 9 \end{array}$	$\begin{array}{r} 1 \\ 2,198 \\ +2,831 \\ \hline 29 \end{array}$	$\begin{array}{r} 1\,1 \\ 2,198 \\ +2,831 \\ \hline 029 \end{array}$	$\begin{array}{r} 1\,1 \\ 2,198 \\ +2,831 \\ \hline 5,029 \end{array}$

Calculator 2198 $+$ 2831 $=$ *5029.*

The students read 5,029 pages.
Is this answer reasonable? Why or why not?

■ **Write About Math** Estimate and then find the sum of 3,126 + 4,507 + 6,289. Then explain each step of the operation and how to record it. Is your answer reasonable? Why or why not?

Check Understanding

For another example, see Set E, pages 96–97.

1. Estimate the sum of 5,643 + 2,587. Then use paper and pencil to find the sum. **Remember** to add the ones first.

2. 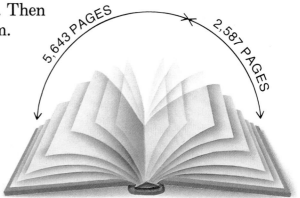 **Calculator** Use a calculator to find the sum in Exercise 1.

3. Would you use paper and pencil or a calculator to find 2,975 + 1,225? Explain your answer.

Practice

For More Practice, see Set E, pages 98–99.

Tell whether you would use paper and pencil or a calculator. Then find each sum.

4.	6,817 + 1,240	**5.**	1,975 + 5,062	**6.**	5,690 + 596	**7.**	7,126 + 2,008
8.	460 1,615 + 3,209	**9.**	528 3,379 + 1,314	**10.**	5,168 719 + 2,420	**11.**	807 1,261 + 8,037
12.	3,409 + 3,401	**13.**	5,678 + 2,321	**14.**	1,282 + 19,829	**15.**	23,458 + 24,983

Problem Solving

Tell whether you would use mental math, paper and pencil, or a calculator. Then solve each problem.

16. Last summer the library lent 3,836 books in June, 4,036 books in July, and 5,259 books in August. About how many books did the library lend last summer?

17. In August, the library lent 1,928 mysteries and 897 more novels than mysteries. Find the total number of novels and mysteries lent by the library during August.

77

Subtracting Thousands

Build Understanding

Saltwater Fish	Weight	Year Caught
Atlantic halibut	250 lb	1981
bluefin tuna	1,496 lb	1979
blue shark	437 lb	1979
tiger shark	1,780 lb	1964
white shark	2,664 lb	1959

A. Jessica is the sports reporter for a local newspaper. She is using a chart for a feature article about some of the biggest fish ever caught. Jessica wants to compare the weights of the tiger shark and the white shark.

She needs to find 2,664 − 1,780.

Estimation   First, she estimates the difference.

3,000 − 2,000 = 1,000

Then she finds the actual difference.

Paper and Pencil

> Subtract the ones. Rename to show 10 more tens. Subtract the tens. ➡

```
  5 16
2,6̸ 6̸ 4    6 hundreds and 6 tens equals
−1,7 8 0    5 hundreds and 16 tens.
───────
     8 4
```

> Rename to show 10 more hundreds. Subtract the hundreds and thousands.

```
 1 1516
2,6̸ 6̸ 4    2 thousands and 6 hundreds equals
−1,7 8 0    1 thousand and 15 hundreds.
───────
   8 8 4
```

Calculator

2664 [−] 1780 [=] 884.

The difference in the record weights of the white shark and the tiger shark is **884** pounds.

B. Find 1,700 − 360.

There are no ones.
Rename to show 10 tens.
Subtract.

Use addition to check
subtraction.
Check:

```
      6 10
  1,7̸0 0        7 hundreds      1,3 4 0
 −  3 6 0       equals         +  3 6 0
  ‾‾‾‾‾‾‾       6 hundreds      ‾‾‾‾‾‾‾
  1,3 4 0       and 10 tens.    1,7 0 0
```

■ **Write About Math** How many years after
the record white shark was caught was the record
tiger shark caught?

Check Understanding

For another example, see Set F, pages 96–97.

Copy and complete each exercise. First estimate
each difference.

1. 8,5 4 6
  − 6,1 2 4
  ‾‾‾‾‾‾‾

2. 4,0 9 0
  − 2,9 0 0
  ‾‾‾‾‾‾‾

3. 3,9 0 0
  − 3,2 8 7
  ‾‾‾‾‾‾‾

4. 5,0 0 0
  − 2,4 6 8
  ‾‾‾‾‾‾‾

Practice

For More Practice, see Set F, pages 98–99.

Tell whether you would use paper and pencil or a
calculator. Find each difference.

5. 1,847
  − 673

6. 3,703
  − 582

7. 8,545
  − 6,922

8. 4,922
  − 3,837

9. 6,100
  − 964

10. 2,184
  − 1,269

11. 7,000
  − 5,603

12. 4,836
  − 3,817

13. 2,493
  − 1,607

14. 7,000
  − 4,158

15. 8,435
  − 6,097

16. 5,245
  − 3,852

17. 3,901 − 568

18. 1,482 − 1,206

19. 1,800 − 1,491

20. 4,301 − 4,201

21. 9,001 − 991

22. 4,000 − 999

Problem Solving

Solve each problem. Use the table on page 78 for Problems 23–28.

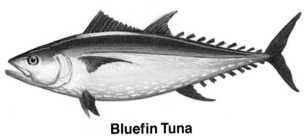

Bluefin Tuna

Black Marlin

Atlantic Halibut

White Shark

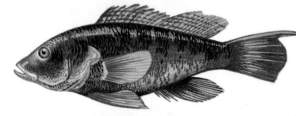

Black Sea Bass

23. How much more does the record bluefin tuna weigh than the record blue shark?

24. The record black marlin weighed 64 pounds more than the record bluefin tuna. How much did the black marlin weigh?

25. The record Atlantic halibut weighs 100 pounds less than the record Pacific halibut. What is the weight of the record Pacific halibut?

26. A typical white shark weighs 1,700 pounds. How much more does the record white shark weigh than the typical white shark?

27. Joe Mizelle, Sr., caught a record black sea bass in 1979. In 1987, Joe Mizelle, Jr., caught a black sea bass 12 ounces heavier than the fish caught in 1979. How many years passed between these two records?

28. About 1610, American settlers began to hunt whales. In 1971, the federal government outlawed whaling in the United States. For how many years was whaling allowed in America?

Clem's Chowder Clem helps to fill take-out orders at his parents' restaurant. One day, Clem had to make up 2-quart orders of clam chowder, but there were no 2-quart containers left.

29. How could Clem measure out 2 quarts of clam chowder using only 3-quart and 4-quart containers?

30. If Clem had only 5-quart and 3-quart containers, how could he measure out 4 quarts?

Midchapter _____ Checkup

Add or subtract mentally.
1. 468 + 300   **2.** 5,355 − 2,000   **3.** 6,725 + 50   **4.** 4,850 − 700

Estimate each sum or difference.

5. 6,989	**6.** 3,392	**7.** 5,835	**8.** 8,470
− 1,736	+ 5,249	+ 1,290	− 5,936

Tell whether you would use mental math, paper and pencil, or a calculator. Then find each answer.

9. 45	**10.** 4,560	**11.** 6,849	**12.** 490
+ 78	− 300	+ 7,482	− 210

13. Write the number 4 thousands, 13 hundreds, 1 ten, 15 ones in standard form.

Rename the number at the right to show
14. 10 more ones.   **15.** 10 more tens.

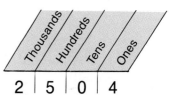

Find each sum or difference.
16. 7,245 + 2,806   **17.** 8,534 − 3,791   **18.** 5,400 − 2,907

Problem Solving WORKSHOP

Real-Life Decision Making

Suppose you go to your aunt's house for a week's vacation. She is willing to take you to several attractions, but she does not want to drive more than 400 miles during the week. You can visit only one major attraction in a day, and you will stay at your aunt's house each night.

Space Museum

Aunt's House

8 mi

37 mi

49 mi

78 mi

Sea Life Park

35 mi

12 mi

Buster Bronco's Ranch

29 mi

26 mi

30 mi

Wild Animal Zoo

Splashing Waters

1. What is the shortest round-trip distance from your aunt's house to Sea Life Park?

2. What is the shortest round-trip distance to Splashing Waters?

3. Decide which attractions you want to visit. List the routes you will take to each attraction and the round-trip distance. Make sure that the total distance is less than 400 miles.

Critical-Thinking Activity

Five runners finished a race. Alice came in first. Brad came in last. Darren was ahead of Cathleen. Ellen was just behind Cathleen. Who came in second?

Explore with a Computer

Use the *Spreadsheet Workshop Project* for this activity.
The Neighborhood Project collects papers, glass, and cans
for recycling. They collected 11,239 pounds in one month.

1. They want to collect the same amount this month. The captain
has recorded the pounds collected so far for this month. Estimate the
amounts missing in the table that would allow them to reach their goal.

2. At the computer, type your estimates in the spreadsheet. Is
your total too high or too low? Change the amounts so the total
pounds collected is exactly 11,239.

Paper	Glass	Cans	Total
	932	824	
2,207	1,273		
1,536		706	
			11,239

Number-Sense Project

Look back at pages 66-67.

1. Two scientists estimated the population of seals on an island.
One estimate was 4,500 and the other was 3,700. Find the difference
between the estimates.

2. 🖩 **Calculator** In the spring,
Northern fur seals migrate
2,500 miles in about 120 days.
Divide to find out about
how many miles they
travel each day.

Choose an Operation

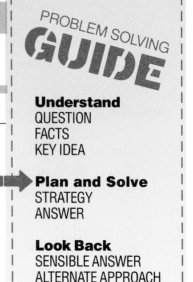

Build Understanding

The youngest person to become President of the United States was Theodore Roosevelt. He was born in 1858 and became President at the age of 42. In what year did Theodore Roosevelt become President of the United States?

Understand   QUESTION   In what year did Theodore Roosevelt become President of the United States?

FACTS   Roosevelt was born in 1858. He became President at the age of 42.

KEY IDEA   Roosevelt became President 42 years after he was born.

**Plan and Solve**   STRATEGY   Add Roosevelt's age to the year that he was born to find the year he became President.

$$\begin{array}{r} 1858 \\ +\ \ 42 \\ \hline 1900 \end{array}$$

ANSWER   Theodore Roosevelt became President in 1900.

Look Back   ALTERNATE STRATEGY   Starting with 1858, count 4 tens and then 2 ones.

1858	1868	1878	1888	1898	1900
$+10$	$+10$	$+10$	$+10$	$+2$	

The answer using either method is 1900.

■ **Talk About Math**   Theodore Roosevelt served as President from 1901 until 1909. Explain how you would find the number of years he served as President.

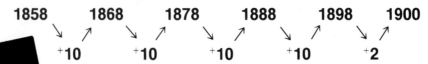

Theodore Roosevelt was the 26th President of the United States.

Check Understanding

Tell whether you would add or subtract the missing numbers to solve the problem.

1. John Adams became President in ▓▓. His son, John Quincy, became President ▓▓ years later. In what year did John Quincy Adams become President?

2. Grover Cleveland's first term as President ended in ▓▓. He served a second term as President starting in ▓▓. How many years passed between his two terms?

Practice

Solve each problem.

3. John F. Kennedy was another young President. He was born in 1917 and elected President in 1960. How old was he when he was elected President?

4. The oldest person to be elected President was Ronald Reagan. He was born in 1911 and was elected President 69 years later. In what year was he elected President?

5. Thomas Jefferson was elected President in 1800 at the age of 57. What was the year of his birth?

6. Abraham Lincoln was born in 1809 and elected President at the age of 51. In what year was he elected President?

7. George Washington, the first President, was born in 1732 and died in 1799. How old was he when he died?

8. Franklin Delano Roosevelt was President from 1933 until 1945. How many years was he President?

9. In 1858 Abraham Lincoln became nationally famous for his debates with Stephen Douglas. The Nixon-Kennedy debates in 1960 were the first televised debates between candidates. How many years separated these famous debates?

10. The Emancipation Proclamation was issued by President Abraham Lincoln in 1862. The Civil Rights Act was signed by President Lyndon Johnson 102 years later. In what year was the Civil Rights Act signed into law?

Estimating with Money

Build Understanding

When you solve problems that involve money, you may not need exact answers. You may be able to solve a problem faster by rounding to the nearest dollar or to the nearest 10 dollars.

A. Harold has $20. Does he have enough money to buy shorts and a sports bag?

shorts	$6.95	Round to the nearest dollar.	$7
sports bag	$9.98	Round to the nearest dollar.	+ $10
			$17

The total price will be about $17. Harold has enough money.

B. Jerry has $100. He wants to buy a sweatsuit, running shoes, and a jacket. Does he have enough money?

sweatsuit	$28.95	$30	
running shoes	$38.95	$40	Each price has been rounded to the nearest 10 dollars.
jacket	$40.99	+ $40	
		$110	

The total price will be about $110. Jerry does not have enough money.

■ **Talk About Math** Why does it seem reasonable to round to the nearest dollar in Example A and to the nearest 10 dollars in Example B?

$5.95 T-SHIRTS

SHORTS $6.95

RUNNING SHOES $38.95

SWEAT SUIT $28.95

JACKET $40.99

SPORTS BAG $9.98

Check Understanding

For another example, see Set G, pages 96–97.

Round each of these amounts to the nearest dollar.

1. $4.95   **2.** $6.25   **3.** $8.50   **4.** $13.79   **5.** $19.95

Round each of these amounts to the nearest 10 dollars.

6. $18.45   **7.** $24.12   **8.** $46.00   **9.** $72.99   **10.** $87.98

Practice

For More Practice, see Set G, pages 98–99.

Estimate each sum by rounding to the nearest dollar.

11. $1.90	**12.** $7.68	**13.** $30.06	**14.** $28.79	**15.** $41.22
0.74	2.04	2.42	9.94	6.80
+ 2.35	+ 1.80	+ 3.52	+ 46.07	+ 1.75

Estimate each sum by rounding to the nearest 10 dollars.

16. $58.15	**17.** $24.57	**18.** $83.12	**19.** $36.43	**20.** $242.18
22.13	10.35	9.49	25.81	117.24
+ 15.80	+ 43.03	18.75	41.90	+ 351.92
		+ 32.28	+ 2.71	

Mixed Practice   Use mental math, paper and pencil, or a calculator to find each answer. Explain your method.

21. 30 + 40   **22.** 810 − 240   **23.** 1,023 + 47   **24.** 6,840 − 5,270

Problem Solving

Solve each problem. Use information from the chart on page 86 for Problem 26.

25. Critical Thinking   What is the pattern in the answers to Exercises 21–24?

26. Maria has $20. Does she have enough money to buy 3 pairs of shorts? Explain your answer.

Renaming with Money

Build Understanding

Exploring Dollars and Cents
Materials: Play money (pennies, dimes, $1 bills, and $10 bills)
Groups: 2 to 4 students

A. Combine your money.
  a. Take 2 $10 bills. Then take any number from 11 to 19 of each of the coins and dollar bills. Set aside the other money to make exchanges.

  b. Record the money in a chart.

$10 bills	$1 bills	Dimes	Pennies

  c. Make as many exchanges as you can. Exchange 10 pennies for a dime, 10 dimes for a $1 bill, and 10 $1 bills for a $10 bill. Record the exchanges.

B. Combine your money.
  a. Take 2 $10 bills. Then take any number from 1 to 9 of each of the coins and dollar bills. Set aside the other money to make exchanges.

  b. Record the money in a chart.

  c. Make an exchange to show 10 more pennies. Next, make an exchange to show 10 more dimes. Make a final exchange to show 10 more $1 bills. Record the exchanges on the chart.

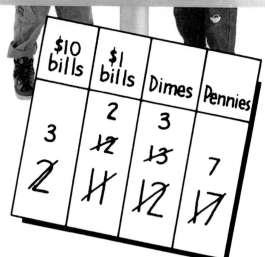

■ **Write About Math** How does the amount of money you started with compare to the amount you had after making the exchanges in Activity A? in Activity B?

Check Understanding

For another example, see Set H, pages 96–97.

Use play money to answer each question.

1. Take 24 dimes and 3 $1 bills. Exchange dimes for $1 bills. How many dimes do you have left? How many $1 bills do you have now?

2. Take 2 $1 bills and 4 pennies. Make exchanges to show 10 more pennies. How many $1 bills, dimes, and pennies do you have now?

Practice

For More Practice, see Set H, pages 98–99.

For Exercises 3–11, copy each chart and use it to record trades.

Trade to show the simplest form.

3.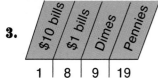

$10 bills	$1 bills	Dimes	Pennies
1	8	9	19

4.

$10 bills	$1 bills	Dimes	Pennies
3	17	5	25

5.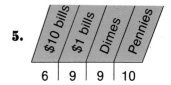

$10 bills	$1 bills	Dimes	Pennies
6	9	9	10

Trade to show 10 more pennies.

6.

$10 bills	$1 bills	Dimes	Pennies
2	1	7	3

7.

$10 bills	$1 bills	Dimes	Pennies
5	3	5	0

8.

$10 bills	$1 bills	Dimes	Pennies
8	4	0	6

Trade to show 10 more dimes.

9.

$10 bills	$1 bills	Dimes	Pennies
6	3	1	5

10.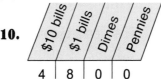

$10 bills	$1 bills	Dimes	Pennies
4	8	0	0

11.

$10 bills	$1 bills	Dimes	Pennies
4	0	2	6

Reading ——— Math

Numbers and Symbols Write each amount of money in words.

1. 1,225¢   **2.** $122.50   **3.** $1,225   **4.** $12.25

Adding and Subtracting Money

Build Understanding

A. Sarah Lightfoot bought paper and a pack of blank disks for her computer. The paper cost $24.95 and the disks cost $10.97. How much did Sarah pay for the two items?

Find $24.95 + $10.97.

Estimation Since $24.95 is about $25 and $10.97 is about $11, Sarah spent about $25 + $11, or $36.

Paper and Pencil   ▦ **Calculator**

$$\begin{array}{r} \$24.95 \\ +\ \ 10.97 \\ \hline \$35.92 \end{array}$$

24 ⎕.⎕ 95 ⎕+⎕ 10 ⎕.⎕ 97 ⎕=⎕

Display: *35.92*

The two items cost $35.92. Why is this answer reasonable?

B. If Sarah gave the clerk $40.00, how much money did she get back?

Find $40.00 − $35.92.

Estimation Rounding to the nearest dollar, $35.92 is about $36. $40 − $36 = $4

Paper and Pencil   ▦ **Calculator**

$$\begin{array}{r} \$40.00 \\ -\ \ 35.92 \\ \hline \$\ \ 4.08 \end{array}$$

40 ⎕−⎕ 35 ⎕.⎕ 92 ⎕=⎕

Display: *4.08*

She received $4.08.

■ **Write About Math** Paul used a calculator to find $50 − $48.20. The calculator displayed 1.8. How much money is this?

Check Understanding

For another example, see Set I, pages 96–97.

Copy and complete each exercise. First estimate
each sum or difference.

1. $42.57
   + 26.51
   $ ▦ ▦.▦ ▦

2. $66.52
   − 35.47
   $ ▦ ▦.▦ ▦

3. $50.00
   − 17.21
   $ ▦ ▦.▦ ▦

4. $98.56
   + 2.44
   $ ▦ ▦ ▦.▦ ▦

Practice

For More Practice, see Set I, pages 98–99.

Add or subtract. **Remember** to write the dollar
sign and the cents point in each answer.

5. $7.25
   + 0.59

6. $13.04
   + 7.88

7. $61.73
   + 80.64

8. $96.73
   + 61.58

9. $54.37
   + 12.84

10. $6.75
    − 0.93

11. $15.02
    − 7.03

12. $83.48
    − 35.26

13. $70.00
    − 20.92

14. $62.95
    − 28.47

15. $579.01
    + 947.32

16. $648.20
    − 75.82

17. $7,406.91
    − 5,782.76

18. $4,200.15
    + 538.49

Problem Solving

Read for the facts. Then solve each problem.

19. ▦ **Calculator** Sarah's new disk holds
    368,640 bytes of data. If she copies a program
    that uses 124,836 bytes, how many bytes
    will be left on the disk?

20. There are 66 keys on Sarah's computer
    keyboard. There is one key for each digit
    and one key for each letter. How many keys
    are not numbers or letters?

21. Sarah paid $799 for her computer. She paid
    $189.95 for an extra disk drive. How much
    did the computer and extra disk drive cost?

TIPS FOR PROBLEM SOLVERS

Be flexible. If you get
stuck, try another idea.

Multiple-Step Problems

Build Understanding

Mr. Wood is shopping at the supermarket. He wants to spend only $15 for groceries.

He puts the following items into his shopping cart: milk for $1.89, fruit for $2.74, cereal for $2.79, and chicken for $4.32. Will he spend more than $15?

PROBLEM SOLVING GUIDE

|||➤ **Understand**
QUESTION
FACTS
KEY IDEA

Plan and Solve
STRATEGY
ANSWER

Look Back
SENSIBLE ANSWER
ALTERNATE APPROACH

|||➤ **Understand**   QUESTION Will Mr. Wood spend more than $15 for his groceries?

FACTS Mr. Wood wants to buy items for $1.89, $2.74, $2.79, and $4.32.

KEY IDEA The actual amount for the groceries is not needed. An estimated sum can be compared to $15.

Plan and Solve STRATEGY Estimate the total price of the items. Round the price of each item up to the nearest dollar.

$1.89 + $2.74 + $2.79 + $4.32

 $2 + $3 + $3 + $5 = $13

Compare this amount to $15.
$13 < $15

ANSWER Mr. Wood will not spend more than $15 on groceries.

Look Back SENSIBLE ANSWER Since each price was rounded up to the nearest dollar, the total price would not be more than $13.

$1.89

$2.74

$2.79

$4.32

Why should you round up to the nearest dollar when you are estimating sums of money?

Check Understanding

Answer the questions about the following problem.
The groceries that Mrs. Ruth bought totaled $43.72 and the tax was $3.06. How much change should Mrs. Ruth receive from $50.00?

1. What was Mrs. Ruth's total bill?

2. How much change should she receive?

Practice

Solve each problem.

3. Mr. Huber bought a tube of toothpaste for $2.50. The tax was $0.16. If he used a coupon for $0.45 off the price of the toothpaste, how much did he pay?

4. Ms. Cooper wanted to buy a $2.79 carton of orange juice and some bread. A loaf of bread cost $1.19. Could she buy 2 loaves of bread and the juice with $5.00?

5. Mrs. Kym paid $3.94 for lettuce, tomatoes, and peas. She paid $0.99 for the lettuce and $1.87 for the tomatoes. How much did she pay for the peas?

6. Mr. Louis used a $0.20 coupon on Double Coupon Day. On this day, the store takes off double the coupon's value. How much will Mr. Louis pay for a $1.98 box of rice?

7. The regular price of a package of cheese was $2.89. During a sale the cheese sold for $0.34 less. How much would you pay for the cheese if you used a $0.40 coupon?

8. John works as a bagger at a grocery store. He worked 3 hours on Tuesday afternoon and 5 hours on Saturday. If he is paid $5 an hour, how much did he earn that week?

9. Mrs. Kane bought 2 cartons of eggs for $1.19 each, detergent for $6.89, and rolls for $1.50. Did she spend more than $10.00?

10. Mr. Howard's grocery bill totaled $25.76. How much will he have to pay if he uses a 45¢ coupon and a 75¢ coupon?

Problem Solving REVIEW

Solve each problem.

Six Longest Rivers in the World

River	Length (Kilometers)
Nile	6,632
Amazon	6,400
Mississippi	5,936
Ob-Irtysh	5,536
Yangtze	5,440
Huang Ho	4,800

1. How much longer is the longest river than the shortest in the list above?

2. Erin bought 4 packages of seeds for $0.50 each. She also bought some pots that cost $3.00 each and a trowel that cost $5.00. The cashier gave Erin $1.00 change from a twenty-dollar bill. How many pots did Erin buy?

3. A 13-oz hammer cost $0.59 in 1900. In 1989, a 13-oz hammer cost $16.49. How much more did the hammer cost in 1989?

4. A pony express rider earned $25.00 a week in 1860. If he spent $4.79 for food during the week, how much money would he have left?

5. Shawna played number tic-tac-toe. She won a game by covering numbers that totaled 17. What numbers did she cover?

6	1	8
7	9	4
3	5	2

6. **Data File** Use data from pages 102-103. Jim and Laurie had breakfast at Marie's restaurant. Jim ordered Stuffed French Toast and Laurie ordered Silver Dollar Pancakes. What was the total cost for the two breakfasts?

7. **Make a Data File** Find money-off coupons in newspapers or magazines. Make a chart showing the items, the original price, the coupon value, and the price with the coupon.

Calculating Minds

The game show, Calculating Minds, had two puzzles. Read the directions and solve the puzzles.

1.

Choose any 2-digit number.

Multiply by 5.

Add 20.

Divide by 5.

Subtract 4.

What does your display show?

2.

Choose any 3-digit number.

Multiply by 3.

Multiply by 5.

Divide by 15.

Subtract 44.

Add 44.

What does your display show?

3. Do each puzzle 3 times using a different starting number each time. What did you notice about the starting number of each try and the ending number?

4. To win the Bonus Round, you must write a set of directions similar to Exercises 1 and 2. Test the directions by trying several different starting numbers. Remember, the display at the end must always show the starting number.

Reteaching

Set A   pages 68–69

Find 6,375 − 200. Think of 200 as 2 hundreds. Then subtract 2 from the hundreds digit.

$$6{,}375 - 200 = 6{,}175$$

Remember that 20 is 2 tens, 200 is 2 hundreds, and 2,000 is 2 thousands. Add or subtract mentally.

1. 2,197 − 40   **2.** 4,682 + 5,000

Set B   pages 70–71

Estimate the sum by rounding both numbers to the nearest thousand.

5,235 + 7,609
↓   ↓
5,000 + 8,000 = 13,000

Remember that the digit in the place to be rounded stays the same if the digit to its right is less than 5. Estimate each sum or difference.

1. 7,382 + 3,642   **2.** 4,585 − 2,609

Set C   pages 72–73

Find 164 − 78.

Mental Math

Think: 78 is 2 less
     than 80.
164 − 80 = 84
84 + 2 = 86

Paper and Pencil

$$\begin{array}{r} 164 \\ -\ 78 \\ \hline 86 \end{array}$$

Calculator   164 − 78 = 86

Remember that paper and pencil can sometimes be as fast as a calculator. Tell whether you would use paper and pencil, mental math, or a calculator. Then find each answer.

1. $\begin{array}{r} 86 \\ +49 \\ \hline \end{array}$ **2.** $\begin{array}{r} 354 \\ -132 \\ \hline \end{array}$ **3.** $\begin{array}{r} 7{,}246 \\ -6{,}219 \\ \hline \end{array}$

Set D   pages 74–75

Rename the number in standard form.

thousands	hundreds	tens	ones
4	6	13	9

Standard form: 4,739

Remember that 10 tens equals 100 and 10 hundreds equals 1,000. Show the number in standard form.

1.

thousands	hundreds	tens	ones
8	12	4	6

Set E   pages 76–77

Find 3,289 + 2,732.
Estimate: 3,000 + 3,000 = 6,000

$\begin{array}{r} 3{,}287 \\ +2{,}732 \\ \hline 9 \end{array}$ $\begin{array}{r} 1\ \ \\ 3{,}287 \\ +2{,}732 \\ \hline 19 \end{array}$ $\begin{array}{r} 1\ 1\ \\ 3{,}287 \\ +2{,}732 \\ \hline {,}019 \end{array}$ $\begin{array}{r} 1\ 1\ \\ 3{,}287 \\ +2{,}732 \\ \hline 6{,}019 \end{array}$

Remember to estimate the sum to be sure your answer makes sense. Tell whether you would use paper and pencil or a calculator. Then add.

1. $\begin{array}{r} 4{,}735 \\ +2{,}276 \\ \hline \end{array}$ **2.** $\begin{array}{r} 8{,}462 \\ +2{,}161 \\ \hline \end{array}$

Set F   pages 78–79

Find 7,458 − 3,762.

Rename to show 10 more tens.	Rename to show 10 more hundreds.

$$\begin{array}{r} 3\ 15 \\ 7,\cancel{4}\cancel{5}8 \\ -\ 3,7\ 6\ 2 \\ \hline 9\ 6 \end{array}$$

$$\begin{array}{r} 6\ 1315 \\ 7,\cancel{4}\cancel{5}8 \\ -\ 3,7\ 6\ 2 \\ \hline 3,6\ 9\ 6 \end{array}$$

Remember to estimate the difference to be sure your answer makes sense. Tell whether you would use paper and pencil, mental math, or a calculator. Find each difference.

1. $\begin{array}{r} 2,736 \\ -\ \ \ \ 454 \\ \hline \end{array}$ 2. $\begin{array}{r} 5,467 \\ -\ 3,673 \\ \hline \end{array}$

Set G   pages 86–87

Estimate the sum by rounding to the nearest dollar.

$$\begin{array}{rcr} \$21.75 & \rightarrow & \$22 \\ \$11.15 & \rightarrow & 11 \\ +\ \ \$3.50 & \rightarrow & +\ \ \ 4 \\ \hline & & \$37 \end{array}$$

Remember that the number of dollars stays the same if the number of cents is less than 50 cents. Estimate each sum by rounding to the nearest dollar.

1. $6.48 + $3.85 + $2.05

2. $32.19 + $7.85 + $2.50

Set H   pages 88–89

Trade to show the simplest form.

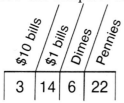

$10 bills	$1 bills	Dimes	Pennies
3	14	6	22

14 $1 bills → 1 $10 bill and
4 $1 bills
22 pennies → 2 dimes and 2 pennies
Simplest form: $44.82.

Remember that trading $10 bills, $1 bills, dimes, and pennies is like renaming with thousands, hundreds, tens, and ones.

Trade to show the simplest form.

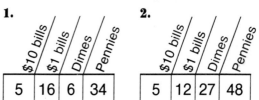

1.
$10 bills	$1 bills	Dimes	Pennies
5	16	6	34

2.
$10 bills	$1 bills	Dimes	Pennies
5	12	27	48

Set I   pages 90–91

Find $21.35 + $11.89.
Estimate: $21.35 + $11.89 is about
$21 + $12, or $33.

Paper and Pencil

$$\begin{array}{r} 1\ 1 \\ \$21.35 \\ +\ 11.89 \\ \hline \$33.24 \end{array}$$

⊞ Calculator

21 ⬚ . ⬚ 35 ⊕ 11 ⬚ . ⬚ 89 ⊜
33.24

Remember to write the dollar sign and the cents point in each answer.

Add or subtract.

1. $\begin{array}{r} \$6.45 \\ +\ \ 0.37 \\ \hline \end{array}$ 2. $\begin{array}{r} \$52.48 \\ +\ 12.63 \\ \hline \end{array}$

3. $\begin{array}{r} \$19.08 \\ -\ \ 8.11 \\ \hline \end{array}$ 4. $\begin{array}{r} \$60.00 \\ -\ 30.88 \\ \hline \end{array}$

More Practice

Set A   pages 68–69

Add or subtract mentally.

1. 508 + 300
2. 207 + 40
3. 637 − 400
4. 4,083 + 30

5. 5,634
   − 400

6. 2,744
   − 30

7. 13,470
   + 3,000

8. 36,814
   − 5,000

Set B   pages 70–71

For Exercises 1–10, estimate each sum or difference.
Round each number to the nearest thousand.

1. 4,930
   + 2,514

2. 3,115
   + 8,392

3. 7,653
   − 3,499

4. 9,392
   − 5,681

5. 4,189
   7,340
   + 3,482

Use front-end digits. Adjust your estimate.

6. 4,268
   + 3,832

7. 46,782
   + 85,306

8. 5,245
   3,981
   + 6,029

9. 53,397
   17,180
   + 39,288

10. 4,389
    8,421
    + 9,506

Set C   pages 72–73

Tell whether you would use paper and pencil, mental
math, or a calculator. Then find each answer.

1. 89
   + 47

2. 5,864
   − 3,647

3. 386
   + 424

4. 8,103
   + 1,014

5. 695
   − 426

6. 35 + 47 + 6
7. 307 + 592 + 2,183
8. 5,976 − 2,588

9. 8,743 − 500
10. 5,024 − 3,986
11. 2,397 + 78

Set D   pages 74–75

Rename to show the number in standard form.

1.

thousands	hundreds	tens	ones
5	3	12	4

2.

thousands	hundreds	tens	ones
6	12	2	16

Copy each chart. Rename to show 10 more tens.

3.

thousands	hundreds	tens	ones
3	5	2	6

4.

thousands	hundreds	tens	ones
4	4	0	8

Set E   pages 76–77

Tell whether you would use paper and pencil or a calculator. Then find each sum.

1. 8,432
   + 1,745

2. 2,846
   + 4,382

3. 7,871
   + 690

4. 5,023
   + 4,115

5. 4,612 + 5,304 + 793

6. 9,467 + 2,853 + 501

Set F   pages 78–81

Tell whether you would use paper and pencil or a calculator. Then find each difference.

1. 2,938
   − 584

2. 4,859
   − 463

3. 9,646
   − 7,835

4. 6,833
   − 5,745

5. 8,614 − 427

6. 3,600 − 3,278

7. 5,846 − 5,618

Set G   pages 86–87

Estimate the sums in Exercises 1–3 by rounding to the nearest dollar. In Exercises 4–5, estimate the sums by rounding to the nearest ten dollars.

1. $2.60
    3.10
  + 0.91

2. $6.88
    2.66
  + 2.02

3. $18.12
    3.34
  + 4.62

4. $36.72
    18.04
  + 22.69

5. $49.82
    8.20
  + 32.65

Set H   pages 88–89

1. Trade to show the simplest form.

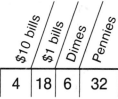

$10 bills	$1 bills	Dimes	Pennies
4	18	6	32

2. Trade to show 10 more pennies.

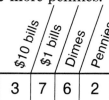

$10 bills	$1 bills	Dimes	Pennies
3	7	6	2

3. Trade to show 10 more dimes.

$10 bills	$1 bills	Dimes	Pennies
8	0	2	6

Set I   pages 90–91

Add or subtract.

1. $8.64
  + 0.27

2. $17.08
  + 6.74

3. $53.81
  + 60.52

4. $87.92
  + 70.29

5. $64.28
  + 21.93

6. $5.45
  − 0.82

7. $18.05
  − 6.07

8. $64.37
  − 46.12

9. $75.68
  − 37.39

10. $60.00
   − 40.78

Enrichment

Quick Sums

Quickly! Find the sum of the numbers 1 through 10. Can you do it? Here is a shortcut.

1 + 2 + 3 + 4 + 5 + 6 + 7 + 8 + 9 + 10

Find the sum of the first and last numbers.

$$1 + 10 = 11$$

Do the second and the next-to-last numbers have the same sum?

$$2 + 9 = 11$$

Find all the pairs of numbers that have a sum of 11.

$$3 + 8 = 11$$
$$4 + 7 = 11$$
$$5 + 6 = 11$$

The shortcut shown on this page was discovered by the German mathematician, Karl Friedrich Gauss (1777–1855).

Did you use all the numbers from 1 through 10?

What is each sum? How many sums of 11 are there?

The sum of each pair of numbers is 11.

There are 5 sums of 11. $5 \times 11 = $ ▦

The sum of the numbers 1 through 10 is 55.

Use the shortcut to find these sums.

1. 4 + 5 + 6 + 7 + 8 + 9

2. 5 + 6 + 7 + 8 + 9 + 10

3. 4 + 6 + 8 + 10 + 12 + 14

4. 1 + 5 + 9 + 13 + 17 + 21

5. The odd numbers 1 through 19

6. The even numbers 2 through 28

7. Will the shortcut work for an odd number of numbers? How can you change the shortcut to work for these numbers?

3 + 6 + 9 + 12 + 15 + 18 + 21

Chapter 3 Review/Test

Add or subtract mentally.

1. 7,618 + 1,000   **2.** 3,416 − 400

Estimate each sum or difference. Round each number to the nearest thousand.

3.   4,168
     + 7,885

4.   4,866
     − 4,184

5. Estimate 6,124 + 3,246 using only front-end digits.

Tell whether you would use mental math, paper and pencil, or a calculator. Then find each answer.

6.   292
     + 69

7.   1,630
     − 1,000

8. Rename to show the number in standard form.

Thousands	Hundreds	Tens	Ones
4	16	6	2

Find each sum or difference.

9.   4,126
     + 3,514

10.   5,244
      + 1,682

11.   1,658
      − 479

12.   4,000
      − 1,782

Estimate by rounding to the nearest dollar.

13. $7.28
         1.42
      + 3.67

14. $2.65
         7.63
      + 1.25

15. Copy the chart. Trade to show the simplest form.

$10 bills	$1 bills	Dimes	Pennies
1	11	13	7

Add or subtract.

16. $127.89
      +   71.63

17. $3,165.78
      −   2,865.98

18. Mrs. Mendez paid $39.50 for a new telephone and $89.95 for an answering machine. What was the total cost of her purchases?

19. George Bush was born in 1924. How old was he when he was elected President in 1988?

Read this problem. Then answer Items 20 and 21.

Mr. Stewart bought a book for $19.95. The tax was $1.20. He gave the clerk $25.00. How much change did he receive?

20. Which would you do *first* to solve this problem?
   a. Subtract $1.20 from $19.95.
   b. Add $1.20 and $25.00.
   c. Add $19.95 and $1.20.
   d. Add $19.95, $1.20, and $25.00.

21. Solve the problem.

22. **Write About Math** Explain why you chose the computation method you used for Item 7.

1. Graph
The graph shows estimates of population from 1710–1780.

2. Menu
Maria's Restaurant
The Menu shows selections from the children's section.

3. Chart
Baseball Standings
W is the number of wins.
L is the number of losses.

4. Diagram
The Diagram gives statistics about Cary's cat.

1. Graph

Colonial Population Estimates	
Year	**Population**
1710	332,000
1720	466,000
1730	629,000
1740	906,000
1750	1,171,000
1760	1,594,000
1770	2,148,000
1780	2,780,000

Each is **⚱** 500,000

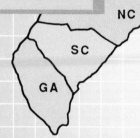

2. Menu

Maria's RESTAURANT

BACON AND EGG MUFFIN
$1.95
A fried egg and bacon covered with melted American cheese, on a toasted English muffin.

KIDS' FRENCH TOAST
$1.95
Traditional style egg-dipped bread grilled golden brown. Served with a sausage link.

STUFFED FRENCH TOAST
$2.45
Egg-dipped bread, stuffed with berries and grilled until golden.

KIDS' SCRAMBLE
$2.45
Two eggs scrambled with cheddar cheese.

SILVER DOLLAR PANCAKES
$1.85
Six mini-pancakes served with your choice of bacon strips or a sausage link.

3. Baseball Standings

Baseball Standings

National League

East Division	W	L
Montreal	55	41
New York	51	44
Chicago	51	44
St Louis	47	44
Pittsburgh	39	53
Philadelphia	37	45
West Division	**W**	**L**
San Fransisco	58	38
Houston	53	42
San Diego	47	49
Cincinnati	45	51
Los Angeles	44	52
Atlanta	40	56

American League

East Division	W	L
Baltimore	53	40
New York	46	48
Boston	44	47
Tronto	46	49
Cleveland	45	48
Milwukee	43	51
Detroit	33	59
West Division	**W**	**L**
California	55	38
Oakland	53	39
Kansas City	53	42
Texas	51	43
Seattle	45	49
Minnesota	37	54
Chicago	39	56

4. Cary's Cat

Length: 16 inches

Age: 12 months

Weight: 10 pounds

Height: 11 inches

NH MA CT RI NJ DE

103

Cumulative Review/Test Chapters 1-3

1. Which number in the following sentence is used to order?

In waiting room 4 on the 3rd floor, there are 5 people waiting.

a. 4   **c.** 5
b. 3rd   **d.** none of these

2. What is the correct standard form for 7 hundreds 8 ones?

a. 78   **c.** 708
b. 780   **d.** 700

3. Round 628 to the nearest ten.

a. 620   **c.** 630
b. 600   **d.** 700

4. Multiply.

5×9

a. 36   **c.** 54
b. 45   **d.** 63

5. Subtract.

$120 - 30$

a. 9   **c.** 70
b. 90   **d.** 80

6. Estimate the sum. Round each number to the nearest hundred.

$172 + 307$

a. 500   **c.** 400
b. 480   **d.** 380

7. Which digit in 5,824 is in the hundreds place?

a. 5   **c.** 2
b. 8   **d.** 4

8. What is the standard form for 35 hundreds?

a. 35   **c.** 350
b. 305   **d.** 3,500

9. Which number is greatest?

a. 4,251   **c.** 2,541
b. 4,521   **d.** 1,542

10. Round 7,628 to the nearest thousand.

a. 7,000   **c.** 7,600
b. 8,000   **d.** 7,700

11. Which digit in 93,124,687 is in the millions place?

a. 9   **c.** 1
b. 3   **d.** 2

12. Add.

$3,618 + 200$

a. 5,618   **c.** 3,638
b. 3,818   **d.** 3,620

13. Add.

$$6,124 + 2,958$$

a. 8,072
b. 8,082
c. 9,082
d. 9,182

14. Estimate 316 + 208 by using front-end digits.

   a. 500   **c.** 530
   b. 600   **d.** 5

15. Rename to show the number in standard form.

Thousands	Hundreds	Tens	Ones
3	12	5	4

   a. 31,254   **c.** 4,254
   b. 13,254   **d.** 3,264

16. Subtract.

$$\begin{array}{r} 2,618 \\ -\,1,399 \\ \hline \end{array}$$

   a. 1,381
   b. 1,209
   c. 1,329
   d. 1,219

17. Subtract.

$$\begin{array}{r} \$50.00 \\ -\ \ 16.79 \\ \hline \end{array}$$

   a. $34.79
   b. $34.21
   c. $33.21
   d. $33.20

Use the pictograph to answer Item 18.

Records Sold

Mon.	⊙ ⊙ ⊙ ⊙
Tues.	⊙ ⊙ ⊙
Wed.	⊙ ⊙ ⊙ ⊙ ◖
Thurs.	⊙ ⊙
Fri.	⊙ ⊙ ⊙ ⊙ ⊙

Each ⊙ stands for 10 records.

18. How many records were sold on Wednesday?

   a. 30 records   **c.** 45 records
   b. 40 records   **d.** 185 records

19. A kilometer is 1,000 meters. How many kilometers are in 6,000 meters?

   a. 6   **c.** 600
   b. 60   **d.** 6,000

20. Mrs. McClean had $928.32 in her savings account. Then she spent $198.28 for a plane ticket. How much did she have left in her savings account?

   a. $730.04   **c.** $740.04
   b. $1126.60   **d.** $830.04

21. Alice bought a hamburger for $1.95 and milk for $0.60. She gave the clerk $5.00. How much change did she receive?

   a. $2.55   **c.** $1.45
   b. $2.45   **d.** $3.45

Read the problem below. Then answer Item 22.

Ida has a nickel and 3 other coins. The value of all the coins is 26¢. What are the coins?

22. Which statement is another way of asking what you are trying to find in this problem?

   a. Find 3 coins with a value of 26 cents.
   b. What is the number of coins that Ida has?
   c. What is the value of the coins that Ida has?
   d. Find 3 coins whose value is 21 cents.

Time and Measurement 4

Did You Know:
In one minute
most adults read
300 words.

Number-Sense Project

Estimate

Estimate how many capital letters of the alphabet you can print in 1 minute. Begin with *A* and continue, in order, with the other letters of the alphabet.

Gather Data

Time yourself. Try it 3 times. Leave extra space between each try.

Analyze and Report

Make a graph or draw a picture showing the results of each of your three tries. Compare your results with those of your classmates.

107

Time: Clocks

Build Understanding

Do you leave for school before noon? You write the hours between midnight and noon with A.M. Do you go to bed before midnight? You write the hours between noon and midnight with P.M.

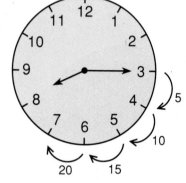

A. John leaves for school at 8:15 A.M. It takes John 20 minutes to get to school. At what time does John get there? Look at the clock at the right. Count by fives to twenty. John gets to school at 8:35 A.M.

B. Cara takes 15 minutes to get to school. She arrives at 8:00 A.M. Look at the clock at the right. Count back 15 minutes. At what time does she leave? Cara leaves at 7:45 A.M.

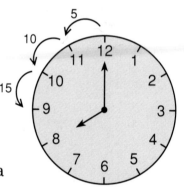

C. At 10:40 A.M., how many minutes is it until Cara eats lunch at 12:05 P.M.?

It is 60 minutes, or 1 hour, from 10:40 A.M. until 11:40 A.M.

It is 25 minutes more from 11:40 A.M. until 12:05 P.M.

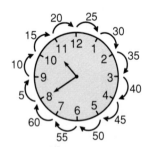

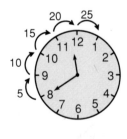

It is 85 minutes, or 1 hour and 25 minutes, from 10:40 A.M. until Cara eats lunch at 12:05 P.M.

■ Talk About Math When you look at a standard clock face, how do you know whether it is A.M. or P.M.?

Check Understanding

For another example, see Set A, pages 134–135.

Write the time shown under each clock.

1.

75 minutes later

2.

20 minutes earlier

3.

13 minutes later

4. Write the times you go to school and go to bed.

5. How much later is the time shown on the clock in Exercise 2 than the time on the clock in Exercise 1?

Practice

For More Practice, see Set A, pages 136–137.

Write each time. **Remember** to use A.M. or P.M.

6. 23 minutes after 1:00 P.M.

7. 20 minutes before 1:00 P.M.

8. 30 minutes after 10:15 A.M.

9. 1 hour 15 minutes after 11:25 P.M.

How much time has passed between

10. 2:40 P.M. and 4:45 P.M.?

11. 8:30 A.M. and 8:30 P.M.?

Problem Solving

Read for the facts. Then solve each problem.

12. Paco weeded from 11:00 A.M. to 12:00 P.M. and from 1:00 P.M. to 2:55 P.M. How long did he spend weeding?

13. Una goes to sleep at 9:00 P.M. She gets up 9 hours and 15 minutes later. At what time does Una get up?

Time: Calendar

Build Understanding

Can you find the Presidents' birthdays on the calendar?

A. Abraham Lincoln was born on February 12. What day of the week is that on the calendar? February 12 falls on a Monday in the year shown.

B. George Bush was born on June 12. How long is it from Lincoln's birthday to Bush's birthday? If you count each day, starting with February 13, you find that Bush's birthday is **120** days after Lincoln's birthday.

C. Is there an easier way to solve the problem in Example B? You can count weeks and then count days.

From February 12 to February 19 is **1** week. It is another week from February 19 to February 26, and so on. From February 12 to June 11 is **17** weeks. From June 11 to June 12 is one day.

Bush's birthday is **17** weeks and **1** day after Lincoln's birthday.

■ **Talk About Math** James Madison's birthday falls on the third Friday in March for the year shown. Explain how you would find the day on which Madison was born.

110

Check Understanding

For another example, see Set B, pages 134–135.

Jimmy Carter's birthday is October 1.
James Polk's birthday is 32 days later. Use the
calendar on page 110 to answer the questions.

1. In what month is Polk's
birthday?

2. On what day of the week is Polk's
birthday?

Practice

For More Practice, see Set B, pages 136–137.

Use the calendar on page 110 to answer the questions.

3. Franklin Roosevelt's birthday is
the fifth Tuesday in January.
What date is his birthday?

4. John Kennedy's birthday is 1 day
after the fourth Monday in May.
When is his birthday?

5. Calvin Coolidge was born on
July 4. Martin Van Buren's
birthday is exactly 22 weeks later.
What date is that?

6. On what day of the week is
Lyndon Johnson's birthday if it
is 7 weeks and 5 days after
Coolidge's birthday?

Problem Solving

Use the calendar on page 110 to help you solve these problems.

7. Critical Thinking On May 3,
Mr. Jay said that a history book
report was due in 10 days. The
students wondered if he was
serious. Why?

8. **Calculator** Add the number
of days in each month to get the
total number of days in the year.

Skills Review pages 72–73, 76–81

Use a calculator, pencil and paper, or mental math to find
each answer. Tell which method you used and why.

1. 905 − 623   **2.** 497 + 386   **3.** 8,000 − 5,000   **4.** 5,391 + 3,487

5. 1,500 + 399 + 101   **6.** 3,468 + 602 + 75   **7.** 8,000 − 99

Use Data from a Table

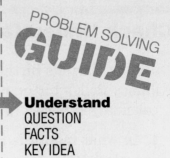

Build Understanding

The Savez family arrived at the El Paso Zoo on Wednesday at 11:15 A.M. and stayed until it closed. How long did they stay?

		OPEN	CLOSE
State Capitol	Daily	8:00 A.M.	5:00 P.M.
El Paso Zoo	M–F	9:30 A.M.	4:15 P.M.
	S–S	10:00 A.M.	5:00 P.M.
The Alamo	M–S	9:00 A.M.	5:30 P.M.
	Sun.	10:00 A.M.	5:30 P.M.
Lyndon Johnson Space Center	Daily	9:00 A.M	5:00 P.M.

PROBLEM SOLVING GUIDE

Understand
QUESTION
FACTS
KEY IDEA

Plan and Solve
STRATEGY
ANSWER

Look Back
SENSIBLE ANSWER
ALTERNATE APPROACH

Understand   QUESTION   How much time passes from 11:15 A.M. until the zoo closes?

FACTS   The table shows that the zoo closes at 4:15 P.M.

KEY IDEA   You need to find how much time passes between 11:15 A.M. and 4:15 P.M.

Plan and Solve   Count on from 11:15 to 4:15.

ANSWER   The Savez family spent 5 hours at the zoo.

Look Back   The answer is reasonable because it is a whole number of hours. Both times are 15 minutes after the hours.

■ **Write About Math**   Explain how you would find the time the Alamo opens on Tuesday.

112

Check Understanding

Use the data in the table on page 112 to answer these questions.

1. At what time does the El Paso Zoo open on Sunday?

2. How long is the State Capitol open on Saturday?

Practice

Use the data in the table on page 112 to answer these questions.

3. Floyd arrived at the Space Center when it opened and stayed until 1:30 P.M. How long did he stay?

4. On Friday, Raymond worked at the El Paso Zoo from opening time until 11:30 A.M. How many hours did he work?

5. How many hours a day is the Space Center open?

6. Tara arrived at the Space Center at 2:15 P.M. and stayed until it closed. How long did she stay?

7. How many hours longer is the Alamo open on Saturday than on Sunday?

8. On Monday, how much longer is the State Capitol open than the zoo?

Choose a **Strategy**

A Capital Idea   Today at the Capitol, one person arrived at 8:00 A.M. for the first tour. Each hour after that three more people arrived than had come the hour before.

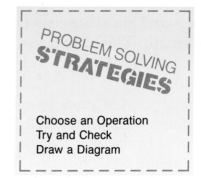

PROBLEM SOLVING STRATEGIES

Choose an Operation
Try and Check
Draw a Diagram

9. The last tour started at 4:00 P.M. How many people arrived for that tour?

10. 🖩 **Calculator**   How many people toured the Capitol today?

Customary Units of Length

Build Understanding

A. Rita measured two chestnut oak acorns to the nearest half inch. Each was about $1\frac{1}{2}$ *inches* long. Why did one look longer?

Sometimes you need a more exact measurement to compare lengths. You can measure the acorns to the nearest quarter inch.

Most rulers do not name the fractions on them. Rita made her own paper ruler and wrote fractions on it. Having the fractions made it easier to read measurements.

Rita used her paper ruler to measure the acorns again. The shorter one was nearer $1\frac{1}{4}$ inches. The longer one was nearer $1\frac{1}{2}$ inches.

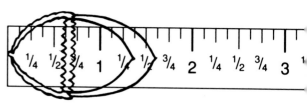

B. Would you measure the height of an oak tree in inches? The *foot* and the *yard* are other customary units of length. There are 3 feet in 1 yard.

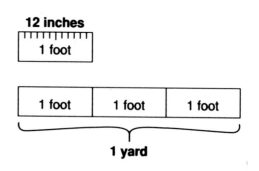

C. Would you use yards to measure the distance to another city? The *mile* is used to measure long distances. There are 5,280 feet or 1,760 yards in 1 mile.

■ **Talk About Math** Explain why you need different units of measurement.

Check Understanding

For another example, see Set C, pages 134–135.

Use your ruler in Exercises 1 and 2.

1. How long is this bur oak acorn to the nearest inch? nearest half inch? nearest quarter inch?

2. How long is this California live oak acorn to the nearest inch? nearest half inch? nearest quarter inch?

3. Why do you sometimes measure to the nearest quarter inch rather than to the nearest half inch?

4. Why are long distances usually measured in miles rather than in inches?

Practice

For More Practice, see Set C, pages 136–137.

Use a ruler to measure the length of each acorn to the nearest inch, nearest half inch, and nearest quarter inch.

5. Northern red oak

6. Pin oak

7. Water oak

Use your ruler to measure each of the following in feet and inches.

8. height of your desk

9. length of your arm

10. your height

11. the height of a classmate

Estimation Which unit (inch, foot, yard, or mile) would you use to measure

12. the distance from home to school?

13. the length of the classroom?

14. the length of a pen?

Use a ruler to help you draw a picture of an acorn the size given.

15. $1\frac{1}{2}$ inches long, 1 inch wide

16. $\frac{1}{2}$ inch wide, $1\frac{1}{4}$ inches long

Choose the most sensible measure.

17. length of a shoe
   10 in.   10 ft   10 mi

18. distance between two towns
   5 ft   5 yd   5 mi

Copy and complete each sentence.

19. There are ▦ inches in 1 yard.

20. There are ▦ feet in 2 yards.

Problem Solving

Solve each problem.

21. Mental Math Rita had 5 acorns. Each was about 2 inches long. If she lined them up end to end, about how long would the line be?

22. Number Sense Andy collected 200 acorns. He put them side by side in a row. Would you measure the length of the row in yards or miles?

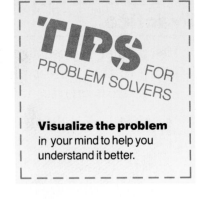

TIPS FOR PROBLEM SOLVERS

Visualize the problem in your mind to help you understand it better.

Look at your answers for Exercises 5–7
to answer the questions.

23. Which of the acorns is the
shortest? Did you need to
measure to the nearest inch,
nearest half inch, or nearest
quarter inch to tell?

24. Which of the acorns is the
longest? Did you need to
measure to the nearest inch,
nearest half inch, or nearest
quarter inch to tell?

Midchapter ———— Checkup

Answer the questions.

1. What time will it be
20 minutes after 7:20 A.M.?

2. How much times passes between
8:00 A.M. and 11:00 A.M.?

Use the calendar months at the
right to answer the questions.

3. What date is 20 days after the
first Monday in May?

4. How many days after May 29
is June 29?

Use the table to answer the questions.

		OPEN	CLOSE
Davis-Inn	Monday–Thursday	9:00 A.M.	6:00 P.M.
	Friday–Saturday	9:00 A.M.	8:00 P.M.
	Sunday	Noon	8:00 P.M.
Parker Diner	Monday–Friday	7:30 A.M.	11:30 P.M.
	Saturday	9:00 A.M.	9:00 P.M.
	Sunday	CLOSED	

5. At what time does the Davis
Inn open on Tuesdays?

6. How many hours is the Parker
Diner open on Wednesdays?

Explore as a Team

1. Which *shape* do you think you are?

   a. *a square:* Your height is the same length as your arm span.

   b. *a tall rectangle:* Your height is greater than your arm span.

   c. *a short rectangle:* Your height is less than your arm span.

2. Measure and compare your height and arm span.

3. Are you the shape you thought you were?

TIPS FOR
WORKING TOGETHER
Help keep your group on task.

Visual-Thinking Activity

Michelle's watch is 15 minutes fast.
Christine's watch is 10 minutes slow.
Paul's watch is 5 minutes fast.
What is the correct time?

Real-Life Decision Making

You need to be at the softball field by 8:30 Saturday morning. It takes you about 15 minutes to ride your bike to the field. You usually take 45 minutes to shower, dress, and eat breakfast. You like to have about a half hour to play or work on your computer in the morning.

Decide. What time will you set your alarm to get up?

Number-Sense Project

Look back at pages 106-107.

1. Choose only 1 capital letter or several capital letters to print in 1 minute.

2. Think about the 26 letters of the alphabet. Do you think you can print one or some of them quicker than you can print others? Explain.

3. Time yourself. For 1 minute each time print the capital letter or letters of your choice. Try it a total of 3 times.

4. Make a graph or draw a picture to show your results.

Metric Units of Length

Build Understanding

A. You already know about *centimeters* (cm) and *meters* (m). Try drawing a ladybug that is 1 cm long. Check it with your ruler. It takes 100 one-centimeter ladybugs to make 1 meter.

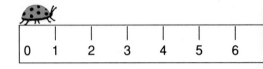

Name three objects in the classroom that are about 1 meter.

100 centimeters is 1 meter.
100 cm = 1 m

B. A *decimeter* is the same as 10 centimeters. This twig is one decimeter (dm) long. The ladybug is 1 cm long.

10 centimeters is 1 decimeter.
10 cm = 1 dm

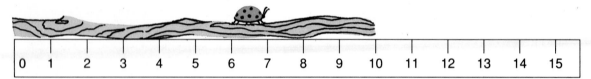

C. Would you measure the distance to your home in centimeters? The *kilometer* (km) is used to measure longer distances.

1,000 meters is 1 kilometer.
1,000 m = 1 km

■ **Talk About Math**   Name three objects in the classroom that are about 1 decimeter.

Check Understanding

For another example, see Set D, pages 134–135.

Use a metric ruler and the picture of the butterfly on page 121 for Exercises 1 and 2.

1. What is the wingspan of the forewings to the nearest cm?

2. What is the wingspan of the forewings to the nearest dm?

3. Would you use cm, dm, or m to measure how far a butterfly flies from flower to flower? Explain your answer.

4. Would you use m or km to measure how far the Monarch butterfly flies from Mexico to Canada? Explain your answer.

Monarch Butterfly

ForeWing

Antenna

Hind Wing

Abdomen

This butterfly is classified as a milkweed butterfly because the caterpillar feeds on milkweed plants.

Practice

For More Practice, see Set D, pages 136–137.

Use a metric ruler and the picture of the butterfly to find each length to the nearest centimeter.

5. wingspan of the hind wings

6. length from top of head to tip of abdomen

7. length from top of forewing to bottom of hind wing

8. width of one forewing

Use a metric ruler to draw lines that have the following lengths.

9. 3 cm **10.** 2 dm **11.** 13 cm **12.** 3 dm

13. 8 cm **14.** 20 cm **15.** 1 dm 3 cm **16.** 30 cm

Estimation Choose the most sensible measure.

17. length of a thumb

3 cm   3 dm   3 m

18. width of a thumb

1 cm   1 dm   1 m

19. length of a palm

1 cm   1 dm   1 m

20. distance across the room

8 cm   8 m   8 km

21. distance between two cities

8 cm   8 m   8 km

22. height of a front door

2 cm   2 m   2 km

Temperature: Celsius and Fahrenheit

Build Understanding

Do you know the temperature right now? A thermometer gives the temperature. Temperature is measured in units called **degrees**.

A. Look at the thermometers. The number next to the top of the liquid is the temperature. On the Celsius thermometer, it is 35 degrees (35°C).

When it is 35°C, what is the Fahrenheit temperature? Look at that thermometer. The liquid is halfway between 90 and 100. It is 95 degrees Fahrenheit (95°F).

B.

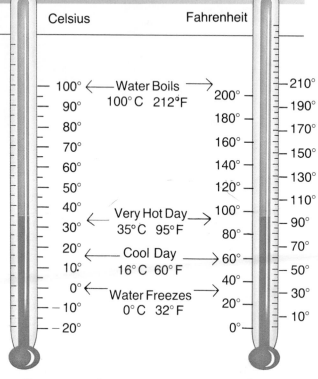

On some thermometers, every degree is marked. On others, every two degrees are marked. Both of the thermometers at the left read 77°C.

■ **Talk About Math**   How are the Celsius and Fahrenheit thermometers different?

Check Understanding

For another example, see Set E, pages 134–135.

1. **Estimation**   Snow is falling outside. What might the Fahrenheit temperature read?

2. A thermometer reads about 20°. Do you need to wear a heavy coat outdoors?

3. **Mental Math**   If the temperature rose 4 degrees, what would the thermometer in Exercise 2 read?

4. What is the temperature in degrees Celsius?

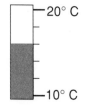

Practice

For More Practice, see Set E, pages 136–137.

Choose the more sensible temperature for each outdoor activity.

5. building a snowman
    26°F   56°F

6. swimming outdoors
    20°C   48°C

7. running on the beach
    56°F   106°F

8. ice-skating outdoors
    10°F   10°C

Write the temperature shown.

9.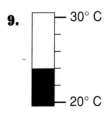

10.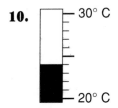

11.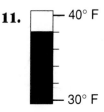

12.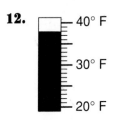

13.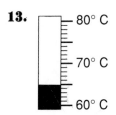

14.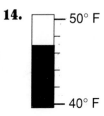

Problem Solving

Solve these problems. Use the thermometers on these pages to help you.

15. The temperature is 26°C. If it goes up 8°, what will it be?

16. The temperature is 26°C. If it goes down 8°, what will it be?

17. The temperature is 6°F. If it goes up 8°, what will it be?

18. The temperature is 16°F. If it goes down 3°, what will it be?

19. Ann's cookbook said a roast should be cooked until the meat thermometer reads 70°. Would this be Celsius or Fahrenheit?

20. Critical Thinking Scott says that the temperature will rise 20 degrees today. Would you notice the change more if it were measured in degrees Fahrenheit or degrees Celsius?

Measuring Perimeter

Build Understanding

A. Do you know how to measure the distance
around a triangle? The distance around a figure
is called the *perimeter*. You can add the lengths
of the sides to find the answer.

7 + 5 + 4 = 16

The perimeter of this triangle is
16 centimeters.

7 cm

5 cm

4 cm

B.

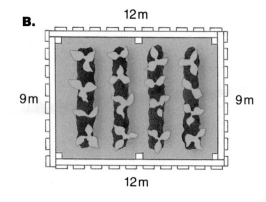

12m

9m

9m

12m

Sam and Eric want to put a fence around
a garden. The garden is in the shape of a
rectangle. The length is **12** meters and the
width is **9** meters. Look at how each boy
found the perimeter.

Eric measured each side
and added.

12 + 12 + 9 + 9 = 42

Sam measured two sides and added.

12 + 9 = 21

Then he said, "This is halfway around.
I can double my answer."

21 + 21 = 42

Both Eric and Sam found the perimeter to be **42** meters.

■ **Talk About Math** When might it be helpful
to know how to find the perimeter at home?

Check Understanding

For another example, see Set F, pages 134–135.

1. Use a ruler to find the perimeter
   in centimeters of this figure.

2. Use the measurements given to find the perimeter.

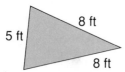

8 ft
5 ft
8 ft

3. All the sides are the same length. Find the perimeter.

3 m

Practice

For More Practice, see Set F, pages 136–137.

Use a centimeter ruler to find the perimeter of each figure.

4.

5.

Use the measurements given to find the perimeter of each figure.

6.

42 cm
22 cm
39 cm
56 cm

7.

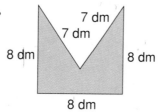

7 dm
7 dm
8 dm
8 dm
8 dm

8.

8 in.
2 in.
2 in.
6 in.
10 in.

9. rectangle

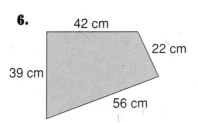

6 ft
3 ft
3 ft
6 ft

10. rectangle

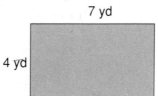

7 yd
4 yd

11. square

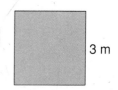

3 m

Problem Solving

Read for the facts. Then answer the questions.

12. A triangular shawl has two sides each 60 cm long and one side 80 cm long. How many centimeters of fringe would you buy to sew on all the edges?

13. A rectangular room has a perimeter of 14 yards. The room is 3 yards wide. How long should a carpet be to cover the floor completely?

Finding Area by Counting Squares

Build Understanding

A. How Big Is Your Hand?
Materials: Grid paper
Groups: With a partner

a. Place your hand on top of the grid paper. Keep your fingers and thumb together.

b. Have your partner trace around your hand with a pencil.

c. Count the number of full squares inside the tracing of your hand. Each square is 1 square unit.

d. Look at the parts of squares around the edges of your tracing. About how many full squares, or square units, would they make?

e. Add your totals for Steps c and d.

In square units, what is the **area**, or surface, covered by your hand?

B. Square units can be different sizes.

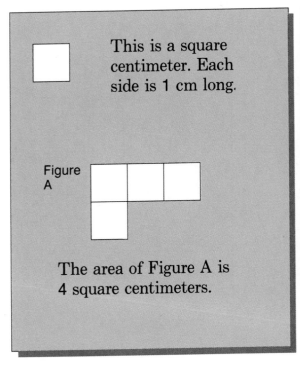

This is a square centimeter. Each side is 1 cm long.

Figure A

The area of Figure A is 4 square centimeters.

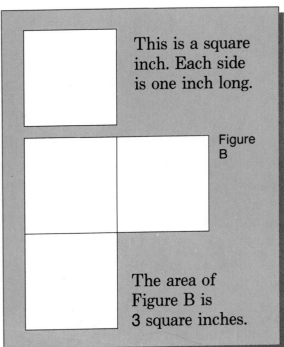

This is a square inch. Each side is one inch long.

Figure B

The area of Figure B is 3 square inches.

■ **Talk About Math** When might you use square units at home?

Check Understanding

For another example, see Set G, pages 134–135.

Use the figures in Example B to help you answer Exercises 1–4.

1. How does a square centimeter differ from a square inch?

2. How do you find the area of a figure?

3. Is Figure A or B larger?

4. Which is larger, a figure that is 4 square centimeters or one that is 4 square inches?

How many square units are in each figure?

5.
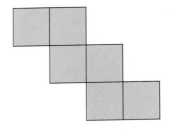

6.
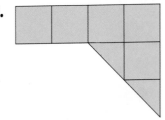

Practice

For More Practice, see Set G, pages 136–137.

Find the area in square centimeters.

7.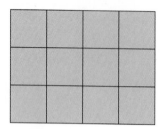

8.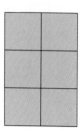

9.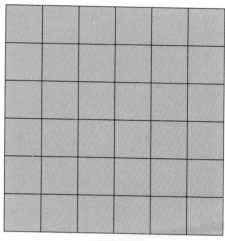

Mixed Practice Find the perimeter of each figure. Then find the area in square centimeters.

10.

11.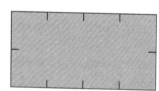

12.

13. Marta drew a rectangle with sides 3 inches and 4 inches. Draw the rectangle and find its area.

14. Jeff drew a rectangle 8 inches long and 4 inches wide. Draw the rectangle and find its area.

Find the area. Each square is a square centimeter.

15.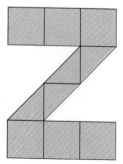

16.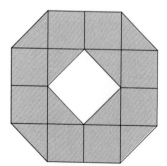

Problem Solving

17. On grid paper draw a figure that has an area of 17 square units. Compare your figure with those of your classmates.

18. Critical Thinking If two figures each have an area of 4 square centimeters, must they have the same perimeter? Explain.

19. Marcia has 6 one-inch squares to make a figure. Draw some of the figures that Marcia could make.

Explore ———— Math

A figure made of squares that are the same size in which each square shares at least one of its sides with another square is called a **polyomino**.

20. These are five-square polyominoes.

 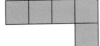

These are *not* five-square polyominoes. Why not?

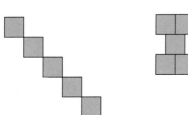

21. These two five-square polyominoes are *not* different from each other. Why not?

22. Can you find 12 different five-square polyominoes? Try to draw them.

Solve a Simpler Problem

Build Understanding

Lee keeps track of her activities. Today she played guitar from 2:58 P.M. to 3:53 P.M. How long did she practice?

Understand   Lee knows when she began and ended practice. She needs a way to find the number of minutes from 2:58 P.M. to 3:53 P.M.

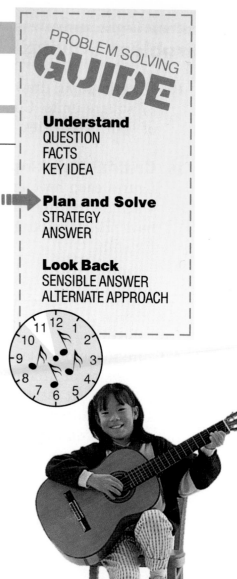

Plan and Solve   STRATEGY   Lee could count minutes, but she can also solve a simpler problem.

2:58 to 3:58 is 60 minutes.
3:53 to 3:58 is 5 minutes.
60 − 5 = 55

ANSWER   Lee practiced 55 minutes.

Look Back   It is 60 minutes from 3:53 back to 2:53. Lee began 5 minutes later, at 2:58.

■ **Write About Math**   Write a problem that would be easier to solve by counting than by solving a simpler problem.

PROBLEM SOLVING
GUIDE

Understand
QUESTION
FACTS
KEY IDEA

Plan and Solve
STRATEGY
ANSWER

Look Back
SENSIBLE ANSWER
ALTERNATE APPROACH

Check Understanding

Suppose Lee practiced from 2:46 P.M. to 3:13 P.M.

1. Is 2:46 P.M. closer to 2:45 P.M. or to 3:00 P.M.?

2. Is 3:13 P.M. closer to 3:00 P.M. or to 3:15 P.M.?

3. How much time is between 2:45 P.M. and 3:15 P.M.?

4. How long did Lee practice?

Practice

Read for the facts. Then solve the problems.

5. Lee did math homework from 5:32 P.M. to 6:06 P.M. How long did she spend on her homework?

6. Lee left the house at 7:27 A.M. and got to school at 7:56 A.M. How long did it take her to get to school?

7. At 2:16 P.M., Lee joined the basketball game, which ended at 2:43 P.M. How long did Lee play?

8. Lee went to a movie that began at 6:06 P.M. and ended at 7:58 P.M. How long was the movie?

Use Data Use the table on page 112 to solve the problem.

9. Lee arrived at the El Paso Zoo 3 minutes after it opened on Saturday. She left at 11:27 A.M. How long did she stay?

Reading ———— Math

Numbers Match each situation on the left with the correct time span on the right. Use each time span only once.

1. Lee practiced more than half an hour.

a. 2:58 P.M. to 3:26 P.M.

2. Lee practiced for almost one hour.

b. 4:32 P.M. to 5:40 P.M.

c. 3:02 P.M. to 3:38 P.M.

3. Lee practiced just under half an hour.

d. 4:08 P.M. to 5:03 P.M.

4. Lee practiced more than one hour.

Problem Solving REVIEW

Solve each problem.

1. There are exactly 8,829 people in the village of Riverlake. What would be a sensible rounded number to put on a road sign giving the population?

2. Carlos was born in 1981. His great-grandfather was born exactly 100 years earlier. When was his great-grandfather born?

3. The temperature in early May near the border of New York State and Canada was 15°. Was it Fahrenheit or Celsius? What was the weather like that day?

4. Melissa wants to put a wallpaper border around her room. The room is 9 feet wide and 12 feet long. How many feet of border paper should she buy?

5. Riverlake Central School sells T-shirts in sizes small, medium, large, and extra-large. The colors available are blue and gold. Make a tree diagram to show the different choices.

6. A newspaper reported that a town meeting passed a law by a show-of-hands vote. The reported vote was 523 to 179. Does this report make sense? Why or why not?

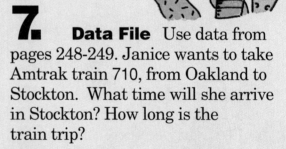

7. **Data File** Use data from pages 248-249. Janice wants to take Amtrak train 710, from Oakland to Stockton. What time will she arrive in Stockton? How long is the train trip?

8. **Make a Data File** Look at a map of your area. Find 3 places that are about 100 miles from your home. List them in alphabetical order.

Explore with a Calculator

Number Scramble Game

1. In a game of Number Scramble, Sheldon has these game tiles on his rack.

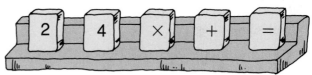

He can use the numbers and signs more than once to make the display shown on his card.

Display 36

This is the sequence he keyed into his calculator.

4 × 4 × 2 + 4 =

Another sequence made by using some of the same keys is

24 + 4 + 4 + 4 =

2. Play Number Scramble. The rack of game tiles and the display card are given for each exercise.

a. 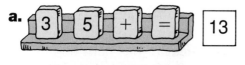 13

e. 0 1 4 − = 2

b.  18

f. 2 4 + = 66

c. 4 7 × + = 56

g. 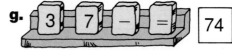 74

d. 5 9 × − = 36

h.  28

3. Choose the operation signs and tell the sequence needed to make the display using only the numbers given.

a.  20

b.  51

Reteaching

Set A   pages 108–109

Lou gets up at 6:45 A.M. School starts at 8:15 A.M. How many minutes is it until school begins?

It is 60 minutes, or 1 hour, from 6:45 A.M. until 7:45 A.M.

It is 30 minutes from 7:45 A.M. until 8:15 A.M.

It is 90 minutes, or 1 hour and 30 minutes, from 6:45 A.M. until school begins at 8:15 A.M.

Remember to write *A.M.* for the hours between midnight and noon. Write *P.M.* for the hours between noon and midnight.

How much time has passed between

1. 2:20 P.M. and 4:30 P.M.?

2. 6:30 A.M. and 11:15 A.M.?

3. 12:15 P.M. and 3:05 P.M.?

Set B   pages 110–111

George Washington was born on February 22. Thomas Jefferson was born on April 13. How many weeks and days are there from Washington's birthday to Jefferson's birthday?

Use the calendar on page 110. It is one week from February 22 to March 1. It is another week to March 8, and so on. From February 22 to April 12 is 7 weeks. From April 12 to April 13 is 1 day. Jefferson's birthday is 7 weeks and 1 day after Washington's birthday.

Remember that the months of the year do not all have the same number of days.

Use the calendar on page 110 to answer the questions.

1. Andrew Jackson's birthday is the third Thursday in March. What date is his birthday?

2. Ronald Reagan was born on February 6. Harry Truman's birthday is exactly 13 weeks later. What date is that?

Set C   pages 114–117

How long is the pencil to the nearest inch? nearest half inch? nearest quarter inch?

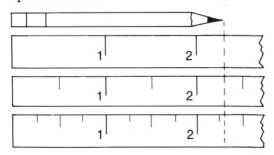

Remember that the smaller the unit of measurement on a ruler, the more exact is the measurement.

Use a ruler to measure the length to the nearest inch, nearest half inch, and nearest quarter inch.

1.

2.

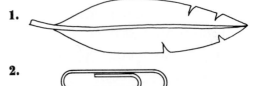

Set D   pages 120–121

Ten paper clips laid side-by-side make about 1 decimeter. The length of 10 football fields is about one kilometer. **Remember** that the kilometer is used to measure long distances.

1. Find the length of this paper clip to the nearest centimeter.

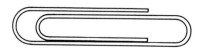

2. Draw a line 4 centimeters long.

Set E   pages 122–123

What is the temperature on the thermometer?
Every two degrees is marked. Count by two to 46°C.

-50°C

-40°C

Remember that the intervals between numbers on the Celsius scale are larger than those on the Fahrenheit scale.

Write each temperature.

1. 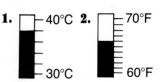 -40°C

-30°C

2. -70°F

-60°F

Set F   pages 124–125

Find the perimeter of this figure. It is a baseball "diamond."

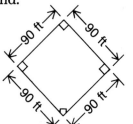

90 ft   90 ft

90 ft   90 ft

Add: 90 + 90 + 90 + 90 = 360 feet

Remember that perimeter means the distance around a figure.

Find the perimeter.

1.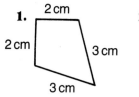
2 cm
2 cm   3 cm
3 cm

2.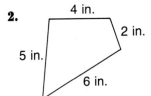
4 in.
2 in.
5 in.
6 in.

Set G   pages 126–129

Find the area in square units.

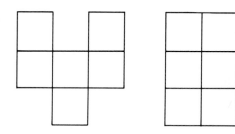

Count the number of squares. Both figures have areas of 6 square units.

Remember that the area of a figure is the number of square units needed to cover the figure.

Find the area in square units.

1.   **2.**

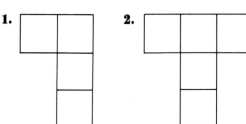

More Practice

Set A   pages 108–109

Write each time.

1. 27 minutes after 5:00 P.M.

2. 15 minutes before 7:00 P.M.

3. 40 minutes after 9:00 A.M.

4. 1 hour 25 minutes after 8:00 A.M.

How much time has elapsed between

5. 3:10 P.M. and 5:15 P.M.?

6. 8:45 A.M. and 10:55 A.M.?

Set B   pages 110–111

Use the calendar on page 110 to answer the questions.

1. Theodore Roosevelt's birthday is the fourth Saturday in October. What date is his birthday?

2. Woodrow Wilson's birthday is 1 day before the fifth Saturday in December. What date is this?

3. James Madison was born on March 16. James Polk's birthday is exactly 33 weeks later. When is his birthday?

4. Ulysses Grant was born on April 27, and Calvin Coolidge was born on July 4. How long is it from Grant's birthday to Coolidge's?

Set C   pages 114–117

Use your ruler to measure the length of each object to the nearest inch, nearest half inch, and nearest quarter inch.

1.

2.

Use a ruler

3. to measure the width of your desk to the nearest inch.

4. to draw a leaf that is $1\frac{1}{2}$ inches long, and $\frac{3}{4}$ inches wide.

Estimation   Which unit (inch, foot, yard, or mile) would you use to measure

5. the length of a zipper?

6. the height of the classroom wall?

7. the distance to the next town?

Choose the most sensible answer.

8. Length of a toothbrush
   a. 6 in.   **b.** 6 ft   **c.** 6 yd

9. Height of a floor lamp
   a. 5 ft   **b.** 5 yd   **c.** 5 mi

Set D   pages 120–121

Use a metric ruler to find the length of each insect.

1.

2.

3.

Estimation   Choose the most sensible answer.

4. Width of a door
   a. 1 cm   **b.** 1 m   **c.** 1 km

5. Length of a car
   a. 4 cm   **b.** 4 m   **c.** 4 km

Set E   pages 122–123

Choose the most sensible temperature for each of the following.

1. Making ice cubes
   a. 10° C   **b.** 30° F

2. A cup of hot cocoa
   a. 40° C   **b.** 70° F

3. A comfortable room
   a. 22° C   **b.** 85° F

Write the temperature shown on each thermometer.

4.

5.

6.

Set F   pages 124–125

Use a centimeter ruler to find the perimeter of each figure.

1.    2.

Use the measurements given to find the perimeter of each figure.

3.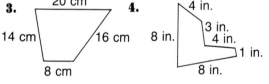
   20 cm
   14 cm   16 cm
   8 cm

4.
   4 in.
   8 in.   3 in.   4 in.   1 in.
   8 in.

Set G   pages 126–129

Find each area in square centimeters.

1.

2.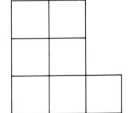

3.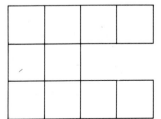

Enrichment

Time Zones

As you travel across the United States, the time changes as you enter different time zones.

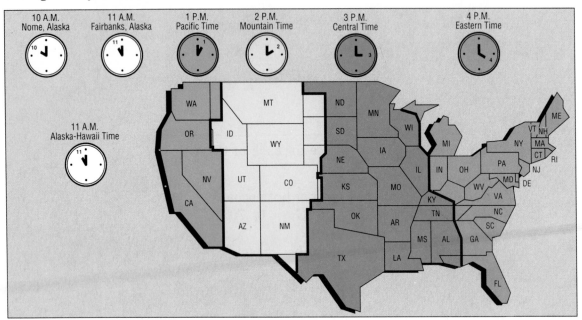

Use the map to answer the following questions.
Name the time zone that is

1. 1 hour later than Pacific Time.

2. 2 hours later than Hawaii Time.

3. 3 hours earlier than Eastern Time.

When it is 11:00 A.M. in Minnesota, what time is it in

4. Wyoming?

5. New York?

6. Hawaii?

For Exercises 7–11, is it a good idea to make the telephone call at the time shown? Why or why not?

You live in:	It is:	You want to call:
7. Massachusetts.	7 A.M.	your grandmother in Colorado.
8. Oregon.	8 A.M.	your friend in Ohio before school.
9. Hawaii.	7 A.M.	your aunt in South Carolina.
10. Nome, Alaska.	6 P.M.	your pen pal in Maine.
11. Virginia.	10 A.M.	a business office in California.

Chapter 4 Review/Test

Write the time.

1. 20 minutes before 3:00 P.M.

Use the calendar to answer Items 2 and 3.

2. What date is 10 days after the first Monday in April?

April						
S	M	T	W	T	F	S
1	2	3	4	5	6	7
8	9	10	11	12	13	14
15	16	17	18	19	20	21
22	23	24	25	26	27	28
29	30					

3. Derek's birthday is April 22. Sue's birthday is 5 days later. On what day of the week is Sue's birthday?

Use the data in the table to answer Items 4 and 5.

		OPEN	CLOSE
Bank	M–F	9:00 A.M.	4:00 P.M.
Post Office	M–S	8:30 A.M.	5:00 P.M.
Grocery	Daily	7:00 A.M.	10:00 P.M.

4. How many hours a day is the post office open?

5. Which data in the table must be used to answer this problem?

Bonny worked at the grocery from opening time until 2:00 P.M. How long did she work?

6. Give the length of the nail to the nearest inch, nearest half inch, and nearest quarter inch.

7. Choose the most sensible measure for the length of a sofa.
6 in.   6 ft   6 mi

8. Give the length of the nail to the nearest centimeter.

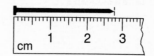

9. Choose the more sensible temperature for snow skiing.
25°F   25°C

10. Find the perimeter.

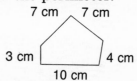

11. How many feet of fencing are needed to enclose a rectangular pen that is 12 ft by 10 ft?

12. Find the area in square units.

13. Delila babysat from 6:20 P.M. to 7:40 P.M. How long did she babysit?

14. **Write About Math** Look at the calendar for April on this page. What is the date of the first Sunday in May? Explain how you got your answer.

Multiplication Facts

5

Penny	Abraham Lincoln
Nickel	Thomas Jefferson
Dime	Franklin D. Roosevelt
Quarter	George Washington
Half Dollar	John F. Kennedy

Number-Sense Project

Estimate
Tell how you could estimate the number of pennies you see. About how many pennies are there? Estimate the amount of money shown here.

Gather Data
Count how many of each type of coin there are except for the pennies. Compute the amount of money for each type. Then find the grand total for all the coins except the pennies.

Analyze and Report
Compare your estimate to the actual amount.

141

Relating Multiplication and Addition

Build Understanding

Look at the toys pictured below. Choose 4 of any item and find the total cost. Explain how you found the total.

Suppose you want to buy 4 turtles. You can find the total cost by adding or by multiplying.

Addition $7 + 7 + 7 + 7 = 28$
Multiplication $4 \times 7 = 28$

So, 4 turtles cost 28¢.

■ **Talk About Math** Suppose you buy one of each item. Can you multiply to find the total cost? Why or why not?

Check Understanding

For another example, see Set A, pages 170–171.

Write an addition sentence for each problem. Use the prices given above.

1. What is the cost of 3 robots?

2. What is the cost of 5 dinosaurs?

3. What is the cost of a bird and a dinosaur?

4. What is the cost of a bird and a turtle?

Practice

For More Practice, see Set A, pages 172–173.

Copy and complete each number sentence.

5. 9 + 9 = ▦
2 × 9 = ▦

6. 8 + 8 + 8 = ▦
3 × 8 = ▦

7. 6 + 6 + 6 + 6 = ▦
4 × 6 = ▦

8. 4 + 4 + 4 = ▦
3 × 4 = ▦

9. 5 + 5 + 5 + 5 + 5 = ▦
5 × 5 = ▦

10. 5 + 5 = ▦
2 × 5 = ▦

Add. Then write the related multiplication sentence.

11. 3 + 3 + 3 + 3

12. 2 + 2 + 2 + 2 + 2

13. 7 + 7 + 7 + 7 + 7

14. 9 + 9 + 9 + 9

15. 6 + 6 + 6 + 6 + 6 + 6

16. 1 + 1 + 1

Problem Solving

Solve each problem. Use prices from the pictures on page 142.

17. How much did Alex spend for a turtle, a dinosaur, and a bird?

18. Find two ways that you could spend 35¢.

19. To find the cost of two robots and two birds, Marsha added 5 and 6 to get 11, and then added 11 more. Find the cost another way.

20. **Estimation** Can you buy more than 10 birds for a dollar? Can you buy more than 20 birds for a dollar?

Choose a _____ Strategy

Even Sums You can use even numbers to get a sum of 10. For example,
2 + 4 + 4 = 10.

21. List 4 other ways that you can use even numbers to make a sum of 10. You may use numbers more than once.

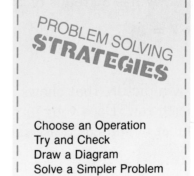

PROBLEM SOLVING STRATEGIES

Choose an Operation
Try and Check
Draw a Diagram
Solve a Simpler Problem

Multiplication by 2 Through 5; Arrays

Build Understanding

There are 3 rows of stars with
7 stars in each row in the picture
shown at the right.

A picture with rows and columns is
called an **array**. Each row has the
same number of objects. Each
column has the same number of
objects.

When you have an array of objects,
you can write two multiplication
sentences.

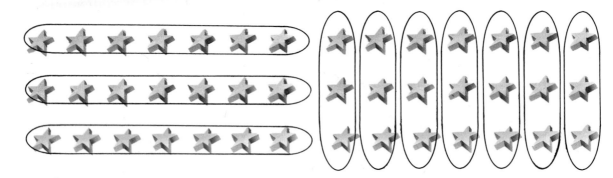

When you group the stars by rows,
the array has 3 groups of 7 stars.

3 × 7 = 21

When you group the stars by
columns, the array has
7 groups of 3 stars.

7 × 3 = 21

Draw a picture that shows 7 rows of stars with 3
in each row. Does your picture have the same
number of stars as those shown above?
Why?

Talk About Math How does knowing that
5 × 9 is 45 help you find 9 × 5? If 37 × 6 is
222, what is 6 × 37?

Check Understanding

For another example, see Set B, pages 170–171.

Write two multiplication sentences for each picture.

1.  **2.**

Draw an array to show each fact. Then find the product.

3. 8×3 **4.** 7×2 **5.** 6×4 **6.** 9×3 **7.** 7×3 **8.** 8×2

Practice

For More Practice, see Set B, pages 172–173.

Find each product. Draw arrays if necessary.

9. 6×3 **10.** 9×2 **11.** 7×4 **12.** 5×9 **13.** 6×2 **14.** 8×4

15. 5×8 **16.** 3×8 **17.** 4×8 **18.** 4×9 **19.** 6×5 **20.** 3×7

21. 3×6 **22.** 7×5 **23.** 9×5 **24.** 4×4 **25.** 3×9 **26.** 2×6

Problem Solving

Use the rectangle for Problems 27–29. Each square is 1 centimeter by 1 centimeter.

27. What is the length?

28. What is the width?

29. Can multiplication be used to find the area? Why or why not?

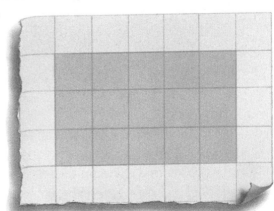

Draw each rectangle on centimeter grid paper. Then find the area.

30. 6 cm by 2 cm   **31.** 3 cm by 9 cm

Multiplication with 6

Build Understanding

Barbara Reddig is a seamstress. Sometimes she buys strips of buttons that have six buttons on each. How many buttons would there be on 9 strips?

9 × 6 = 54

There are 54 buttons on 9 strips.

Here is a way to find 9 × 6 without counting all the buttons. How many buttons are on the five strips above the pencil?

5 × 6 = ▦

How many buttons are on the four strips below the pencil?

4 × 6 = ▦

The total of 5 × 6 and 4 × 6 is 9 × 6, or 54.

■ **Talk About Math** Discuss other ways to find the total without counting all of the buttons.

Check Understanding

For another example, see Set C, pages 170–171.

Each strip has 6 buttons. How many buttons are on

1. 3 strips? **2.** 6 strips? **3.** 7 strips? **4.** 8 strips?

Practice

For More Practice, see Set C, pages 172–173.

Copy and complete the table.

5.

×	1	2	3	4	5	6	7	8	9
6									

Find each product.

6. 6×6 **7.** 7×6 **8.** 6×3 **9.** 2×6 **10.** 5×6 **11.** 6×8

12. 6×9 **13.** 6×4 **14.** 8×6 **15.** 9×6 **16.** 6×7 **17.** 4×6

Mixed Practice   Find each product.

18. 4×3 **19.** 2×9 **20.** 4×6 **21.** 9×3 **22.** 9×6 **23.** 4×9

24. 8×6 **25.** 7×4 **26.** 8×3 **27.** 2×5 **28.** 6×7 **29.** 4×5

30. 2×7 **31.** 4×8 **32.** 3×9 **33.** 6×3 **34.** 2×8 **35.** 3×7

Problem Solving

Solve each problem. Use the prices shown at the right.

36. Find the sale price for 6 yards of denim.

37. Find the regular price for 8 yards of corduroy.

38. Find the difference between the regular price and the sale price for a yard of corduroy.

39. A customer bought 8 yards of corduroy on sale. How much money did the customer save?

FABRIC SALE

● **Corduroy**
Regular Price
$6 per yard
Sale Price
$4 per yard

● **Denim**
Regular Price
$4 per yard
Sale Price
$3 per yard

Multiplication with 7

Build Understanding

Chairs have been arranged for a meeting. There are 8 rows of 7 chairs. How many chairs is that altogether?

Think of 8 groups of 7.

8 × 7 = 56

It also can be written as:

$$\begin{array}{r} 7 \\ \times\,8 \\ \hline 5\,6 \end{array}$$

There are 56 chairs.

■ **Talk About Math** How many chairs are in 4 rows? How can you use the product 4 × 7 to find 8 × 7?

Check Understanding

For another example, see Set D, pages 170–171.

Each row has 7 chairs. How many chairs are in

1. 2 rows? **2.** 3 rows? **3.** 5 rows? **4.** 6 rows? **5.** 7 rows?

6. If you know that 8 × 7 is 56, how can you find the product 9 × 7?

7. Will the product 12 × 7 be an odd number or an even number?

Practice

For More Practice, see Set D, pages 172–173.

Find each product.

8.	9.	10.	11.	12.	13.
8 ×7	7 ×6	7 ×2	7 ×7	4 ×7	9 ×7

Mixed Practice   Multiply.

14. 6 × 5   **15.** 4 × 9   **16.** 3 × 4   **17.** 9 × 6   **18.** 7 × 5   **19.** 4 × 7

20. 6 × 8   **21.** 5 × 5   **22.** 3 × 8   **23.** 6 × 7   **24.** 5 × 2   **25.** 4 × 4

26. 3 × 6   **27.** 7 × 3   **28.** 4 × 6   **29.** 8 × 3   **30.** 2 × 9   **31.** 7 × 8

Problem Solving

Solve each problem.

32. There were 7 tables used at the meeting. Six students sat at each table. How many students were there in all?

33. There were 23 boys and 19 girls at the meeting. How many more boys than girls were there?

34. There were 42 students and 6 adults at the meeting. How many people attended the meeting?

35. Allie brought 6 packages of pens to the meeting. Each package had 8 pens. How many pens did she bring? Did she have enough pens for everyone?

Skills ——— Review   pages 14–15, 76–81

Tell whether you would use paper and pencil, mental math, or a calculator. Then find the answer.

1. 49 + 29   **2.** 80 − 39   **3.** 8,300 − 5,130   **4.** 366 + 534

5. 900 − 60   **6.** 1,525 + 200   **7.** 8,209 + 282   **8.** 925 − 725

9. 156 + 749   **10.** 426 − 163   **11.** 783 + 32   **12.** 5,100 − 3,098

Too Much Information

Build Understanding

There are more than <u>300 types</u> of bamboo. One type from China grows as much as <u>3 feet in a day</u>. How much could this bamboo grow in <u>5 days</u>?

PROBLEM SOLVING GUIDE

▶ Understand
QUESTION
FACTS
KEY IDEA

Plan and Solve
STRATEGY
ANSWER

Look Back
SENSIBLE ANSWER
ALTERNATE APPROACH

▶ Understand   QUESTION   How much could this bamboo grow in 5 days?

FACTS   The numerical facts in the problem are underlined.

KEY IDEA   Which facts are needed to solve the problem? Which fact is not needed?

Plan and Solve   STRATEGY   Multiply to find the answer.

5 × 3 = 15

ANSWER   In five days, the bamboo can grow 15 feet.

Look Back   You can add to check your answer.

3 + 3 + 3 + 3 + 3 = 15

■ **Talk About Math**   Suppose another type of bamboo grows 2 feet per day. The bamboo grows in 4 different countries. How much does this bamboo grow in a week? Which facts must you know to solve the problem?

Bamboo stems can be used as fishing poles and in screens, cooking utensils, tools, shoes, paper, and building materials.

Check Understanding

Use the problem at the right to answer questions 1–3.

1. Which underlined facts are needed to solve the problem?

2. Which underlined facts are not needed?

3. Should you add, subtract, multiply, or divide?

4. Solve the problem.

A rubber tree pod contains <u>3 seeds.</u> Each seed is <u>1 inch long.</u> Suppose a branch has <u>6 pods.</u> How many seeds are on the branch?

Practice

Read for the facts. Then solve each problem.

5. Rice that is grown in the United States ripens about 5 months after planting. In Asia, one type of rice ripens in about 3 months. If rice in the United States is planted in mid-April, when will it ripen?

6. A python lays 100 eggs at a time. When the eggs hatch, the young are about 3 feet long. Adult pythons are about 30 feet long. About how much longer is an adult python than a young python?

7. The Amazon River is about 3,900 miles long, and 1,800 miles of the river can be used by ocean freighters. The Nile River is about 4,100 miles long. About how much longer is the Nile than the Amazon?

8. Most coffee trees are about 12 feet tall. Each year, a tree produces about a pound of coffee beans. About how many pounds of coffee beans would be produced by 5 trees?

Multiplication with 8

Build Understanding

In music, vertical bars are used to separate the measures. Nine measures of musical notes are shown below, with 8 notes in each measure. How many notes are shown in all?

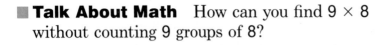

$$9 \times 8 = 72$$

There are 72 notes in 9 measures.

■ **Talk About Math** How can you find 9×8 without counting 9 groups of 8?

Check Understanding

For another example, see Set E, pages 170–171.

Each measure has 8 notes. How many notes will be played in

1. 3 measures?   **2.** 6 measures?   **3.** 4 measures?

4. 8 measures?   **5.** 5 measures?   **6.** 7 measures?

Practice

For More Practice, see Set E, pages 172–173.

Multiply.

7.	8.	9.	10.	11.	12.
3	8	8	9	4	8
×8	×6	×7	×8	×8	×8

Mixed Practice Multiply.

13. 2×6 **14.** 7×4 **15.** 4×3 **16.** 3×9 **17.** 3×8 **18.** 6×4

19. 5×6 **20.** 8×5 **21.** 7×2 **22.** 7×6 **23.** 9×7 **24.** 4×8

25. 6×9 **26.** 7×7 **27.** 8×2 **28.** 4×9 **29.** 6×3 **30.** 7×8

Copy and complete each row of the multiplication chart.

	×	1	2	3	4	5	6	7	8	9
31.	2	2	4	6						
32.	4	4	8							
33.	8	8	16							

Problem Solving

Solve each problem.

34. Some songs have 4 beats in each measure. How many beats are in 8 measures?

35. A song has 20 measures with 4 beats in each. How many beats does the song have?

36. A choir is recording a song that has 4 verses. Each verse lasts 40 seconds. What is the length of the song in minutes and seconds?

Be flexible. If you get stuck, try another idea.

Midchapter ———— Checkup

Multiply. Draw an array if necessary.

1. 5×6 **2.** 7×8 **3.** 3×7 **4.** 8×5 **5.** 6×6

6. Kyle had a music lesson each week for 9 weeks. Each lesson cost $8 and lasted 30 minutes. What was the cost for 8 lessons?

Problem Solving WORKSHOP

Number-Sense Project

Look back at pages 140-141.
Two sisters emptied their piggy banks and counted their money. First, they sorted their coins by type and then counted how many of each type they had. Their counts are shown below.

Lorie's Count

Lydia's Count

Type of Coin	Number
penny	43
nickel	15
dime	21
quarter	8
half-dollar	1
dollar	0

Type of Coin	Number
penny	12
nickel	20
dime	25
quarter	16
half-dollar	4
dollar	1

1. Which sister had the greatest number of coins?

2. Which sister had the greatest number of quarters?

3. Which sister had a total of $10.62?

4. If their mother had 10 coins totaling 78¢, what coins could she have had?

Explore with a Computer

Use the *Number Sense Workshop Project* for this activity.

1. With the **Number-Chart** option you can experiment with patterns in multiplication. Use the **Shade** option to show multiples of 2. Then shade multiples of 4. What happened to the display? What would happen if you shaded multiples of 8?

2. Clear the shading you did above. Experiment with other combinations of shading. What numbers show the same patterns? What numbers *do not* show the same patterns?

Real-Life Decision Making

You are making muffins for your scout group. You need to triple the recipe.

1. The recipe calls for 2 cups of flour. How many cups of flour do you need?

2. The recipe calls for baking muffins for 25 minutes at 350 degrees. You can bake all the muffins at the same time.

    a. How long will you bake the muffins?

    b. At what temperature will you bake the muffins?

Explore as a Team

1. Draw and cut out rectangles with 12 squares.

2. How many different rectangles with 12 squares can you make?

3. Were you able to make a rectangle having a side with 1 square? 2 squares? 3 squares?

4. Make all the rectangles having 25 squares or less.

5. What patterns do you see?

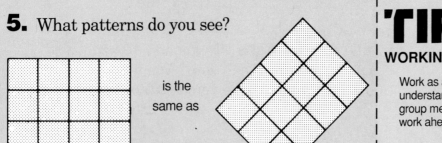

is the same as

TIPS FOR **WORKING TOGETHER**

Work as a group. If you understand, help another group member. Don't work ahead of the others.

Multiplication with 0, 1, and 10

Build Understanding

A. In a game, you are to give each player seven $10 bills and seven $1 bills. What is the total value of the ones that each player gets? What is the total value of the tens?

Count the ones.

$1	$1	$1	$1	$1	$1	$1
1	2	3				

7 × 1 = 7

Count by tens.

$10	$10	$10	$10	$10	$10	$10
10	20					

7 × 10 = 70

The value of the ones is $7 and the value of the tens is $70.

B. Copy and complete each sentence. Are your answers the same? Why?

0 + 0 + 0 = ▦   **3 × 0 = ▦**

■ **Talk About Math** If you add 10 zeros, will the sum be more than zero? What is the sum of 50 zeros? What is the sum of 100 zeros?

Check Understanding

For another example, see Set F, pages 170–171.

For each exercise, tell which item is not equal to the others.

1. 7×10
7 tens
7×1
70

2. 10 tens
10×10
100
$10 + 10$

3. $6 + 10$
60
6 tens
6×10

4. 3×10
$3 + 0$
3 tens
30

5. 40
4×10
4×0
4 tens

Practice

For More Practice, see Set F, pages 172–173.

Find each product.

6. 8×0 **7.** 4×10 **8.** 1×7 **9.** 6×0 **10.** 7×10 **11.** 0×4

12. 8×10 **13.** 5×1 **14.** 0×2 **15.** 10×3 **16.** 8×1 **17.** 1×9

Problem Solving

Critical Thinking   Solve each problem. Each student has only tens and ones.

18. Mel has $33 in bills. He has more than one $10 bill. He has more ones than tens. How many $1 bills does he have?

19. Jill has less than $50. She has four $10 bills. She has fewer ones than tens. She has 6 bills in all. How many ones does she have?

20. Angie has nine $1 bills. She has more than seven $10 bills. She has fewer tens than ones. How much money does she have?

21. Ted has fewer than ten $10 bills. He has more than three $1 bills. The number of tens is twice the number of ones. How much money does he have?

Multiplication with 9

Build Understanding

There are 9 pennies in each stack. How many pennies are in 4 stacks of 9?

Find 4 x 9

Think 4 x 10

An easy way to multiply nines is to think of tens, and then subtract. Think of 4 × 10, or 40. Then subtract 4.

4 × 9 = 36

There are 36 pennies in 4 stacks.

■ **Write About Math** Explain how to find 6 × 9. Then draw a picture to show how your method works.

Check Understanding

For another example, see Set G, pages 170–171.

Find each product.

1. 2 × 10 = ▦
   2 × 9 = ▦

2. 9 × 10 = ▦
   9 × 9 = ▦

3. 3 × 10 = ▦
   3 × 9 = ▦

4. 8 × 10 = ▦
   8 × 9 = ▦

5. 5 × 10 = ▦
   5 × 9 = ▦

6. 7 × 10 = ▦
   7 × 9 = ▦

Practice

For More Practice, see Set G, pages 172–173.

Find each product.

7.	8.	9.	10.	11.	12.
9 × 8	6 × 9	5 × 9	9 × 9	9 × 4	7 × 9

Mixed Practice   Complete each row of the table.
Look for and describe patterns.

x	5	10	9	6	3
13. 2					
14. 4					
15. 3					
16. 7					
17. 1					
18. 8					

Calculator   Find each product. Then add the digits
in the product. What do you notice?

For example, 9 $\times$ 382 $=$ 3438 and 3 $+$ 4 $+$ 3 $+$ 8 $=$ 18

19. 9 × 52   **20.** 9 × 68   **21.** 9 × 37   **22.** 9 × 84   **23.** 9 × 99

24. 9 × 578   **25.** 9 × 627   **26.** 9 × 112   **27.** 9 × 813   **28.** 9 × 333

Problem Solving

Solve each problem.

29. Jane had 9 stacks of dimes. There were 5 coins in each stack. How many dimes did she have?

30. Use Data   Would 3 quarters be enough to buy 9 toy turtles? Use data from page 142.

31. Critical Thinking   Jill has 57¢ in a piggy bank. There are 6 coins in the bank. What coins does she have?

32. Mark has 6 dimes. He has 3 more dimes than nickels. He has 2 fewer dimes than pennies. How much money does he have?

Another Meaning of Multiplication

Build Understanding

A landscape designer planted 4 shrubs in the front yard of a house. Three times as many shrubs will be planted in the backyard. How many shrubs will be planted in the backyard?

Draw 3 rows of four Xs to represent the shrubs in the backyard. What does each row of Xs represent?

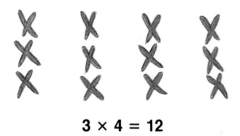

$$3 \times 4 = 12$$

There will be 12 shrubs in the backyard.

■ **Talk About Math** When you say that 12 is 3 times as many as 4, you are comparing 12 and 4. What is another way to compare 12 and 4? How many more shrubs will be planted in the backyard than in the front yard?

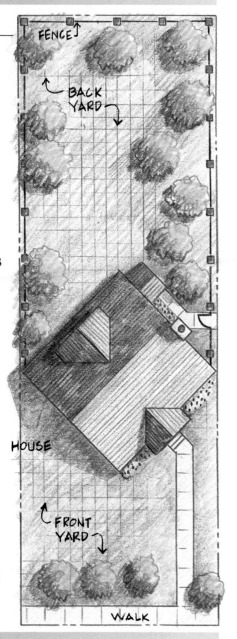

Check Understanding

For another example, see Set H, pages 170–171.

Answer each question. Draw pictures if necessary.

1. What number is 4 times as many as 6?

2. What number is 9 times as many as 5?

Practice

For More Practice, see Set H, pages 172–173.

For each exercise write the number that is 3 times as many.

3. 7   **4.** 9   **5.** 3   **6.** 8   **7.** 10   **8.** 6

For each exercise write the number that is 7 times as many.

9. 8   **10.** 4   **11.** 9   **12.** 6   **13.** 3   **14.** 10

Mental Math   Travis spent 10 minutes weeding the garden. Write the amount of time that is

15. 3 times as long.   **16.** 2 times as long.   **17.** 5 times as long.

18. 6 times as long.   **19.** 8 times as long.   **20.** 9 times as long.

Problem Solving

Solve each problem.

21. David planted 2 maple trees. He planted five times as many birch trees as maple trees. How many birch trees did he plant?

22. Julia planted twice as many flower bulbs as Jay. She planted 7 more than he did. How many flower bulbs did Jay plant?

Explore ————— Math

Use the diagrams to help you solve each problem.

23. The length of the rose garden is ▦ times the length of the marigold garden.

24. The area of the rose garden is ▦ square feet, and the area of the marigold garden is ▦ square feet.

25. The area of the rose garden is ▦ times the area of the marigold garden.

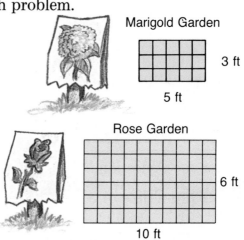

Marigold Garden

3 ft

5 ft

Rose Garden

6 ft

10 ft

Multiples

Build Understanding

Exploring Multiples
Materials: Hundred-square charts, crayons

a. Write the number 3 several times and find the sum. Since each addend is 3, the total must be a *multiple* of 3.

Is it possible to use 3s as addends to get a sum of 10? of 12?

b. Fill in the numbers from 1 to 100 on a 100-square chart. Choose a crayon and color the square with the number 3. Then color every third box up to 100. These numbers are the multiples of 3 between 1 and 100.

■ **Talk About Math** How else might you find multiples of 3? If 78 is a multiple of 3, what is the next multiple of 3? If 91 is a multiple of 7, what is the next multiple of 7?

Check Understanding

For another example, see Set I, pages 170–171.

Answer each question.

1. Is 22 a multiple of 3?

2. Is 24 a multiple of 3?

3. Write the next 4 multiples of 5.
5, 10, 15, ▦, ▦, ▦, ▦

4. Is 47 a multiple of 5? How do you know?

162

Practice

For More Practice, see Set I, pages 172–173.

Write 6 multiples of each number.

5. Multiples of 2

6. Multiples of 4

7. Multiples of 6

8. Multiples of 7

9. Multiples of 8

10. Multiples of 9

11. Multiples of 10

12. Multiples of 100

13. Multiples of 11

Answer *yes* or *no*.

14. Is 18 a multiple of 4?

15. Is 36 a multiple of 6?

16. Is 21 a multiple of 7?

17. Is 81 a multiple of 8?

Problem Solving

Copy the chart at the right.

18. Circle all the multiples of 4. List them.

19. Put a triangle over the multiples of 6. List them.

20. Which numbers are multiples of both 4 and 6?

1	2	3	4	5	6	7	8	9	10
11	12	13	14	15	16	17	18	19	20
21	22	23	24	25	26	27	28	29	30
31	32	33	34	35	36	37	38	39	40
41	42	43	44	45	46	47	48	49	50
51	52	53	54	55	56	57	58	59	60
61	62	63	64	65	66	67	68	69	70
71	72	73	74	75	76	77	78	79	80
81	82	83	84	85	86	87	88	89	90
91	92	93	94	95	96	97	98	99	100

Use the chart if necessary. Find a number that is a multiple of both

21. 3 and 5.   **22.** 2 and 3.   **23.** 3 and 4.   **24.** 4 and 6.   **25.** 6 and 8.

26. ▥ **Calculator**   Use your calculator to find multiples of 12.

Step 1: Enter 12 into the calculator.

Step 2: Press ⊞ 12 ⊜.

Step 3: Keep pressing ⊞ 12 ⊜ to get more multiples of 12.

(On some calculators you can just keep pressing ⊜.)

Missing Factors and Factoring

Build Understanding

A. Electricity is measured in *watts*. Suppose each light bulb in a chandelier uses 10 watts of electricity. If the chandelier uses a total of 80 watts of electricity, how many bulbs are there?

Think of multiplication. The number of bulbs times the number of watts used by one bulb is the total number of watts used by the chandelier.

▦	×	**10**	=	**80**
factor		*factor*		*product*

Since $8 \times 10 = 80$, the ***missing factor*** is 8. So, the chandelier has 8 bulbs.

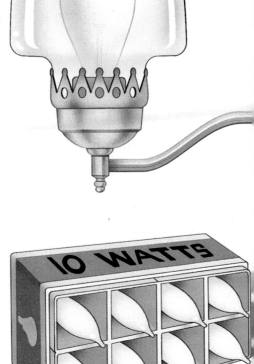

The *watt* was named for the Scottish engineer and inventor James Watt.

B. In each diagram below, the number at the top is the product of the factors below it. Copy and complete each diagram.

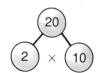

The missing factor is 7.

The missing factor is 6.

■ **Write About Math** Can you make a different diagram with factors for 20? for 49? for 18?

Check Understanding

For another example, see Set J, pages 170–171.

Copy and complete each sentence. Sometimes you will find more than one answer.

1. $5 \times \text{▦} = 25$ **2.** $\text{▦} \times \text{▦} = 12$ **3.** $\text{▦} \times \text{▦} = 36$ **4.** $\text{▦} \times \text{▦} = 40$

Practice

For More Practice, see Set J, pages 172–173.

Copy and complete each number sentence.
Some exercises have more than one answer.

5. $7 \times \text{▦} = 35$ **6.** $\text{▦} \times 8 = 24$ **7.** $\text{▦} \times 4 = 12$ **8.** $6 \times \text{▦} = 18$

9. $9 \times \text{▦} = 63$ **10.** $3 \times \text{▦} = 12$ **11.** $\text{▦} \times 6 = 48$ **12.** $7 \times \text{▦} = 42$

13. $5 \times \text{▦} = 35$ **14.** $\text{▦} \times 4 = 16$ **15.** $\text{▦} \times 7 = 28$ **16.** $\text{▦} \times 8 = 56$

17. $9 \times \text{▦} = 27$ **18.** $\text{▦} \times 8 = 64$ **19.** $\text{▦} \times \text{▦} = 54$ **20.** $\text{▦} \times \text{▦} = 44$

Copy and complete each diagram. **Remember** that the top number
must be the product of the two other numbers.

21.   **22.**   **23.**   **24.**

Problem Solving

Number Sense Choose numbers from the
screen so that the paragraph makes sense.

25. A color television uses about ▦ watts of
electricity. A television uses more watts than
a radio, which uses only about ▦ watts.
Watching television for an hour costs about
▦ cents. The cost for listening to a radio is
about ▦ cent each hour.

Reading ——— Math

Vocabulary Answer each question.

1. What is the product in Exercise 8?

2. What is the missing factor in Exercise 12?

3. What is the given factor in Exercise 15?

Write a Number Sentence

PROBLEM SOLVING GUIDE

Understand
QUESTION
FACTS
KEY IDEA

➤ **Plan and Solve**
STRATEGY
ANSWER

Look Back
SENSIBLE ANSWER
ALTERNATE APPROACH

Build Understanding

A number sentence shows how numbers are related to each other. In the situation below, replace ○, △, and □ with numbers that make sense. What number sentence can you write?

For an art project, each of ○ students will need △ cups. Altogether, the students will need □ cups.

Understand The situation is about equal groups. The total number of cups must be the product of the numbers chosen for ○ and △.

➤ **Plan and Solve** STRATEGY Suppose that 6 students need 9 cups each. Then the total must be 54 cups. Write a multiplication sentence.

ANSWER $6 \times 9 = 54$ or $9 \times 6 = 54$

Look Back Try other numbers for ○, △, and □.

■**Talk About Math** How can you tell if the numbers make sense in the situation?

Check Understanding

Write a number sentence for the situation. Then change the numbers and write another number sentence.

1. Margie drew pictures of 8 dinosaurs. Pat drew 15 dinosaurs, which was 7 more than the number Margie drew.

2. There are 7 tables in the art room, and 8 students can sit at each table. Altogther, 56 students can sit at the tables.

Practice

Replace ○, △, and □, with numbers that make sense.
Then write a number sentence.

3. Jeff took ○ sheets of art paper from a package of △ sheets. There were □ sheets of paper left.

4. To make mobiles, each student cut ○ inches of yarn into △ pieces of the same length. Each short piece was □ inches long.

5. The art teacher got ○ new boxes of paint. Each box contained △ jars. Altogether, there were □ new jars of paint.

6. Milton combined ○ ounces of red paint with △ ounces of yellow paint. Then he had □ ounces of orange paint.

Choose a 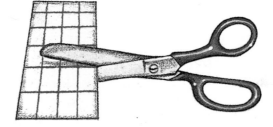 **Strategy**

Cut It Out   When learning about area, Lucita's class cut rectangles out of grid paper and then compared the dimensions of the rectangles to their areas.

Lucita's twin sister, Rita, cut out a rectangle that was twice as long as it was wide. Rita's rectangle had an area of 18 square units.

Bill's rectangle was also twice as long as it was wide, but the width of this rectangle was exactly the same as the length of Rita's.

The rectangle that Ronald cut out was just as long as Bill's. Ronald's rectangle was 4 times as long as it was wide.

Lucita's rectangle was just as wide as Ronald's and twice as long as it was wide.

7. What were the dimensions of Rita's rectangle?

8. What were the dimensions of Bill's rectangle? What was its area?

9. What was the area of Ronald's rectangle?

10. What was the area of Lucita's rectangle?

Problem-Solving Review

Solve each problem.

1. About 47,000 people attended a football game. Of this number, 19,000 were women. About how many men attended the game?

2. Ed goes to sleep at 9:30 P.M. and wakes up at 6 A.M. Elise goes to sleep at 8:00 P.M. and wakes up at 5:15 A.M. Who sleeps more?

3. Emily wants to buy sheet music for the piano. Each song sheet costs $2.97. She made $10 babysitting last night. How many songs can she buy?

4. John earns $4.00 an hour stocking shelves in a department store. On Sundays and holidays, he earns overtime pay of $6.00 an hour. He has to work 20 hours of regular time before he is allowed to work overtime. He has 28 hours free to work this week. What is the most he can earn at this job this week?

5. Shine shampoo sells for $2 for a 16-ounce bottle. Wavy shampoo sells for $3 for a 24-ounce bottle. Lisa bought 5 bottles of each kind. How much did she spend?

6. **Data File** Use data from pages 248-249 and a calculator. What are the round-trip distances between Boyne Falls, Michigan, and Chicago, Illinois? and Toledo, Ohio? Which trip is longer?

7. **Make a Data File** Look in an atlas to find 3 rivers in your state. Write them in order from longest to shortest.

Explore with a Calculator

Outer Space Multiplication

1. Is 42 a multiple of 6? Start with 42 and keep subtracting 6 until the number in the display is less than the number you are subtracting. If you get a display of 0, then 42 is a multiple of 6.

42 ⊟ 6 ⊟ 6 ⊟ 6 ⊟ 6 ⊟ 6 ⊟ 6 ⊟ 6 ⊜

This sequence will work also.

42 ⊟ 6 ⊜ ⊜ ⊜ ⊜ ⊜ ⊜ ⊜

2. In this video game, you have to put each numbered rocket on the correct planet. Some rockets may go on more than one planet. Some rockets may not go on any planet.

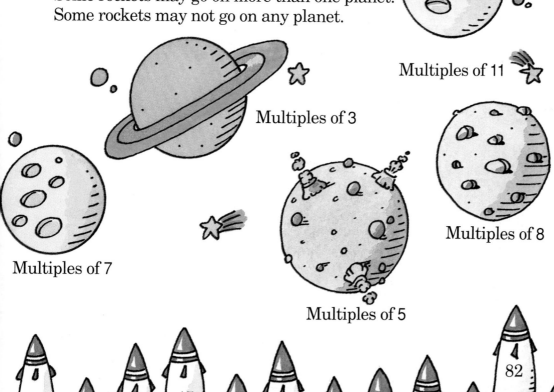

Multiples of 11

Multiples of 3

Multiples of 8

Multiples of 7

Multiples of 5

55   91   44   45   30   120   104   112   63   82   73   165

Reteaching

Set A   pages 142–143

How much will 4 dogs cost?
Addition: 8 + 8 + 8 + 8 = 32
Multiplication: 8 × 4 = 32
So, 4 dogs will cost 32¢.

Remember that multiplication is repeated addition.

Add. Then write the related multiplication sentence.

1. 4 + 4 + 4   **2.** 5 + 5 + 5 + 5

Set B   pages 144–145

Write a multiplication sentence for each picture.

3 × 4 = 12   4 × 3 = 12

Remember that factors can be written in any order.

Find each product.

1. 3 × 5   **2.** 4 × 2   **3.** 3 × 3

4. 5 × 6   **5.** 2 × 8   **6.** 2 × 5

Set C   pages 146–147

There are 6 balloons in a bag. How many balloons are in 7 bags?

5 × 6 = 30   2 × 6 = 12

The total is 7 × 6, or 42 balloons.

Remember that you can multiply if all the groups are the same size.

Multiply.

1. 6 × 2   **2.** 6 × 5   **3.** 6 × 3

4. 8 × 6   **5.** 4 × 6   **6.** 6 × 6

Set D   pages 148–149

There are 7 days in a week. How many days are in 3 weeks?

Think of 3 groups of 7.

X X X X X X X
X X X X X X X
X X X X X X X

There are 21 days in 3 weeks.

3 × 7 = 21

Remember that you can use 2 × 7 to find 4 × 7, 6 × 7, and 8 × 7.

Multiply.

1. 4 × 7   **2.** 7 × 8   **3.** 6 × 7

4. 7 × 9   **5.** 7 × 6   **6.** 7 × 7

Set E   pages 152–153

A ticket for a concert costs $8. How much do 3 tickets cost?

Think of 3 groups of 8 dollar bills. This is 3 × 8 = 24, or $24.

Remember that the products of 8 × 3 and 3 × 8 are the same. Multiply.

1. 5   **2.** 7   **3.** 3 × 8   **4.** 6 × 8
      × 8   × 8

Set F pages 156–157

a. Four student tickets at $1 each cost
$1 + $1 + $1 + $1 = $4.
4 × 1 = 4, or $4

b. Four adult tickets at $10 each cost
$10 + $10 + $10 + $10 = $40.
4 × 10 = 40, or $40

Remember that if a factor is 0, the product is 0. If a factor is 1, the product is the other factor. Multiply.

1. 10
× 5

2. 1
×9

3. 10
× 9

4. 8
×1

Set G pages 158–159

To find 3 × 9, think of 3 × 10. Then subtract 3 from 3 × 10.

3 × 10 = 30, and 30 − 3 = 27.
So 3 × 9 = 27.

Remember that you can find the product of 9 and any number by finding 10 times the number and then subtracting the number from the product. Find each product.

1. 4 × 9   **2.** 9 × 6   **3.** 8 × 9

Set H pages 160–161

Ted planted 3 violets. He planted 5 times as many pansies. How many pansies did he plant?

Violets   Pansies
X   X X X X X
X   X X X X X
X   X X X X X

5 × 3 = 15

Remember that doubling means to multiply by 2 and tripling means to multiply by 3.

For each exercise double the number. Then triple the given number.

1. 3   **2.** 4   **3.** 8

4. 5   **5.** 10   **6.** 0

Set I pages 162–163

Is 26 a multiple of 4? Count by 4s until you reach 26 or pass 26.

4 8 12 16 20 24 28

So 26 is not a multiple of 4.

Remember that when you count by a number you are finding its multiples.

1. Is 28 a multiple of 6?

2. Is 36 a multiple of 4?

Set J pages 164–165

Find the missing factor in
7 × ▦ = 42.

Think: What number times 7 is 42?

Since 7 × 6 = 42, the missing factor is 6.

Remember that you can use a family of facts to find the missing factor.

1. 5 × ▦ = 45   **2.** ▦ × 9 = 72

3. 8 × ▦ = 0   **4.** 1 × ▦ = 17

More Practice

Set A   pages 142–143

Copy and complete each number sentence.

1. 8 + 8 = ▦
   2 × 8 = ▦

2. 6 + 6 + 6 = ▦
   3 × 6 = ▦

3. 7 + 7 + 7 + 7 = ▦
   4 × 7 = ▦

Add. Then write the related multiplication sentence.

4. 4 + 4 + 4 + 4

5. 9 + 9 + 9

6. 3 + 3 + 3 + 3 + 3

Set B   pages 144–145

Find each product. You may draw arrays to help you.

1. 7 × 2   **2.** 3 × 4   **3.** 5 × 5   **4.** 8 × 5   **5.** 2 × 5   **6.** 3 × 3

7. 4 × 5   **8.** 5 × 7   **9.** 5 × 8   **10.** 4 × 6   **11.** 5 × 4   **12.** 2 × 9

Set C   pages 146–147

Find each product.

1. 2 × 6   **2.** 6 × 5   **3.** 6 × 9   **4.** 3 × 6   **5.** 8 × 6   **6.** 4 × 6

Mixed Practice   Find each product.

7. 2 × 4   **8.** 5 × 4   **9.** 7 × 6   **10.** 5 × 8   **11.** 6 × 6   **12.** 9 × 3

Set D   pages 148–149

Find each product.

1. 3
   × 7

2. 7
   × 5

3. 6
   × 7

4. 7
   × 9

5. 4
   × 7

6. 7
   × 8

Mixed Practice   Multiply.

7. 6 × 4   **8.** 7 × 2   **9.** 9 × 4   **10.** 7 × 7   **11.** 4 × 3   **12.** 5 × 7

Set E   pages 152–153

Multiply.

1. 5
   × 8

2. 8
   × 4

3. 6
   × 8

4. 8
   × 3

5. 7
   × 8

6. 8
   × 9

Mixed Practice   Multiply.

7. 7 × 9   **8.** 9 × 6   **9.** 8 × 2   **10.** 4 × 7   **11.** 8 × 8   **12.** 9 × 3

Set F pages 156–157

Find each product.

1. 0×7 **2.** 5×10 **3.** 8×1 **4.** 1×4 **5.** 3×10 **6.** 5×0

Set G pages 158–159

Find each product.

1. $\begin{array}{r} 9 \\ \times 3 \\ \hline \end{array}$ **2.** $\begin{array}{r} 4 \\ \times 9 \\ \hline \end{array}$ **3.** $\begin{array}{r} 9 \\ \times 7 \\ \hline \end{array}$ **4.** $\begin{array}{r} 9 \\ \times 5 \\ \hline \end{array}$ **5.** $\begin{array}{r} 2 \\ \times 9 \\ \hline \end{array}$ **6.** $\begin{array}{r} 9 \\ \times 9 \\ \hline \end{array}$

Mixed Practice Find each product.

7. 8×9 **8.** 3×6 **9.** 9×1 **10.** 6×9 **11.** 3×10 **12.** 0×8

Set H pages 160–161

For each exercise write the number that is 5 times as many.

1. 5 **2.** 3 **3.** 8 **4.** 7 **5.** 4 **6.** 9

For each exercise write the number that is 4 times as many.

7. 4 **8.** 8 **9.** 6 **10.** 9 **11.** 5 **12.** 7

Set I pages 162–163

Write 6 multiples of each number.

1. 3 **2.** 5 **3.** 6 **4.** 8 **5.** 4 **6.** 20

Answer each question.

7. Is 22 a multiple of 4? **8.** Is 35 a multiple of 7? **9.** Is 49 a multiple of 9?

Set J pages 164–165

Copy and complete each number sentence.

1. $3 \times \boxed{} = 30$ **2.** $\boxed{} \times 2 = 16$ **3.** $7 \times \boxed{} = 21$ **4.** $10 \times \boxed{} = 20$

5. $6 \times \boxed{} = 30$ **6.** $4 \times \boxed{} = 32$ **7.** $\boxed{} \times 5 = 45$ **8.** $\boxed{} \times 8 = 48$

Copy and complete each diagram.

9.   **10.**   **11.**   **12.** 45, ×

Enrichment

Rules, Rules, Rules!

Judy was visiting her father at his office. One of the things that she saw from his window were lots of cars in the parking lot. She counted the cars. Then she wondered how many tires there were. She thought to herself, "If I know the number of cars, I can multiply by 4 to find the number of tires." Using a pencil and paper she found on a nearby desk, she wrote this rule:

$4 \times \square = \bigcirc$

where $\square$ represented the number of cars in the lot and $\bigcirc$ represented the number of tires.

Then she started to complete the following chart using the rule:

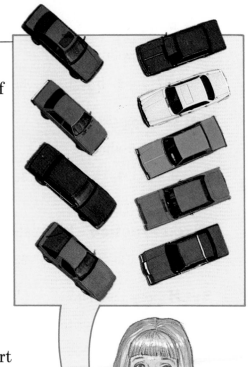

$\square$	1	2	3	4	5	6	7	8	9
$\bigcirc$	4	8	12						

1. Copy and complete Judy's chart.

Use Judy's rule to find the number of tires if the number of cars in the parking lot is

2. 10.   **3.** 15.   **4.** 48.   **5.** 187.

6. Copy and complete the chart if the rule is $\square + 5 = \triangle$.

$\square$	3	5	8	16	25	56	67	98	109
$\triangle$									

Write a rule for each chart.

7.

$\square$	1	2	3	4	5	6	7
$\bigstar$	8	16	24	32	40	48	56

8.

$\square$	1	2	3	4	5	6	7
$\diamond$	0	1	2	3	4	5	6

Chapter 5 Review/Test

Find each sum. Then write the related multiplication sentence.

1. 7 + 7 + 7 + 7 + 7

2. 9 + 9 + 9

Write two multiplication sentences for each picture.

3. ★ ★ ★ ★ ★
★ ★ ★ ★ ★
★ ★ ★ ★ ★

4. ★ ★
★ ★
★ ★
★ ★

Find each product. Draw an array for each product.

5. 8 × 3   **6.** 6 × 5

7. Tickets to a play cost $6 each. What is the cost of 4 tickets?

Find each product.

8. 6
    × 7

9. 7
    × 3

10. 8
     × 7

11. Selma bought 7 decals. Each one cost 8 cents. How much did she spend?

12. Which underlined facts are needed to solve the problem?

There are 5 pencils in each package. The cost of each pencil is 7 cents. Celeste bought 3 packages of pencils. How many pencils did she buy?

Multiply.

13. 8 × 4   **14.** 9 × 9   **15.** 9 × 8

16. 0 × 5   **17.** 1 × 7   **18.** 10 × 5

19. Eduardo had 9 stacks of checkers. There were 4 checkers in each stack. How many checkers did he have?

20. Ardis read 5 times as many pages of a magazine as Sue. Sue read 4 pages. How many pages did Ardis read?

Write 6 multiples of each number.
21. 5   **22.** 7

Answer *Yes* or *No*.
23. Is 21 a multiple of 3?

24. Is 28 a multiple of 9?

Copy and complete each sentence.
25. 6 × ▦ = 36   **26.** ▦ × 8 = 72

27. Replace ◯, △, and ☐ with numbers that make sense. Then write a number sentence.

A gardener planted ◯ rows of tomatoes. Each row had △ tomatoes. In all, there were ☐ tomatoes.

28. Write About Math You have to explain multiplication to someone who only knows how to add. How will you explain that 3 × 6 is equal to 18?

Division Facts

Number-Sense Project

Estimate
Predict which activity listed under "Did You Know:" will be the most popular choice of your classmates for a class party.

Gather Data
You have 5 points to rate the activities. Rate at least two activities. For example, someone might give picnicking 4 points and fishing 1 point. Someone else may give each of 5 activities 1 point. Add up the points from the whole class for each activity. Which received the most points?

Analyze and Report
Compare this method of choosing the most popular activity to taking a vote in which each student has 1 vote. What are the advantages and disadvantages of the two systems?

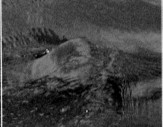
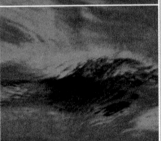

Did You Know: People 12 years and older were asked what they like to do in their spare time in a U.S. Census. The top 10 were these:

1. Swimming
2. Walking
3. Visiting zoos, amusement parks or fairs
4. Driving for pleasure
5. Picnicking
6. Sightseeing
7. Watching sports events
8. Fishing
9. Bicycling
10. Boating

177

Grouping and Sharing

Build Understanding

Groups Galore!
Materials: Cubes or small objects
Groups: With a partner

A. Each of you take a handful of cubes. Combine your cubes. Count them. Then make as many groups of 3 as you can. How many groups can you make? How many cubes are left over?

With ⬚ cubes you can form ⬚ groups of 3 cubes with ⬚ cubes left over.

B. Divide the same cubes into 3 equal groups. How many cubes are in each group? How many cubes are left over?

With ⬚ cubes you can form 3 groups of ⬚ cubes with ⬚ cubes left over.

■ **Talk About Math** Katie made 8 groups of 3 cubes. Suppose she rearranges them into 3 groups. How many cubes will be in each group? How do you know?

Check Understanding

For another example, see Set A, pages 206–207.

Choose the words that make a true sentence.

1. With 15 cubes you can form
   a. 2 groups of
   8 cubes.
   b. 3 groups of
   5 cubes.
   c. 4 groups of
   4 cubes.

2. With 22 cubes you can form
   a. 4 groups of 5
   with 2 left over.
   b. 3 groups of 7
   with 2 left over.
   c. 3 groups of 6
   with 3 left over.

Practice

For More Practice, see Set A, pages 208–209.

Use cubes to find the number of groups and the
number of cubes left over.

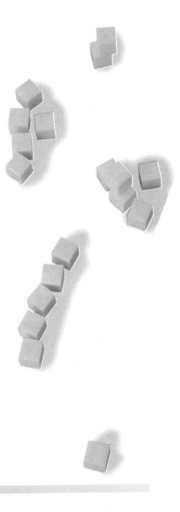

Number of cubes	Number of cubes in each group	Number of groups	Number of cubes left over
15	5	**3.**	**4.**
32	4	**5.**	**6.**
26	6	**7.**	**8.**
27	3	**9.**	**10.**
30	8	**11.**	**12.**
21	2	**13.**	**14.**

Use cubes to find the number of cubes in each group
and the number of cubes left over.

Number of cubes	Number of groups	Number of cubes in each group	Number of cubes left over
18	3	**15.**	**16.**
20	5	**17.**	**18.**
35	6	**19.**	**20.**
27	4	**21.**	**22.**
25	7	**23.**	**24.**
24	9	**25.**	**26.**

Problem Solving

Use cubes to find each answer.

27. Number Sense John made
4 groups of 6 with 24 cubes.
How many groups of 6 could he
make with 48 cubes?

28. Ken formed 3 groups of 7 with
21 cubes. How many groups of 3
could Ken form with 21 cubes?

29. Ted has 4 groups of 7 cubes with 3 cubes left over.
How many cubes does he have?

Families of Facts

Build Understanding

Draw 3 rows of Xs with the same number of Xs in each row. Now write two multiplication sentences that describe your picture.

Nancy drew the picture at the right.

She wrote two multiplication sentences about her picture.

3 × 4 = 12   Think: 3 rows of 4 is 12.

4 × 3 = 12   Think: 4 columns of 3 is 12.

She can also write two division sentences about her picture.

12 ÷ 4 = 3   Think: 12 divided into rows of 4 is 3 rows.

12 ÷ 3 = 4   Think: 12 divided into columns of 3 is 4 columns.

These four number sentences form a *family of facts*.

■**Write About Math** Write the complete family of facts for the picture that you drew.

Check Understanding

For another example, see Set B, pages 206–207.

Complete the family of facts for each picture.

1.
```
X X X X X X X
X X X X X X X
X X X X X X X
X X X X X X X
X X X X X X X
```
$5 \times 7 = 35$

$\blacksquare \times \blacksquare = 35$

$35 \div \blacksquare = \blacksquare$

$35 \div \blacksquare = \blacksquare$

2.
```
X X X
X X X
X X X
```
$3 \times \blacksquare = \blacksquare$

$9 \div \blacksquare = \blacksquare$

3. Draw eight rows of Xs with the same number of Xs in each row. Write the family of facts for your picture.

4. Draw a picture for a family of facts which has only two number sentences. Write the family of facts.

Practice

For More Practice, see Set B, pages 208–209.

Write the other facts from each family.

5. $2 \times 7 = 14$ **6.** $5 \times 3 = 15$ **7.** $6 \times 6 = 36$ **8.** $9 \times 4 = 36$

9. $72 \div 8 = 9$ **10.** $49 \div 7 = 7$ **11.** $40 \div 5 = 8$ **12.** $3 \div 1 = 3$

Choose the three numbers that can make a family. Then write the four related sentences.

13. 3   5   10   2   12

14. 21   3   24   6   8

15. 8   63   6   9   54

16. 3   28   7   4   24

17. 50   4   100   200   10

18. 📱 **Calculator**   42   2,242   46   51   2,142

Problem Solving

19. Amy had 18 quarters that she arranged in equal stacks. How many stacks did she have if she had 75 cents in each stack? Draw a picture and write a family of facts to solve the problem.

Dividing by 2 Through 5

Build Understanding

Farmers plant alfalfa in their fields to restore nitrogen to the soil. Nitrogen is a valuable plant nutrient. Alfalfa is a nutritious food for animals.

A farmer stored 35 bags of alfalfa seed in piles of 5. How many piles of bags were there?

How many groups of 5 are in 35?
Find 35 ÷ 5.
Since 5 × 7 = 35, you know that 35 ÷ 5 = 7.

Quotient

$$35 \div 5 = 7$$

Dividend Divisor

Quotient

$$5)\overline{35} = 7$$

Divisor Dividend

The farmer had 7 piles of 5 bags.

■**Talk About Math** To find 20 ÷ 4, what multiplication sentence would help you?

Have you ever put alfalfa sprouts on your salad?

Check Understanding

For another example, see Set C, pages 206–207.

Write the multiplication sentence that helps you find the quotient. Then write the quotient.

1. 2)16 **2.** 4)24 **3.** 3)12 **4.** 5)25

5. 10 ÷ 2 = ▦ **6.** 40 ÷ 5 = ▦ **7.** 3 ÷ 3 = ▦ **8.** 42 ÷ 7 = ▦

Practice

For More Practice, see Set C, pages 208–209.

Write the quotient. **Remember** that you can use
a multiplication fact to help you.

9. $45 \div 5$ **10.** $8 \div 4$ **11.** $24 \div 3$ **12.** $18 \div 2$ **13.** $24 \div 4$

14. $0 \div 3$ **15.** $2 \div 2$ **16.** $0 \div 2$ **17.** $36 \div 4$ **18.** $28 \div 4$

19. $3\overline{)21}$ **20.** $4\overline{)0}$ **21.** $4\overline{)32}$ **22.** $5\overline{)5}$ **23.** $2\overline{)14}$

24. $5\overline{)15}$ **25.** $3\overline{)27}$ **26.** $3\overline{)18}$ **27.** $4\overline{)20}$ **28.** $5\overline{)30}$

For Exercises 29–34, tell whether you would use
paper and pencil, mental math, or a calculator.
Then find each sum or difference.

29. $\begin{array}{r} 952 \\ -\ 875 \end{array}$ **30.** $\begin{array}{r} 6,357 \\ +\ 1,643 \end{array}$ **31.** $\begin{array}{r} 32,853 \\ +\ 11,126 \end{array}$ **32.** $\begin{array}{r} 8,762 \\ -\ 8,628 \end{array}$

33. $587 + 213 + 52$ **34.** $1,408 + 571 + 3,678$

Problem Solving

Solve each problem.

35. It takes 20 bags of feed to fill 5 troughs. How many bags of feed are needed to fill each trough?

36. Mental Math Last year a farmer planted rows that were 860 feet long. This year he made each row 50 feet longer. How long is each row?

Reading ——— Math

Vocabulary Answer each question.

1. If the dividend is 6 and the divisor is 3, what is the quotient?

2. If the divisor is 2 and the quotient is 4, what is the dividend?

3. If the dividend is 4 and the quotient is 1, what is the divisor?

183

Dividing by 6

Build Understanding

Do you own a wristwatch? The first wristwatch was owned by Empress Josephine, wife of Napoleon, in 1809.

Today, watches can be bought in many sizes, shapes, and colors. There are 30 modern watches pictured at the right. How many groups of 6 watches are there?

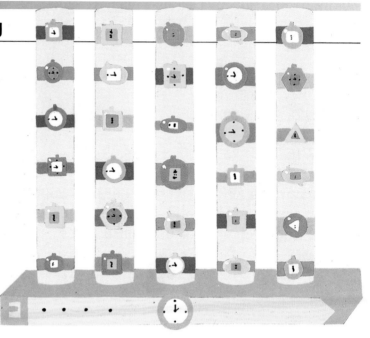

Divide 30 by 6.

There are 5 groups of 6 watches.

$$30 \div 6 = 5$$

■ **Talk About Math** How can you use the array of watches to find $30 \div 5$?

Check Understanding

For another example, see Set D, pages 206–207.

Divide. Copy the picture and circle groups of 6.

1.
X X X X X X
X X X X X
X X X X X

$18 \div 6 = $ ▦

2.
X X X X X X
X X X X X X
X X X X X X
X X X X X X

$24 \div 6 = $ ▦

3.
X X X X X X X X
X X X X X X X X
X X X X X X X X
X X X X X X X X
X X X X X X X X
X X X X X X X X

$48 \div 6 = $ ▦

Practice

For More Practice, see Set D, pages 208–209.

Divide. Draw a picture and circle groups of 6 if necessary.

4. $6\overline{)18}$ **5.** $6\overline{)0}$ **6.** $6\overline{)30}$ **7.** $6\overline{)42}$ **8.** $6\overline{)6}$

9. $6\overline{)12}$ **10.** $6\overline{)48}$ **11.** $6\overline{)24}$ **12.** $6\overline{)54}$ **13.** $6\overline{)36}$

Mixed Practice   Divide.

14. $5\overline{)25}$ **15.** $3\overline{)18}$ **16.** $2\overline{)16}$ **17.** $6\overline{)6}$ **18.** $4\overline{)20}$

19. $6\overline{)36}$ **20.** $2\overline{)10}$ **21.** $5\overline{)40}$ **22.** $3\overline{)21}$ **23.** $6\overline{)12}$

24. $32 \div 4$ **25.** $14 \div 2$ **26.** $27 \div 3$ **27.** $8 \div 4$

28. $3 \div 3$ **29.** $35 \div 5$ **30.** $0 \div 4$ **31.** $54 \div 6$

Problem Solving

Solve each problem.

32. In 1893, Robert Ingersoll sold watches for $1.00 each. How many years was this after Empress Josephine first owned a wristwatch?

33. Sandglasses have been used since the 15th century to measure time. How many times would the sand need to run out of a 3-minute sandglass to measure 21 minutes?

Explore ———— Math

Calculator   Use a calculator to find each quotient.

34. $52 \div 2$ **35.** $52 \div 4$ **36.** $84 \div 3$ **37.** $84 \div 6$

38. $96 \div 4$ **39.** $96 \div 8$ **40.** $140 \div 5$ **41.** $140 \div 10$

42. What happens to the quotient when the divisor is doubled?

Dividing by 7

Build Understanding

A cast is applied by a doctor to hold the broken bone in position so that it will mend properly. Did you ever break a bone? How long did you need to wear a cast?

Suppose you need to wear a cast for 42 days. How many weeks is this?

There are 7 days in one week. You can find how many 7s there are in 42 by using a number line.

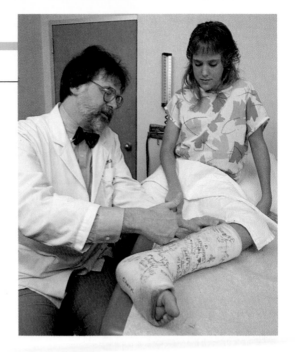

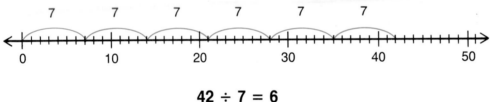

$$42 \div 7 = 6$$

You need to wear a cast for 6 weeks.

■ **Talk About Math** Explain how this same number line describes $42 \div 6 = 7$.

Check Understanding

For another example, see Set E, pages 206–207.

Complete the division sentence.

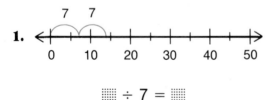

1. $\boxdot \div 7 = \boxdot$

2. $\boxdot \div \boxdot = 5$

3. $56 \div 7 = \boxdot$ **4.** $28 \div 7 = \boxdot$ **5.** $63 \div 7 = \boxdot$

Practice

For More Practice, see Set E, pages 208–209.

Divide. Use a number line if necessary.

6. $7\overline{)14}$ **7.** $7\overline{)28}$ **8.** $7\overline{)7}$ **9.** $7\overline{)56}$ **10.** $7\overline{)0}$

11. $7\overline{)63}$ **12.** $7\overline{)21}$ **13.** $7\overline{)49}$ **14.** $7\overline{)35}$ **15.** $7\overline{)42}$

Mixed Practice   Find each quotient.

16. $15 \div 3$ **17.** $49 \div 7$ **18.** $30 \div 5$ **19.** $0 \div 2$

20. $7 \div 7$ **21.** $48 \div 6$ **22.** $14 \div 7$ **23.** $36 \div 4$

Problem Solving

Solve each problem.

24. A child's bone fracture may heal in as little as **21** days. How many weeks is this?

25. It may take **6** weeks for soft bone to form after a break and another **12** weeks for it to be replaced by harder bone. How many weeks is this in all?

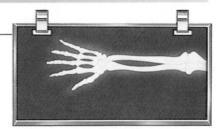

X-rays were discovered by Wilhelm Roentgen (1845–1923).

Midchapter Checkup

Draw cubes to help you complete Exercises 1–2.

1. With 33 cubes you can form ▦ groups of 4 cubes with ▦ cubes left over.

2. With 51 cubes you can form 6 groups of ▦ cubes with ▦ cubes left over.

3. Write the family of facts using 3, 8, and 24.

4. Write the other 3 facts from the family with $4 \times 5 = 20$.

Divide.

5. $28 \div 4$ **6.** $36 \div 6$ **7.** $14 \div 7$ **8.** $27 \div 3$

9. $18 \div 6$ **10.** $56 \div 7$ **11.** $20 \div 5$ **12.** $10 \div 2$

Explore as a Team

1. Predict the *average* number of letters in the first names of your classmates.

2. Use 1-inch square paper to write each of the letters of your first names in a different square. Cut out the squares. Put the names of each person in the group along different lines.

3. Move the letters until you have the same number of letters on each line. Put any extra letters to the side.

4. What is the average number of letters in the first names in your group? (Do not count the extra letters.)

5. Compare your group's results with the other groups in your class.

TIPS FOR **WORKING TOGETHER**
To make sure your group understands the task or solution have each group member say it in his or her own words, summarize the steps, or give an example.

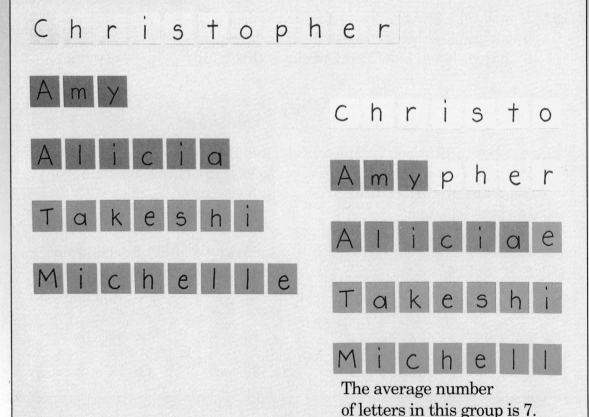

The average number of letters in this group is 7.

Number-Sense Project

Look back at pages 176-177.

1. If you choose your favorite activity by giving 5 points to two or more activities, what is the greatest number of points you can give one activity?

2. If you could give 10 points to 2 or more activities, what is the greatest number of points you could give one activity?

3. Do you think it would be better to let each student just cast 1 vote or to let each student share 5 points among two or more activities? Why?

MATH Laugh

Two mothers and two daughters divided $21 in dollar bills evenly among themselves. Each received an equal number of dollar bills. How could this be?

ANSWER: A grandmother, a mother, and a daughter each get $7.

Critical Thinking Activity

1. Complete the *magic square* so that each row, column, and diagonal has the same sum.

2. If you divided each number by 3, would you still have a *magic square*?

24	?	12
3	15	?
?	21	6

Too Little Information

PROBLEM SOLVING
GUIDE

➤ **Understand**
QUESTION
FACTS
KEY IDEA

Plan and Solve
STRATEGY
ANSWER

Look Back
SENSIBLE ANSWER
ALTERNATE APPROACH

Build Understanding

Cozy Corner Bookstore received a shipment of 8 cartons of books. Each of 2 workers unpacked the same number of books. How many books did each worker unpack?

➤ **Understand**   QUESTION   How many books did each worker unpack?

FACTS   You know the number of cartons of books and the number of workers that are unpacking.

KEY IDEA   Although you know the number of cartons of books, you do not know how many books there are in all. This problem contains too little information to solve it.

■ **Talk About Math**   Suppose the problem stated that each carton contained 10 books. Now could the problem be solved? Explain your answer.

Check Understanding

Choose the fact needed to solve the problem.

1. There were 20 books sold on Monday morning. Each customer bought the same number of books. How many customers did the store have that morning?

   a. Number of books each customer bought
   b. Total cost of all the books sold

Practice

Choose the fact needed to solve each problem.

2. Joe bought a book for $4.95 and a sports magazine. How much change did he receive from $10.00?

   a. Cost of the sports magazine

   b. Amount of money Joe brought to the store

3. The store sold 42 books worth $245 on Saturday morning and 56 books in the afternoon. What were the total sales for the day?

   a. Total number of books sold

   b. Cost of books sold in the afternoon

4. Chuck bought some books on sale for $4 each. What was his total bill?

   a. Original price of the books

   b. How many books Chuck bought

5. Tom worked at the bookstore from 9:00 A.M. until 4:00 P.M. How much money did he make that day?

   a. The store hours

   b. Tom's pay per hour

6. Tom has 54 books to display on shelves. Each shelf is 6 feet long. How many shelves will he need?

   a. Number of books displayed on one shelf

   b. Number of shelves in each bookcase

7. Monica read 129 pages of a book with 14 chapters. How many more pages must she read to finish the book?

   a. Number of pages in each chapter

   b. Number of pages in the book

8. Rewrite Problem 2 to include enough information so that the problem can be solved. Then solve the problem.

9. **Use Data** Norbert read a book about Abraham Lincoln. He discovered that his own birthday is 6 days after Lincoln's. What day is Norbert's birthday? Use data from page 110.

Who is the author and what is the title of the last book that you read for enjoyment?

Dividing by 8

Build Understanding

Have you ever worked on a patchwork quilt? Does someone in your family have a patchwork quilt?

Patchwork is an American needle art. Quilts sewn by the colonists from the cloth of worn clothes and scraps of fabric provided warm bedcovers and beautiful pieces of art.

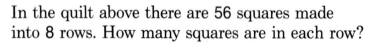

In the quilt above there are 56 squares made into 8 rows. How many squares are in each row?

$$56 \div 8 = 7 \quad \text{or} \quad 8\overline{)56}^{\,7}$$

There are 7 squares in each row.

■ **Talk About Math** What other division fact can be shown using the squares of the quilt? Explain your answer.

192

Check Understanding

For another example, see Set F, pages 206–207.

Copy and complete this multiplication table.

×	0	1	2	3	4	5	6	7	8	9
8	**1.**	**2.**	**3.**	**4.**	**5.**	**6.**	**7.**	**8.**	**9.**	**10.**

Use the multiplication table to find each quotient.

11. 24 ÷ 8   **12.** 40 ÷ 8   **13.** 0 ÷ 8   **14.** 72 ÷ 8

Practice

For More Practice, see Set F, pages 208–209.

Divide.

15. 8)64   **16.** 8)8   **17.** 8)16   **18.** 8)48   **19.** 8)0

20. 8)32   **21.** 8)56   **22.** 8)72   **23.** 8)40   **24.** 8)24

Mixed Practice   Tell whether you would use paper and pencil, mental math, or a calculator. Then find each answer.

25. 257 × 8   **26.** 250 + 750   **27.** 888 − 801

28. 100 × 3   **29.** 2,080 − 1,192   **30.** 80 ÷ 8

Problem Solving

Solve each problem.

31. At a quilting bee, 64 squares were to be sewn. If 8 people shared the work equally, how many squares did each person sew?

32. Estimation   A 30-inch ribbon is cut into 8 equal sections to be used in decorating a quilt. About how many inches long is each section?

Dividing by 1 and 10

Build Understanding

A. Leo Ames is a caterer. He packs 10 servings of chicken on each tray for delivery. How many trays of chicken will he need for 60 servings? Find 60 ÷ 10. Think 6 × 10 = 60.

60 ÷ 10 = 6

Leo needs 6 trays of chicken.

B. Find 6 ÷ 1.

Think of 1 group of six, 1 × 6 = 6.

6 ÷ 1 = 6

■ **Talk About Math** Can you find 5 ÷ 0? Is there a number that can make the sentence 0 × ▦ = 5 true?

Check Understanding

For another example, see Set G, pages 206–207.

Complete each sentence.

1. 50 = ▦ tens

50 = ▦ × 10

50 ÷ 10 = ▦

2. 7 = ▦ ones

7 = ▦ × 1

7 ÷ 1 = ▦

3. 40 = ▦ tens

40 = ▦ × 10

40 ÷ 10 = ▦

4. 30 ÷ 10 = ▦

5. 0 ÷ 10 = ▦

6. 8 ÷ 1 = ▦

Practice

For More Practice, see Set G, pages 208–209.

Think of groups or place value to find each quotient.

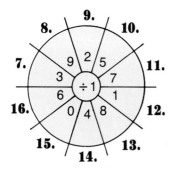

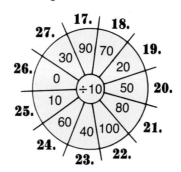

28. What pattern do you see in your answers when you divide by 1?

29. What pattern do you see in your answers when you divide by 10?

Problem Solving

When Mr. Ames packs his delivery truck to serve a party, he packs 10 items in each carton. Find the number of cartons he needs to pack for each item in the chart.

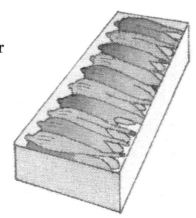

Item	Number of servings needed	Number of cartons
Barbecue beef	70	**30.**
Potato salad	50	**31.**
Corn on the cob	40	**32.**

Dividing by 9

Build Understanding

Laura is a milliner, or hat maker.
She is making small bows
for trimming hats. How
many 9-inch pieces can
she cut from 72 inches
of ribbon?

Find 72 ÷ 9.

Count by 9s to 72.

9 18 27 36 45 54 63 72

72 ÷ 9 = 8

Laura can cut 8 pieces of ribbon.

■ **Talk About Math** Suppose you divided a number
by both 10 and 9. Which quotient would be greater?
Explain your answer.

Check Understanding

For another example, see Set H, pages 206–207.

Laura is cutting a yard (36 inches) of striped ribbon
into 9-inch pieces. How many 9-inch pieces will she
have?

1. Count by 9s to 36.
9 ▦ ▦ ▦

2. Fill in the blank.
▦ × 9 = 36

3. Divide.
36 ÷ 9

Practice

For More Practice, see Set H, pages 208–209.

Divide.

4. $9\overline{)27}$ **5.** $9\overline{)9}$ **6.** $9\overline{)45}$ **7.** $9\overline{)0}$ **8.** $9\overline{)18}$

9. $9\overline{)72}$ **10.** $9\overline{)54}$ **11.** $9\overline{)36}$ **12.** $9\overline{)81}$ **13.** $9\overline{)63}$

Mixed Practice   Divide.

14. $24 \div 6$ **15.** $6 \div 2$ **16.** $30 \div 6$ **17.** $18 \div 9$

18. $28 \div 7$ **19.** $18 \div 3$ **20.** $63 \div 9$ **21.** $27 \div 9$

22. $9 \div 1$ **23.** $72 \div 8$ **24.** $80 \div 10$ **25.** $48 \div 8$

26. $0 \div 5$ **27.** $32 \div 4$ **28.** $45 \div 9$ **29.** $42 \div 7$

Problem Solving

Solve each problem.

30. Critical Thinking In Exercises 4–13, compare the quotient to the tens digit of the dividend. What pattern do you see?

31. How many 9-inch pieces of ribbon can Laura cut from a piece of ribbon that is 30 inches long?

Choose a _____ Strategy

Letter Finish Five friends ran a race. Runner B finished the race right behind Runner E. Runner D finished last. Runner C finished ahead of Runner A. Two runners finished between Runners A and C.

32. Who won the race?

PROBLEM SOLVING STRATEGIES

Choose an Operation
Try and Check
Draw a Diagram
Solve a Simpler Problem
Write a Number Sentence

Division and Fractions; Equal Parts

Build Understanding

Have you ever gone to a science fair? What types of projects did you enjoy? What kind of science project would you like to do?

The students at Fox School received 18 awards at the Science Fair. One sixth of these science projects involved experiments with plant growth. How many projects involved plant growth?

Find one sixth of 18. To find one sixth of 18, divide the projects into 6 equal groups.

18 ÷ 6 = 3

There were 3 projects on plant growth.

■ **Talk About Math** One third of the award-winning projects were weather experiments. How many weather projects was this?

Check Understanding

For another example, see Set I, pages 206–207.

Match each question with the division sentence you would use to answer it.

1. What is $\frac{1}{6}$ of 12? **a.** 12 ÷ 3 = 4

2. What is $\frac{1}{4}$ of 12? **b.** 12 ÷ 4 = 3

3. What is one half of 12? **c.** 12 ÷ 6 = 2

4. What is one third of 12? **d.** 12 ÷ 2 = 6

Practice

For More Practice, see Set I, pages 208–209.

Divide to find each part.

5. one ninth of 81   **6.** one sixth of 18   **7.** one eighth of 24

8. one third of 21   **9.** one fifth of 30   **10.** one tenth of 50

11. $\frac{1}{5}$ of 35   **12.** $\frac{1}{3}$ of 27   **13.** $\frac{1}{8}$ of 40   **14.** $\frac{1}{2}$ of 6

15. $\frac{1}{4}$ of 28   **16.** $\frac{1}{10}$ of 90   **17.** $\frac{1}{6}$ of 36   **18.** $\frac{1}{9}$ of 45

Problem Solving

Solve each problem.

19. One fifth of the 500 students at Fox School entered a science project. How many students was this?

20. In Ellen's project, $\frac{1}{7}$ of her 21 plants bloomed on the 35th day of growth. How many plants was this?

21. Critical Thinking The 32 students who won awards represent $\frac{1}{8}$ of all students that entered the fair. How many entered?

Compare problems to help you relate new problems to ones you've solved before.

Skills _____ Review   pages 38–41

Copy and complete.
1. 3,800 = ▦ hundreds   **2.** 650 = ▦ tens

Write the number that is
3. 100 more than 2,349.   **4.** 1,000 less than 68,750.

Write the number in standard form.
5. five thousand, two hundred six   **6.** ninety thousand, forty-one

Division with Remainders

Build Understanding

Robin is making necklaces for the
Craft Fair. She needs 5 red beads
for each necklace. She has 32 beads.
How many necklaces can she make?
How many beads will she have left over?

Find $5\overline{)32}$.

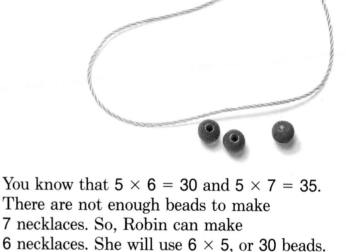

You know that $5 \times 6 = 30$ and $5 \times 7 = 35$.
There are not enough beads to make
7 necklaces. So, Robin can make
6 necklaces. She will use 6×5, or 30 beads.
To find the number of beads left over,
subtract 30 from 32.

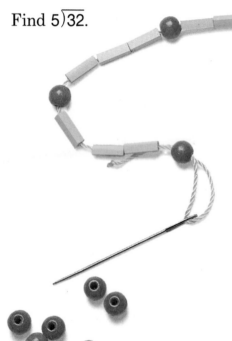

$$
\begin{array}{r}
6\ \text{R2} \\
5\overline{)3\,2} \\
-3\,0 \\
\hline
2 \leftarrow \text{remainder}
\end{array}
$$

The **remainder** should be less
than the divisor. Write the
remainder beside the quotient.

Robin can make 6 necklaces.
She will have 2 beads left over.

■ **Talk About Math** Suppose Robin uses
7 beads in each necklace. Will she be able to
make more or fewer necklaces with 32 beads?
Explain your answer.

Check Understanding

For another example, see Set J, pages 206–207.

Copy and fill in the boxes to find
each quotient and remainder.

1.
```
     7 R ▦
  3)2 2
  −2 1
     ▦
```

2.
```
     6 R ▦
  8)5 2
  −▦▦
    ▦
```

3.
```
     ▦ R ▦
  7)3 4
  −▦▦
    ▦
```

Practice

For More Practice, see Set J, pages 208–209.

Find each quotient and remainder.

4. 5)23   5. 4)26   6. 6)49   7. 3)19   8. 7)51

9. 5)39   10. 2)11   11. 4)38   12. 6)27   13. 8)20

14. 3)14   15. 9)55   16. 4)23   17. 7)64   18. 6)41

19. 5)44   20. 3)17   21. 9)33   22. 8)59   23. 7)44

Mixed Practice   Divide.

24. 4)24   25. 3)26   26. 6)30   27. 5)35   28. 8)54

Problem Solving

Solve each problem.

29. Robin has 25 cents to buy large beads for necklaces. The beads cost 8 cents each. How many beads can she buy? How much money will she have left over?

30. Robin makes 60 cents on every necklace that she sells. How much money does she make on a sale of 4 necklaces?

31. Robin made 9 necklaces with 7 beads in each necklace. She had 3 beads left over. How many beads did she have when she started?

Make a Table

Build Understanding

Pete has 5 books and Bob has 6 books to stack. Each stack must have an equal number of books. How many different ways could each boy stack his books?

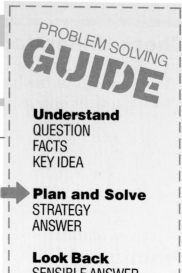

PROBLEM SOLVING
GUIDE

Understand
QUESTION
FACTS
KEY IDEA

Plan and Solve
STRATEGY
ANSWER

Look Back
SENSIBLE ANSWER
ALTERNATE APPROACH

Understand How many different ways can each boy stack his books if each stack must have the same number of books?

Plan and Solve

STRATEGY Organize the ways in a table. Start with 1 stack. How many books are in 1 stack? Then try 2 stacks. Check to see if the number of books can be divided by 2 with no remainder. Then try 3 stacks, and so on.

Pete's 5 books		Bob's 6 books	
Number of stacks	Number in each stack	Number of stacks	Number in each stack
1	5	1	6
2	–	2	3
3	–	3	2
4	–	4	–
5	1	5	–
–	–	6	1

ANSWER Pete can stack 5 books in 2 different ways. Bob can stack 6 books in 4 different ways.

Look Back SENSIBLE ANSWER Look at the first and third columns. All stacks are recorded. The answers make sense.

■ **Talk About Math** Can you stack 4 books in more than 2 different ways? Explain your answer.

202

Check Understanding

For Exercises 1–4, suppose you had **8** books to stack.

1. Could you make 1 stack? How many books would be in the stack?

2. Could you make 2 equal stacks? How many books would be in each stack?

3. Copy and complete the table at the right.

4. How many different ways could you stack the books?

Number of stacks	Number in each stack
1	
2	

Practice

For Problems 5–12, make a table to find how many ways the books can be arranged in equal stacks.

5. 12 books   **6.** 17 books   **7.** 10 books   **8.** 18 books

9. 15 books   **10.** 13 books   **11.** 9 books   **12.** 24 books

Explore ——— Math

Prime Numbers Numbers that have only 2 factors (ways to stack) are called ***prime numbers***. Numbers that have more than 2 factors (ways to stack) are called ***composite numbers***.

Here is a way to find the prime numbers less than 100:
a. List the whole numbers from 1 to 100. Cross out 1 because it is neither prime nor composite. Circle 2, the first prime number. Then cross out all numbers that have 2 as a factor.
b. Circle the next number that is not crossed out. It is the next prime number. Then cross out all numbers that have it as a factor. Continue this process.

13. List the prime numbers between 1 and 100.

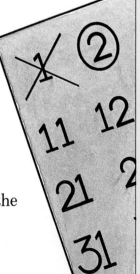

Solve each problem.

1. A number is between 14 and 40. It has a 3 in the ones place. It is prime. What is the number?

2. Arnie put his autographed baseballs in 3 rows. There are 4 baseballs in each row. If he puts the baseballs in 2 rows, how many will be in each row?

3. Margie has 2 quarters, 2 dimes, and 4 nickels. What coins can she use to buy lemonade from the machine?

4. There are 3 cassette tapes in a package. How many packages will you have to buy to get 23 tapes?

5. Laura earns $1 for each of the first 50 bookbags she sells. She earns $2 for each bookbag over 50. If she sells 57 bookbags, how much will she earn?

6. Frank is shorter than Ed. Ed is shorter than Gene. Cliff is the tallest. Name the boys from tallest to shortest.

7. **Data File** Use data from pages 248-249. In what order will the phases of the moon occur?

8. **Make a Data File** For six team sports, find the number of players on a team. How many teams could your class form for each sport?

Explore with a Calculator

Play 1, 2, 3, 4

1. Look at each of these cards. Decide which operation signs, $+$, $-$, $\times$, or $\div$, should go in the boxes so the sequence will equal the display shown. You do not need to use all the signs.

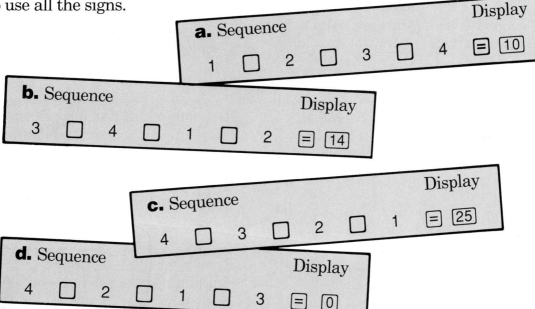

a. Sequence   Display

1 ☐ 2 ☐ 3 ☐ 4 = 10

b. Sequence   Display

3 ☐ 4 ☐ 1 ☐ 2 = 14

c. Sequence   Display

4 ☐ 3 ☐ 2 ☐ 1 = 25

d. Sequence   Display

4 ☐ 2 ☐ 1 ☐ 3 = 0

2. Look at each of these cards. Decide where the numbers, 1, 2, 3, or 4, should replace the ■ so the sequence will equal the display shown. Use each number only once.

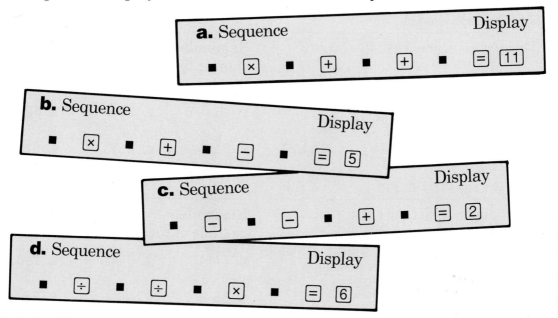

a. Sequence   Display

■ × ■ + ■ + ■ = 11

b. Sequence   Display

■ × ■ + ■ − ■ = 5

c. Sequence   Display

■ − ■ − ■ + ■ = 2

d. Sequence   Display

■ ÷ ■ ÷ ■ × ■ = 6

Reteaching

Set A pages 178–179

With 12 cubes you can form 3 groups of 4 cubes with 0 cubes left over.

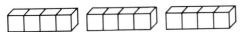

With 12 cubes you can form 2 groups of 5 cubes with 2 cubes left over.

Remember that each group has the same number of cubes.

Write the number of groups and the number of cubes left over.

1. 16 cubes, 4 cubes in each group

2. 16 cubes, 3 cubes in each group

Set B pages 180–181

You know that $3 \times 7 = 21$ and $7 \times 3 = 21$ are related. These facts give two more related facts:

$21 \div 3 = 7$ and $21 \div 7 = 3$.

Remember that a family of facts has two multiplication and two division sentences if the factors are different.

1. Write the other facts from the family of $3 \times 9 = 27$.

Set C pages 182–183

Ed stacked 24 bales of hay in piles of 4. How many piles were there?

Find $24 \div 4$.
Since $4 \times 6 = 24$, you know that $24 \div 4 = 6$.

Ed stacked 6 piles.

Remember to use a related multiplication fact to help you solve a division problem. Divide.

1. $27 \div 3$ **2.** $20 \div 4$ **3.** $16 \div 2$

4. $5\overline{)30}$ **5.** $5\overline{)0}$ **6.** $4\overline{)28}$

Set D pages 184–185

This picture shows that $18 \div 6 = 3$.

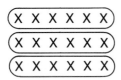

Remember that the dividend is the number being grouped or shared. Divide.

1. $48 \div 6$ **2.** $24 \div 6$ **3.** $12 \div 6$

4. $6\overline{)18}$ **5.** $6\overline{)30}$ **6.** $6\overline{)54}$

Set E pages 186–187

This number line shows that $21 \div 7 = 3$.

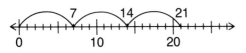

Remember that the dividend is a multiple of the divisor. Divide.

1. $7\overline{)14}$ **2.** $7\overline{)42}$ **3.** $7\overline{)0}$

4. $56 \div 7$ **5.** $28 \div 7$ **6.** $63 \div 7$

206

Set F   pages 192–193

This scarf has 24 rectangles arranged in rows of 8. How many rows are there?

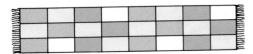

Since 24 ÷ 8 = 3, there are 3 rows.

Remember that you can use a multiplication table to help you find a quotient. Divide.

1. 8)$\overline{32}$ **2.** 8)$\overline{72}$ **3.** 8)$\overline{0}$

4. 16 ÷ 8   **5.** 40 ÷ 8   **6.** 64 ÷ 8

Set G   pages 194–195

One ice cube tray holds 10 ice cubes. How many trays are needed for 40 cubes?

Think: 40 ÷ 10 = 4

So, 4 trays are needed.

Remember that when the divisor is 1, the quotient equals the dividend.

1. 80 ÷ 10   **2.** 50 ÷ 10   **3.** 0 ÷ 1

4. 10)$\overline{60}$ **5.** 1)$\overline{7}$ **6.** 1)$\overline{3}$

Set H   pages 196–197

How many 9-member teams can be formed with 45 softball players?

Find 45 ÷ 9.
Since 9 × 5 = 45, 45 ÷ 9 = 5.

So, 5 teams can be formed.

Remember that counting by 9s is the same as writing the multiples of 9.

1. 36 ÷ 9   **2.** 54 ÷ 9   **3.** 0 ÷ 9

4. 3)$\overline{27}$ **5.** 4)$\overline{36}$ **6.** 7)$\overline{63}$

Set I   pages 198–199

To find one fifth of 30, divide 30 into 5 equal groups.

Thus, $\frac{1}{5}$ of 30 means 30 ÷ 5, or 6.

Remember that the denominator of the fraction is the divisor.

Divide to find each part.

1. $\frac{1}{4}$ of 16   **2.** $\frac{1}{3}$ of 21   **3.** $\frac{1}{8}$ of 24

Set J   pages 200–201

Lou uses 7 charms in each bracelet she makes. She has 50 charms. How many bracelets can she make? How many charms will be left over?

$$\begin{array}{r} 7 \text{ R1} \\ 7)\overline{50} \\ -\underline{49} \\ 1 \end{array}$$

She can make 7 bracelets, and 1 charm will be left over.

Remember that the remainder should be less than the divisor.

1. 4)$\overline{21}$ **2.** 3)$\overline{17}$ **3.** 9)$\overline{19}$

4. 7)$\overline{26}$ **5.** 8)$\overline{34}$ **6.** 5)$\overline{31}$

7. 6)$\overline{45}$ **8.** 7)$\overline{41}$ **9.** 9)$\overline{74}$

More Practice

Set A   pages 178–179

Use cubes to find the number of groups and the number of cubes left over.

Number of cubes	Number of cubes in each group	Number of groups	Number of cubes left over
21	3	**1.** _____	**2.** _____
34	4	**3.** _____	**4.** _____
27	8	**5.** _____	**6.** _____

Set B   pages 180–181

Write the other factors from each family.

1. $3 \times 8 = 24$ **2.** $8 \times 7 = 56$ **3.** $15 \div 3 = 5$ **4.** $32 \div 8 = 4$

Choose the three numbers that can make a family.
Then write the four related sentences.

5. 2 4 9 3 36   **6.** 32 5 35 7 8   **7.** 5 7 45 42 9

Set C   pages 182–183

Write the quotient.

1. $35 \div 5$ **2.** $16 \div 4$ **3.** $21 \div 3$ **4.** $25 \div 5$ **5.** $16 \div 2$

6. $4\overline{)28}$ **7.** $3\overline{)15}$ **8.** $4\overline{)36}$ **9.** $2\overline{)12}$ **10.** $5\overline{)40}$

Set D   pages 184–185

Divide.

1. $6\overline{)42}$ **2.** $6\overline{)54}$ **3.** $6\overline{)36}$ **4.** $6\overline{)0}$ **5.** $6\overline{)24}$

Set E   pages 186–187

Divide.

1. $7\overline{)21}$ **2.** $7\overline{)42}$ **3.** $7\overline{)35}$ **4.** $7\overline{)14}$ **5.** $7\overline{)49}$

Mixed Practice   Divide.

6. $7\overline{)63}$ **7.** $6\overline{)48}$ **8.** $7\overline{)28}$ **9.** $6\overline{)30}$ **10.** $7\overline{)56}$

Set F   pages 192–193

Divide.

1. $8\overline{)24}$ 2. $8\overline{)40}$ 3. $8\overline{)56}$ 4. $8\overline{)0}$ 5. $8\overline{)32}$

Mixed Practice   Divide.

6. $64 \div 8$ 7. $18 \div 6$ 8. $48 \div 8$ 9. $45 \div 5$ 10. $72 \div 8$

Set G   pages 194–195

Divide.

1. $1\overline{)3}$ 2. $10\overline{)30}$ 3. $1\overline{)5}$ 4. $10\overline{)50}$ 5. $10\overline{)0}$

6. $4 \div 1$ 7. $60 \div 10$ 8. $90 \div 1$ 9. $20 \div 10$ 10. $70 \div 10$

Set H   pages 196–197

Divide.

1. $9\overline{)36}$ 2. $9\overline{)72}$ 3. $9\overline{)27}$ 4. $9\overline{)9}$ 5. $9\overline{)45}$

Mixed Practice   Divide.

6. $32 \div 8$ 7. $81 \div 9$ 8. $21 \div 3$ 9. $90 \div 10$ 10. $3 \div 1$

11. $63 \div 9$ 12. $0 \div 7$ 13. $54 \div 9$ 14. $28 \div 7$ 15. $18 \div 9$

Set I   pages 198–199

Divide to find each part.

1. one third of 24   2. one fifth of 50   3. one ninth of 72

4. $\frac{1}{2}$ of 14   5. $\frac{1}{5}$ of 25   6. $\frac{1}{3}$ of 12   7. $\frac{1}{8}$ of 64

Set J   pages 200–201

Find each quotient and remainder.

1. $3\overline{)28}$ 2. $5\overline{)18}$ 3. $7\overline{)48}$ 4. $9\overline{)52}$ 5. $6\overline{)51}$

6. $4\overline{)29}$ 7. $4\overline{)38}$ 8. $9\overline{)35}$ 9. $6\overline{)32}$ 10. $8\overline{)44}$

Mixed Practice   Divide.

11. $2\overline{)17}$ 12. $7\overline{)35}$ 13. $3\overline{)23}$ 14. $4\overline{)32}$ 15. $5\overline{)43}$

Enrichment

Multiplication and Division Patterns

Multiplication sentences supply the clues you can use to detect the mystery quotients.

Since $3 \times 4 = 12$, you also know $12 \div 4 = 3$ and $12 \div 3 = 4$.

Since $20 \times 6 = 120$, you know $120 \div 6 = $ ▦ and $120 \div 20 = $ ▦.

Since $161 \times 25 = 4,025$ you know $4,025 \div 25 = $ ▦ and $4,025 \div 161 = $ ▦.

Use these clues to find the mystery quotients.

$10 \times 14 = 140$
$33 \times 18 = 594$
$102 \times 86 = 8,772$
$13 \times 95 = 1,235$
$40 \times 201 = 8,040$
$8 \times 548 = 4,384$
$22 \times 57 = 1,254$
$15 \times 53 = 795$
$103 \times 39 = 4,017$

1. $795 \div 15 = $ T

2. $1,235 \div 95 = $ N

3. $140 \div 14 = $ H

4. $594 \div 18 = $ O

5. $4,384 \div 8 = $ Y

6. $795 \div 53 = $ T

7. $8,772 \div 86 = $ I

8. $4,017 \div 39 = $ L

9. $4,384 \div 548 = $ P

10. $1,254 \div 22 = $ M

11. $8,040 \div 201 = $ C

12. $4,017 \div 103 = $ M

If your detective work is correct, you will find the guilty party by ordering your answers least to greatest and writing the letters.

? ? A ? ? ? ?   F A ? ?   F A ? ? ? ?

Chapter 6 Review/Test

1. Choose the phrase that makes a true sentence.

With 21 cubes, you can form
a. 10 groups of 2.
b. 7 groups of 3.
c. 5 groups of 4.

Write the other facts from each family.

2. $7 \times 5 = 35$ **3.** $48 \div 6 = 8$

Write the quotient.

4. $30 \div 5$ **5.** $4\overline{)36}$

6. $6\overline{)30}$ **7.** $8 \div 1$

8. $7\overline{)21}$ **9.** $42 \div 7$

10. $32 \div 8$ **11.** $8\overline{)40}$

12. $63 \div 9$ **13.** $9\overline{)36}$

14. There are 35 days left until the end of the year. How many weeks is that?

15. Choose the fact needed to solve the following problem.

Susan is putting photos in an album that holds 6 photos per page. How many pages will she fill?

a. number of photos Susan has
b. cost of the album

16. Paul is cutting a 54-inch board into 9-inch pieces. How many pieces will he have?

For Items 17–19, complete each sentence.

17. $60 = $ ▦ tens   **18.** $60 = $ ▦ $\times 10$

19. $60 \div 10 = $ ▦

Divide to find each part.
20. one fifth of 30   **21.** $\frac{1}{4}$ of 24

Find each quotient and remainder.

22. $7\overline{)25}$ **23.** $9\overline{)39}$

24. George has 16 dog biscuits to share equally among 3 puppies. How many biscuits can each puppy have? How many biscuits will be left over?

25. Suppose you have 14 books to put into stacks. You want the same number of books in each stack. Copy and complete the table below to find out how many different ways there are of stacking the books.

Number of Stacks	Number in Each Stack
1	▦

26. Write About Math Write another phrase for Item 1 that makes a true sentence. Draw a picture to show each sentence.

Geometry

7

Did You Know: Today there are over 30,000 malls in the United States. Over half of all retail businesses are located in malls today.

2
You are here

Number-Sense Project

Estimate
Which person in your family does most of the shopping? Predict the 3 types of stores this person shops in the most.

Gather Data
Once each day for a week, interview the person in your family who shops the most. Tally the types of stores they shopped in during the previous 24 hours.

Analyze and Report
Total the tally marks for the week. Write a sentence telling how your estimate compared with the data you collected. Compare your results with those of other students.

Polygons

Build Understanding

A. *Polygons* are closed figures that have straight sides. The sides of polygons meet at points called *vertices*. Sides *AB* and *BC* meet at *vertex B*. Name the other sides and vertices of this 9-sided polygon.

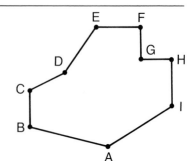

B. Some polygons have names.

Triangle	Quadrilateral	Pentagon	Hexagon	Octagon
3 sides	4 sides	5 sides	6 sides	8 sides

■ **Talk About Math**   Can a polygon have only 2 sides? Why?

Check Understanding

For another example, see Set A, pages 242–243.

1. Which figures are not polygons? Why?

a.   **b.**   **c.**   **d.**   **e.**

 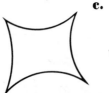  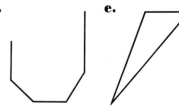

Name the polygon, its sides, and its vertices. How many sides and vertices does the polygon have?

2.

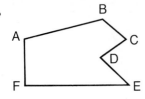

3.

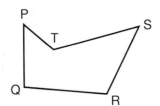

4.

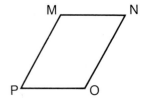

214

Practice

For More Practice, see Set A, pages 244–245.

How many sides and vertices does each polygon have?

5. Triangle   **6.** Quadrilateral   **7.** Pentagon

8. Hexagon   **9.** Octagon   **10.** Decagon

11. If a polygon has 30 vertices, how many sides does it have?

12. If a polygon has 25 sides, how many vertices does it have?

How are the figures alike? How are they different?

13.
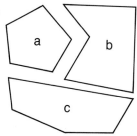

14.
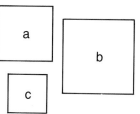

15.
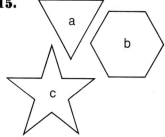

Problem Solving

16. Look at home, school, or outdoors for examples of at least 5 different polygonal shapes. Make a pencil drawing of each example and outline the polygons in color.

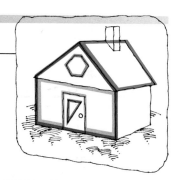

Reading **Math**

This wedge of cheese suggests polygonal shapes for sides.

1. Name the polygons that you can see from this view of the wedge.

2. Name the polygons that cannot be seen from this view of the wedge.

3. Draw the wedge as if you were viewing it directly from above. How many polygons can be seen?

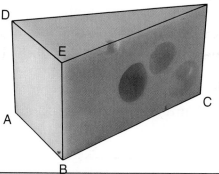

Slides, Flips, and Turns

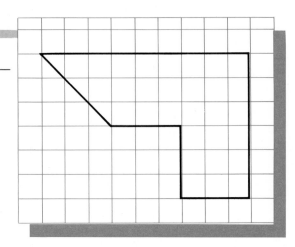

Build Understanding

ACTIVITY

Move That Polygon!
Materials: Grid paper, tracing paper
Groups: With a partner

Draw the polygon on grid paper. Trace it. Cut out the tracing and place it on the polygon. Then make the following moves.

a. *Slide* the tracing 3 square lengths to the right. To show how the polygon looks after sliding it, draw around the tracing. You can slide a polygon in any direction on the grid paper. Slide it in a different direction and draw it.

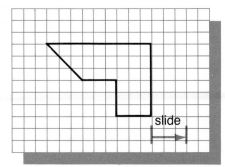

b. *Flip* the tracing over a line. You must pick up the tracing and turn it over when flipping a polygon. Draw the polygon in its new position. A polygon can be flipped over any line on the paper. Flip the polygon over a different line and draw it.

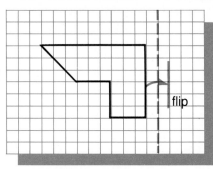

c. *Turn* the tracing about one of the vertices of the polygon. Draw the polygon in its new position. You can turn a polygon about any point on the paper. Choose a different vertex. Turn the polygon about it in a counterclockwise direction and draw it.

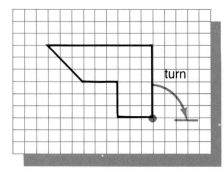

■ **Talk About Math**   How far should a flipped polygon be from its flip line?

Check Understanding

For another example, see Set B, pages 242–243.

Copy each polygon on grid paper. Then draw each in its new position.

1. Flip

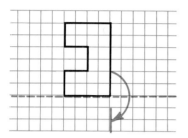

2. Slide

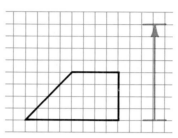

3. Turn

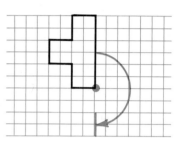

Practice

For More Practice, see Set B, pages 244–245.

Draw a rectangle on grid paper. Trace it. Cut out the tracing and place it on the rectangle. Show 3 possible positions as it turns

4. about a vertex.

5. about a point in the middle of a side.

Tell how each polygon was moved. Write *flip, slide,* or *turn.*

6.

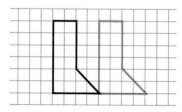

7.

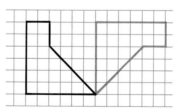

8.

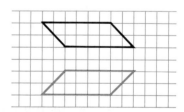

9.

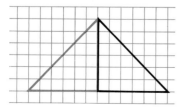

10.

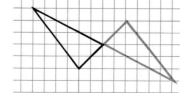

11.

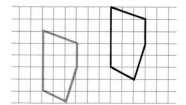

Copy each polygon on grid paper. Draw and label a slide, flip, and turn of each. Choose your own moves.

12.    **13.** 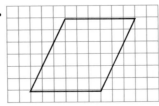   **14.**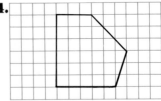

Problem Solving

15. Three flips of the polygon given in the activity create the pattern below. Make a pattern of your own. You can use any combination of slides, flips, and turns.

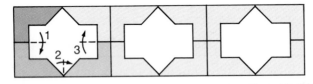

  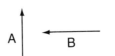

Use slides, flips, turns, or a combination of moves so that Arrow A is on Arrow B. Write the order of the moves you used.

16.　A　B　　**17.**　A　B　　**18.**　A　←　B　　**19.**　A　→　B

20. Draw a polygon and turn it about a point that is outside the polygon.

21. Use Data Copy Figure A on page 127. Trace the figure again so that when the two figures are placed together they form a rectangle. What is the area of the rectangle?

22. ▦ Calculator What is the greatest number of these figures that can be made on a 10 by 10 piece of grid paper?

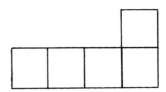

Explore _____ **Math**

Cagey Cages or Closed Curves

The lion trainer is outside the cage. Is the lion inside the cage or outside the cage?

A simple closed curve has an inside and an outside. In the curve at the right, points A, B, and C are in the inside. Points D, E, and F are outside the curve.

Imagine a straight line segment whose two endpoints are inside the curve. How many times does the segment cross the curve between these inside points?

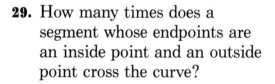

23. A and B   **24.** A and C   **25.** B and C

How many times does the segment cross the curve between these outside points?

26. D and F   **27.** D and E   **28.** E and F

29. How many times does a segment whose endpoints are an inside point and an outside point cross the curve?

30. If you know the location of one point, how can you determine the location of another?

31. Is the lion inside the cage or outside the cage?

The rabbit is outside the figure. Are these carrots inside or outside the figure?

32. S

33. T

34. X

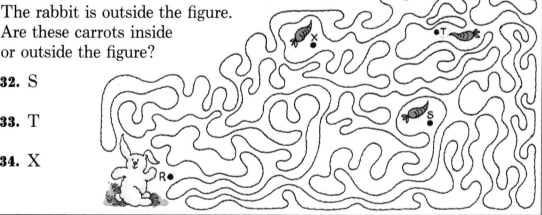

Congruence

Build Understanding

Congruent figures have the same shape and size. If a figure can be moved so that it fits exactly on another figure, the figures are congruent.

If you could place one of the place mats in this table setting on top of the other place mat, they would fit exactly. The shapes of the place mats are congruent.

Sometimes you can decide if two polygons are congruent just by looking at them.

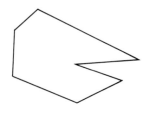

A.

The triangles are congruent.

B.

The squares are not congruent.

Sometimes you will want to trace one of the polygons and place the tracing on the other polygon to check if it fits exactly. Try it with these examples.

C.

These polygons are congruent.

D.

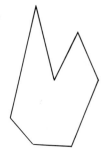

These polygons are not congruent.

■**Talk About Math**   Tell how you moved one
polygon on the other in Examples C and D. Did you
use a flip, slide, turn, or a combination of moves?

Check Understanding
For another example, see Set C, pages 242–243.

Are the shapes of these placemats congruent?

1. 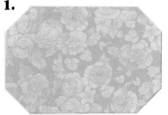   **2.**

Practice
For More Practice, see Set C, pages 244–245.

Which polygons are congruent to the first polygon?

3.    a   b   c

4. 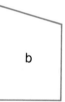   a   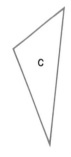 b   c

5.    a   b   c

Problem Solving

6. Critical Thinking   If 2 polygons are congruent, must they
have the same area? If 2 polygons have the same area, must
they be congruent? Explain your answers.

221

Use Data from a Picture

PROBLEM SOLVING
GUIDE

→ **Understand**
QUESTION
FACTS
KEY IDEA

Plan and Solve
STRATEGY
ANSWER

Look Back
SENSIBLE ANSWER
ALTERNATE APPROACH

Build Understanding

Juan is a carpenter. He is going to make shelves for a bookcase. How many 3-foot shelves can he make from these 2 boards?

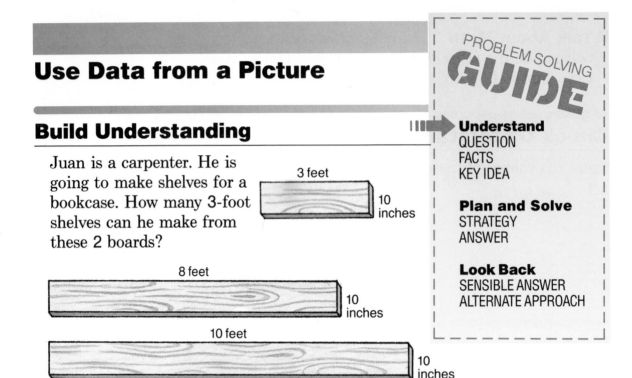

3 feet
10 inches

8 feet
10 inches

10 feet
10 inches

→ Understand   QUESTION   How many shelves can be made?

FACTS   The boards measure 8 feet and 10 feet. Each shelf must be 3 feet long.

KEY IDEA   Find how many 3-foot sections are in each board.

Plan and Solve   Mark off 3-foot sections on each board. Add to find the total number of shelves.

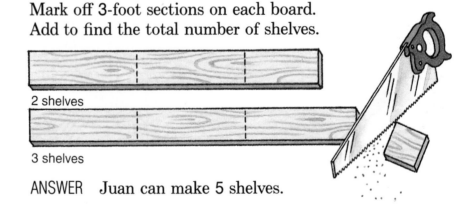

2 shelves

3 shelves

ANSWER   Juan can make 5 shelves.

Look Back   The total length of the boards is 18 feet. If Juan had one 18-foot board, 6 shelves could be made. Therefore, 5 shelves is a reasonable answer.

■ **Talk About Math**   Why can't Juan make 6 shelves?

Check Understanding

How much is not used for shelves in the

1. 8-foot board?

2. 10-foot board?

Suppose that the 2 boards are to be cut into shelves of equal lengths with no parts of the boards left over.

3. What is the largest size shelf that can be made?

4. How many of these shelves can be made?

Practice

Use the 8-foot and 10-foot boards given in the example for Exercises 5–8.

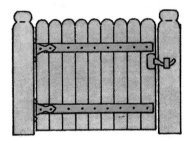

4 feet

10 inches

5 feet

10 inches

5. How many 4-foot shelves can Juan make from the boards?

6. How many 5-foot shelves can he make?

7. In Exercises 5–6, which shelf length has the least amount of board left over?

8. A gate needs 9 vertical slats, each measuring 5 inches by 5 feet. How many vertical slats can be made from the boards?

9. **Mental Math**   Juan's carpentry crew is going to make built-in bookcases for 50 new houses. Every house will have 2 bookcases with 4 shelves apiece. How many shelves are needed in all?

10. **Estimation**   Two carpenters can finish about 5 bookcases in one day. If Juan works along with his crew of 5, about how many days should it take them to finish the job described in Exercise 9?

Juan's Carpentry Shop

Symmetry

Build Understanding

A. If you could fold this triangular shape along the dotted line, the two parts would match. The line is called the *line of symmetry*. A polygon is *symmetric* if it has at least one line of symmetry.

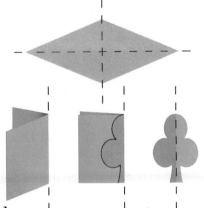

B. Some shapes have more than one line of symmetry. This shape has two lines of symmetry.

C. You can make a symmetric shape. Fold a sheet of paper in half. Draw a shape that begins and ends on the fold line. Cut out the shape and open it.

■ **Talk About Math** Explain how you would fold a sheet of paper to make a symmetric shape with two lines of symmetry.

Check Understanding

For another example, see Set D, pages 242–243.

1. Which figures show a line of symmetry?

a.   **b.**   **c.** 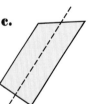 **d.**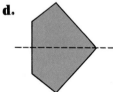

How many lines of symmetry does each figure have?

2.  **3.**  **4.**   **5.**

Practice

For More Practice, see Set D, pages 244–245.

How many lines of symmetry does each figure have?

6.

7.

8.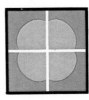

9.

10.

11.

12.

13.

Problem Solving

Visual Thinking What shape will you get after cutting and opening the paper?

14.

15.

16.

17.

18. Critical Thinking How many lines of symmetry does a circle have?

Midchapter ✓ Checkup

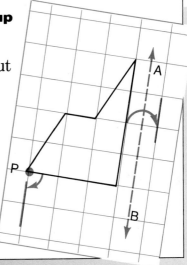

Draw the polygon at the right on grid paper.
1. Flip it over the line.
2. Slide it up 5 squares.
3. Turn it about point P.

4. Draw a polygon that has one line of symmetry. Then draw a polygon that is congruent to it.

5. How many boards measuring 6 inches by 3 feet can be made from boards that are 1 foot by 12 feet and 1 foot by 15 feet?

Problem Solving **WORKSHOP**

Number-Sense Project

Look back at pages 212-213.
This blueprint shows part of a mall.

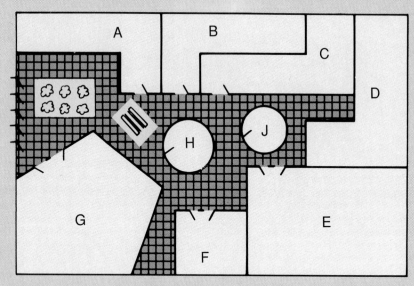

1. Which businesses have congruent floor plans?

2. Which store is shaped as a pentagon?

3. Which business has the same floor plan as A, except it has been flipped?

4. Name a business which does not have a floor plan shaped like a polygon.

Explore with a Computer

Use the *Geometry Workshop Project* for this activity.

1. Make a pattern of triangles and squares. Use the **Draw** option to make a square and a triangle. The sides of the square and the triangle should be the same length. Check the lengths using the **Measure** option.

2. Move the square or the triangle so the two shapes touch.

3. Use the **Copy** option to make copies of the square and triangle. Place the copies anywhere on the screen.

4. Try the **Flip** and **Turn** options to make an interesting pattern.

Explore as a Team

1. Use toothpicks to make *square designs*.

2. Keep a record of how many squares you make.

3. How many different *square designs* can you make with less than 25 whole toothpicks?

TIPS FOR WORKING TOGETHER

Tell someone when he or she does or says something that helps you.

Square Design	Number of Toothpicks	Number of Squares
□	4	1
	12	5
	17	8

Math-at-Home Activity

1. Make a puzzle using a 3-inch by 5-inch card.

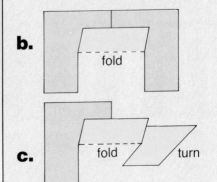

a. $2\frac{1}{2}$ in. $2\frac{1}{2}$ in. $1\frac{1}{2}$ in. cut fold cut cut $1\frac{1}{2}$ in.

b. fold

c. fold turn

2. Tape the puzzle onto a larger card.

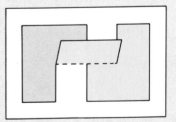

3. Give people in or around your home a piece of paper and scissors to make the puzzle. Keep a tally of how many people were and were not able to make the object.

227

Lines

Build Understanding

A. The straight path from point A to point B is *segment* AB. It is also called segment BA. Points A and B are the *endpoints* of segment AB. Two line segments are congruent if they have the same length.

The sides of a polygon are segments. Name the sides of polygon $GHJKL$.

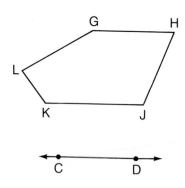

B. A segment is part of a *line*. A line goes on and on in both directions. Line CD is pictured at the right. It is also called line DC.

C. A *ray* is part of a line that goes on and on in one direction. It has one endpoint. Ray EF is pictured at the right. When naming a ray, always name its endpoint first. Describe ray FE.

D. Lines PQ and RS are *intersecting lines*. They meet or intersect at point O.

E. Lines WX and YZ are *parallel lines*. They have no points in common. They do not intersect.

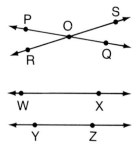

■ Talk About Math

What kind of lines are suggested by the rails of this train track? Can the rails suggest intersecting lines, too? Explain your answer.

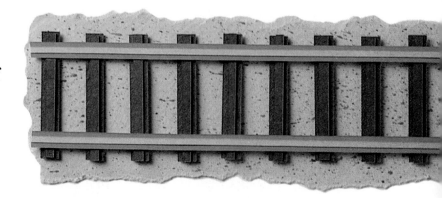

Check Understanding

For another example, see Set E, pages 242–243.

Name each line or part of a line.

1.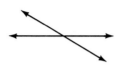

2.

3.

Tell whether the lines are intersecting lines or parallel lines. **Remember** that lines go on and on.

4.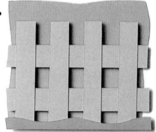

5.

6.

Practice

For More Practice, see Set E, pages 244–245.

Tell whether each picture suggests lines, segments, rays, intersecting lines, or parallel lines.

7.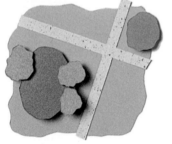

8.

9.

Draw two segments that

10. are congruent. **11.** are parallel. **12.** intersect.

How do you tell if 2 line segments are

13. congruent? **14.** intersecting? **15.** parallel?

Problem Solving

16. Visual Thinking Find an example of two lines that are neither parallel nor intersecting. Explain your answer.

Angles and Right Angles

Build Understanding

How might a carpenter's square be used in the construction of a home? Do the following activity to help you answer this question.

Draw and Compare Angles
Materials: 2 cardboard strips, fastener
Groups: With a partner

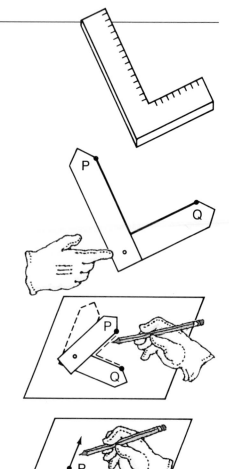

A. Join 2 strips of cardboard with a fastener. Mark one strip *P* and the other *Q*.

Place the strips on your paper. Hold the *Q*-strip in place and move the *P*-strip to a new position. Place a pencil point at *P* and draw along the inner edges to *Q*.

Remove the strips. Extend the segments and draw arrowheads for rays. This is an **angle**. It is called angle *POQ* or angle *QOP*. It can be written ∠*POQ* or ∠*QOP*. Point *O* is called the **vertex** of the angle. Use the strips to draw another angle.

B. An angle that forms a square corner is called a **right angle**. You can test for right angles by using the square corner of a card.

You can also use the strips to decide if an angle is a right angle. Place the strips around the corner of a card. Draw the position of the strips.

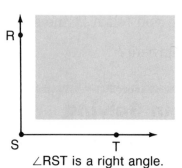

∠RST is a right angle.

c. When lines *PR* and *QS* intersect at point *O*, they form four angles—angles *POQ, QOR, ROS,* and *SOP*.

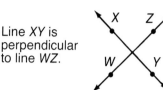

When two lines intersect to form four right angles, the lines are **perpendicular** to each other.

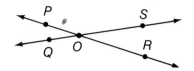

Line *XY* is perpendicular to line *WZ*.

If you know that ∠*ABC* is a right angle, then you know that ray *BA* is perpendicular to ray *BC*. You also know that segment *AB* is perpendicular to segment *BC*.

If segment *AB* is perpendicular to segment *BC*, is ∠*ABC* a right angle?

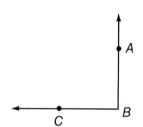

D. You can use a card to compare an angle to a right angle.

Place a corner of a card on the vertex of the given angle and an edge along a ray. If the other ray is covered by the card, the angle is less than a right angle. How can you tell if an angle is greater than a right angle?

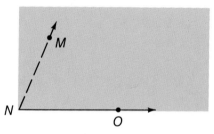

∠ *MNO* is less than a right angle.

E. Two angles are congruent if the tracing of one angle exactly fits on the other angle.

Explain why ∠*PQR* is congruent to ∠*XYZ*.

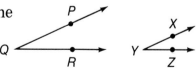

F. The sides of a polygon meet to form angles. Name the angles in polygon *ABCDE*.

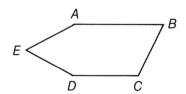

■ **Talk About Math** How might a carpenter's square be used in construction?

Check Understanding

For another example, see Set F, pages 242–243.

1. Use the strips to draw two right angles.
What can you say about all right angles?

2. Is segment *DE* perpendicular to
segment *EF*? Why?

3. Which angle is greater than a
right angle?

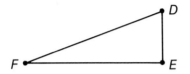

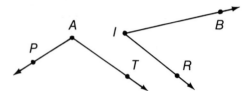

Practice

For More Practice, see Set F, pages 244–245.

Use these angles to answer Exercises 4–7.

a.   **b.**   **c.**   **d.**   **e.**

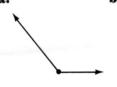   

f.   **g.**   **h.**   **i.**   **j.**

   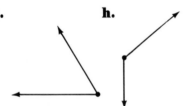   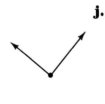   

Which angles are
4. right angles?

5. less than right angles?

6. congruent?

7. greater than right angles?

Name the right angles and perpendicular segments.

8.   **9.**   **10.**

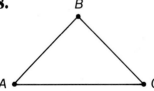   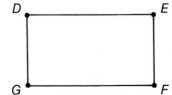   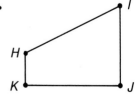

Problem Solving

Use the corner of a card or the strips to decide if the angle is a right angle. If it is not a right angle, tell whether it is less than or greater than a right angle. Explain your answers.

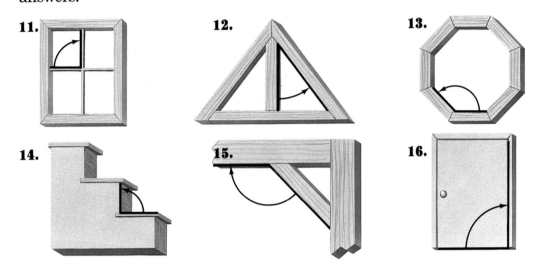

11.

12.

13.

14.

15.

16.

Choose a ▮ Strategy

Lots of Lots   The Jones family used fencing to divide their property into lots.

17. How much fencing did they use?

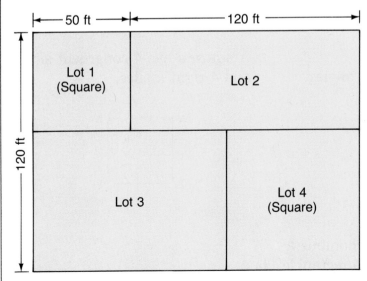

PROBLEM SOLVING
STRATEGIES

Choose an operation.
Try and check.
Draw a diagram.
Solve a simpler problem.
Write a number sentence.
Make a table.

233

Types of Quadrilaterals

Build Understanding

Many artists use geometric shapes.

Look for quadrilaterals that have right angles, parallel sides, or congruent sides.

This painting by Piet Mondrian (1872–1944) is at the Tate Gallery in London.

Some quadrilaterals have special names.

A. The opposite sides of a *parallelogram* are parallel and congruent.

B. A *rhombus* has 4 congruent sides.

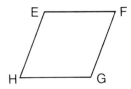

C. A *rectangle* has 2 pairs of congruent sides and 4 right angles.

D. A *square* has 4 congruent sides and 4 right angles.

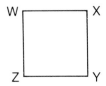

■ **Talk About Math** Is a rhombus a parallelogram? Is a square a rectangle? Is a square a rhombus? Explain your reasoning.

Check Understanding

For another example, see Set G, pages 242–243.

Name the quadrilaterals. How are the two
quadrilaterals alike? different?

1. a.  **b.** **2. a.** **b.**

Practice

For More Practice, see Set G, pages 244–245.

Is the figure a parallelogram? Write *yes* or *no*.

3. **4.** **5.**  **6.**

Use grid paper to draw a quadrilateral with

7. four right angles.

8. congruent sides.

9. two pairs of congruent parallel sides.

10. two pairs of congruent parallel sides and four right angles.

11. Name the quadrilaterals that you drew in Exercises 7–10. Which exercises could have two or more answers? Explain.

12. Draw a quadrilateral with two pairs of congruent sides that is not a parallelogram.

Problem Solving

13. Number Sense Choose numbers from the tags so that the paragraph makes sense.

Eva needs a new rug for her square-shaped room. She measured one side to be ▦ feet. The area of the floor is ▦ square feet. She also wants to carpet her closet which is shaped like a rectangle. Its dimensions are ▦ feet by ▦ feet. The area of the closet floor is ▦ square feet. In all, Eva needs ▦ square feet of carpeting.

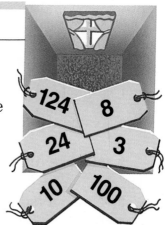

235

Circles

Build Understanding

You have seen many things that have the shape of a circle.

A. Point *O* is the **center** of the circle. A circle is named by its center point. This is circle *O*.

B. A **radius** is a line segment whose endpoints are the center of the circle and a point of the circle. Segment *OP* is a radius.

C. A **diameter** is a line segment that goes through the center of a circle and whose endpoints are on the circle. Segment *RS* is a diameter.

■ **Talk About Math** Given a circle, how many diameters does it have? How many radii? How many centers?

The golden age of the circus began about 1870 in the United States.

Check Understanding

For another example, see Set H, pages 242–243.

Use the circle at the right.

1. Name the circle.

2. Name a diameter.

3. Name a radius.

4. Mary traced around the bottom of a can. Then she cut out the circle and folded it in half. When she opened it, she marked the fold line in red. What is the name of the red segment? What do you know about it?

5. If Mary were to fold the circle in half again and mark the new segment in blue, what can you say about the two segments?

6. Sketch a circle. Find its center and label it O. Draw a diameter and label it AB. Name a radius of your circle.

Problem Solving

Copy and complete the table.
Use a centimeter ruler to measure.

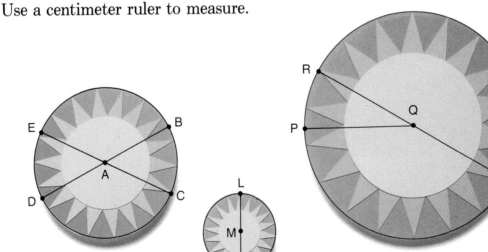

	Circle Q	Circle A	Circle M
Name a diameter.	7.	8.	9.
Name a radius.	10.	11.	12.
Length of a diameter	13.	14.	15.
Length of a radius	16.	17.	18.

19. Use Problems 7–18 to write a sentence that compares the radius and diameter of any circle.

Use Logical Reasoning

Build Understanding

Liberty School celebrated its 50th anniversary with an open house. All of the students and teachers were given T-shirts and hats with the school colors. The pictures below represent the distribution in one of the classrooms.

A. How many students are wearing blue T-shirts or yellow hats?

Understand
QUESTION
FACTS
KEY IDEA

▶ **Plan and Solve**
STRATEGY
ANSWER

Look Back
SENSIBLE ANSWER
ALTERNATE APPROACH

Understand   A student is wearing a blue T-shirt *or* a yellow hat if he or she is wearing (1) a blue T-shirt, (2) a yellow hat, or (3) both a blue T-shirt and a yellow hat.

▶ **Plan and Solve**   STRATEGY   Count the students who meet the conditions in (1), (2), and (3).

ANSWER   Nine are wearing blue T-shirts, 7 are wearing yellow hats, and 5 are wearing both. The students that are wearing both have been counted twice. So $9 + 7 - 5$, or 11, students are wearing blue T-shirts or yellow hats.

Look Back   Since 5 of the 16 students are not wearing blue T-shirts or yellow hats, it makes sense that 11 students are.

B. How many students are wearing blue T-shirts and yellow hats?

A student is wearing a blue T-shirt *and* a yellow hat if he or she is wearing both items. By counting we find that there are 5 students wearing blue T-shirts and yellow hats.

■ **Talk About Math**   If the teacher in this classroom is wearing a blue hat and a blue T-shirt, how many people are wearing blue T-shirts or yellow hats? blue T-shirts and yellow hats?

Check Understanding

Suppose that the committee did not order enough T-shirts and hats and that this is the distribution in one classroom. How many students are wearing

1. blue T-shirts and yellow hats?

2. blue T-shirts or yellow hats?

Practice

Write a sentence about these students with respect to the colors of their T-shirts and pennants using the word

3. *or.*   **4.** *and.*

Five students in a class of 23 have a cat and a dog, 10 have only a dog, and 4 have only a cat. How many students have

5. cats or dogs?   **6.** no cats or dogs?

7. Number Sense   Use numbers from the square that make sense in the sentence.

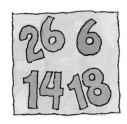

Of the ▦ students in the classroom, ▦ students wore blue, ▦ students wore black, and ▦ students wore blue and black. More students wore blue than black.

Problem-Solving Review

Solve each problem.

1. Gayla placed her international doll collection on 4 shelves with 6 dolls on a shelf. Draw an array to find out how many dolls Gayla has.

2. Solve this riddle. Always a quadrilateral, sticky on one side, when you put me on a letter, I go for a ride.

3. Jason and Ryan each bought a poster. Rolled up, the posters are the same length. Are the posters congruent? How could you find out for sure?

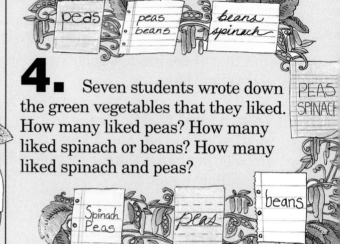

4. Seven students wrote down the green vegetables that they liked. How many liked peas? How many liked spinach or beans? How many liked spinach and peas?

5. Use data from pages 248-249. What is the total distance a baseball player would travel around the bases if he hit a homerun on a major league field? On a little league field? If the bases were vertices, what type of quadrilateral would they form?

6. Collect at least 6 newspaper headlines that use exact numbers or number estimates. When might exact numbers be needed? When might estimates be needed?

Explore with a Calculator

Pyramid Puzzles

To complete the pyramid puzzles, you need to discover how the numbers in the blocks relate to each other.

1.

108	
33	75

| 9 | 24 | 51 | 47 |

2.

6,900

1,821

814 | 1,007

137 | 596 | 671

3.

6,005

2,599

1,128

784

932 | 149

843 | 89 | 106 | 43

Reteaching

The sides of a polygon meet at points called vertices. You use the vertices to name the sides. The number of sides determines the name of a polygon.

Remember that a polygon is a closed figure and its sides are straight.

Name the polygon, its sides, and its vertices.

1.   2.

Set B   pages 216–218

There are 3 ways to move a polygon.

Slide: The polygon moves in any direction as though it were on a sled.

Flip: The polygon flips over a line like a page in a book.

Turn: The polygon turns on a vertex as though the vertex were nailed down.

Remember that you can use a tracing to see how a figure moved.

Tell how the polygon was moved. Write *flip*, *slide*, or *turn*.

1.

2.

Set C   pages 220–221

Two figures are congruent if one of them can be moved so that it fits exactly on the other figure.

Since these polygons have the same shapes but different sizes, they are *not* congruent.

Remember you can trace a figure and place it on another to see if it fits exactly.

Which polygons are congruent to the first polygon?

1.

Set D   pages 224–225

A square has 4 lines of symmetry because there are 4 ways that you can fold it so that one half of the figure fits the other half exactly.

Remember that a polygon is symmetric if it has at least one line of symmetry.

How many lines of symmetry does each figure have?

1.   2.

Set E   pages 228–229

A segment is named by its two endpoints. A line is also named by two points, but a line has no endpoints. A ray is also named by two points, but only one of these is an endpoint.

Remember that parallel lines never intersect.

1. Draw two parallel lines.

2. Draw two intersecting segments.

3. Draw a ray.

Set F   pages 230–233

All angles are one of three types:

a. Right angles
b. Less than a right angle
c. More than a right angle

The corner of each page in this book forms a right angle.

Remember that right angles can be formed by lines, segments, or rays that are perpendicular.

1. Which angle is less than a right angle?

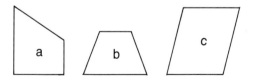

Set G   pages 234–235

A parallelogram has opposite sides that are parallel and congruent.

Side *AB* is parallel and congruent to side *DC*. Side *AD* is parallel and congruent to side *BC*.

Remember that a parallelogram may also be a rhombus, a rectangle, or a square.

1. Which of these figures is a parallelogram?

Set H   pages 236–237

Why isn't segment *AB* a diameter of this circle?

The endpoints of segment *AB* are on the circle, but segment *AB* does not go through the center of the circle.

Remember that a radius of a circle is like a spoke on a bicycle wheel.

1. Name each radius in the circle at the left.

2. Name the diameter of the circle at the left.

More Practice

Set A pages 214–215

How are the figures alike? How are they different?

1.

2.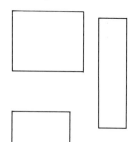

3.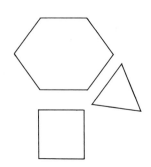

Set B pages 216–218

Tell how each polygon was moved. Write *flip*, *slide*, or *turn*.

1.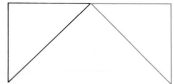

2.

3.

Set C pages 220–221

Which polygons are congruent to the first polygon?

1.   a b c

2.   a b c

Set D pages 224–225

How many lines of symmetry does each figure have?

1.

2.

3.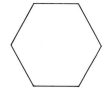

4.

Set E pages 228–229

Tell whether the picture suggests lines, segments, rays, intersecting lines, or parallel lines.

1.

2.

3.

Set F pages 230–233

Use these angles to answer Exercises 1–4.

a.   b.   c.   d.   e.

Which angles are

1. right angles?

2. less than right angles?

3. congruent?

4. greater than right angles?

Set G pages 234–235

Is the figure a parallelogram? Write *Yes* or *No*.

1.   2.    3.   4.    5.

Give the exercise numeral of every figure shown above that can be called

6. a rhombus.

7. a square.

8. a rectangle.

Set H pages 236–237

Use the circle at the right.

1. Name the circle.

2. Name the diameter.

3. Name each radius.

Enrichment

Similar Figures

Millie, the artist, likes to duplicate patterns when she decorates a room. For example, the curtains in her kitchen have the same pattern as the floor tiles, but the pattern is twice the size. She uses dot paper to enlarge or reduce a pattern.

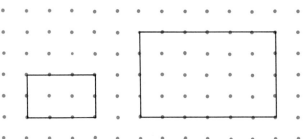

Figures that have the same shape are *similar figures*. In the similar figures shown above, each side of the large figure is twice as long as the corresponding side of the small figure.

Copy the figure at the right. Then draw a similar figure with sides that are

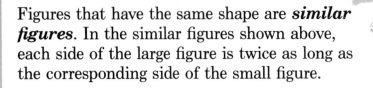

1. twice as long.   2. three times as long.

3. half as long.   4. the same length.

5. Draw your own dot figure. Then repeat Exercises 1–4.

6. If two figures are congruent, are they always similar?

7. If two figures are similar, are they always congruent?

8. Are all rectangles similar? Explain your answer.

9. Draw a simple tile design inside a square. Then draw the corresponding design inside a square whose dimensions are twice as long.

Chapter 7 Review/Test

1. Name the polygon, its sides, and its vertices.

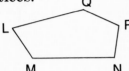

2. If a polygon has 12 sides, how many vertices does it have?

3. Tell how the polygon was moved. Write flip, slide, or turn.

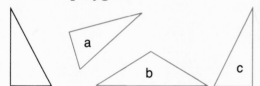

4. Which polygons are congruent to the first polygon?

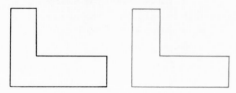

5. In all, how many boards 6 inches wide and 2 feet long can be cut from the boards shown?

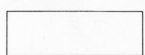

6. How many lines of symmetry does this figure have?

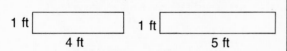

7. What shape will you get after cutting and opening the paper?

Tell whether the lines are intersecting lines or parallel lines.

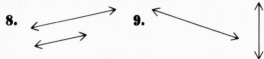

8.   9.

10. Which angle is greater than a right angle?

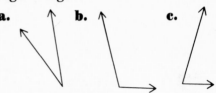

a.   b.   c.

11. Is *DEFG* a parallelogram? Write *Yes* or *No*.

Refer to circle *S* to answer Items 12 and 13. Name a

12. diameter.

13. radius.

14. Which number sentence gives the solution to this problem?

   In a class of 20 students, 4 are both in the band and on the softball team, 5 are only in the band, and 2 are only on the softball team. How many are in the band or on the softball team?
   a. $20 - 4 = 16$
   b. $5 + 2 = 7$
   c. $4 + 5 + 2 = 11$
   d. $5 + 2 - 4 = 3$

15. **Write About Math** Is the letter F symmetric? Explain.

1. Train Schedule
This schedule shows train times between Oakland, California, and Stockton, California.

2. Chart
This chart shows information about the sun, moon and planets for August 11, 1989.

3. Map
This map shows the number of miles from Boyne Falls to different cities.

4. Diagram
The diagram shows the number of calories in an average cheeseburger.

5. Diagram
This diagram shows the difference between a major league baseball field and a little league baseball field.

2. Chart

Skywatch

- **Sunset today:** 8:39 p.m.
- **Sunrise tomorrow:** 6:36 a.m
- **Moonrise:** 4:49 p.m.
- **Moonset:** 1:19 a.m. Saturday.
  New moon: Aug. 31.
  First moon: Sept 8.
  Full moon: Aug 16.
  Last moon Aug. 23.
- **Mercury:** Not visible.
- **Venus:** 6° W 9 p.m.
- **Mars:** Not visible.
- **Jupiter:** 31° E 6 a.m.
- **Saturn:** 22° SSE 9:30 p.m.

1. Amtrak Trains

All trains daily.

	S.Joaquin 708	Zephyr 6	S.Joaquin 710	Starlight 14
Oakland Lv	7:25a	11:50a	*5:15p*	*8:54p*
Berkeley ● Lv	7:31a	—	*5:21p*	—
Richmond ■ Lv	7:39a	*12:03p*	*5:29p*	*9:07p*
Martinez Lv	8:10a	*12:33p*	*6:00p*	*9:38p*
Suisun-Fairfield ● Lv	—	*12:53p*	—	—
Antioch-Pittsburgh● Lv	8:33a	—	*6:23p*	—
Stockton Lv	9:10a	—	*7:00p*	—

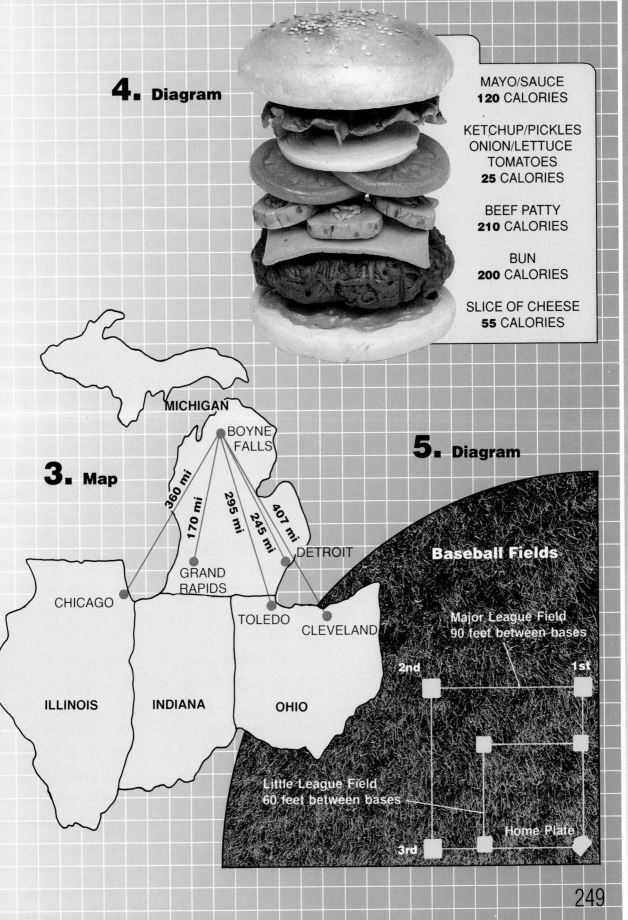

4. Diagram

MAYO/SAUCE
120 CALORIES

KETCHUP/PICKLES
ONION/LETTUCE
TOMATOES
25 CALORIES

BEEF PATTY
210 CALORIES

BUN
200 CALORIES

SLICE OF CHEESE
55 CALORIES

3. Map

MICHIGAN

BOYNE FALLS

360 mi

170 mi

295 mi

245 mi

407 mi

GRAND RAPIDS

DETROIT

CHICAGO

TOLEDO

CLEVELAND

ILLINOIS

INDIANA

OHIO

5. Diagram

Baseball Fields

Major League Field
90 feet between bases

2nd

1st

Little League Field
60 feet between bases

3rd

Home Plate

1. Round 8,189 to the nearest thousand.

a. 8,000   c. 8,200
b. 9,000   d. 10,000

2. Which digit in 72,168,945 is in the millions place?

a. 7   c. 1
b. 2   d. 6

3. Add.

$$\begin{array}{r} 4,368 \\ + 2,799 \\ \hline \end{array}$$

a. 6,057
b. 5,167
c. 6,167
d. 7,167

4. Estimate the sum. Round each number to the nearest hundred.

307 + 582

a. 800   c. 890
b. 900   d. 880

5. Write the time.

12 minutes before 8:00 A.M.

a. 7:48 A.M.   c. 8:12 P.M.
b. 8:12 A.M.   d. 8:38 A.M.

6. What is the length of the nail to the nearest quarter inch?

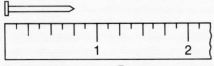

a. $\frac{1}{2}$ inch   c. $\frac{7}{8}$ inch
b. $\frac{3}{4}$ inch   d. 1 inch

7. Choose the most sensible measure for the length of a new pencil.

a. 17 mm   c. 17 dm
b. 17 cm   d. 17 m

8. Find the perimeter.

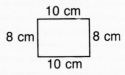

a. 80 cm   c. 80 ft
b. 18 cm   d. 36 cm

9. Which sentence is a related multiplication sentence for 6 + 6 + 6 + 6 + 6?

a. $5 \times 6 = 30$
b. $2 \times 15 = 30$
c. $10 \times 3 = 30$
d. $6 \times 6 = 36$

10. Which number is a multiple of 5?

a. 28   c. 45
b. 18   d. all of these

11. Multiply.

7×10

a. 7   c. 70
b. 17   d. 700

12. Choose the words to make a true sentence.

With 21 cubes, you can form
a. 7 groups of 3
b. 11 groups of 2
c. 5 groups of 5
d. 8 groups of 3

13. Divide.

$63 \div 9$

a. 8
b. 7
c. 6
d. 9

14. Find $\frac{1}{4}$ of 12.

a. 3   **c.** 48
b. 4   **d.** 16

15. Tell how the polygon was moved.

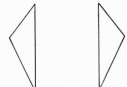

a. flip   **c.** turn
b. slide   **d.** none of these

16. Which angle is greater than a right angle?

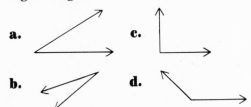

a.   **c.**

b.   **d.**

17. Which segment is a diameter?

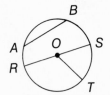

a. Segment AB
b. Segment RS
c. Segment RO
d. Segment OT

18. The telephone bill for the Hall family was $48.26 in April and $37.27 in May. How much more was the phone bill in April than in May?

a. $85.53   **c.** $10.01
b. $11.99   **d.** $10.99

19. A rectangular pen is 8 feet long by 6 feet wide. How many feet of fencing are needed to enclose the pen?

a. 14 feet   **c.** 28 feet
b. 48 feet   **d.** 24 feet

20. In a class of 24 students, 3 play only on the soccer team, 6 play only on the baseball team, and 4 play on both the soccer team and baseball team. How many are on either the soccer team or the baseball team?

a. 20 students   **c.** 13 students
b. 16 students   **d.** 9 students

21. Jeffrey has 25 decals that he will give away to 4 friends. Each friend will receive the same number. How many decals will be left over?

a. 6 decals   **c.** 5 decals
b. 1 decal   **d.** 4 decals

Read the problem below. Then answer Item 22.

Each tray holds 10 rolls. There are 8 trays. Each roll costs 9 cents. What is the cost of 1 tray of rolls?

22. Which of the underlined facts are needed to solve this problem?

a. 10 rolls and 8 trays
b. 10 rolls and 9 cents
c. 8 trays and 9 cents
d. All of the above

Multiplication
Computation

Did You Know: Wisconsin has more dairy cows than any other state. Each day, the cows produce about 8 million gallons of milk. This is enough milk to fill about 130 million small cartons.

Number-Sense Project

Estimate
Estimate how many students in your school ordered milk with lunch today.

Gather Data
Find out how many students in your class usually order milk. List the other classes in the school. Estimate the number of students in each class that ordered milk.

Analyze and Report
To estimate the number of cartons for the school, add the estimates for each class. Ask the office for the actual number. Compare your estimate with the actual number.

253

Multiplying Tens

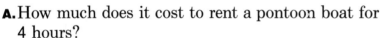

Build Understanding

Mary Tibbs is the manager at Martin's Marina. The chart at the right shows boat rental rates.

A. How much does it cost to rent a pontoon boat for 4 hours?

The rental cost is $30 per hour. Think of 4 groups of 30. You can add or multiply.

30 + 30 + 30 + 30 = 120

4 × 30 = 120   4 × 3 tens = 12 tens

The cost for 4 hours is $120.

B. Estimation   About how much would it cost to rent a motorboat for 8 hours?

Since 22 is close to 20, find 8 × 20.

8 × 20 = 160   8 × 2 tens = 16 tens

The cost would be about $160.

■ **Talk About Math**   Explain how you can multiply a one-digit number and a multiple of ten mentally. In Example B, is the estimate less than or greater than the exact product? Why?

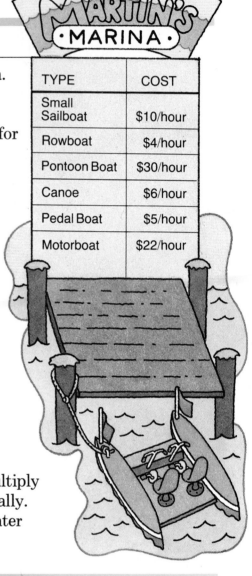

TYPE	COST
Small Sailboat	$10/hour
Rowboat	$4/hour
Pontoon Boat	$30/hour
Canoe	$6/hour
Pedal Boat	$5/hour
Motorboat	$22/hour

Check Understanding

For another example, see Set A, pages 286–287.

Complete each number sentence.

1. 3 × 50 = 3 × 5 ▦ = 15 tens

So 3 × 50 = ▦.

2. 3 × 60 = 3 × 6 tens = ▦ tens

So 3 × 60 = ▦.

3. 3 × 70 = ▦

4. 3 × 80 = ▦

Practice

For More Practice, see Set A, pages 288–289.

Mental Math   Multiply.

5. 3 × 10 **6.** 6 × 10 **7.** 9 × 10 **8.** 5 × 10 **9.** 3 × 50

10. 6 × 50 **11.** 9 × 50 **12.** 5 × 50 **13.** 7 × 20 **14.** 7 × 40

15. 7 × 60 **16.** 7 × 80 **17.** 4 × 60 **18.** 5 × 20 **19.** 40 × 8

20. 80 × 2 **21.** 9 × 70 **22.** 7 × 90 **23.** 8 × 90 **24.** 90 × 8

Estimation   Estimate the product. Tell whether your estimate is greater than or less than the actual product.

25. 4 × 81 **26.** 7 × 33 **27.** 5 × 67 **28.** 3 × 88 **29.** 76 × 2

30. 8 × 29 **31.** 61 × 4 **32.** 48 × 7 **33.** 3 × 43 **34.** 25 × 6

Problem Solving

Solve each problem. Use data from page 254.

35. Before a person uses a rental motorboat, Martin's Marina requires a deposit of $50 and a rental payment for 1 hour. How much must be paid before a person uses a motorboat?

36. Kasha and her friends rented a pedal boat for 2 hours and a sailboat for 3 hours. How much did they pay for the rental at Martin's Marina?

TIPS FOR PROBLEM SOLVERS

Don't give up. Some problems take longer than others.

Multiplying 2-Digit Numbers: Area Models

Build Understanding

A hallway is 26 feet long and 8 feet wide. Find the number of square-foot floor tiles used to cover it.

In the diagram, each small square is 1 square foot. Without counting each tile, find how many tiles are in 8 rows of 26.

26 feet

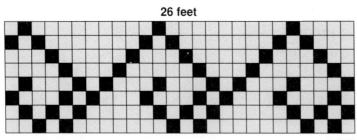

8 feet

You can divide the large diagram into smaller parts. Part A of the diagram below has 8 rows of 20 squares. Part B has 8 rows of 6 squares. First, multiply to find the number of squares for each part. Then add the parts to find the total.

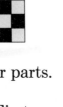

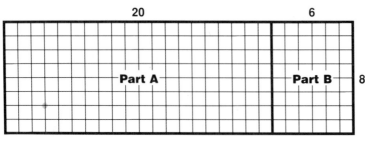

20   6

Part A   Part B 8

Part A 160 $8 \times 20 = 160$
Part B   48 $8 \times 6 = 48$
Total   208

The multiplication sentence below shows the total number of tiles.

Number of rows   Number of tiles in each row

$$8 \times 26 = 208$$

It takes **208** tiles to cover the hallway.

■ **Talk About Math** Are there other ways to divide the rectangle in the Example into two parts? Do you think one way is better than another? Why?

Check Understanding

For another example, see Set B, pages 286–287.

Name the part of the rectangle that matches each sentence.

1. $7 \times 30 = 210$ **2.** $7 \times 5 = 35$

3. Write a multiplication sentence to show the area of the rectangle.

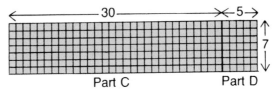

Part C   Part D

Practice

For More Practice, see Set B, pages 288–289.

Draw a rectangle on grid paper for each multiplication sentence. Divide the rectangle into two parts and show the number of squares for each part.

4. $4 \times 11 = 44$ **5.** $34 \times 2 = 68$ **6.** $6 \times 13 = 78$ **7.** $27 \times 2 = 54$

Find each product. Draw a rectangle if necessary.

8. 10×6 **9.** 14×3 **10.** 31×7 **11.** 23×4 **12.** 15×8

13. 25×9 **14.** 41×2 **15.** 5×29 **16.** 3×18 **17.** 5×36

Problem Solving

Explore ———— Math

Solve each problem by drawing rectangles on grid paper.

18. A piece of felt is 9 inches wide and 25 inches long. How many rectangles, each 5 inches by 9 inches, can be cut from it?

19. Draw as many different rectangles as you can that have an area of 36 square units. List their dimensions.

Multiplying Tens and Ones

Build Understanding

Centerville has 3 fire stations. Each fire station has 24 firefighters. How many firefighters does the city have in all?

Since each fire station has the same number of firefighters, you can multiply. Find 3 × 24.

Estimation Estimate the product first.
Since 3 × 20 = 60, you know 3 × 24 > 60.
Since 3 × 30 = 90, you know 3 × 24 < 90.
So 3 × 24 is between 60 and 90.

Place-Value Materials

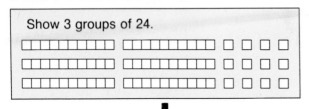
Show 3 groups of 24.

↓

Trade 10 ones for a ten.
Make other trades if you can.

↓

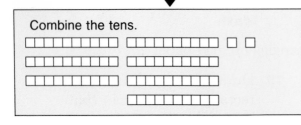
Combine the tens.

Paper and Pencil

Write the problem.
Multiply the ones.

$$\begin{array}{r} 24 \\ \times\ 3 \\ \hline \end{array}$$ 3 × 4 ones = 12 ones

Write the ones.
Rename 10 ones as 1 ten.

$$\begin{array}{r} \overset{1}{2}4 \\ \times\ 3 \\ \hline 2 \end{array}$$ 12 ones = 1 ten 2 ones

Multiply the tens. Add the extra ten. Write the tens.

$$\begin{array}{r} \overset{1}{2}4 \\ \times\ 3 \\ \hline 72 \end{array}$$ 3 × 2 tens = 6 tens
6 tens + 1 ten = 7 tens

Centerville has 72 firefighters in all.

■ **Talk About Math** Why is this answer reasonable?

Check Understanding

Copy and complete. Use place-value models if necessary.

1.
```
   12
 ×  4
 ▨▨8
```

2.
```
    2
   29
 ×  3
 ▨▨7
```

3.
```
   53
 ×  2
 ▨▨6
```

4.
```
    4
   68
 ×  5
 ▨▨0
```

5.
```
   81
 ×  9
 ▨▨9
```

6. Norma found 68 × 5 by thinking of 60 × 5 and
   8 × 5. Then she added 300 + 40. Does her method
   give the same result as Exercise 4?

Practice

Multiply.

7.
```
   39
 ×  2
```

8.
```
   11
 ×  8
```

9.
```
   13
 ×  5
```

10.
```
   27
 ×  3
```

11.
```
   18
 ×  4
```

12.
```
   72
 ×  4
```

13.
```
   83
 ×  3
```

14.
```
   51
 ×  5
```

15.
```
   74
 ×  2
```

16.
```
   31
 ×  6
```

17.
```
   46
 ×  4
```

18.
```
   29
 ×  7
```

19. 8 × 27   20. 45 × 9   21. 6 × 47   22. 35 × 8   23. 29 × 9

Problem Solving

Read for the facts. Then solve each problem.

24. The city has 8 fire trucks. Each
holds 42 gallons of gas. How
many gallons of gas does it take
to fill all 8 trucks?

25. The firefighters answered 125
alarms in March and 216 in
April. How many alarms were
answered in March and April?

Skills _____ Review   pages 142–143

Add. Then write the related multiplication sentence.

1. 20 + 20 + 20   2. 15 + 15 + 15 + 15   3. 8 + 8 + 8 + 8 + 8

4. 38 + 38   5. 100 + 100 + 100   6. 75 + 75 + 75 + 75

Multiplying Hundreds

Build Understanding

A. Each fire truck has a 500-gallon water tank. If 3 trucks respond to a fire call, how much water will they take to the fire?

Think of 3 groups of 500. You can add or multiply.

500 + 500 + 500 = 1,500

3 × 500 = 1,500   3 × 5 hundreds = 15 hundreds

The trucks will take 1,500 gallons of water to the fire.

B. Estimation   Estimate 5 × 174.

Round 174 to the nearest hundred. Since 174 rounds to 200, find 5 × 200.

5 × 200 = 1,000   5 × 2 hundreds = 10 hundreds

So 5 × 174 is about 1,000.

■ **Talk About Math**   Explain how you can multiply a one-digit number and a multiple of one hundred mentally. In Example B, is the estimate less than or greater than the actual product? Why?

Check Understanding

For another example, see Set D, pages 286–287.

Complete each number sentence.

1. 700 = ⬚ hundreds

2. 20 hundreds = ⬚

3. 3 × 6 hundreds = ⬚ hundreds

4. 8 hundreds × 5 = ⬚ hundreds

5. 726 is about ⬚ hundreds.

6. 283 is about ⬚ hundreds.

Practice

For More Practice, see Set D, pages 288–289.

Mental Math   Multiply.

7. 4 × 100   **8.** 6 × 100   **9.** 100 × 9   **10.** 3 × 600   **11.** 8 × 500

12. 9 × 500   **13.** 5 × 500   **14.** 7 × 600   **15.** 7 × 800   **16.** 900 × 7

17. 600 × 4   **18.** 500 × 6   **19.** 400 × 8   **20.** 800 × 2   **21.** 300 × 1

Estimation   Estimate the product. Tell whether your estimate is greater than or less than the actual product.

22. 3 × 816   **23.** 645 × 7   **24.** 254 × 4   **25.** 8 × 967   **26.** 766 × 2

27. 350 × 6   **28.** 5 × 850   **29.** 7 × 486   **30.** 5 × 732   **31.** 997 × 4

Problem Solving

Solve each problem.

32. The fire truck had 3 hoses, each 400 feet long. If they were hooked together, how far would they reach?

33. The city ordered 12 new fire trucks for its 3 fire stations. How many trucks will each station get?

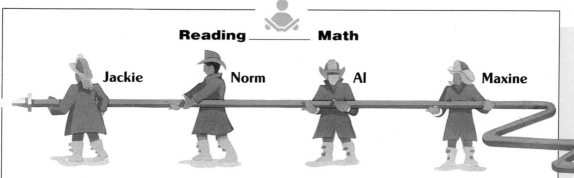

Reading ———— Math

Jackie   Norm   Al   Maxine

Refer to the diagram as you read each statement. Tell if the statement is *true* or *false*.

1. Maxine is behind Al and in front of Norm.

2. Norm is behind Jackie or Maxine.

3. Jackie is directly in front of Al.

4. Norm is in front of Maxine.

Exploring Multiplication of 3-Digit Numbers

Build Understanding

ACTIVITY

Dollars, Dollars, Dollars
Materials: Play money
($100 bills, $10 bills, $1 bills)
Groups: 3 to 4 students

a. Imagine that you are earning money at a job. As a group, choose a 3-digit number less than 300 for the amount you earn each week. Show this amount of money using play money.

b. Next, show two more sets of the same amount. Combine the three amounts. How many ones, tens, and hundreds are there?

c. Suppose you take the money to a bank to exchange or trade bills so that the total amount has the least number of bills. How many ones, tens, and hundreds are there?

d. How much would you earn in 3 weeks?

■**Talk About Math** What are two possible trades that you might make and still have the same amount of money?

Check Understanding

$100	$100		$10	$10	$10		$1	$1	$1	$1	$1
$100	$100		$10	$10	$10		$1	$1	$1	$1	$1
$100	$100		$10	$10	$10		$1	$1	$1	$1	$1
$100	$100		$10	$10	$10		$1	$1	$1	$1	$1

1. What exchanges can you make to show this amount of money using the least number of bills?

2. How much money is in each row? How many rows are there?

3. What is the total amount?   **4.** 4 × $235 = ▦

Practice

Use play money or draw pictures to find the products.

5. 2 × $300   **6.** 7 × $102   **7.** 4 × $105   **8.** 8 × $120   **9.** 3 × $308

10. 5 × $240   **11.** 2 × $430   **12.** 4 × $192   **13.** 3 × $245   **14.** 3 × $271

Problem Solving

Mrs. Miles earns $206 per week. How much will she earn in

15. 3 weeks?   **16.** 2 weeks?   **17.** 4 weeks?   **18.** 9 weeks?

Adam earns $134 per month. How much will he earn in
19. 2 months?   **20.** 3 months?   **21.** 6 months?   **22.** 12 months?

23. How can you use your answer to Problem 21 to find the answer to Problem 22?

24. Write a problem that can be solved by multiplying $250 by 3.

25. Explain how you can use your answers to Problems 19 and 20 to find how much Adam will earn in 5 months.

26. Jill earns $240 each month and saves half of her earnings. How long will it take her to save $600?

Multiplying 3-Digit Numbers by 1-Digit Numbers

Build Understanding

The Capitol building in Washington, D.C., has guided tours. On one winter day, 186 visitors toured the Capitol each hour. How many visitors toured the Capitol in 3 hours?

Find 3 × 186.

Estimation Since 186 < 200, will 3 groups of 186 be more or less than 600?

The diagram shows place-value models for 3 groups of 186. Notice that 10 ones can be traded for a ten. Each group of 10 tens can be traded for a hundred. As you study the three steps below, think about how each step is shown with models.

10 tens = 100

10 ones = 1 ten

10 tens = 100

Multiply the ones. Rename if needed.	➡	Multiply the tens. Add any renamed tens. Rename if needed.	➡	Multiply the hundreds. Add any renamed hundreds.

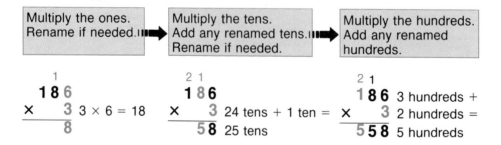

$$\begin{array}{r} {\scriptstyle 1} \\ 18\mathbf{6} \\ \times 3 \\ \hline 8 \end{array}$$ 3 × 6 = 18

$$\begin{array}{r} {\scriptstyle 2\ 1} \\ 1\mathbf{8}6 \\ \times 3 \\ \hline 58 \end{array}$$ 24 tens + 1 ten = 25 tens

$$\begin{array}{r} {\scriptstyle 2\ 1} \\ \mathbf{1}86 \\ \times 3 \\ \hline 558 \end{array}$$ 3 hundreds + 2 hundreds = 5 hundreds

In 3 hours, 558 people toured the Capitol.

■ **Write About Math** Find 6 × 106. Write the steps and explain how you found the product. Explain how you know your answer is reasonable.

Check Understanding

For another example, see Set E, pages 286–287.

Copy and complete. Use place-value models if necessary.

1. ¹
    213
    × 4
    ⧈52

2. ²
    307
    × 3
    ⧈21

3. 181
    × 5
    ⧈5

4. ²³
    235
    × 6
    ⧈,⧈10

5. William found 235 × 6 by thinking of 200 × 6, 30 × 6, and 5 × 6. Then he added 1,200 + 180 + 30. Would his method give the same result as Exercise 4?

Practice

For More Practice, see Set E, pages 288–289.

Multiply.

6. 243
    × 4

7. 279
    × 3

8. 127
    × 6

9. 518
    × 5

10. 229
    × 7

11. 134
    × 9

12. 904
    × 8

13. 398
    × 2

14. 473
    × 9

15. 670
    × 4

16. 8 × 925

17. 5 × 506

18. 931 × 6

19. 7 × 240

20. 604 × 3

Mixed Practice   Tell whether you would use mental math or paper and pencil. Then find each answer.

21. 200 × 8

22. 30 × 4

23. 23 × 3

24. 4 × 902

25. 50 × 7

26. 384 × 6

27. 9 × 225

28. 47 × 5

Problem Solving

Solve each problem.

29. In the spring, as many as 875 visitors tour the Capitol each hour. How many visitors can see the Capitol in 8 hours?

30. The Johnsons began their tour at 3:10 P.M. The tour lasted 45 minutes. At what time was their tour completed?

Multiplying Dollars and Cents

Build Understanding

A. While visiting Washington, D.C., the McFaddens took the Mall Tour on the Tourmobile. If the 3 McFadden children were in elementary school, how much did the children's tickets cost?

TOURMOBILE TICKETS		
Mall Tour	Adults	$7.50
	Ages 3-11	$3.75
Arlington Tour	Adults	$2.50
	Ages 3-11	$1.25
Two-Day Tour	Adults	$12.25
	Ages 3-11	$6.25

Find 3 × $3.75.

Since $3.75 is about $4 and 3 × $4 = $12, the tickets will cost about $12.

Multiply as with whole numbers. Then write the product as dollars and cents.

$$\begin{array}{r} \overset{2\ 1}{\$3.75} \\ \times \quad 3 \\ \hline \$11.25 \end{array}$$

$3.75 = 375¢

1125¢ = $11.25

The children's Tourmobile tickets cost $11.25. This answer is reasonable because $11.25 is close to $12.

B. What is the cost for 4 adults to take a 2-day tour?

Multiply $12.25 × 4.

The cost is $49.00.

$$\begin{array}{r} \$12.25 \\ \times \quad 4 \\ \hline \$49.00 \end{array}$$

■ **Talk About Math**   For Example B, does the answer seem reasonable? Why or why not?

Check Understanding

For another example, see Set F, pages 286–287.

Copy and complete each exercise by writing the product as dollars and cents.

1.	2.	3.	4.	5.
$3.47	$6.07	$0.27	$27.80	$6.34
× 4	× 2	× 9	× 3	× 8
1388	1214	243	8340	5072

Practice

For More Practice, see Set F, pages 288–289.

Multiply. **Remember** to check that your answers are reasonable.

6. $0.05 × 9	**7.** $0.02 × 4	**8.** $0.27 × 9	**9.** $5.13 × 8	**10.** $3.81 × 9
11. $1.33 × 6	**12.** $4.05 × 7	**13.** $16.98 × 8	**14.** $8.60 × 5	**15.** $15.00 × 4

16. 6 × $0.43   **17.** 4 × $6.29   **18.** 8 × $1.07   **19.** 4 × $2.50

20. 9 × $0.58   **21.** 7 × $7.36   **22.** 4 × $32.49   **23.** 7 × $43.65

Problem Solving

Use the table on page 266 to find the cost of

24. 2 adult Mall Tour tickets.

25. 4 children's Arlington Tour tickets.

26. 1 adult Mall Tour and 1 adult Arlington Tour tickets.

27. 2 adult Two-Day Tours and 3 children's Two-Day Tours.

Critical Thinking Without multiplying, explain how much more

28. 3 × $7.75 is than 2 × $7.75.

29. 6 × $3.65 is than 5 × $3.65.

30. 4 × $3.25 is than 4 × $3.00.

31. 6 × $1.25 is than 4 × $1.25.

Midchapter _____ **Checkup**

Multiply.

1. 84 × 9   **2.** 400 × 6   **3.** 193 × 7   **4.** 2 × $307   **5.** $4.90 × 4

Estimate each product.

6. 39 × 4   **7.** 5 × 384

8. Draw a rectangle to help you complete this multiplication sentence: 16 × 4 = ▦.

Problem-Solving Workshop

Real-Life Decision Making

You want to buy a frame for a 10-inch by 14-inch picture. A store sells wood or metal frames in sections that you put together. You need to buy two pairs of sides for each frame. Below are the prices for the pairs of sides.

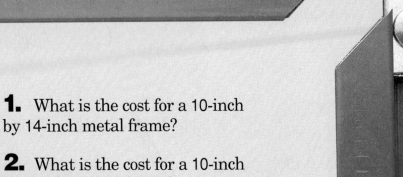

1. What is the cost for a 10-inch by 14-inch metal frame?

2. What is the cost for a 10-inch by 14-inch wood frame?

3. The frame can be larger than the picture if you get a mat board, which costs $2.00. You can spend up to $15. Can you afford to buy a 14-inch by 18-inch frame and a mat board?

4. Decide which size and type of frame to buy.

Pair Length	Cost for Metal	Cost for Wood
8-inch	$4.45	$6.00
10-inch	$4.75	$6.50
12-inch	$5.05	$7.00
14-inch	$5.35	$7.50
16-inch	$5.65	$8.00
18-inch	$6.00	$8.60
20-inch	$6.40	$9.20

Number-Sense Project

Look back at pages 252-253.
The chart shows the number of milk cartons ordered by one school each day for a week.

1. How many cartons did the school order during the week?

2. How many cartons do you think would be ordered during the school year (36 weeks)?

Day	Number of Cartons
Mon.	590
Tues.	610
Wed.	450
Thurs.	600
Fri.	605

Explore with a Computer

Use the *Spreadsheet Workshop Project* for this activity.

1. Sally is planting a rectangular flower garden. Two sides of the garden will be edged by brick walls. Sally has exactly 17 feet of fence to use for the other two sides. What is the area of the garden if its length is 14 feet?

Length x Width = Area
(ft)   (ft)   (sq ft)
14   3

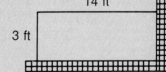

14 ft

3 ft

2. At the computer, change the length of the garden. What happens to the width of the garden? What happens to the area?

3. Can you find the greatest possible area?

269

Find a Pattern

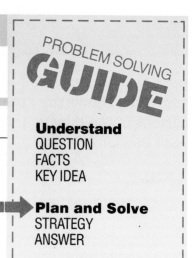

PROBLEM SOLVING GUIDE

Understand
QUESTION
FACTS
KEY IDEA

▌▶**Plan and Solve**
STRATEGY
ANSWER

Look Back
SENSIBLE ANSWER
ALTERNATE APPROACH

Build Understanding

One day Justin boasted, "I can tell if a number is a multiple of 3 mentally." His friends immediately gave him these numbers.

125   **1,116**   **3,021**

Justin thought for a moment and said, "The last two numbers are multiples of 3." His friends used their calculators to divide each number by 3. They discovered that Justin was right. "How did you do that?" they asked. "I found a pattern," said Justin. Then he started the table at the right. What is Justin's method for finding multiples of 3?

X	3	Sum of Digits
1	3	3
2	6	6
3	9	9
4	12	1+2=3
5	15	1+5=6
	18	1+8=9
6		
7	21	

Understand   The multiples of 3 are numbers that have 3 as a factor.

▌▶**Plan and Solve**   STRATEGY   Continue the table until you see a pattern. The pattern for the sum of the digits seems to be 3, 6, 9, 3, 6, and so on. Check the sums for Justin's numbers.

125: 1 + 2 + 5 = 8   The sum is not 3, 6, or 9, so 125 is not a multiple of 3.

1,116: 1 + 1 + 1 + 6 = 9   So 1,116 is a multiple of 3.

3,021: 3 + 0 + 2 + 1 = 6   So 3,021 is a multiple of 3.

ANSWER   Justin knows that a number is a multiple of 3 if the sum of its digits is 3, 6, or 9.

Look Back   Continuing the table of multiples continues the pattern. The answer makes sense.

■Talk About Math   Can you use Justin's method to tell if 81,021 is a multiple of 3? Explain your answer.

Check Understanding

Is the number a multiple of 3? Write *yes* or *no*. Explain your answer.

1. 1,746
2. 43,709
3. 111,999
4. 2,876,973

Practice

Begin tables of multiples for 2 and 5. Look for a pattern in the digits of the multiples. How do you know if a number is

5. a multiple of 2?
6. a multiple of 5?

Tell if the number is a multiple of 2, 3, or 5. If the number is not a multiple of 2, 3, or 5, write *none of these.*

7. 125
8. 687
9. 1,106
10. 3,543
11. 503

12. 224
13. 3,515
14. 23,906
15. 66
16. 660

▦ Calculator   How can you tell if a number is

17. a multiple of 9?
18. a multiple of 4?

Choose a ____ Strategy

How many cows?   A farmer has cows and chickens. There are 18 animals in all. Together they have 48 legs.

19. How many of each animal does the farmer have?

271

Multiplying Using Place Value

Build Understanding

A. An array of 300 objects can be grouped in many ways.
Write multiplication sentences that use multiples of 10.

Hundreds	Tens	Ones
3	**0**	**0**

300 ones	30 tens	3 hundreds
300 groups of 1	30 groups of 10	3 groups of 100
300 × 1 = 300	30 × 10 = 300	3 × 100 = 300

B. Find the missing factors.
Use a place-value chart.

Ten-thousands	Thousands	Hundreds	Tens	Ones
		6	2	0
		5	0	0
	7	0	0	0
	9	1	0	0
4	7	0	0	0
3	0	0	0	0

62 × ▦ = 620

▦ × 10 = 500

700 × 10 = ▦

91 × 100 = ▦

470 × ▦ = 47,000

▦ × 100 = 30,000

■ **Talk About Math**   How can you use a
place-value chart to help you name two multiples
of 10 that are factors of 5,400?

Check Understanding

For another example, see Set G, pages 286–287.

Which item in each list does not belong?

1. 100 tens	2. 7 thousands	3. 1 hundred	4. 6 tens
10 × 100	70 tens	100 ones	600
100 × 1	70 × 10	10 × 10	6 × 10
10 hundreds	700 × 1	10 × 100	60 × 1

5. ▤ **Calculator** Choose a 2-digit number and multiply it by 10. Write the product. Then multiply the product by 10 and write the new product. Divide this product by 100. Explain the result.

Practice

For More Practice, see Set G, pages 288–289.

Find each product.

6. 10 × 6	7. 1,000 × 9	8. 100 × 2	9. 100 × 85
10. 45 × 10	11. 100 × 32	12. 24 × 1,000	13. 219 × 10
14. 100 × 385	15. 10 × 6,142	16. 910 × 100	17. 165 × 1,000

Find each missing factor.

18. 100 × ▦ = 900   19. ▦ × 58 = 5,800   20. 17 × ▦ = 17,000

21. 26 × ▦ = 260   22. ▦ × 100 = 15,000   23. 270 × ▦ = 2,700

Mental Math Multiply the underlined factors first. Then multiply by the other factor to find each product.

24. 25 × 4 × 17   25. 38 × 2 × 5   26. 2 × 91 × 50   27. 5 × 20 × 78

Problem Solving

Solve the problem.

28. **Use Data** Use the chart on page 254. In one month, exactly $600 was collected for canoe rentals. For how many hours were canoes rented during that month?

Multiplying by Multiples of 10

Build Understanding

A. A market gets boxes of lettuce with 24 heads in each box. How many heads of lettuce are in the 40 boxes?

Since each box contains the same number of heads of lettuce, you can use multiplication.

Find 40 × 24.

$$
\begin{array}{r}
2\,4 \\
\times \quad 4 \text{ tens} \\
\hline
9\,6 \text{ tens}
\end{array}
\qquad
\begin{array}{r}
2\,4 \\
\times 4\,0 \\
\hline
9\,6\,0
\end{array}
$$

There are 960 heads of lettuce in 40 boxes.

B. 50 × 70 = ▦

Think of 50 as 5 × 10. Think of 70 as 7 × 10. You can multiply the numbers in any order.

$$50 \times 70 = 5 \times 10 \times 7 \times 10$$
$$= 35 \times 100$$
$$= 3{,}500$$

■ **Talk About Math**   What is another way to find the product in Example B?

More lettuce is grown in California than in any other state.

Check Understanding

For another example, see Set H, pages 286–287.

Copy and complete the chart.

×	7	30	37	67	200	230
4	**1.**	**2.**	**3.**	**4.**	**5.**	**6.**
40	**7.**	**8.**	**9.**	**10.**	**11.**	**12.**

Number Sense   Are the products equal? Tell why or why not.

13. 30 × 20
30 × 2 × 100

14. 24 × 50
24 × 5 × 10

15. 45 × 2 × 10
45 × 20

16. 38 × 70
40 × 70

Practice

For More Practice, see Set H, pages 288–289.

Multiply. **Remember** to think of multiples of 10.

17. 40 × 3

18. 40 × 30

19. 80 × 5

20. 80 × 50

21. 15 × 9

22. 15 × 90

23. 4 × 39

24. 40 × 39

25. 200 × 7

26. 200 × 70

27. 703 × 4

28. 703 × 40

29. 9 × 820

30. 90 × 820

31. 5 × 200

32. 50 × 200

Mixed Practice   Find each product.

33.   30
× 90

34.   128
×   5

35.   91
× 70

36.   49
×   4

37.   804
×   2

38.   692
×   6

Problem Solving

Solve each problem.

39. Tomatoes cost 59¢ a pound. Find the cost of 20 pounds.

40. Carrots cost 30¢ a pound. Find the cost of 17 pounds.

41. A box holds 40 grapefruit. The box could also hold 88 oranges. How many more oranges than grapefruit fit in the box?

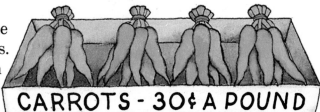

CARROTS - 30¢ A POUND

Estimation

Build Understanding

How many students in your class would like to buy a computer? If you know the cost of each computer, how could you estimate the total cost?

Mrs. Jacobs wants to estimate the cost of 38 computers that cost $624 each. Here are three ways to estimate.

A. Use front-end digits to estimate 624 × 38. Write zeros in place of each digit except the first. Then multiply.

$$
\begin{array}{r}
624 \\
\times\ 38 \\
\hline
\end{array}
\qquad
\begin{array}{r}
600 \\
\times\ 30 \\
\hline
18,000
\end{array}
\qquad 600 \times 3 \text{ tens } = 1,800 \text{ tens}
$$

So, 624 × 38 must be greater than 18,000.

If you could write a computer program, what would you have it do?

B. Find a range for 624 × 38. The product must be greater than 600 × 30, but less than 700 × 40.

600 × 30 = 18,000
700 × 40 = 28,000

Therefore, 624 × 38 is between 18,000 and 28,000.

The computers will cost between $18,000 and $28,000.

C. Round to estimate 624 × 38. 624 is closer to 600 than 700. 38 is closer to 40 than 30.

600 × 40 = 24,000

So 624 × 38 is about 24,000.

■ **Talk About Math** Which estimation method is easiest for you? What are the advantages of each method?

Check Understanding

For another example, see Set I, pages 286–287.

Use the digits 2, 4, 6, and 9 to write two 2-digit factors.

1. Use front-end digits to estimate the product of your two factors.

2. Find a range for the product of your two factors.

3. Use rounding to estimate the product of the two factors.

4.  **Calculator** Find the actual product of the two factors.

Practice

For More Practice, see Set I, pages 288–289.

Find a range for each product.

5. 42 × 30   **6.** 60 × 28   **7.** 78 × 41   **8.** 37 × 19   **9.** 84 × 53

10. 200 × 49   **11.** 533 × 70   **12.** 306 × 61   **13.** 79 × 196   **14.** 63 × 261

Estimate. Choose any method.

15. 71 × 35   **16.** 42 × 18   **17.** 11 × 92   **18.** 44 × 68   **19.** 89 × 88

20. 56 × 324   **21.** 872 × 42   **22.** 329 × 38   **23.** 36 × 542   **24.** 150 × 81

Problem Solving

Estimate the cost of

25. 84 disk cases.   **26.** 43 keyboards.

27. 19 disk cases and a printer.

Computer Items	Price
Disk Case	$ 12
Keyboard	$ 99
Printer	$295

Skills **Review**   pages 266–267

Write each amount using a dollar sign and cents point.

1. 245¢   **2.** 307¢   **3.** 21¢   **4.** 7¢   **5.** 140¢

Write each amount using a cent sign.

6. $5   **7.** $1.98   **8.** $3.50   **9.** $0.30   **10.** $0.08

Multiplying by 2-Digit Numbers: Area Models

Build Understanding

The Vale's family room is 28 feet long and 23 feet wide. What is the area of the family room in square feet?

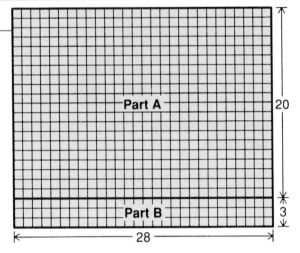

Mr. Vale drew a diagram of the family room. Since there are 23 rows of 28 squares, one way to find the area is to add 23 groups of 28. Is there a faster way?

Part A of the diagram has 20 rows of 28 squares. Part B has 3 rows of 28 squares. Multiply to find the number of squares for each part. Then add the number of squares in each part to find the total.

Part A	Part B	Total
28	28	560
×20	× 3	+ 84
560	84	644

The multiplication sentence below shows the total number of squares.

Number   Number of squares
of rows   in each row

$$23 \times 28 = 644$$

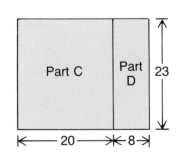

The room has an area of 644 square feet.

■ **Talk About Math** The diagram at the right shows another way to divide the diagram of the family room. What is the area of each part? Is the total area 644 square feet?

Check Understanding

Name the part of the rectangle below that matches each multiplication sentence.

1. 60 × 20 = 1,200

2. 7 × 20 = 140

3. What is the multiplication sentence for the total area of Parts X and Y?

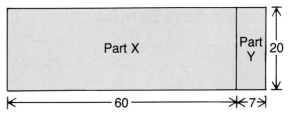

Practice

Draw a rectangle for each multiplication sentence. Divide the rectangle into parts and show the area of each part.

4. 24 × 15 = 360   **5.** 56 × 38 = 2,128   **6.** 23 × 38 = 874

7. 67 × 85 = 5,695   **8.** 79 × 32 = 2,528   **9.** 47 × 96 = 4,512

Find each product. Draw a rectangle if necessary.

10. 18 × 21   **11.** 35 × 42   **12.** 84 × 30   **13.** 37 × 16

14. 29 × 14   **15.** 43 × 62   **16.** 31 × 13   **17.** 25 × 23

Problem Solving

Find the area of a rectangular room that measures

18. 13 ft by 21 ft.   **19.** 36 ft by 25 ft.   **20.** 27 ft by 24 ft.

21. Critical Thinking Describe two ways to find the area of this figure. Then find the area using both ways.

15 ft

5 ft

15 ft

5 ft

15 ft

5 ft

15 ft

15 ft

5 ft

45 ft

Multiplying by 2-Digit Numbers

Build Understanding

A. Mr. Brogan, a drama teacher, needs to know how many tickets to sell for the school play. The auditorium has 26 rows of seats. If each row has 32 seats, how many seats are there?

Find 26 × 32.

First estimate the product.
30 × 30 = 900

Use the model to help you find the exact product.
Think of 26 as 20 + 6.

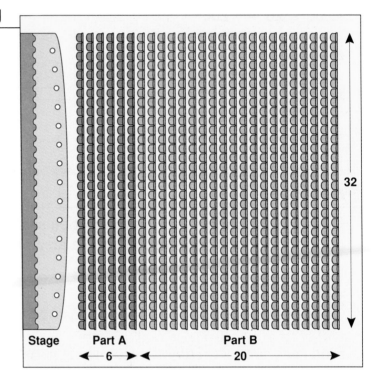

Stage | Part A | Part B
6 | 20 | 32

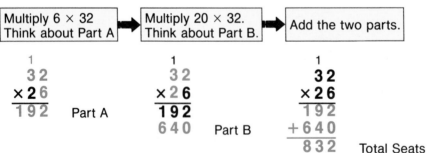

| Multiply 6 × 32 Think about Part A | → | Multiply 20 × 32. Think about Part B. | → | Add the two parts. |

```
   1
   3 2
 × 2 6
 ─────
 1 9 2    Part A
```

```
     1
     3 2
   × 2 6
   ─────
   1 9 2
   6 4 0    Part B
```

```
     1
     3 2
   × 2 6
   ─────
   1 9 2
 + 6 4 0
 ─────
   8 3 2    Total Seats
```

The auditorium has 832 seats. Is this answer reasonable?

B.
```
    5 4 2
  ×   1 8
  ───────
  4 3 3 6
+ 5 4 2 0
─────────
  9,7 5 6
```

C.
```
   $1 1.9 5
  ×      3 2
  ─────────
    2 3 9 0
+ 3 5 8 5 0
──────────
 $3 8 2.4 0
```

■ **Talk About Math** Study the examples at the left. What two factors are multiplied to find each product shown in red? in blue?

Check Understanding

For another example, see Set J, pages 286–287.

Find each product.

1. 5 × 125   **2.** 40 × 125   **3.** 45 × 125   **4.** 45 × $1.25

5. Tell how the answers to Exercises 1 and 2 help you find the answer to Exercise 3.

6. Tell how the answer to Exercise 3 helps you find the answer to Exercise 4.

Practice

For More Practice, see Set J, pages 288–289.

Multiply.

7. 16
     × 41

8. 83
     × 36

9. 52
     × 28

10. 22
      × 33

11. 220
      × 33

12. 103
      × 65

13. 370
      × 21

14. 432
      × 13

15. $8.19
      ×   53

16. $2.65
      ×   65

Tell whether you would use mental math, paper and pencil, or a calculator. Then find each product.

17. 80 × 11   **18.** 12 × 12   **19.** 70 × 100   **20.** 195 × 32

21. 17 × $4.01   **22.** $2.50 × 20   **23.** $73.65 × 42   **24.** 999 × 40

Problem Solving

Mr. Brogan is ordering supplies for making costumes. How many

25. feathers are in 12 packages?

26. yards of braid are in 18 packages?

Find the cost of

27. 15 packages of feathers.

28. 24 packages of braid.

29. 12 packages of feathers and 24 packages of braid.

ITEM	AMOUNT PER PACKAGE	COST PER PACKAGE
Feathers	200	$15.95
Braid	5 yards	$4.39

Deciding When an Estimate Is Enough

PROBLEM SOLVING
GUIDE

▶ **Understand**
QUESTION
FACTS
KEY IDEA

Plan and Solve
STRATEGY
ANSWER

Look Back
SENSIBLE ANSWER
ALTERNATE APPROACH

Build Understanding

Sometimes an estimate is good enough for an answer. At other times an exact answer is needed. The students in Grades 4, 5, and 6 are planning a boat trip. There are 83 people from Grade 4, 75 from Grade 5, and 78 from Grade 6 going on the trip. Should they request a boat that holds up to 150 passengers or one that holds up to 300 passengers? How many tickets will be needed?

Understand   QUESTIONS   What size boat is needed? How many tickets will be needed?

FACTS   There will be 83 people from Grade 4, 75 from Grade 5, and 78 from Grade 6.

KEY IDEA   Estimate the total number of people to find the size of the boat needed. The number of tickets needs to be exact.

Plan and Solve

Estimate to determine the boat size.

$$83 + 75 + 78$$
$$80 + 80 + 80 = 240$$

A boat for 300 people is needed.

Compute to find the exact number of tickets.

$$\begin{array}{r} 83 \\ 75 \\ +78 \\ \hline 236 \end{array}$$

They need 236 tickets.

Look Back   Since each of the three classes has about 80 people going on the trip, the boat that holds 150 is too small.

■ **Talk About Math**   Suppose each class has close to 100 people going on the boat trip. Can you use an estimate of 300 to choose the larger boat?

282

Check Understanding

For each problem, tell if you would estimate or find an exact answer. Then find the answer.

1. The marks on a road map show that the Bradys must travel 312 miles, 208 miles, and 406 miles to reach the ocean. About how far is it to the ocean?

2. Three music classes have 61 students, 56 students, and 49 students. How many song books are needed if each student is to have a book?

Practice

For each problem, tell if you would estimate or find an exact answer. Then find the answer.

3. Laura has $10. Can she buy 3 souvenirs that cost $3.98 each?

4. Joe earns $10.75 an hour. How much does he earn in 4 hours?

5. Sam bought a book for $21.50 and a T-shirt for $13.95. How much did he pay?

6. The boat goes about 28 feet per second. About how many feet does it travel in 5 seconds?

7. One tour boat has 84 seats. If 59 people get on the boat, how many seats will be empty?

8. About 75 postcards are sold each day. Will 3,000 postcards be enough for 28 days?

Choose a ——— Strategy

Paint by Number In a certain town, the houses on each street are numbered in order starting with 1, 2, 3, 4, . . . The town hired Bill Jones to paint each house number on the curb in front of the house. Bill was paid $1 for each digit that he painted.

9. When Bill worked on Polk Street, he earned $576. How many houses are on that street?

> PROBLEM SOLVING
> STRATEGIES
>
> Choose an Operation
> Write an Equation
> Draw a Diagram
> Solve a Simpler Problem
> Write a Number Sentence
> Make a Table
> Use Logical Reasoning
> Find a Pattern

Solve each problem.

1. Each of the 8 members of the Nature Club contributed $30 to go on a field trip. How much did the trip cost?

2. Mr. Bauer bought calendar watches for his 2 nephews. Each watch cost $85. How much did Mr. Bauer pay?

3. I was a three-digit number with digits all the same. When multiplied by one of my digits, 1,776 I became. What number was I?

4. A movie is 2 hours and 10 minutes long. If it begins at 8:30 P.M., what time will it end?

5. Mr. Aouita bought flashlights for each of the 7 members of the Explorers' Club. Each flashlight costs $9.95. What was the total cost of the 7 flashlights?

6. Mrs. Melinta's garden is 24 feet wide and 36 feet long. If she plants strawberries in a 6 foot by 8 foot space, find the area left to plant.

7. **Data File** Use data from pages 388-389. What is the area of Bedroom 2 of the Parkside Model Home?

8. **Make a Data File** Collect food advertisments from newspapers. Make a display showing items that you would buy to feed your family for one day. Find the total cost of these items.

Explore with a Calculator

Math and the Memory Keys

1. Suppose you shopped at Dan's Denim Factory and purchased 2 shirts at $9.95 each and 2 pairs of jeans at $21.50 each. What would be the total cost of your purchases?

You can use the memory keys on your calculator to figure out the total cost.

First, clear your memory by pressing $\boxed{\text{MC}}$.

		Display
Press:	2 $\boxed{\times}$ 9.95 $\boxed{=}$ $\boxed{\text{M+}}$	*19.9*
	2 $\boxed{\times}$ 21.5 $\boxed{=}$ $\boxed{\text{M+}}$	*43.*
	$\boxed{\text{MR}}$	*62.9*

The total cost of your purchase would be $62.90.

DAN'S DENIM FACTORY	
Sweaters	$11.95
Shirts	$9.95
Jeans	$21.50
Shoes	$19.75
Belts	$6.95
Vests	$24.50
Jackets	$35.95
Boots	$42.50
Skirts	$18.45

Most calculators have these memory keys	
$\boxed{\text{MC}}$	Clears the memory.
$\boxed{\text{M+}}$	Adds display to memory.
$\boxed{\text{M−}}$	Subtracts display from memory.
$\boxed{\text{MR}}$	Recalls memory to display.

2. Use the memory keys to determine each bill.

a.

```
1 Sweater
3 Shirts
3 Vests
1 Pr. Shoes

Total ____
```

b.

```
1 Jacket
2 Vests
4 Shirts
3 Skirts

Total ____
```

c.

```
2 Pr. Shoes
3 Sweaters
2 Pr. Jeans

Total ____
```

3. Which two items have a total cost of exactly $57.45?

4. Which two items have a total cost of exactly $64.00?

Reteaching

Set A   pages 254–255

It costs $40 per hour to rent a boat. What is the cost for 4 hours?

40 + 40 + 40 + 40 = 160, or

4 × 40 = 160 ← 4 × 4 tens = 16 tens

The cost for 4 hours is $160.

Remember that multiplication is repeated addition.

Multiply.

1. 50 × 7   **2.** 80 × 3

3. 5 × 60   **4.** 4 × 70

Set B   pages 256–257

Find the product of 6 × 24.

	20	4
6	Part A	Part B

$$\begin{array}{r} 120 \\ + \ 24 \\ \hline 144 \end{array}$$

6 × 24 = 144

Remember to divide the rectangle so that one part is a multiple of 10.

Find each product.

1. 32 × 6   **2.** 18 × 7

3. 26 × 5   **4.** 4 × 31

Set C   pages 258–259

Multiply 4 × 28.

Multiply the ones. Rename 30 ones as 3 tens.

$$\begin{array}{r} 3 \\ 28 \\ \times \ 4 \\ \hline 2 \end{array}$$

$$\begin{array}{r} 3 \\ 28 \\ \times \ 4 \\ \hline 112 \end{array}$$

Multiply the tens. Add the extra tens. 8 tens + 3 tens = 11 tens.

Remember to add the extra tens after you multiply the tens.

Multiply.

1. $\begin{array}{r} 12 \\ \times \ 5 \end{array}$ **2.** $\begin{array}{r} 23 \\ \times \ 6 \end{array}$ **3.** $\begin{array}{r} 47 \\ \times \ 4 \end{array}$

Set D   pages 260–261

A water tank holds 400 gallons. How much water do 3 tanks hold?

400 + 400 + 400 = 1,200

3 × 400 = 1,200 ← 3 × 4 hundreds

The water tank holds 1,200 gallons.

Remember to think of 200 and 500 as 2 hundreds and 5 hundreds.

Multiply.

1. 7 × 200   **2.** 500 × 6

3. 800 × 9   **4.** 8 × 600

Set E   pages 264–265

Multiply 7 × 193.

$$\begin{array}{r} 2 \\ 193 \\ \times \ 7 \\ \hline 1 \end{array}$$

$$\begin{array}{r} 62 \\ 193 \\ \times \ 7 \\ \hline 51 \end{array}$$

$$\begin{array}{r} 62 \\ 193 \\ \times \ 7 \\ \hline 1,351 \end{array}$$

Remember to estimate the product to see if your answer is reasonable.

Multiply.

1. $\begin{array}{r} 146 \\ \times \ 7 \end{array}$ **2.** $\begin{array}{r} 354 \\ \times \ 8 \end{array}$ **3.** $\begin{array}{r} 529 \\ \times \ 3 \end{array}$

Set F pages 266–267

Multiply 6 × $4.72.

Multiply as with whole numbers.

```
    4 1
 $ 4.7 2      $4.72 = 472¢
×      6
 $ 2 8.3 2    2,832¢ = $28.32
```

Remember to write the dollar sign and cents point in the product.

Multiply.

1. $ 0.0 7   **2.** $ 2.1 6
    ×   8   ×   7

Set G pages 272–273

Find the missing factor.

▦ × 67 = 6,700

Thousands	Hundreds	Tens	Ones
6	7	0	0

So, 100 × 67 = 6,700.

Remember you can use a place-value chart to help you find the missing factor. Find each missing factor.

1. ▦ × 27 = 270

2. 46 × ▦ = 46,000

Set H pages 274–275

Multiply 60 × 40.

Think of 60 as 6 × 10.
Think of 40 as 4 × 10.

60 × 40 = 6 × 10 × 4 × 10
         = 24 × 100 = 2,400

Remember to think of multiples of 10. Multiply.

1. 70 × 4   **2.** 30 × 50

3. 400 × 40   **4.** 80 × 600

Set I pages 276–277

Round to estimate 586 × 32.

586 is closer to 600 than 500.
32 is closer to 30 than 40.
600 × 30 = 18,000.

So, 586 × 32 is about 18,000.

Remember to round 3-digit numbers to the nearest hundred and 2-digit numbers to the nearest ten.

Estimate each product.

1. 34 × 17   **2.** 310 × 62

Set J pages 280–281

Multiply 26 × 43.

Think of 26
as 20 + 6.

```
                1
                43
              × 26
6 × 43 ——→    258
20 × 43 ——→   860
             1,118
```

Remember to estimate to check if the product is reasonable.

Multiply.

1. 46   **2.** 57   **3.** 78
   × 13   × 26   × 39

Practice

pages 254–255

Math   Multiply.

1. 4 × 10   2. 7 × 50   3. 80 × 6   4. 5 × 40   5. 90 × 6

Estimation   Estimate the product. Tell whether your estimate is greater than or less than the exact product.

6. 6 × 73   7. 58 × 4   8. 7 × 95   9. 42 × 6   10. 5 × 28

Set B   pages 256–257

Draw a rectangle on grid paper for each multiplication sentence. Divide the rectangle into two parts, and show the number of squares in each part.

1. 6 × 12 = 72   2. 24 × 4 = 96   3. 2 × 28 = 56   4. 3 × 32 = 96

Find each product. Draw a rectangle if necessary.

5. 5 × 10   6. 16 × 4   7. 42 × 3   8. 27 × 5   9. 7 × 34

Set C   pages 258–259

Multiply.

1. 29 × 2   2. 14 × 4   3. 23 × 7   4. 76 × 3   5. 47 × 5

6. 4 × 24   7. 37 × 9   8. 25 × 6   9. 7 × 73   10. 85 × 2

Set D   pages 260–261

Mental Math   Multiply.

1. 7 × 100   2. 100 × 6   3. 7 × 500   4. 9 × 800   5. 4 × 700

Estimation   Estimate the product. Tell whether your estimate is greater than or less than the actual product.

6. 4 × 608   7. 585 × 6   8. 8 × 762   9. 450 × 7   10. 5 × 421

Set E   pages 264–265

Multiply.

1.   268   2.   234   3.   149   4.   374   5.   706
   ×   4   ×   3   ×   5   ×   9   ×   6

6. 2 × 230   7. 408 × 3   8. 7 × 235   9. 904 × 5   10. 840 × 9

Set F   pages 266–267

Multiply.

1. $ 0.0 9
      ×   7

2. $ 0.4 6
      ×   2

3. $ 6.3 4
      ×   8

4. $ 5.0 8
      ×   6

5. $ 1 6.0 0
      ×   3

Set G   pages 272–273

Find each product.

1. 10 × 35   **2.** 36 × 1,000   **3.** 100 × 72   **4.** 592 × 100

Find each missing factor.

5. 100 × ▦ = 700   **6.** ▦ × 37 = 3,700   **7.** 380 × ▦ = 3,800

Mental Math   Multiply the underlined factors first. Then multiply by the other factor to find each product.

8. 5̲ × 2̲ × 49   **9.** 2̲ × 85 × 5̲0̲   **10.** 4̲ × 2̲5̲ × 19   **11.** 5̲ × 67 × 2̲0̲

Set H   pages 274–275

Multiply.

1. 50 × 4   **2.** 70 × 60   **3.** 90 × 630   **4.** 50 × 708

Mixed Practice   Find each product.

5.   40
      × 80

6.   147
      ×   3

7.   84
      × 20

8.   56
      × 6

9.   582
      ×   4

10.   706
       ×   9

Set I   pages 276–277

Find a range for each product.

1. 56 × 40   **2.** 30 × 38   **3.** 49 × 27   **4.** 88 × 187   **5.** 507 × 60

Estimate. Choose any method.

6. 32 × 45   **7.** 24 × 16   **8.** 88 × 12   **9.** 47 × 531   **10.** 669 × 51

Set J   pages 280–281

Multiply.

1.   38
      × 12

2.   62
      × 26

3.   79
      × 31

4.   304
      × 75

5. $ 5.3 7
      ×   4 3

Enrichment

Parentheses and the Distributive Property

Study Examples A and B below. To find each
value, do the operations in parentheses first.

A. Find the value of 8 + (10 × 5).
Multiply 10 and 5 first.
Then add.

$$8 + (10 × 5) =$$
$$8 + 50 =$$
$$58$$

B. Find the value of (8 + 10) × 5.
Add 8 and 10 first.
Then multiply.

$$(8 + 10) × 5 =$$
$$18 × 5 =$$
$$90$$

Recall that a product such as 38 × 7 can be
thought of as 30 × 7 plus 8 × 7. This
relationship can be written as a number sentence
with parentheses.

$$(30 + 8) × 7 = (30 × 7) + (8 × 7)$$

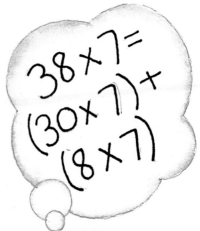

This number sentence is an example of the
distributive property. Instead of multiplying
the sum of 30 + 8 by 7, you can *distribute*,
or spread out, the multiplication.

Find each value. **Remember** to do the
operations in parentheses first.

1. 4 + (6 × 5)   **2.** (4 + 6) × 5

3. (20 × 4) + (9 × 4)   **4.** (20 + 9) × 4

Copy and complete. Then find the value of each
side of the number sentence.

5. (50 + 9) × 3 = (▦ × 3) + (▦ × 3)

6. 7 × (40 + 1) = (7 × ▦) + (7 × ▦)

7. (90 + 5) × 26 = (▦ × 26) + (▦ × 26)

8. 38 × (60 + 8) = (38 × ▦) + (38 × ▦)

Chapter 8 Review/Test

Multiply.

1. 7×80 **2.** 60×5

3. 69×7 **4.** 4×38

5. 8×300 **6.** 700×4

7. 8×726 **8.** 5×840

9. $7 \times \$0.09$ **10.** $9 \times \$2.78$

11. 80×90 **12.** 805×50

13. 86×21 **14.** 27×375

Tell if the number is a multiple of 2, 3, or 5. If the number is not a multiple of 2, 3, or 5, write *none of these*.

15. 714   **16.** 5,189   **17.** 1,850

Find each missing factor.

18. $100 \times \text{▓} = 800$

19. $\text{▓} \times 100 = 13,000$

Estimate each product. Choose any method.

20. 71×52 **21.** 589×62

22. Draw a rectangle for the multiplication sentence below. Divide the rectangle into two parts. Show the area of each part.

$28 \times 30 = 840$

Name the part of the rectangle that matches each sentence.

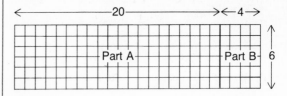

23. $20 \times 6 = 120$ **24.** $4 \times 6 = 24$

25. Write a multiplication sentence to show the area of the rectangle above.

26. What exchange can you make to show this amount of money using the least number of bills?

$100 $10 $10 $10 $10 $10 $1

$100 $10 $10 $10 $10 $10

For Items 27–29, use these facts.

Clare has $20. Cassette tapes cost $3.95 each.

27. Which estimate could you use to find out whether Clare can buy 5 cassettes with her money?
  a. $5 \times 4 = 20$
  b. $20 + 4 = 24$
  c. $5 \times 3 = 15$

28. Can Clare buy 5 cassettes?

29. Can Clare buy 3 cassettes and an $8.25 carrying case?

30. **Write About Math** Explain how you decided whether the number in Item 16 is a multiple of 3.

Division: One-digit Divisors

9

Did You Know: Whole wheat bread contains fiber and important minerals. Bread from commercial bakeries is enriched with vitamins to help prevent certain diseases.

Number-Sense Project

Estimate

Predict how many slices of bread your family will eat in the next 3 days.

Gather Data

Count the number of slices of bread in your house. (If bread is bought during that time, add those slices to the amount.) In 3 days, count how many slices are left.

Analyze and Report

Compute how many slices were used. Compare your results with other students.

Dividing Multiples of 10 and 100

Build Understanding

A. Dawn and two other students received 90¢ for recycling cans. They want to share the money equally. How much money should each student get?

Think of dividing 9 dimes into 3 equal groups.

Each student gets 30¢. You can write this division sentence:
90 ÷ 3 = 30

B. Estimation Another group of students brought 900 cans in 4 large bags. Each bag contained about the same number. About how many cans were in each bag?

Think of 9 hundreds divided by 4. The quotient is 2 hundreds with 1 hundred left over.

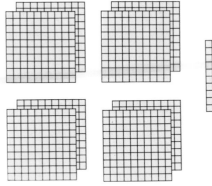

900 ÷ 4 = 200 R100

Each bag contained about 200 cans.

■ **Talk About Math** In Example B, can you be sure that each bag had 200 or more cans? Why or why not?

Check Understanding

For another example, see Set A, pages 316–317.

Complete each problem.

1. 16 tens ÷ 4 = ▦ tens
160 ÷ 4 = ▦

2. 6 hundreds ÷ 3 = ▦ hundreds
600 ÷ 3 = ▦

3. 60 ÷ 5 is about ▦.

4. 70 ÷ 2 is about ▦.

5. 320 ÷ 6 is about ▦.

6. 900 ÷ 2 is about ▦.

Practice

For More Practice, see Set A, pages 318–319.

Mental Math   Divide.

7. 70 ÷ 7

8. 60 ÷ 3

9. 80 ÷ 2

10. 80 ÷ 4

11. 120 ÷ 6

12. 320 ÷ 4

13. 180 ÷ 2

14. 350 ÷ 7

15. 500 ÷ 5

16. 900 ÷ 3

17. 300 ÷ 3

18. 100 ÷ 5

19. 800 ÷ 4

20. 300 ÷ 6

21. 300 ÷ 5

22. 400 ÷ 8

Estimation   Estimate each quotient.

23. 70 ÷ 3

24. 90 ÷ 7

25. 160 ÷ 5

26. 310 ÷ 4

27. 900 ÷ 5

28. 800 ÷ 3

29. 847 ÷ 2

30. 453 ÷ 8

Problem Solving

Number Sense   Use numbers from the cans to make the sentences reasonable.

31. Dawn and her ▦ friends collected a total of ▦ cans. They each collected the same number of cans. Each of the ▦ girls collected ▦ cans.

32. The recycling center was open ▦ hours on Saturday. During that time people brought in ▦ pounds of cans. This was about ▦ pounds per hour.

180   3   60   2

200   4   800

Sharing Dimes and Pennies

Build Understanding

Be Fair!
Materials: Play money (dimes and pennies)
Groups: 2 to 4 students

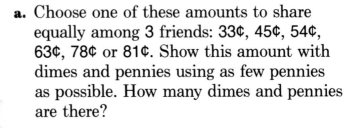

a. Choose one of these amounts to share equally among 3 friends: 33¢, 45¢, 54¢, 63¢, 78¢ or 81¢. Show this amount with dimes and pennies using as few pennies as possible. How many dimes and pennies are there?

b. Divide the dimes into three piles. How many dimes are in each pile? Are there any dimes left over?

c. Trade each leftover dime for ten pennies. How many pennies are there to share?

d. Divide the pennies among the three piles. How many dimes and how many pennies are in each pile? How much money is this? Are there any pennies left over?

■ **Talk About Math**   Why is it necessary to trade the leftover dimes for pennies?

Check Understanding

For another example, see Set B, page 316–317.

Divide the money into equal shares. Then copy and complete the division sentence.

1. 52¢ shared by 4 people
52 ÷ 4 = ▦

Practice

For More Practice, see Set B, pages 318–319.

Use play money to find equal shares. Then copy
and complete the division sentence.

2. 48¢ shared by 4 people
$48 \div 4 = $ ▦

3. 63¢ shared by 3 people
$63 \div 3 = $ ▦

4. 72¢ shared by 9 people
$72 \div 9 = $ ▦

5. 65¢ shared by 5 people
$65 \div 5 = $ ▦

6. 56¢ shared by 4 people
$56 \div 4 = $ ▦

7. 51¢ shared by 3 people
$51 \div 3 = $ ▦

8. 80¢ shared by 5 people
$80 \div 5 = $ ▦

9. $1.35 shared by 3 people
$135 \div 3 = $ ▦

Problem Solving

10. Critical Thinking Find amounts
less than 20¢ that cannot be shared
equally among 4 students. Tell the
pattern you see.

Choose a Strategy

Drink Juice for a Change A juice
machine sells cans of juice for 50¢. The
machine takes only exact change. It accepts
quarters, dimes, and nickels. For example, you
could buy a can of juice with two quarters.

11. Suppose you used only nickels. How many
nickels would you need to buy a can of
juice?

12. Find eight more ways to show 50¢.
Record your answers, telling how many
quarters, dimes, and nickels you used.

PROBLEM SOLVING
STRATEGIES

Choose an Operation
Try and Check
Draw a Diagram
Solve a Simpler Problem
Write a Number Sentence
Make a Table
Use Logical Reasoning
Find a Pattern

Recording Division

Build Understanding

Abe, Ben, and Carl want to share 43¢.
How much money should each receive?

Find 3)‾43. Study how to record each step.

Divide the dimes.	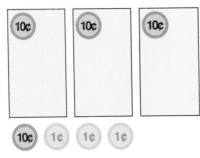	Dimes	Pennies	
		1		1 dime each
		3)4	3	
		− 3		3 dimes shared
		1		1 dime left over

Trade the leftover dime for 10 pennies.		Dimes	Pennies	
		1		
		3)4	3	
		− 3		
		1	3	13 pennies to share

Divide the pennies.	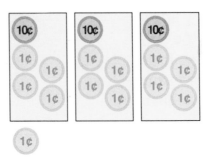	Dimes	Pennies	
		1	4 R1	4 pennies each
				Remainder 1
		3)4	3	
		− 3		
		1	3	
		− 1	2	12 pennies shared
			1	1 penny left over

Each boy receives 14¢. There is 1¢ left over.

■ **Talk About Math**   How can you tell if the
quotient will be greater than or less than 10¢?

Check Understanding

For another example, see Set C, pages 316–317.

Copy and complete. Use dimes and pennies if necessary.

1.

Dimes	Pennies
▦	▦

4)4 8
− ▦
0 8
− ▦
▦

2.

Dimes	Pennies
▦	▦

2)5 6
− 4
▦ ▦
− ▦ ▦
▦

3.

Dimes	Pennies
▦	▦ R▦

3)8 3
− 6
2 ▦
− ▦ ▦
▦

Practice

For More Practice, see Set C, pages 318–319.

Divide. Show dimes and pennies if necessary.

4. 2)28   **5.** 5)57   **6.** 5)65   **7.** 4)85   **8.** 2)50

9. 3)75   **10.** 5)82   **11.** 3)81   **12.** 2)37   **13.** 3)94

14. 3)53   **15.** 3)65   **16.** 4)72   **17.** 2)56   **18.** 5)95

Problem Solving

How much should each person pay?

19. Peanuts shared by three people

20. Popcorn shared by two people

Explore ———— Math

Divide. Write the quotient and remainder.

21. 4)50   **22.** 4)51   **23.** 4)52   **24.** 4)53   **25.** 4)54   **26.** 4)55

27. What are the possible remainders when dividing by 4?

Dividing 2-Digit Numbers by 1-Digit Numbers

Build Understanding

The fourth-grade students at Friendship School were reading stories about Paul Bunyan. The chart shows a typical meal for Paul.

200-pound steak
323 potatoes
250 cups of green beans
76 loaves of bread
58 baked apples
44 gallons of milk

If the bread was baked in batches of 6 loaves, how many complete batches were made? How many loaves were in the last batch?

Find $6\overline{)76}$.

| Divide the tens. ▯▶ | Bring down the ones. ▯▶ | Divide the ones. |

Tens	Ones		Tens	Ones		Tens	Ones
1			1			1	2 R4
6)7	6		6)7	6		6)7	6
−6	6 tens shared.		−6	↓		−6	
1	1 ten left over.		1	6	16 ones to share.		1	6
						−1	2	12 ones shared.
							4	4 ones left over.

There were 12 complete batches. The last batch had 4 loaves.

You can check a division problem using the method shown at the right.

Check

$$\begin{array}{r} 12 \\ \times\ 6 \\ \hline 72 \\ +\ 4 \\ \hline 76 \end{array}$$

■ **Talk About Math** Which of these quotients will be more than 10? How do you know?

$5\overline{)43}$ $4\overline{)62}$ $9\overline{)75}$

Paul Bunyan was a legendary hero in American lumber camps.

300

Check Understanding

For another example, see Set D, pages 316–317.

Copy and complete.

1.
Tens	Ones
1	▦ R▦
7)9	2
−7	
▦	▦
−▦	▦
	▦

2.
Tens	Ones
▦	▦ R▦
4)8	7
−▦	
0	▦
−	▦
	▦

3.
Tens	Ones
	▦ R▦
9)6	5
−▦	▦
	2

Check each problem. If the problem is correct, write OK. If not, write the correct answer.

4. $\overset{9 \text{ R}1}{8)73}$ 5. $\overset{11}{6)68}$ 6. $\overset{16 \text{ R}2}{5)82}$ 7. $\overset{14 \text{ R}1}{7)92}$

Practice

For More Practice, see Set D, pages 318–319.

Use estimation to tell whether the quotient will be greater than or less than 10. Then divide.

8. 8)78   9. 8)96   10. 9)38   11. 5)84   12. 7)62

13. 5)74   14. 4)51   15. 8)92   16. 7)63   17. 6)92

18. 5)40   19. 9)99   20. 7)96   21. 6)76   22. 8)44

Problem Solving

Solve each problem.

23. Hot Biscuit Slim baked batches of 9 apples. How many complete batches did he make for Paul's meal on page 300? How many apples were in the last batch?

24. Paul's toothpicks were 4-foot logs. How many toothpicks could be made from five 12-foot logs?

TIPS FOR PROBLEM SOLVERS

Be confident so you can do your best.

Make a Table

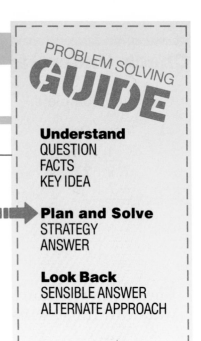

PROBLEM SOLVING GUIDE

Understand
QUESTION
FACTS
KEY IDEA

▐▐▐▶ **Plan and Solve**
STRATEGY
ANSWER

Look Back
SENSIBLE ANSWER
ALTERNATE APPROACH

Build Understanding

Mr. Penn wants to buy a pencil for each of the 25 students in his class. How many different ways can he buy them?

Understand   QUESTION   How many ways can he buy exactly 25 pencils?

FACTS   He must buy blue pencils by the box. There are 4 in each box. Red pencils are sold separately.

KEY IDEA   Find all the ways that he can buy red pencils and boxes of blue pencils.

▐▐▐▶ **Plan and Solve**   STRATEGY   Make a table to show the combinations of pencils that he could buy. Begin with the greatest number of boxes without going over 25 pencils.

ANSWER   There are 7 ways to buy 25 pencils.

Look Back   SENSIBLE ANSWER   He could not buy 7 boxes of blue pencils. Why? The table shows all combinations of pencils using less than 7 boxes of blue pencils. The answer makes sense.

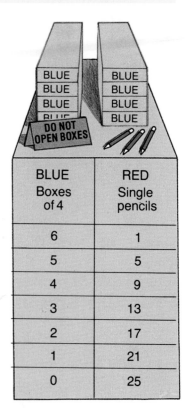

BLUE Boxes of 4	RED Single pencils
6	1
5	5
4	9
3	13
2	17
1	21
0	25

▐ **Talk About Math**   Can Mr. Penn get the exact number of pencils if he decides to buy only blue pencils? Explain your answer.

Check Understanding

Suppose Mr. Penn also decides to buy 3 blue pencils for himself.

1. How many pencils will he need to buy altogether?

2. Copy and complete the table.

3. How many choices does he have?

BLUE Boxes of 4	RED Single Pencils
7	0
6	

Practice

Make a table to help you answer each question.

4. There are 30 students in Mrs. Michal's art class. How many ways can she buy exactly 30 pieces of chalk?

5. If a box of mixed chalk is $1.00 and a box of white is $1.50, which choice is the best buy?

6. Mr. Penn is going to buy large fun-shaped erasers for his students. He is deciding between white elephants which come 3 to a box, and blue whales which are sold separately. How many choices does he have for buying 25 erasers?

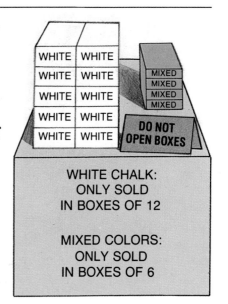

WHITE CHALK:
ONLY SOLD
IN BOXES OF 12

MIXED COLORS:
ONLY SOLD
IN BOXES OF 6

Midchapter  **Checkup**

Divide.

1. $80 \div 4$ 2. $200 \div 5$ 3. $3\overline{)81}$ 4. $6\overline{)74}$ 5. $8\overline{)97}$

6. If you share 72¢ among 4 people, how much money will each person get?

7. Make a table to show the number of choices if Miss MacArthur wants to buy exactly 20 posters.

POSTERS

WHITE: Only sold in packages of 5

MIXED COLORS: Only sold in single sheets

Explore as a Team

Suppose you want to buy one of an item that is priced by the group, such as 2 for 99¢ or 3 for 25¢. You can divide to find the *unit price*, or price for one. If there is a remainder, round the price up to the nearest cent.

3 for 50¢

4 for 72¢

6 for 77¢

5 for 83¢

8 for 99¢

2 for 35¢

1. Look at the price signs. Guess which items have the same unit price.

2. Discuss your guesses with other students on your team. Then compute unit prices. Were your guesses correct?

3. Think of other ways to write the prices so that the unit prices are the same. Write the prices for groups of 8 or fewer items. Discuss your answers with other team members.

4. Make lists of prices that go with each unit price. Find a rule for writing prices that will have a certain unit price.

TIPS FOR
WORKING TOGETHER

Be a good tutor. Make up similar problems or easier ones to help someone understand.

Number-Sense Project

Look back at pages 292-293.

1. A family used 46 slices of bread in 3 days. About how many slices per day was this?

2. A family used 89 slices of bread in 7 days. About how many slices per day was this?

3. A loaf of bread has about 20 slices. A school used 1,000 slices of bread in a day. About how many loaves of bread was this?

MATH Laugh

What occurs once in every minute, twice in every moment, but not once in a thousand years?

ANSWER: The letter M

Math-at-Home Activity

Take a survey of 12 people you know. Ask the people how many times they smile in an average day. Graph the results.

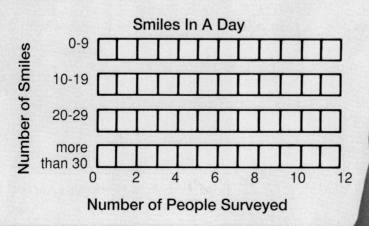

Smiles In A Day

Number of Smiles: 0-9, 10-19, 20-29, more than 30

Number of People Surveyed: 0 2 4 6 8 10 12

Dividing 3-Digit Numbers by 1-Digit Numbers

Build Understanding

A. The chart lists heights of several waterfalls. Bridalveil Falls is how many times as high as a 5-foot tall student?

Divide to find how many 5s are in 620.

Heights of Waterfalls

Big Manitou	165 ft
Akaka	442 ft
Fall Creek	256 ft
Bridalveil	620 ft

Divide the hundreds.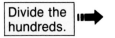

Hundreds	Tens	Ones
1		
5) 6	2	0
− 5		
1		

Bring down the tens. Divide the tens.

Hundreds	Tens	Ones
1	2	
5) 6	2	0
− 5	↓	
1	2	
− 1	0	
	2	

Bring down the ones. Divide the ones.

Hundreds	Tens	Ones
1	2	4
5) 6	2	0
− 5		
1	2	
− 1	0	↓
	2	0
	− 2	0
		0

The waterfall is 124 times as high as a 5-foot tall student.

B. Divide to find how many 9s are in 486.

```
    5 4
9)4 8 6
 −4 5
    3 6
  −3 6
     0
```

■ **Talk About Math** How can you tell if a quotient will be greater than or less than 100?

Bridalveil Falls is in Yosemite National Park in California.

Check Understanding

For another example, see Set E, pages 316–317.

Copy and complete.

1.

Hundreds	Tens	Ones
▦	▦	▦
5) 6	4	5
− 5		
▦	▦	
− ▦	▦	
	▦	▦
	▦	▦
		▦

2.

Hundreds	Tens	Ones
	▦	▦ R ▦
8) 4	6	2
− ▦	▦	
	6	2
	▦	▦
		▦

3. 4)272

4. 7)928

Practice

For More Practice, see Set E, pages 318–319.

Tell whether the quotient will be greater than or less than 100. Then divide.

5. 5)580   **6.** 9)459   **7.** 2)586   **8.** 6)777   **9.** 8)479

For Exercises 10–13, tell whether you would use paper and pencil or mental math. Then find each quotient.

10. 366 ÷ 6   **11.** 500 ÷ 5   **12.** 252 ÷ 4   **13.** 448 ÷ 7

Problem Solving

Solve. Use the chart on page 306.

14. About how high is Taughannock Falls if it is half as high as Akaka Falls?

15. Mental Math About how high is Feather Falls if it is 20 feet higher than Bridalveil Falls?

Reading ——— Math

Numbers and Symbols Match each number sentence with its description.

1. The divisor is 3 and the dividend is 27.

2. A factor is 3 and the product is 27.

3. An addend is 3 and the sum is 27.

A. 3 × 9 = 27

B. 24 + 3 = 27

C. 27 ÷ 3 = 9

Zeros in the Quotient

Build Understanding

A. A rancher is going to repair some 6-foot sections of fence. He has 63 feet of fencing stored in a shed. How many 6-foot sections can he repair?

Find 63 ÷ 6.

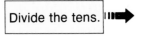

Divide the tens. 	Bring down the ones. Divide the ones.

Tens	Ones
1	
6)6	3
−6	
0	

Tens	Ones	
1	0	R 3
6)6	3	
−6	↓	
0	3	
−	0	
	3	

There are not enough ones to divide by 6. Write 0 in the ones place in the quotient.

The rancher can mend 10 six-foot sections. How much fencing will be left over?

B. Find 824 ÷ 4.

```
   206
4)824
 −8
  02
  −0
   24
  −24
    0
```

There are not enough tens to divide by 4. Write 0 tens in the quotient.

■ Talk About Math

In Example B, tell how you know that 206 is a reasonable answer.

Check Understanding

For another example, see Set F, pages 316–317.

Divide.

1. 5)$\overline{54}$ **2.** 3)$\overline{628}$ **3.** 7)$\overline{845}$ **4.** 6)$\overline{603}$ **5.** 4)$\overline{323}$

Practice

For More Practice, see Set F, pages 318–319.

Divide.

6. 3)$\overline{152}$ **7.** 7)$\overline{75}$ **8.** 4)$\overline{600}$ **9.** 8)$\overline{818}$ **10.** 2)$\overline{861}$

11. 6)$\overline{643}$ **12.** 5)$\overline{505}$ **13.** 3)$\overline{62}$ **14.** 6)$\overline{184}$ **15.** 4)$\overline{803}$

Mixed Practice   Tell whether you would use paper
and pencil or mental math. Then find each quotient.

16. 4)$\overline{84}$ **17.** 6)$\overline{342}$ **18.** 2)$\overline{750}$ **19.** 9)$\overline{369}$ **20.** 7)$\overline{84}$

21. 8)$\overline{576}$ **22.** 5)$\overline{65}$ **23.** 3)$\overline{600}$ **24.** 4)$\overline{76}$ **25.** 9)$\overline{972}$

Problem Solving

Solve each problem.

26. Five ranch hands worked a total
of 50 hours. If each one worked
an equal number of hours, how
many did each work?

27. If 312 bales of hay were loaded
equally onto 3 trucks, how many
bales were on each truck?

Skills _____ **Review**   pages 108–109,
114–115, 120–121

Solve.

1. How many minutes is it from
9:30 A.M. until 10:15 A.M.?

2. How many hours is it from
9 P.M. until 6 A.M.?

Choose the most sensible measure.

3. Length of a baseball bat
35 in.   35 ft   35 yd

4. Height of a flagpole
15 cm   15 m   15 km

Dividing Money

Build Understanding

A. Mrs. Sharpe manages a supermarket. Part of her job is to list the unit prices of the items in the store. For example, 3 pounds of laundry soap cost $4.47. To find the cost per pound, Mrs. Sharpe divides $4.47 by 3.

```
       Dollars  Dimes  Pennies
         $  1  .  4    9
       3)$  4  .  4    7
         - 3
         ─────
            1     4
          - 1     2
          ─────
                  2    7
              -   2    7
              ─────────
                       0
```

Divide the dollars. Write the quotient above the dollars in the dividend. Write a dollar sign and cents point as shown.

How many dollars are remaining? Think of 1 dollar 4 dimes as 14 dimes.

How many dimes are remaining? Think of 2 dimes 7 pennies as 27 pennies.

The laundry soap costs $1.49 per pound.

B. Decide if $73.50 ÷ 7 will be more or less than $10. Then find the actual quotient.

Think of $73.50 as a little more than $70. $70 ÷ 7 = $10. So, the quotient will be a little more than $10.

```
        $ 1 0 . 5 0
      7)$ 7 3 . 5 0
       - 7
       ────
         0 3
       -   0
       ────
           3 5
         - 3 5
         ─────
             0 0
```

■ **Write About Math** Explain how $12 can be shared equally among 8 people.

The next time you are in a supermarket, look for unit pricing labels on the shelves.

For Exercises 1–2, copy and complete each problem. For Exercises 3–4, copy and finish each problem.

1.
$$
\begin{array}{r}
\$1.\blacksquare\blacksquare \\
4\overline{)\$5.40} \\
-4 \\
\hline
1\,\blacksquare \\
-\blacksquare\,\blacksquare \\
\hline
\blacksquare\,\blacksquare \\
-\blacksquare\,\blacksquare \\
\hline
\blacksquare
\end{array}
$$

2.
$$
\begin{array}{r}
\$0.\blacksquare\blacksquare \\
8\overline{)\$2.00} \\
-\blacksquare\,\blacksquare \\
\hline
4\,0 \\
-\blacksquare\,\blacksquare \\
\hline
\blacksquare
\end{array}
$$

3.
$$
\begin{array}{r}
\$6.\blacksquare\blacksquare \\
6\overline{)\$36.72} \\
-36 \\
\hline
\blacksquare
\end{array}
$$

4.
$$
\begin{array}{r}
\$24.\blacksquare\blacksquare \\
3\overline{)\$74.25} \\
-6 \\
\hline
1\,4 \\
-1\,2 \\
\hline
\blacksquare
\end{array}
$$

Estimate to decide if each quotient is greater than or less than $10. Then divide. **Remember** to write a dollar sign and cents point in each quotient.

5. $6\overline{)\$31.80}$ 6. $3\overline{)\$3.75}$ 7. $7\overline{)\$4.41}$ 8. $4\overline{)\$80.24}$

9. $5\overline{)\$24.00}$ 10. $8\overline{)\$80.80}$ 11. $2\overline{)\$6.14}$ 12. $9\overline{)\$7.11}$

For Exercises 13–21, tell whether you will use paper and pencil or mental math. Then divide to find the cost of one item.

13. 3 for $90.60

14. 5 for $6.05

15. 7 for $17.99

16. 6 for $5.76

17. 9 for $9.99

18. 7 for $220.50

19. 5 for $108.30

20. 8 for $23.44

21. 4 for $400.40

Problem Solving

Solve each problem.

22. A 6-ounce box of wild rice costs $1.44. Find the cost per ounce.

23. **Use Data** Refer to the table on page 300. If a gallon of milk costs about $1.59 at the supermarket, how much would Paul Bunyan have paid for milk?

Interpret the Remainder

Build Understanding

Students from Taft School are going to a museum. One adult will be guiding each group of 6 students. No group of students will be larger than 6. How many adults will be needed for 83 students?

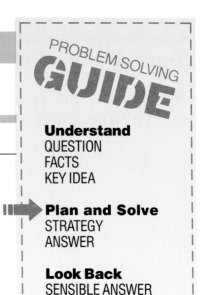

PROBLEM SOLVING
GUIDE

Understand
QUESTION
FACTS
KEY IDEA

Plan and Solve
STRATEGY
ANSWER

Look Back
SENSIBLE ANSWER
ALTERNATE APPROACH

Understand   One adult is needed for each group of 6 or fewer students. You can divide to find the number of groups of 6.

Plan and Solve   STRATEGY   Divide 83 by 6. If there is a remainder, there will be one more group.

$$\begin{array}{r} 13 \text{ R } 5 \\ 6\overline{)83} \\ -6 \\ \hline 23 \\ -18 \\ \hline 5 \end{array}$$

ANSWER   To have an adult for each group, 14 adults will be needed.

Look Back   Fourteen adults can guide 14×6 or 84 students. Since there are 83 students, 14 adults will be enough.

■ **Talk About Math**   How many $6 items can be purchased for $83 at the museum gift shop? Did you use the remainder in your answer?

Check Understanding

Problems 1–4 all use the fact that 52 ÷ 3 = 17 R1. For each problem, tell whether the answer is 17 or 18.

1. How many $3 souvenirs can you buy for $52?

2. How many 3-packs of postcards should you buy if you need 52?

3. How many 3-inch-thick books can make a stack at least 52 inches tall?

4. In a class of 52 students, how many groups of 3 students can be made?

Practice

Solve each problem.

5. Sue wants to buy 5¢ dinosaur stickers at the museum shop. How many stickers can she buy for 88¢?

6. If Sue buys as many 5¢ stickers as she can, how much money will she have left?

7. The museum has 79 Indian arrowheads. Each shelf can display 8 arrowheads. How many shelves are needed to display all the arrowheads?

8. A 7-minute film is shown at the buffalo exhibit. How many times can the whole film be shown in 120 minutes?

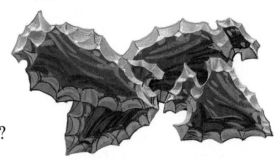

9. **Calculator** Every twelfth person entering the museum on Monday pays no admission cost. Last Monday 986 people entered the museum. How many got in free?

Choose a _____ Strategy

10. **Visit the Museum.** At the museum you can choose to go on 3 different tours, to see 2 different films, and to hear 3 different lectures. How many combinations of choices do you have if you want to go on one tour, see one film, and hear one lecture?

Problem Solving REVIEW

Solve each problem.

1. 3 friends equally shared a package of sunflower seeds that cost $0.93. How much should each person pay?

2. Warren baked 84 blueberry muffins. He divided them equally among 5 friends. How many muffins were left over?

3. Fruit bars come in packages of 3 for $1.29 and separately for $0.50 each. What is the least expensive way Jerome can buy exactly 20 fruit bars?

4. The Sato family is making a 960 mile trip. If they travel about the same distance each of 4 days, how far should they travel each day?

5. Can 9 people share 3,186 baseball cards equally?

6. Ben, Renaldo, Yuri and Steve each threw the discus. Yuri's throw was longest. Ben's throw was 4 feet farther than Renaldo's. Steve's throw was 8 feet shorter than Renaldo's. Whose throw was shortest?

7. **Data File** Use data from pages 388-389. A fruit market sold 72 pecks of apples in one day. How many bushels of apples was this?

8. **Make a Data File** Use unit prices to compare the cost of different size packages of the same item. Is it always cheaper to buy the largest size? Give examples.

Explore with a Calculator

Dartboard Multiplication

This game involves computerized darts and a number board. The computer throws five darts at numbered sections on the screen. The darts always land on a numbered section. The score is the product of the five numbers.

1. Use a calculator to answer these questions.

a. What score is shown by the darts on the board?

b. What is the greatest possible score?

c. What is the least possible score?

d. What numbers could the five darts have landed on if the score was 9,216?

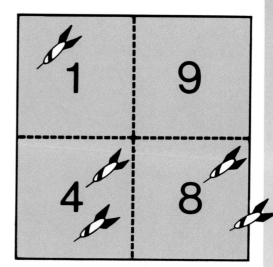

2. Use the number board at the right for these problems. With this number board, the score is the product of the numbers that four darts land on.

a. What is the greatest possible score?

b. What is the least possible score?

c. What numbers could the four darts have landed on if the score was 324?

d. What numbers could the four darts have landed on if the score was 1,600?

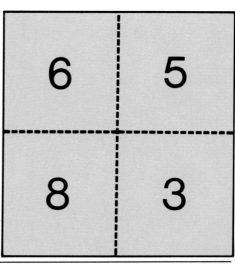

Reteaching

Set A pages 294–295

Find 180 ÷ 3.

18 tens ÷ 3 = 6 tens, or 60

So, 180 ÷ 3 = 60.

Remember that 80 can be thought of as 8 dimes. Divide.

1. 120 ÷ 6   **2.** 250 ÷ 5   **3.** 800 ÷ 4

Set B pages 296–297

Show how to share 52¢ with 4 people.

Give each person 1 dime. Trade the leftover dime for 10 pennies. Give each person 3 pennies.

Each person receives 13¢.

Remember when sharing money equally you trade any leftover dimes for pennies. Use play money to find equal shares. Then copy and complete the division sentence.

1. 54¢ shared by 3 people
54 ÷ 3 = ▓

2. 34¢ shared by 2 people
34 ÷ 2 = ▓

Set C pages 298–299

Four students want to share 57¢.

Dimes	Pennies
1	

4)5 7
− 4

| 1 | ← Trade 1 dime for 10 pennies. |

Dimes	Pennies
1	4

4)5 7
− 4

1	7
− 1	6
	1

Each will receive 14¢.
There will be
1¢ left over.

Remember that the quotient will be greater than 10¢ if the tens digit is greater than the divisor.

Divide. Show dimes and pennies if necessary.

1. 2)32   **2.** 4)29   **3.** 2)57

4. 3)69   **5.** 5)63   **6.** 4)60

Set D pages 300–301

Find 6)86.

Tens	Ones
1	

6)8 6
− 6

| 2 | |

Tens	Ones
1	4 R2

6)8 6
− 6

2	6
− 2	4
	2

Remember that the quotient will be less than 10 if the tens digit is less than the divisor. Divide.

1. 6)59   **2.** 4)52   **3.** 8)76

4. 5)76   **5.** 7)60   **6.** 9)89

7. 3)81   **8.** 4)95   **9.** 6)75

Set E pages 306–307

Find 584 ÷ 4.

Hundreds	Tens	Ones		Hundreds	Tens	Ones		Hundreds	Tens	Ones
1				1	4			1	4	6
4)5	8	4		4)5	8	4		4)5	8	4
−4				−4				−4		
1				1	8			1	8	
				−1	6			−1	6	
					2				2	4
								−	2	4
										0

Remember that the quotient will be greater than 100 if the hundreds digit is greater than the divisor. The quotient will be less than 100 if the hundreds digit is less than the divisor.

Tell whether the quotient will be greater than or less than 100. Then divide.

1. 6)504   **2.** 8)928

3. 7)647   **4.** 4)533

5. 3)285   **6.** 5)639

Set F pages 308–309

Find 625 ÷ 3.

```
     2
 3)625
  −6
   02 ← There are not
        enough tens to
        divide by 3.
```

```
    208 R1
 3)625
  −6
   02
  − 0
    25
  −24
    1
```

Remember that zeros are sometimes needed in a quotient.

Divide.

1. 4)162   **2.** 5)54   **3.** 3)906

4. 6)654   **5.** 7)743   **6.** 5)153

Set G pages 310–311

Find $78.40 ÷ 8.

```
        $ 9.8 0
 8)$ 7 8.4 0
  −   7 2
      6 4
    − 6 4
        0 0
      − 0 0
```

Remember to write a dollar sign and cents point in the quotient.

Divide.

1. 4)$37.20   **2.** 3)$6.81

3. 6)$61.80   **4.** 7)$50.40

5. 9)$82.98   **6.** 5)$52.40

7. 8)$9.84   **8.** 6)$5.04

More Practice

Set A pages 294–295

Mental Math Divide.

1. 50 ÷ 5
2. 60 ÷ 2
3. 90 ÷ 3
4. 40 ÷ 2

5. 150 ÷ 5
6. 160 ÷ 4
7. 540 ÷ 9
8. 600 ÷ 3

9. 400 ÷ 5
10. 300 ÷ 3
11. 200 ÷ 5
12. 100 ÷ 2

Estimation Estimate the quotient.

13. 80 ÷ 6
14. 60 ÷ 5
15. 130 ÷ 4
16. 290 ÷ 7

17. 600 ÷ 4
18. 500 ÷ 3
19. 700 ÷ 3
20. 900 ÷ 4

Set B pages 296–297

Use play money to find equal shares. Then copy and
complete the division sentence.

1. 24¢ shared by 3 people
   24 ÷ 3 = ▦

2. 64¢ shared by 4 people
   64 ÷ 4 = ▦

3. 75¢ shared by 5 people
   75 ÷ 5 = ▦

4. 60¢ shared by 4 people
   60 ÷ 4 = ▦

5. 84¢ shared by 7 people
   84 ÷ 7 = ▦

6. 45¢ shared by 3 people
   45 ÷ 3 = ▦

Set C pages 298–299

Divide. Show dimes and pennies if necessary.

1. $2\overline{)34}$
2. $4\overline{)45}$
3. $5\overline{)62}$
4. $4\overline{)48}$
5. $5\overline{)75}$

6. $2\overline{)47}$
7. $4\overline{)61}$
8. $3\overline{)84}$
9. $2\overline{)68}$
10. $5\overline{)83}$

Set D pages 300–301

Use estimation to tell whether the quotient will be
greater than or less than 10. Then divide.

1. $7\overline{)64}$
2. $6\overline{)72}$
3. $8\overline{)58}$
4. $9\overline{)81}$
5. $6\overline{)95}$

6. $5\overline{)94}$
7. $8\overline{)66}$
8. $5\overline{)60}$
9. $6\overline{)79}$
10. $7\overline{)78}$

Set E pages 306–307

Tell whether the quotient will be greater than or less than 100. Then divide.

1. $4\overline{)484}$ **2.** $6\overline{)546}$ **3.** $8\overline{)304}$ **4.** $9\overline{)747}$ **5.** $5\overline{)625}$

6. $6\overline{)666}$ **7.** $8\overline{)712}$ **8.** $4\overline{)504}$ **9.** $9\overline{)486}$ **10.** $7\overline{)644}$

For Exercises 11–15, tell whether you would use paper and pencil or mental math. Then find each quotient.

11. $4\overline{)400}$ **12.** $6\overline{)720}$ **13.** $7\overline{)357}$ **14.** $8\overline{)416}$ **15.** $3\overline{)858}$

Set F pages 308–309

Divide.

1. $4\overline{)123}$ **2.** $6\overline{)65}$ **3.** $8\overline{)824}$ **4.** $3\overline{)61}$ **5.** $7\overline{)766}$

6. $6\overline{)242}$ **7.** $4\overline{)414}$ **8.** $5\overline{)154}$ **9.** $7\overline{)215}$ **10.** $9\overline{)988}$

Mixed Practice   Tell whether you would use paper and pencil or mental math. Then find each quotient.

11. $3\overline{)363}$ **12.** $4\overline{)848}$ **13.** $7\overline{)91}$ **14.** $5\overline{)85}$ **15.** $8\overline{)352}$

16. $4\overline{)64}$ **17.** $9\overline{)810}$ **18.** $3\overline{)258}$ **19.** $4\overline{)600}$ **20.** $7\overline{)630}$

Set G pages 310–311

Estimate to decide whether each quotient is greater than or less than $10. Then divide.

1. $3\overline{)\$6.93}$ **2.** $6\overline{)\$7.32}$ **3.** $5\overline{)\$60.85}$ **4.** $2\overline{)\$5.36}$ **5.** $9\overline{)\$90.18}$

6. $7\overline{)\$8.47}$ **7.** $4\overline{)\$46.52}$ **8.** $6\overline{)\$73.86}$ **9.** $5\overline{)\$8.65}$ **10.** $9\overline{)\$8.28}$

For Exercises 11–19, tell whether you would use paper and pencil or mental math. Then divide to find the cost of one item.

11. 4 for $8.16   **12.** 6 for $4.86   **13.** 7 for $27.30

14. 8 for $12.80   **15.** 3 for $7.86   **16.** 9 for $8.10

17. 3 for $45.63   **18.** 4 for $15.64   **19.** 5 for $9.20

Enrichment

Divisibility

One number is *divisible* by another number if the remainder is zero when you divide.

A. Is 245 divisible by 5?

```
     4 9
5)2 4 5
  2 0
    4 5
    4 5
      0     The remainder is zero.
```

Yes, 245 is divisible by 5.

B. Is 245 divisible by 3?

```
     8 1 R2
3)2 4 5
  2 4
    0 5
      3
      2     The remainder is not zero.
```

No, 245 is not divisible by 3.

C. ▦ **Calculator** When a remainder is 0, the calculator shows the quotient as a whole number.

615 ÷ 3 = 205.
So, 615 is divisible by 3.

D. When the remainder is not 0, the calculator shows the quotient as a decimal.

737 ÷ 8 = 92.125
        ↑
These digits show that
there is a remainder.

So, 737 is not divisible by 8.

Is the first number divisible by the second number? Write yes or no.

1. 72; 4 **2.** 63; 7 **3.** 92; 3 **4.** 75; 5 **5.** 84; 7

6. 385; 5 **7.** 192; 3 **8.** 576; 6 **9.** 395; 9 **10.** 504; 8

11. 2,770; 4 **12.** 4,424; 7 **13.** 9,407; 9 **14.** 1,882; 8

Chapter 9 Review/Test

1. Divide the money into equal shares. Then copy and complete the division sentence.

93¢ shared by 3 people
$93 \div 3 = $ ▦

Estimate each quotient.

2. $330 \div 4$ **3.** $70 \div 3$

Divide.

4. $60 \div 6$ **5.** $180 \div 3$

6. $400 \div 5$ **7.** $800 \div 2$

8. $3\overline{)29}$ **9.** $2\overline{)36}$

10. $7\overline{)60}$ **11.** $9\overline{)70}$

12. $6\overline{)245}$ **13.** $8\overline{)352}$

14. $4\overline{)203}$ **15.** $7\overline{)707}$

16. $5\overline{)\$25.75}$ **17.** $3\overline{)\$9.15}$

Solve each problem.

18. How many teams of 4 can be obtained from a group of 23 students?

19. Ally is buying bread sticks that cost 8¢ each. She has 50¢ to spend. If she buys as many as possible, how much money will she have left?

Read the following problem. Then answer Items 20–22.

Mrs. Chan is buying marker pens for the 22 students in her class. The markers come in red and yellow. The red markers are sold in boxes of 3. The yellow markers are sold separately. In how many ways can Mrs. Chan buy exactly 22 markers?

20. Which of the following has the same meaning as the question in the problem?

  a. How many red markers are there in 3 boxes?
  b. How many boxes should Mrs. Chan buy to get 22 red markers?
  c. How many ways are there of buying exactly 22 markers?

21. Make a table to show all the ways Mrs. Chan can buy markers for her students.

22. Solve the problem.

23. **Write About Math** Write a word problem that could be solved by using the division shown in Item 17.

Geometry and Measurement

10

Did You Know: Jason Bright grew a 260-pound watermelon in Arkansas. Ed Gancarz grew a $595\frac{1}{2}$-pound green squash in New Jersey. Charlotte and David Knutsen grew an $8\frac{1}{2}$-pound lemon in California.

ZERO   TARE

WEIGHT

UNIT PRICE

3.77 LB.

0.44 $/L

CAPACITY
30 × 0.01LB.

Number-Sense Project

Estimate
Do you think people are more likely to give high estimates or low estimates of weight?

Gather Data
Choose three items that are heavier than a book, but light enough for you to hold. Have 5 people estimate the weight of each item in pounds.

Analyze and Report
Weigh each item, then compare the estimates. Were more estimates high or low? Write a summary telling what you found.

Solid Shapes

Build Understanding

ACTIVITY

A. Construct a Castle
Materials: Ruler, scissors, tape
Groups: 3 to 6 students

a. The patterns shown are for a *cylinder*, a *cube*, and a *cone*. Each person in the group traces the pattern for one of these three solid shapes.

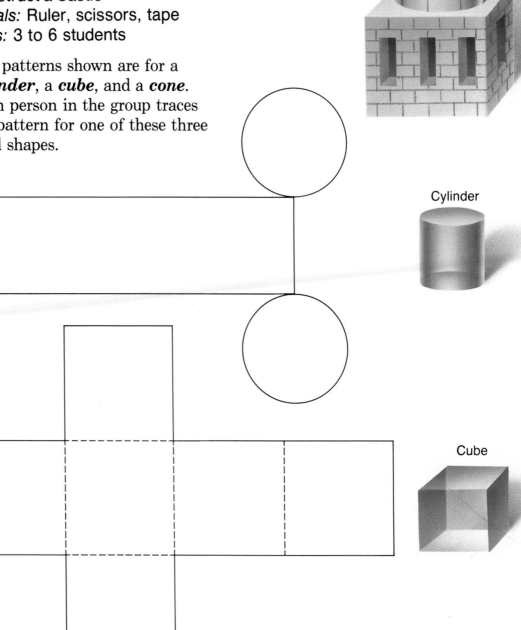

Cylinder

Cube

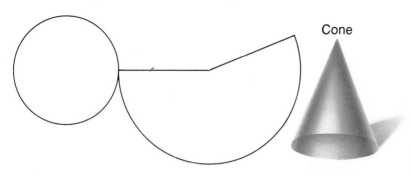
Cone

b. Cut on the solid lines and fold on the dashed lines. Then tape to make the solid shape. Before taping you may want to draw and color windows, vines, tiles, and bricks on the patterns to make each shape look like part of a castle.

c. As a class, tape together as many shapes as you want to use to build a castle.

This is Neuschwantstein Castle in Bavaria, Germany.

B. Here are pictures of two other solid shapes.

The ***rectangular prism*** has 6 flat surfaces. They are called ***faces***. The ***sphere*** has no faces.

Rectangular Prism 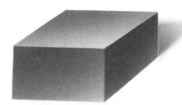   Sphere

■ **Talk About Math** All of the six faces of a cube are the same size and shape. Is a cube a rectangular prism? Explain.

Check Understanding

For another example, see Set A, pages 346–347.

Match the name of each solid shape with a lettered part of the knight.

1. Sphere

2. Cone

3. Cube

4. Cylinder

5. Rectangular prism

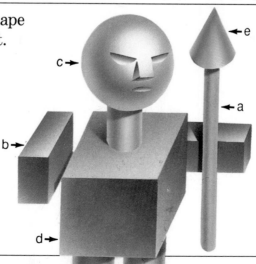

Practice

For More Practice, see Set A, pages 348–349.

Write *cone*, *cylinder*, *cube*, *sphere*, or *rectangular prism* to name each object.

6. Crayon box

7. Unsharpened pencil

8. Paint funnel

9. Ball of yarn

10. Paste bucket

11. Art box with six square sides

Give the shape of the faces for each solid. **Remember** that faces are flat surfaces.

12. Package of art paper

13. Jar of paint

Problem Solving

Visual Thinking Suppose you wanted to add this tower to the castle you built in Activity A.

14. Which two patterns would you use?

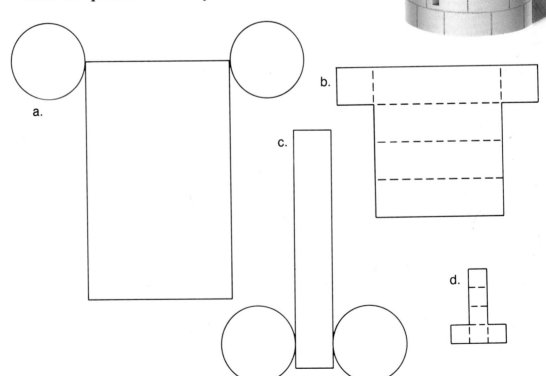

a.

b.

c.

d.

Visual Thinking Suppose you could cut each pattern on the solid lines and fold on the dashed lines. Could you use the pattern to make the solid shape? Explain.

Pattern   Solid Shape

15.

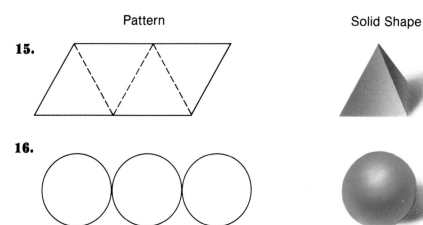

16.

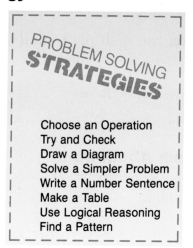

Choose a _____ Strategy

Uncovering Numbers
Mr. Nugent uses square blocks to build patios. He uses redwood boards to create separate sections. Mr. Nugent got dirt on these patio plans. Find the numbers that are covered with dirt.

PROBLEM SOLVING STRATEGIES

Choose an Operation
Try and Check
Draw a Diagram
Solve a Simpler Problem
Write a Number Sentence
Make a Table
Use Logical Reasoning
Find a Pattern

17.   **18.**

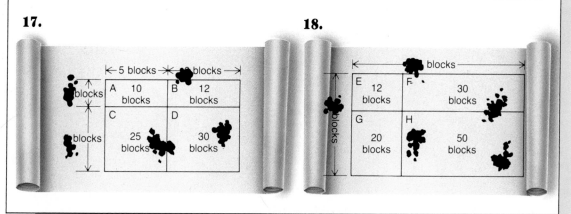

Volume

Build Understanding

A. Cory works in the shipping department of a
school-supply company. A teacher ordered
30 sets of centimeter cubes. Each set contains
24 cubes. A centimeter cube measures 1 cm on
each side. One cube has a *volume* of one cubic
centimeter. What is the volume of one set of
24 cubes?

1 cubic centimeter

Cory used this arrangement to stack one set of
24 cubes for shipping. Because each cube has a
volume of 1 cubic centimeter, the volume of the
rectangular prism formed by the stacked cubes is
24 cubic centimeters.

B. You can multiply to find the volume of the solid
shape Cory formed.

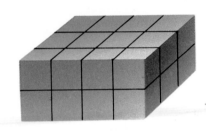

Layers		Rows		Cubes in each row		Volume
2	×	3	×	4	=	24 cubic centimeters

You can write
cm^3 for cubic
centimeters.

■ **Talk About Math** In Example A, would the volume
have changed if Cory stacked the cubes differently?
Explain.

Check Understanding

For another example, see Set B, pages 346–347.

Cory plans to ship these stacks of inch cubes.
Find the volume of each solid shape. **Remember**
to include cubic inches in your answers.

1.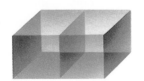

2.

3.
2 in.
2 in.
4 in.

4. A 2-layer stack of 5 rows that have 2 cubes in each row

Practice

For More Practice, see Set B, pages 348–349.

Count the cubes to find the volume. **Remember**
to use the label "cubic inches" or "cubic
centimeters" in each of your answers.

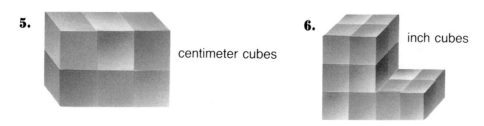

5. centimeter cubes

6. inch cubes

Find the volume. **Remember** to label each unit of measure.

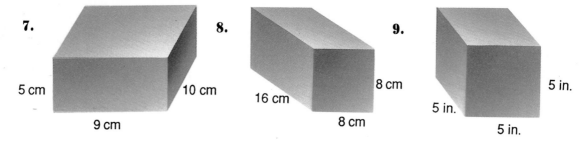

7. 5 cm 10 cm 9 cm

8. 16 cm 8 cm 8 cm

9. 5 in. 5 in. 5 in.

Problem Solving

Solve each problem.

10. Use Data   Refer to the polygon in
Exercise 3 on page 217. Suppose it is on
centimeter grid paper. If you stacked 4
layers of centimeter cubes on the
polygon to make a solid shape, what
would be the volume of the solid?

TIPS FOR
PROBLEM SOLVERS

Take risks. Try your
hunches, they often work.

Critical Thinking   Find the width, labeled w.

11.

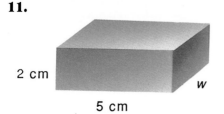

2 cm   5 cm w

Volume = 30 cm^3

12.

3 in.   3 in. w

Volume = 18 cubic inches

Customary Weights: Ounces and Pounds

Build Understanding

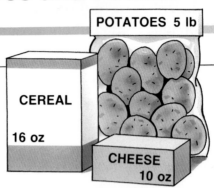

A. Do you read the weights printed on packages of food?

The **ounce** (oz) and the **pound** (lb) are customary units used to measure weight.

A slice of bread weighs about 1 ounce.

A loaf of bread weighs about 1 pound.

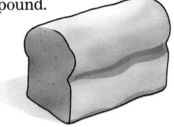

Each of these quantities of things weighs about 1 ounce.

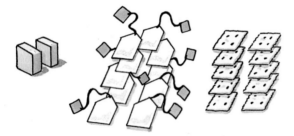

Each of these quantities of things weighs about 1 pound.

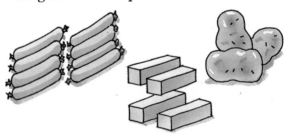

B. There are 16 ounces in 1 pound. To change pounds to ounces, multiply the number of pounds by 16.

If each slice of bread weighs 1 ounce, how many slices of bread are in a 1-pound loaf?

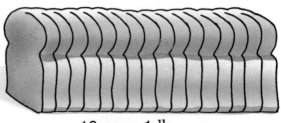

16 oz = 1 lb

■ **Talk About Math** Why do you think it makes sense to measure some objects in ounces and others in pounds?

330

Check Understanding

For another example, see Set C, pages 346–347.

Estimation Would you use ounces or pounds to measure the weight of each object?

1. A horse

2. 3 mushrooms

Find the missing numbers.

3. 10 pounds = ▦ ounces

4. 5 pounds = ▦ ounces

Practice

For More Practice, see Set C, pages 348–349.

Estimation Tell whether an ounce or a pound would be the more sensible unit for the weight of a

5. box of toothpicks.

6. bag of flour.

7. dozen apples.

8. slice of cheese.

9. bag of potatoes.

10. dozen peanuts.

For Exercises 11–16, tell whether you would use mental math, paper and pencil, or a calculator to find each answer. Then find the missing numbers.

11. 16 oz = ▦ lb

12. 4 lb = ▦ oz

13. 100 lb = ▦ oz

14. 18 oz = ▦ lb ▦ oz

15. 36 oz = ▦ lb ▦ oz

16. 58 lb = ▦ oz

Number Sense Choose weights from the tags at the right. Complete the paragraph so that it makes sense.

17. Scottie went grocery shopping. He bought one ▦ package of cream cheese, a ▦ box of corn flakes, a ▦ chicken and a ▦ turkey.

Problem Solving

Critical Thinking Solve each problem. Explain your answers.

18. If two grocery products are in packages of the same size, must they weigh the same?

19. If two grocery products weigh the same, must they fit in packages of the same size?

Metric Mass: Grams and Kilograms

Build Understanding

A. *Grams* (g) and **kilograms** (kg) are metric units used for measuring *mass*.

A large paper clip is about one gram.   A science book is about one kilogram.

Each of these quantities has a mass of about 1 gram.

Each of these objects has a mass of about 1 kilogram.

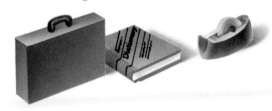

B. How many grams are in 4 kilograms?

There are 1,000 grams in 1 kilogram. To change kilograms to grams, multiply the number of kilograms by 1,000.

4 × 1,000 = 4,000

There are 4,000 grams in 4 kilograms.

■ **Write About Math**   How would you find the number of kilograms in 6,000 grams? Write a rule for changing grams to kilograms.

Check Understanding

For another example, see Set D, pages 346–347.

Estimation   Tell whether you would measure each object in grams or kilograms.

1. An envelope   **2.** A backpack   **3.** A desk   **4.** A pencil

Compare. **Remember** to use >, <, or = .

5. 1 kg ▦ 400 g   **6.** 3 kg ▦ 3,000 g

Practice

For More Practice, see Set D, pages 348–349.

Estimation Choose the more sensible measure.

7. Cheeseburger
   180 g   180 kg

8. Can of soup
   312 g   312 kg

9. Watermelon
   3 g   3 kg

10. Dime
    2 g   2 kg

11. Brick
    1 g   1 kg

12. Car
    1,500 g   1,500 kg

Use mental math or paper and pencil to change each mass to grams. Tell which method you used.

13. 2 kilograms

14. 5 kilograms

15. 14 kilograms

Problem Solving

Solve each problem.

16. If one lunch box weighs 425 grams, will 3 lunch boxes be more or less than a kilogram? What is the total mass of the 3 lunch boxes? Did you add, subtract, multiply, or divide?

17. The school cafeteria uses about 500 grams of salt a week. How many grams should the cook buy to store a 10-week supply of salt? How many kilograms is that?

Midchapter  Checkup

Name each solid shape.

1.
2.
3.
4.
5.

Find each volume.

6. A carton is 10 inches long, 6 inches wide, and 5 inches high.

7.
   7 cm   7 cm   7 cm

Find each missing number.

8. 4 lb = ▦ oz

9. 1,000 g = ▦ kg

10. 7 kg = ▦ g

Problem Solving WORKSHOP

Explore as a Team

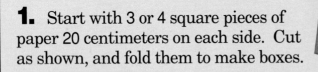

1. Start with 3 or 4 square pieces of paper 20 centimeters on each side. Cut as shown, and fold them to make boxes.

2. Record the measurements of each box. Which box has the greatest volume?

3. Have a contest. Cut other squares of paper the same size. See which group can make a box with the greatest volume.

TIPS FOR **WORKING TOGETHER**

Remember, you can disagree without being disagreeable.

Number-Sense Project

Look back at pages 322-323.
Jamie wanted to weigh her dog and cat. She weighed herself while holding each pet and recorded these results.

Jamie	72 lb
Jamie and Fluffy (the cat)	81 lb
Jamie and Max (the dog)	107 lb

1. How much did Fluffy weigh?

2. How much did Max weigh?

Critical Thinking Activity

If the longest side of a triangle is 10 cm, what can you say about the perimeter?

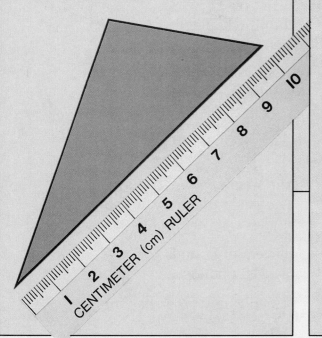

Real-Life Decision Making

1. Which box of dog biscuits is the better buy?

2. When would it be better to buy the other box?

335

Use Alternate Strategies

PROBLEM SOLVING
GUIDE

Understand
QUESTION
FACTS
KEY IDEA

Plan and Solve
STRATEGY
ANSWER

→ **Look Back**
SENSIBLE ANSWER
ALTERNATE APPROACH

Build Understanding

Each of the new shelving units at Sam's Sight and Sound Store has this label:

> **UNSAFE for loads over 100 pounds**

John has 40 portable CD (compact disk) players that he wants to display on one unit. Each machine weighs 48 ounces. Can one shelving unit safely hold 40 CD players?

Understand   Each shelving unit can hold up to 100 pounds. There are 40 CD players. Each player weighs 48 ounces. To solve the problem, express the weights in the same unit.

Plan and Solve   STRATEGY   Find the weight of 40 CD players in ounces.
40 CD players × 48 ounces = 1,920 ounces

Change 100 pounds to ounces so you can compare.
100 pounds × 16 = 1,600 ounces

ANSWER   Since 1,920 > 1,600, one shelving unit cannot safely hold 40 CD players.

→ **Look Back**   ALTERNATE APPROACH   Find the weight of a CD player in pounds. Since 16 ounces equals 1 pound, you know that 48 ounces equals 3 pounds.

Find the weight of 40 CD players in pounds.
3 pounds × 40 CD players = 120 pounds

So 120 pounds cannot be placed safely on a shelving unit that holds 100 pounds.

■ **Talk About Math** Can you think of a third approach toward solving this problem? Explain.

Check Understanding

Use the following facts to answer Problems 1–2:

> John has 50 AM/FM clock radios. Each weighs 32 ounces.

1. Use the strategy given in the Plan and Solve of the Example to tell if one shelving unit can safely support 50 radios.

2. Use the strategy given in the Look Back of the Example to check your answer to Problem 1.

Practice

Can the shelving unit safely support the weight?

3. Each shelving unit supports up to 20 pounds. There are 120 cassette tapes. Each weighs 2 ounces.

4. Each shelving unit supports up to 20 kilograms. There are 90 cans of sauce. Each weighs 225 grams.

5. Each shelving unit supports up to 4 pounds. There are 10 cans, each containing 6 ounces of styling mousse.

6. Each shelving unit supports up to 40 kilograms. There are 12 jars with 600 quarters in each. A jar weighs 300 grams. A quarter weighs 6 grams.

Reading ———— Math

Diagrams and Pictures
For each three-dimensional figure, tell which point is
1. closest to you.

2. farthest from you.

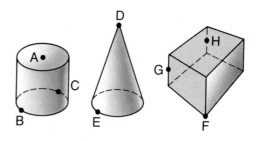

Customary Capacity: Cups, Pints, Quarts, and Gallons

Build Understanding

A. Chef Yus teaches a cooking class. In his class, he uses the customary units, *cups*, *pints*, *quarts*, and *gallons*, to measure liquids.

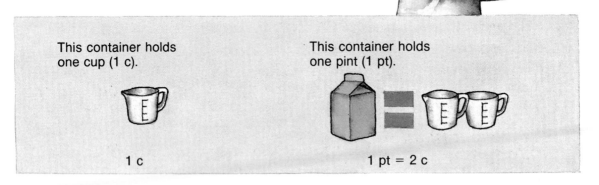

This container holds one cup (1 c).

1 c

This container holds one pint (1 pt).

1 pt = 2 c

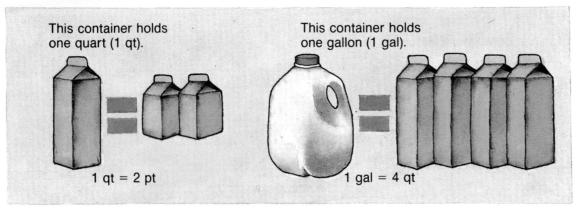

This container holds one quart (1 qt).

1 qt = 2 pt

This container holds one gallon (1 gal).

1 gal = 4 qt

B. The chef has a recipe calling for 2 gallons of tomato sauce. How many quart jars of tomato sauce should he use?

Number of gallons	Quarts in 1 gallon	Total quarts
2	× 4	= 8

There are 8 quarts in 2 gallons. The chef should use 8 jars.

■ **Talk About Math**   How many quarts are in a half gallon? How many cups are in a half pint? Explain your answers.

Check Understanding

For another example, see Set E, pages 346–347.

Chef Yus has pans that hold 1 cup, 1 gallon, 1 pint, and 1 quart.

1. Arrange the pans in order from largest to smallest.

2. Write the abbreviation for each unit of measurement.

Estimation   Choose the most sensible unit of measure.

3. Coffee mug
  c   pt   qt   gal

4. Bucket
  c   pt   qt   gal

5. Baby bottle
  c   pt   qt   gal

Practice

For More Practice, see Set E, pages 348–349.

Estimation   Choose the more sensible measure.

6. Water glass
  1 c   1 qt

7. Teakettle
  2 qt   2 gal

8. Milk-shake glass
  1 gal   1 pt

9. Kitchen sink
  20 pt   20 gal

10. Juice pitcher
  2 c   2 qt

11. Soup bowl
  2 c   2 qt

Mixed Practice   Find each missing number.

12. 2 qt = ▒ pt

13. 3 gal = ▒ qt

14. 3 pt = ▒ c

15. 10 lb = ▒ oz

16. 32 oz = ▒ lb

17. 4 pt = ▒ c

Problem Solving

Explore ———— Math

Find each sum. If necessary, use four 1-quart containers, three 1-pint containers, and one 1-cup container. Measure the amounts given in the addends. Then pour each amount into larger containers to find each sum.

18.   4 pt 1 c
       + 2 pt 1 c

19.   2 pt
       + 1 pt 4 c

20.   2 qt 1 pt
       + 1 qt 1 pt

Metric Capacity: Milliliters and Liters

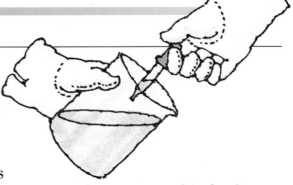

Build Understanding

The **_milliliter_** and **_liter_** are metric units used to measure liquid.

A. Fourth-grade students were examining the effects of different liquids on the growth of bean plants. They used eyedroppers to measure small amounts of liquid. An eyedropper holds about one milliliter (mL) of liquid.

The liquids were stored in beakers that each held one liter (L).

$$1,000 \text{ mL} = 1 \text{ L}$$

B. The teacher had a large bottle. Its label was marked "4,000 mL of distilled water." How many liters of distilled water were in the bottle?

Number of milliliters	Number of milliliters in 1 liter	Number of liters in 4,000 milliliters
4,000 ÷	1,000 =	4

There were 4 liters of distilled water in the bottle.

■ **Talk About Math** Tell why you think mathematicians use a capital L to abbreviate the word *liter* but use lower-case letters for all other metric units.

Check Understanding

For another example, see Set F, pages 346–347.

Estimation Tell whether liters or milliliters are the more sensible units of measure for

1. an eyedropper.　　**2.** a science lab sink.　　**3.** a test tube.

Which measure is more appropriate for

4. a plant watering can?　　**5.** a vitamin bottle?　　**6.** a spoon?

　2 L　　2 mL　　　　30 mL　　30 L　　　　5 mL　　5 L

Practice

For More Practice, see Set F, pages 348–349.

Change each to liters.

7. 3,000 mL   **8.** 7,000 mL   **9.** 9,000 mL   **10.** 20,000 mL

Mixed Practice   Find each missing number.

11. 10,000 mL = ▦ L   **12.** 5,000 g = ▦ kg

13. 4 L = ▦ mL   **14.** 8 kg = ▦ g

15. 6,000 mL = ▦ L   **16.** 12,000 g = ▦ kg

Problem Solving

Solve each problem.

17. Mental Math Tom made fertilizer. He had 1,525 mL of distilled water. He added 50 mL of liquid sodium phosphate. How many milliliters of fertilizer has he made?

18. **Calculator** Thu Lee mixed 1,080 mL of fertilizer in a bucket. She wants to put an equal amount into each of 6 jars. How much should she put into each jar?

Skills _____ **Review**   pages 108–109

Read the time on the clock. Use that time to solve each problem.

1. 10 minutes earlier   **2.** 15 minutes later

3. 4 hours later   **4.** 50 minutes later

5. 25 minutes later   **6.** 6 hours earlier

7. If the time is 5:05 now, how many minutes ago was the time on the clock?

Draw a Picture

PROBLEM SOLVING
GUIDE

Understand
QUESTION
FACTS
KEY IDEA

IIII➡ **Plan and Solve**
STRATEGY
ANSWER

Look Back
SENSIBLE ANSWER
ALTERNATE APPROACH

Build Understanding

Tom is planning a memory game for a party. He will divide his guests into 6 teams. How many games must he schedule for each team to play every other team once?

Understand   There are 6 teams. Each team plays the other teams once.

IIII➡**Plan and Solve**   STRATEGY   Draw a picture. Let 6 points represent the 6 teams. Let each line segment between two points represent a game. Draw and count the line segments between Team 1 and each of the other teams. Then draw and count the line segments from Team 2 to each of the teams other than Team 1, and so on.

ANSWER   Fifteen line segments were drawn. This means Tom must schedule 15 games.

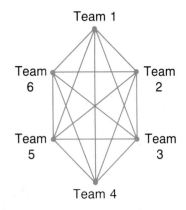

Look Back   ALTERNATE APPROACH   Make a list of all the games to be played. There are 15 games.

Teams 1 and 2	Teams 2 and 3	Teams 3 and 5
Teams 1 and 3	Teams 2 and 4	Teams 3 and 6
Teams 1 and 4	Teams 2 and 5	Teams 4 and 5
Teams 1 and 5	Teams 2 and 6	Teams 4 and 6
Teams 1 and 6	Teams 3 and 4	Teams 5 and 6

Talk About Math   Explain why the following statement is wrong: If each team has to play 5 other teams, there will be 6×5, or 30 games.

Check Understanding

Read the problem given below. Then find the answers to Problems 1–4.

Five boys played a game to get the highest score. Oliver's score was higher than both Pete's and Mike's, but Oliver was not the winner. Neil's score placed him just after Oliver. Two boys scored between Robbie and Pete.

Lowest Scorer _____•_____ Highest Scorer

Oliver

1. Copy the picture. Show Neil in relation to Oliver.

2. Show Pete and Mike in relation to Oliver. Can you tell in what order to place them?

3. Since two boys scored between Robbie and Pete, where do you place Pete? Robbie? Mike?

4. List the players in order with the winner first.

Practice

Draw a picture to help you solve each problem.

5. Tom and some guests sat at a round table for a card game. Tom took the top card from a pile of 13 cards and passed the pile to the right. Each person took the top card and passed the pile to the right until Tom took the last card. List the possible number of people that could have been playing the game.

6. Julie and Carol live 12 blocks apart. They decided to meet part way between their houses and go to Tom's party together. Both girls left home at the same time. Julie rode her bike 2 blocks for every 1 block that Carol walked. How far from home was each girl when they met?

7. When 4 friends met, they each shook hands with one another. How many handshakes were there?

8. Suppose Tom used 21 cards in Problem 5 and he took the first and last cards. How many players could have played?

Solve each problem.

1. Pavel has 2 books that are each 4 inches wide, 6 inches long, and 1 inch thick. Can he ship them in a 4-inch by 5-inch by 4-inch box?

2. Marie needs 2 pounds of mushrooms for a recipe. She has three 12-ounce jars of mushrooms. Does she have enough?

3. Aaron has a box 8 centimeters wide and 11 centimeters long. If the volume of the box is 264 cubic centimeters, what is the depth of the box?

4. Five stuffed teddy bears weigh 188 grams each. Do they weigh more or less than a kilogram? How much more or less?

5. How many handshakes are needed for 7 people to shake hands with one another?

6. Amy made 72 ounces of jam. How many 6-ounce jars can she fill?

7. **Data File** Use data from pages 388-389. Which container holds more, B or E? How much more?

8. **Make a Data File** Find out the record weights for three different animals. Make a chart to show your data.

Problem Solving REVIEW

Explore with a Calculator

The Clear Advantage

Calculators have a key labeled $\boxed{\text{C/CE}}$ or $\boxed{\text{ON/C}}$.
Both keys work the same way.

Press: 5 $\boxed{+}$ 2   2 is in the display

Press: $\boxed{\text{ON/C}}$ Pressing $\boxed{\text{ON/C}}$ once clears the last
                          number entered.

Press: 6   The 2 is replaced with 6.

Press: $\boxed{=}$ Pressing the $\boxed{=}$ sign gives 11, the sum
                          of 5 and 6.

CAUTION: The display is cleared when the $\boxed{\text{ON/C}}$ is pressed twice

1. Guess what the display will show when $\boxed{=}$ is
pressed. Then press each sequence. Compare the results
to your guesses.

a. 9 $\boxed{+}$ 4 $\boxed{\text{ON/C}}$ $\boxed{\text{ON/C}}$ 7 $\boxed{+}$ 5 $\boxed{=}$

b. 8 $\boxed{-}$ 2 $\boxed{\text{ON/C}}$ 6 $\boxed{=}$

c. 4 $\boxed{\times}$ 7 $\boxed{\text{ON/C}}$ 5 $\boxed{=}$

2. Pepe wanted to add the prices
on the sales slip with his calculator.
When he entered the cost of the paper
he pressed $35.00 by mistake. Tell
what he should do to correct it. Then
find the cost of the school supplies.

pens	$2.35
scissors	1.39
glue	.99
crayons	1.68
pencils	2.05
paper	3.50
lunch box	2.45
ruler	.29
pencil case	1.19
5 notebooks	4.98

345

Reteaching

Set A   pages 324–327

The shapes of a few common objects are given below.

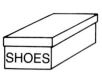
SHOES

rectangular prism

cube

SOUP

cylinder

sphere

cone

Remember that a cube is a special type of rectangular prism.

Write *cone, cylinder, cube, sphere,* or *rectangular prism* to name each object.

1.

2.

Set B   pages 328–329

Find the volume of this figure. Each cube stands for 1 cubic inch.

There are 3 layers of cubes. Each layer has 4 rows. Each row has 3 cubes.

Layers	Rows	Cubes in a row	Volume
3	× 3	× 4	= 36

The volume is 36 cubic inches.

Remember to include cubic inches in your answer.

Count the inch cubes to find the volume.

1.

2.

Set C   pages 330–331

How many ounces are in 5 pounds?

Since there are 16 ounces (oz) in 1 pound (lb), there are 5 × 16 ounces or 80 ounces in 5 pounds.

Remember that to change pounds to ounces, you multiply the number of pounds by 16.

Tell whether you would use mental math, paper and pencil, or a calculator to find each answer. Find the missing numbers.

1. 3 lb = ▦ oz

2. 8 lb = ▦ oz

3. 10 lb = ▦ oz

4. 37 lb = ▦ oz

5. 20 lb = ▦ oz

6. 100 lb = ▦ oz

Set D pages 332–333

How many grams are in 6 kilograms?

Since 1 kilogram equals 1,000 grams, 6 kilograms = 6 × 1,000 grams, or 6,000 grams.

Remember that you can change kilograms to grams by multiplying the number of kilograms by 1,000.

Use mental math or paper and pencil to change from kilograms to grams. Tell which method you used.

1. 3 kilograms   2. 7 kilograms

3. 8 kilograms   4. 10 kilograms

5. 19 kilograms   6. 25 kilograms

Set E pages 338–339

Write 4 gallons in
a. quarts   b. pints   c. cups

a. Since 1 gallon = 4 quarts, 4 gallons equals 4 × 4 quarts, or 16 quarts.

b. Since 1 quart = 2 pints, 16 quarts equals 16 × 2 pints, or 32 pints.

c. Since 1 pint = 2 cups, 32 pints equals 32 × 2 cups, or 64 cups.

Remember that you multiply to change a larger unit of measure to a smaller unit of measure.

Fill in each missing number.

1. 5 gal = ▦ qt   2. 10 qt = ▦ pt

3. 8 qt = ▦ pt   4. 6 pt = ▦ c

5. 18 pt = ▦ c   6. 9 gal = ▦ qt

Set F pages 340–341

Write 5 liters in milliliters.

Since 1 liter (L) = 1,000 milliliters (mL), 5 L = 5 × 1,000 mL, or 5,000 mL.

Write 8,000 milliliters in liters.

Since 1,000 mL = 1 L, 8,000 mL = 8,000 ÷ 1,000, or 8 L.

Remember that you divide to change a smaller unit of measure to a larger unit of measure.

Mixed Practice Fill in each missing number.

1. 6 L = ▦ mL

2. 8 L = ▦ mL

3. 5,000 mL = ▦ L

4. 7,000 mL = ▦ L

5. 25,000 mL = ▦ L

More Practice

Set A pages 324–327

Write *cone, cylinder, cube, sphere,* or *rectangular prism* to name each object.

1.

2.

3.

4.

5.

6.

Set B pages 328–329

Count the cubes to find the volume.

1.  centimeter cubes

2. inch cubes

Find the volume.

3. 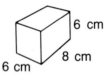 6 cm 8 cm 6 cm

4. 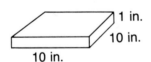 1 in. 10 in. 10 in.

5. 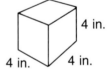 4 in. 4 in. 4 in.

Set C pages 330–331

Estimation Tell whether ounces or pounds would be the more sensible weight of

1. a sack of sugar.

2. an ice cube.

3. a postal letter.

4. a watermelon.

5. a slice of bread.

6. a bag of onions.

For Exercises 7–12, tell whether you would use mental math, paper and pencil, or a calculator to find each answer. Then find the missing numbers.

7. 32 oz = ▦ lb

8. 6 lb = ▦ oz

9. 9 lb = ▦ oz

10. 7 lb = ▦ oz

11. 40 lb = ▦ oz

12. 48 oz = ▦ lb

Set D pages 332–333

Estimation Choose the more sensible measure.

1. Shoelace
   1 g   1 kg

2. Couch
   100 g   100 kg

3. Bumble bee
   2 kg   2 g

4. Dictionary
   2 g   2 kg

5. Egg
   55 g   55 kg

6. Screwdriver
   57 g   57 kg

Use mental math or paper and pencil to change kilograms to grams. Tell which method you used. Write each answer.

7. 4 kilograms

8. 9 kilograms

9. 22 kilograms

Set E pages 338–339

Estimation Choose the more sensible measure.

1. Dog's water bowl
   2 c   2 gal

2. Cream pitcher
   1 c   1 qt

3. Bath tub
   15 qt   15 gal

4. Sand pail
   2 qt   2 gal

5. Baby's bottle
   1 c   1 qt

6. Wading pool
   25 pt   25 gal

Mixed Practice Fill in each missing number.

7. 3 qt = ▦ pt

8. 6 gal = ▦ qt

9. 8 pt = ▦ c

10. 5 lb = ▦ oz

11. 48 oz = ▦ lb

12. 10 pt = ▦ c

Set F pages 340–341

Change each to liters.

1. 4,000 mL

2. 8,000 mL

3. 10,000 mL

4. 5,000 mL

Mixed Practice Fill in each missing number.

5. 11,000 mL = ▦ L

6. 6,000 g = ▦ kg

7. 4,000 mL = ▦ L

8. 6 L = ▦ mL

9. 9 kg = ▦ g

10. 30 L = ▦ mL

11. 20,000 mL = ▦ L

12. 11,000 g = ▦ kg

13. 2 kg = ▦ g

Enrichment

Number Patterns

An interesting sequence of numbers was discovered by the mathematician Fibonacci. The Fibonacci sequence begins like this:

1 1 2 3 5 8 13 . . .

More numbers in this sequence can be found by using an addition pattern.

Answer each question to help you find the pattern.

1. What is the sum of the first and second numbers in the sequence?

2. What is the third number in the sequence?

3. What is the sum of the second and third numbers in the sequence?

4. What is the fourth number in the sequence?

5. What is the sum of the third and fourth numbers in the sequence?

6. What is the fifth number in the sequence?

7. What pattern do you see?

8. Write the next four numbers.

1 1 2 3 5 8 13 ▦ ▦ ▦ ▦

9. Find the addition pattern in this sequence.

1 1 1 3 5 9 17 . . .

10. Find the next four numbers in the sequence in Exercise 9.

Chapter 10 Review/Test

Write *cone, cylinder, cube, sphere,* or *rectangular prism* to name the shape of each object.

1. Basketball   **2.** Soup can

3. Cracker box   **4.** Funnel

Choose the more sensible measure.

5. Weight of a sack of apples
   30 oz   30 lb

6. Capacity of a car's gas tank
   16 pt   16 gal

7. Capacity of a can of motor oil
   1 mL   1 L

Find each missing number.

8. 6 lb = ▦ oz

9. 48 oz = ▦ lb

10. 3 kg = ▦ g

11. 4,000 g = ▦ kg

12. 5 gal = ▦ qt

13. 4 qt = ▦ pt

14. 5,000 mL = ▦ L

15. 4 L = ▦ mL

16. How many centimeter cubes will fit into this box?

2 cm 3 cm 2 cm

17. What is the volume of the box in Item 16?

18. Find the volume.

6 cm 8 cm 20 cm

19. A shelf can hold 50 pounds. Is it safe to put 60 cans that each weigh 12 ounces on the shelf?

20. A can holds 354 mL of juice. Will 3 of these cans hold more or less than a liter?

Read the following problem. Then answer Items 21–23.

After a ball game, the 5 members of Bob's team each said "Goodbye" to every other member once. How many times was "Goodbye" said?

21. Which of these sentences could be completed to answer this problem?
   a. "Goodbye" was said ▦ times.
   b. Bob said "Goodbye" ▦ times.
   c. ▦ team members said "Goodbye" to Bob.
   d. Each player said "Goodbye" ▦ times.

22. Draw a picture that shows the solution to the problem.

23. Solve the problem.

24. **Write About Math** Explain why the measure you chose for Item 7 is the more sensible one.

Fraction Concepts

Did You Know: Approximately 75 acres of pizza are consumed in the United States every day. An acre is 43,560 square feet.

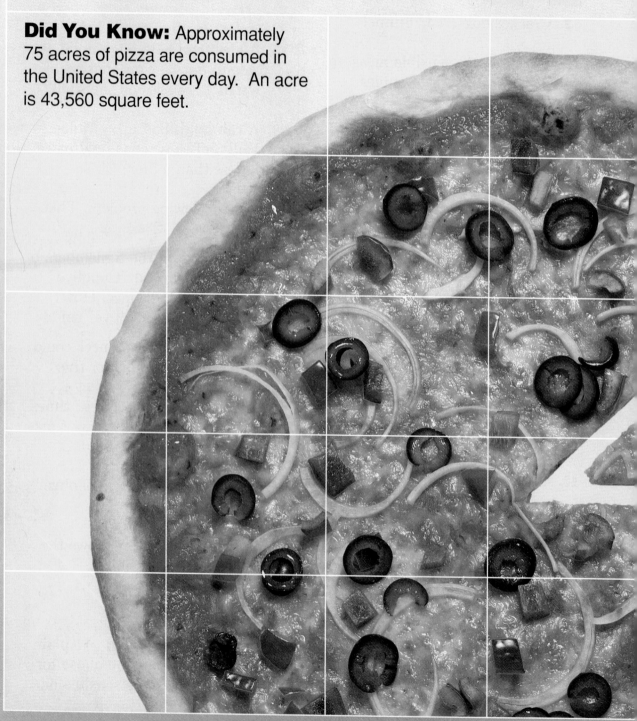

Number-Sense Project

Estimate
Predict what kinds of pizza toppings are the most popular.

Gather Data
Ask 5 people to tell which of the pizza toppings in the coupon they would choose. (More than one topping can be chosen.)

Analyze and Report
Make a table of the results from your entire class. Was your prediction correct?

Pizza
SpecialCoupon

Sausage
Pepperoni
Mushrooms
Green peppers
Onions
Olives

Part of a Whole

Build Understanding

A *fraction* can be used to name a part of a whole.

A. The flag of Peru is divided into 3 equal parts. Two of the three parts are red. This can be written as the fraction two thirds.

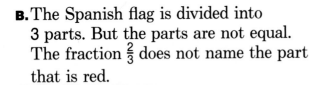

Number of red parts → **2** ← *Numerator*
Number of equal parts → **3** ← *Denominator*

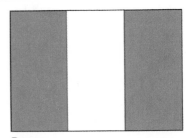
Peru

B. The Spanish flag is divided into 3 parts. But the parts are not equal. The fraction $\frac{2}{3}$ does not name the part that is red.

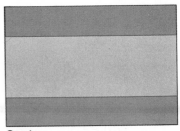
Spain

■ **Talk About Math**   The flag of the United States is red, white, and blue. Is $\frac{1}{3}$ of the flag red? Explain your answer.

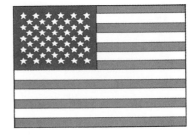
U.S.

Check Understanding

For another example, see Set A, pages 382–383.

Answer the following questions about the flag of Mauritius that is pictured at the right.

1. How many parts are there?

2. Are all the parts equal?

3. How many of the parts are yellow?

4. What fraction of the flag is yellow?

Mauritius

5. What fraction of the flag is black?

Practice

For More Practice, see Set A, pages 384–385.

Write a fraction to show how much of the figure is shaded.

6.

7.

8.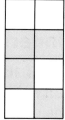

9.

10.

11.

Write a fraction for each phrase. **Remember** that the denominator tells the number of equal parts.

12. Four sevenths   **13.** Two fifths   **14.** Three tenths

Estimation Choose the fraction that best shows how full each container is.

15.

$\frac{3}{4}$ $\frac{1}{2}$ $\frac{1}{4}$

16.

$\frac{2}{3}$ $\frac{1}{2}$ $\frac{1}{3}$

17.

$\frac{7}{8}$ $\frac{5}{8}$ $\frac{3}{8}$

18.

$\frac{10}{10}$ $\frac{5}{10}$ $\frac{1}{10}$

Problem Solving

Answer the questions about the pictured flags.

19. The primary colors are red, yellow, and blue. What fraction of France's flag is a primary color?

20. What part of France's flag is red? What part is not red?

21. Johnny said that the flag of Colombia is $\frac{1}{3}$ red. Is he correct? Why?

France

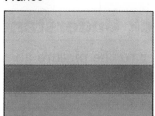

Colombia

Part of a Set

Build Understanding

A. In the *set* of 16 people in the Center City Wind Players, 4 play the clarinet. What part of the set, or fraction of the players, plays the clarinet?

Since there are 4 clarinet players, you can say that $\frac{4}{16}$ of the players play the clarinet.

$\dfrac{4}{16}$ ← Number of clarinet players
← Total number of players

B. The 9 woodwind players play clarinet, saxophone, or flute. What fraction of the woodwind players plays the clarinet?

Since 4 woodwind players play clarinet, $\frac{4}{9}$ of the woodwind players play clarinet.

$\dfrac{4}{9}$ ← Number of clarinet players
← Total number of woodwind players

■ **Write About Math** Why are the denominators different in Examples A and B?

What type of instrument would you like to play?

Check Understanding

For another example, see Set B, pages 382–383.

Refer to the picture above. What fraction of the

1. players are women?

▦ ← Number of women players
▦ ← Total number of players

2. players play the tuba?

▦ ← Number of tuba players
▦ ← Total number of players

356

Practice

For More Practice, see Set B, pages 384–385.

What fraction of the

3. music books are open?

4. instrument cases are black?

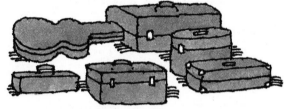

5. notes are half notes (𝅗𝅥)?

6. flutists are playing?

Mixed Practice   For Exercises 7–12, tell if the fraction is a fraction of a set or a fraction of a whole.

7. One half of a peach

8. Two fifths of the marbles in a bag

9. Two thirds of the books on a shelf

10. Three fourths of a quart of juice

11. Six tenths of the balloons in a box

12. One fourth of a floor washed

Problem Solving

Use the information pictured on page 356 to solve Problems 14–15.

13. What fraction of the letters in the word SAXOPHONE are Os? What fraction of the letters are not Os?

14. Trumpets and trombones are brass wind instruments. What fraction of all the players play brass wind instruments?

15. Last night, one of the clarinetists was absent. What fraction of the clarinet players was present?

16. The players perform on Thursdays, Fridays, and Saturdays. On what fraction of the days of the week do they perform?

Comparing Fractions

Build Understanding

A. Mrs. Hill tests recipes for a food company.

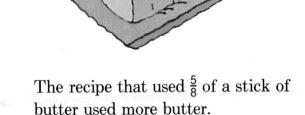

One muffin recipe used $\frac{5}{8}$ of a stick of butter.

Another muffin recipe used $\frac{3}{8}$ of a stick of butter.

Which recipe used more butter?

The butter in both recipes is measured in eighths of a stick of butter. Since $5 > 3$, $\frac{5}{8} > \frac{3}{8}$.

The recipe that used $\frac{5}{8}$ of a stick of butter used more butter.

B. Compare $\frac{2}{5}$ and $\frac{2}{3}$.

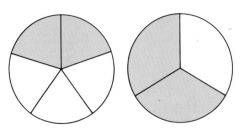

In both circle fraction models, 2 pieces are shaded. Notice that fifths are smaller than thirds in the models, so $\frac{2}{5} < \frac{2}{3}$.

■ **Talk About Math** If two fractions have the same denominator, which fraction is greater? If two fractions have the same numerator, which fraction is greater?

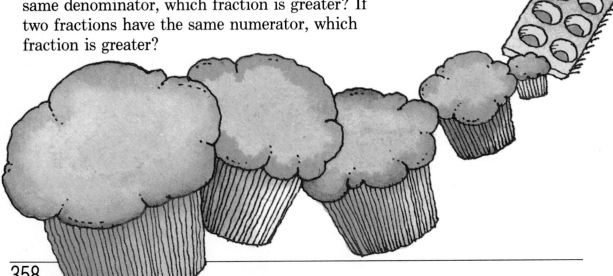

Check Understanding

For another example, see Set C, pages 382–383.

Compare the fractions. Use < or >.

1.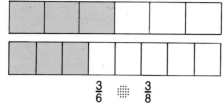

$$\frac{3}{6} \;\vcenter{\hbox{⣿}}\; \frac{3}{8}$$

2.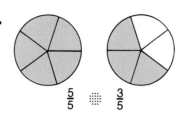

$$\frac{5}{5} \;\vcenter{\hbox{⣿}}\; \frac{3}{5}$$

Practice

For More Practice, see Set C, pages 384–385.

Compare the fractions. Use < or >.

3.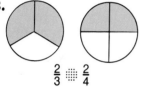

$$\frac{2}{3} \;\vcenter{\hbox{⣿}}\; \frac{2}{4}$$

4.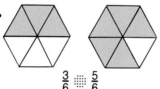

$$\frac{3}{6} \;\vcenter{\hbox{⣿}}\; \frac{5}{6}$$

5.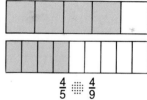

$$\frac{4}{5} \;\vcenter{\hbox{⣿}}\; \frac{4}{9}$$

6. $\frac{1}{5} \;\vcenter{\hbox{⣿}}\; \frac{2}{5}$

7. $\frac{8}{10} \;\vcenter{\hbox{⣿}}\; \frac{5}{10}$

8. $\frac{3}{8} \;\vcenter{\hbox{⣿}}\; \frac{3}{4}$

9. $\frac{1}{2} \;\vcenter{\hbox{⣿}}\; \frac{0}{2}$

10. $\frac{5}{6} \;\vcenter{\hbox{⣿}}\; \frac{5}{10}$

11. $\frac{1}{7} \;\vcenter{\hbox{⣿}}\; \frac{1}{3}$

12. $\frac{7}{9} \;\vcenter{\hbox{⣿}}\; \frac{9}{9}$

13. $\frac{10}{12} \;\vcenter{\hbox{⣿}}\; \frac{5}{12}$

Problem Solving

Solve each problem.

14. Mrs. Hill used $\frac{1}{4}$ cup of sugar and $\frac{1}{3}$ cup of flour in a recipe. Did she use more sugar or more flour?

15. Mrs. Hill filled one loaf pan $\frac{6}{8}$ full of bread dough and a second pan $\frac{5}{8}$ full. Which pan contained less dough?

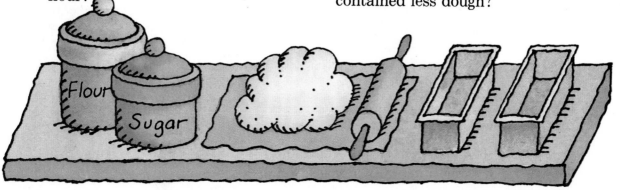

Equal Fractions

Build Understanding

A. The sub sandwiches in Sally's Sub Shop are made with French bread. To make a Super Sub, Sally cuts a loaf of bread in half and uses $\frac{1}{2}$ of the loaf. To make a Regular Sub, Sally cuts a loaf of bread into 4 equal pieces and uses one piece, or $\frac{1}{4}$ of the loaf.

Compare the amount of bread in one Super Sub to the amount of bread in two Regular Subs.

Compare $\frac{1}{2}$ and $\frac{2}{4}$.

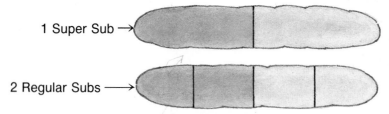

1 Super Sub →

2 Regular Subs →

The picture shows that $\frac{1}{2}$ of a loaf is the same size as $\frac{2}{4}$ of a loaf.

So $\frac{1}{2}$ and $\frac{2}{4}$ are ***equal fractions***.

B. You can use fraction strips to find equal fractions.

$\dfrac{2}{3} = \dfrac{}{6}$

$\frac{1}{3}$	$\frac{1}{3}$	$\frac{1}{3}$

Place the fraction strip for thirds above the fraction strip for sixths. Shade 2 of the thirds.

$\dfrac{2}{3} = \dfrac{4}{6}$

$\frac{1}{6}$	$\frac{1}{6}$	$\frac{1}{6}$	$\frac{1}{6}$	$\frac{1}{6}$	$\frac{1}{6}$

Shade the same part of the fraction strip for sixths. How many sixths were shaded to equal 2 of the thirds?

■ **Talk About Math** Explain how you would use fraction strips to find the missing numerator in these equal fractions: $\frac{3}{5} = \frac{}{10}$.

360

Check Understanding

For another example, see Set D, pages 382–383.

Use the fraction strips shown to find the equal fractions.

1.

$\frac{1}{3}$	$\frac{1}{3}$	$\frac{1}{3}$

$\frac{1}{9}$	$\frac{1}{9}$	$\frac{1}{9}$	$\frac{1}{9}$	$\frac{1}{9}$	$\frac{1}{9}$	$\frac{1}{9}$	$\frac{1}{9}$	$\frac{1}{9}$

$$\frac{1}{3} = \frac{\boxed{}}{9}$$

2.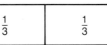

$\frac{1}{4}$	$\frac{1}{4}$	$\frac{1}{4}$	$\frac{1}{4}$

$\frac{1}{8}$	$\frac{1}{8}$	$\frac{1}{8}$	$\frac{1}{8}$	$\frac{1}{8}$	$\frac{1}{8}$	$\frac{1}{8}$	$\frac{1}{8}$

$$\frac{\boxed{}}{4} = \frac{6}{8}$$

Use fraction strips to find

3. four fractions equal to $\frac{1}{2}$.

4. two fractions equal to $\frac{2}{3}$.

Practice

For More Practice, see Set D, pages 384–385.

Use fraction strips to find the equal fractions.

5. $\frac{1}{3} = \frac{\boxed{}}{6}$

6. $\frac{\boxed{}}{4} = \frac{4}{8}$

7. $\frac{\boxed{}}{3} = \frac{9}{9}$

8. $\frac{1}{2} = \frac{\boxed{}}{10}$

9. $\frac{4}{8} = \frac{\boxed{}}{2}$

10. $\frac{4}{5} = \frac{\boxed{}}{10}$

11. $\frac{3}{9} = \frac{\boxed{}}{3}$

12. $\frac{6}{8} = \frac{\boxed{}}{4}$

13. $\frac{2}{3} = \frac{\boxed{}}{9}$

14. $\frac{3}{6} = \frac{\boxed{}}{2}$

15. $\frac{10}{10} = \frac{\boxed{}}{6}$

16. $\frac{0}{4} = \frac{\boxed{}}{2}$

17. $\frac{\boxed{}}{6} = \frac{2}{3}$

18. $\frac{\boxed{}}{8} = \frac{1}{4}$

19. $\frac{\boxed{}}{9} = \frac{4}{6}$

20. $\frac{\boxed{}}{5} = \frac{4}{10}$

Problem Solving

Solve each problem. Use fraction strips if necessary.

21. Sally cut $\frac{1}{2}$ of a loaf of bread into 4 equal slices. What fraction of the entire loaf is one slice?

22. Sally sold 36 sub sandwiches to the lunchtime crowd. If $\frac{1}{3}$ of the sandwiches were Super Subs, how many Super Subs did she sell?

Mixed Numbers

Build Understanding

A. Joan had $1\frac{3}{4}$ pizzas left after serving pizza at a party. Numbers like $1\frac{3}{4}$ are *mixed numbers*.

A mixed number is made up of a whole number and a fraction.

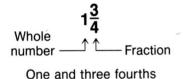
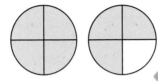

Whole number ─── Fraction

One and three fourths

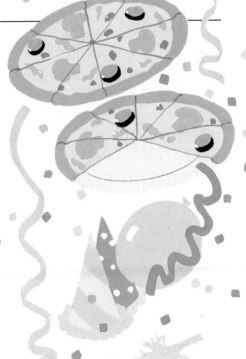

B. Each pizza was divided into 4 equal pieces, or fourths. Seven fourths were left.

$1\frac{3}{4} = \frac{7}{4}$

■ **Talk About Math** How would you draw a picture to show five halves?

Check Understanding

For another example, see Set E, pages 382–383.

Refer to the picture at the right for Exercises 1–4.

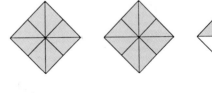

1. How many whole figures are shaded?

2. Each figure is divided into how many equal parts?

3. How many parts of the third figure are shaded?

4. What mixed number describes the picture?

Practice

For More Practice, see Set E, pages 384–385.

Write the mixed number.

5. Three and one third

6. Two and two fourths

7. One and five eighths

8. Four and five tenths

9. For Exercises 5–8, sketch figures to show the mixed numbers.

Write a fraction and a mixed number for each group of pictures.

10.

11.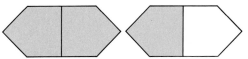

12.

13.

Problem Solving

Answer each question.

14. Joan served 7 pints of frozen yogurt at the party. There are 2 pints in a quart. How many quarts of frozen yogurt did she serve?

15. **Critical Thinking** How do you know if a fraction is greater than 1, less than 1, or equal to 1?

Skills ———— Review   pages 68–69

Mental Math   Add or subtract mentally.

1.	482 + 300	**2.**	720 + 50	**3.**	2,781 + 4,000	**4.**	6,391 + 700	**5.**	5,083 + 60
6.	587 − 70	**7.**	645 − 400	**8.**	7,385 − 50	**9.**	4,652 − 3,000	**10.**	8,904 − 400

Fractions in Measurement

Build Understanding

A. Mrs. Jackson sewed a $\frac{1}{2}$ inch button on her granddaughter's teddy bear.

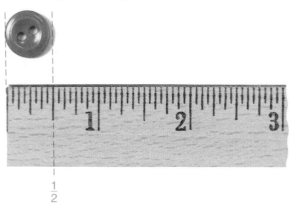

If you divide an inch into two equal parts, each part is one half of an inch.

B. She used $4\frac{3}{4}$ inches of thread.

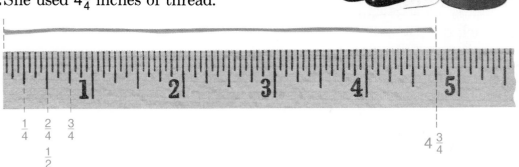

If you divide an inch into four equal parts, each part is one fourth inch.

Notice that the same mark on this ruler shows $\frac{2}{4}$ inch and $\frac{1}{2}$ inch.

■ Talk About Math What do you do when the end of an object being measured falls between the marks on the ruler?

Check Understanding

For another example, see Set F, pages 382–383.

Use the ruler to find the length of each piece of trim.

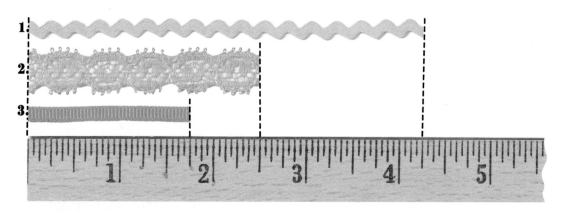

Practice

For More Practice, see Set F, pages 384–385.

Use a ruler to measure each object.

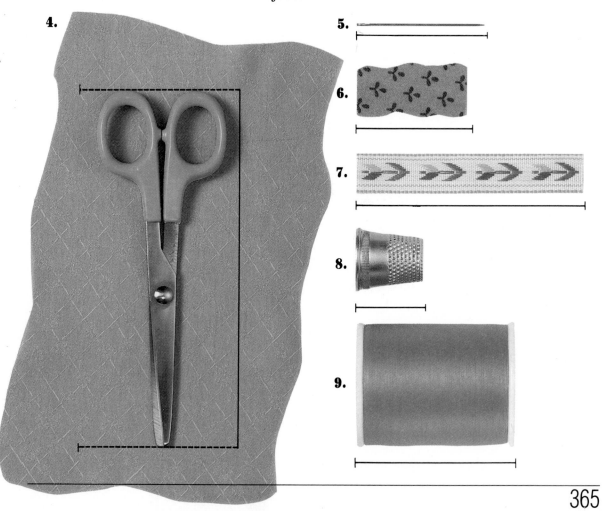

Problem Solving

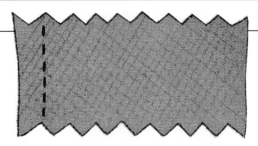

Use a ruler for Problems 10–12.

10. Measure the distance from the stitching to the edge of the fabric at the right.

11. Use your ruler to draw a segment $2\frac{3}{4}$ inches long.

12. Use your ruler to draw a segment $4\frac{1}{2}$ inches long.

13. Number Sense Use lengths from the basket to make the sentence reasonable.

The length $2\frac{3}{4}$ in. is large compared to ▦, small compared to ▦, and about the same as ▦.

14. 📱 **Calculator** On many rulers, an inch is divided into 16 equal parts. Each part is $\frac{1}{16}$ of an inch. Is $\frac{112}{16}$ inches more or less than 8 inches?

Press: 112 ÷ 16 =

🏭

Choose a _____ Strategy

Buttons, Buttons, Buttons Jane bought only red buttons and blue buttons. Carol bought only red buttons and yellow buttons. Jane spent 31¢ and Carol spent 75¢.

15. What did each girl buy?

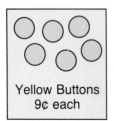

Yellow Buttons
9¢ each

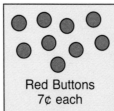

Red Buttons
7¢ each

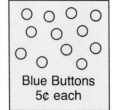

Blue Buttons
5¢ each

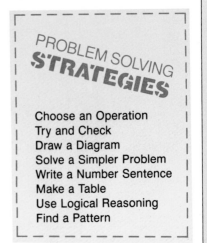

PROBLEM SOLVING
STRATEGIES

Choose an Operation
Try and Check
Draw a Diagram
Solve a Simpler Problem
Write a Number Sentence
Make a Table
Use Logical Reasoning
Find a Pattern

What fraction of the figure is shaded?

1.

2.

3.

What fraction of the

4. coins are pennies?

5. silver coins are dimes?

Compare the fractions. Use < or >.

6. $\frac{2}{3}$ ⬚ $\frac{2}{5}$ **7.** $\frac{4}{4}$ ⬚ $\frac{2}{4}$ **8.** $\frac{6}{8}$ ⬚ $\frac{6}{10}$ **9.** $\frac{4}{9}$ ⬚ $\frac{7}{9}$

Use the fraction strips to find the equal fractions.

10.

$\frac{1}{4}$	$\frac{1}{4}$	$\frac{1}{4}$	$\frac{1}{4}$

$\frac{1}{8}$	$\frac{1}{8}$	$\frac{1}{8}$	$\frac{1}{8}$	$\frac{1}{8}$	$\frac{1}{8}$	$\frac{1}{8}$	$\frac{1}{8}$

$$\frac{3}{4} = \frac{⬚}{8}$$

11.

$\frac{1}{6}$	$\frac{1}{6}$	$\frac{1}{6}$	$\frac{1}{6}$	$\frac{1}{6}$	$\frac{1}{6}$

$\frac{1}{2}$	$\frac{1}{2}$

$$\frac{⬚}{6} = \frac{1}{2}$$

Write a fraction and a mixed number to describe each group of pictures.

12.

13.

Give the length of each segment.

14.

15.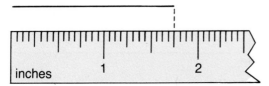

Problem Solving WORKSHOP

Real-Life Decision Making

Today is a very hot day. You and your friends can ride bikes to Crystal Lake to go swimming, or to Skittles Playground to play.

Crystal Lake
$2\frac{1}{3}$ **miles**

Skittles Playground
$2\frac{1}{4}$ **miles**

1. You and your friends are looking at this sign. Are you closer to the lake or the playground?

2. Decide whether you will go to the lake or the playground today.

Math-at-Home Activity

Play *Up to the Right Corner* with someone at home. Draw 16 dots, 4 in each row and column. The first player starts at the bottom left corner. Take turns drawing a line segment connecting two dots. You may draw up *or* to the right. You cannot change direction during one turn. The winner is the first player to land on the dot in the upper right corner.

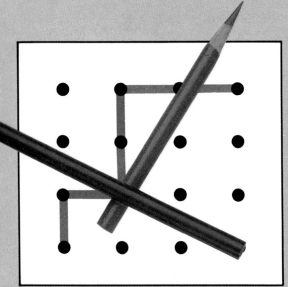

Explore with a Computer

Use the *Fractions Workshop Project* for this activity.

Nancy and Steve are having a computer game tournament. They are going to play a set of 36 games.

1. Suppose Nancy has won $\frac{1}{4}$ of the set. At the computer, shade this fraction. How many games has Nancy won?

2. Steve has won $\frac{1}{3}$ of the set. Shade this fraction. Who has won the most games?

3. They have tied 12 times. Show this number. What is this fraction?

4. How many games do they have left to play? Write this number as a fraction.

Number-Sense Project

Look back at pages 352-353.

One class interviewed 100 people. The class made this table of people's choices for pizza toppings.

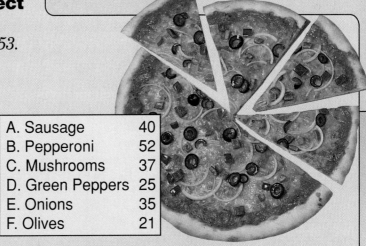

A. Sausage	40
B. Pepperoni	52
C. Mushrooms	37
D. Green Peppers	25
E. Onions	35
F. Olives	21

1. Explain how you know that some people chose more than one topping.

2. What fraction of the people selected green peppers? olives?

Use Data from a Picture

PROBLEM SOLVING
GUIDE

IIII➡ **Understand**
QUESTION
FACTS
KEY IDEA

Plan and Solve
STRATEGY
ANSWER

Look Back
SENSIBLE ANSWER
ALTERNATE APPROACH

Build Understanding

Jim Kern bought a compact disc (CD) on sale at The Music Shop. How much did he save if the CD regularly sells for $16?

IIII➡ **Understand**   QUESTION   How much did Jim save by buying the CD on sale?

FACTS   The CD regularly sells for $16. Look in the picture below for information about a sale at The Music Shop. The sign in the window says "$\frac{1}{4}$ off all CDs."

KEY IDEA   Jim saved $\frac{1}{4}$ of the regular price.

Plan and Solve   STRATEGY   Find $\frac{1}{4}$ of $16. $16 \div 4 = 4

ANSWER   Jim Kern saved $4 by buying the CD on sale.

Look Back   Think of putting sixteen $1 bills into 4 equal groups. There would be four $1 bills in each group. So $\frac{1}{4}$ of $16 is $4.

■**Talk About Math**   How much did Jim Kern pay for the CD?

Look for fractions on store signs the next time you go shopping.

Check Understanding

Use data from the picture on page 370. The roast beef sandwich, the Lunch Special at Joe's Diner, regularly costs $3.75. What is the savings on the roast beef sandwich when it is the day's special?

1. What facts do you need to solve this problem?

2. What operation would you use to solve this problem?

3. Find the savings on the roast beef sandwich special.

Practice

Solve each problem. Use the picture on page 370.

4. Mr. and Mrs. Lopez each had the Lunch Special at Joe's Diner. What was the bill for their meals?

5. Leo had 17 customers today at his barber shop. What fraction of his customers received a free newspaper?

6. How many degrees must the noon temperature rise to reach the predicted high temperature of 92°F?

7. Mrs. Thomas bought a dozen blueberry muffins at Millie's Bakery. How much did she pay for the 12 muffins?

8. What fraction of the people walking down Main Street are carrying packages?

9. At 9:00 P.M., the temperature was 71°F. How much did the temperature change since noon?

10. Jason has 45¢, Brian has 38¢, Ben has 50¢, and Mike has 27¢. Do the boys have enough money to buy 4 blueberry muffins at Millie's Bakery?

11. Kevin saved $5 by buying some CDs on sale at The Music Shop. How much would he have had to pay for the CDs if they had not been on sale?

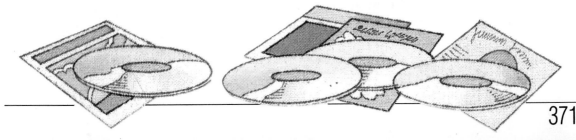

Using the Number Line

Build Understanding

A. Drawing and Marking Lines in Fractional Parts
Materials: Fraction strips

You can use fraction strips to draw number lines.

a. Draw a line. Place the fraction strip for halves below the line. Mark and label the points for $\frac{0}{2}$, $\frac{1}{2}$, and $\frac{2}{2}$ as shown.

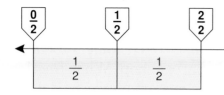

b. Slide the fraction strip to the right so that the left end is on the point marked $\frac{2}{2}$. Mark $\frac{3}{2}$ and $\frac{4}{2}$ on the number line. Repeat until you have marked $\frac{6}{2}$ on your line.

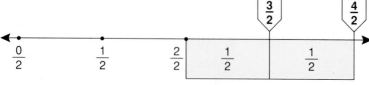

c. Draw another line below and parallel to your halves number line. Mark off a segment that is the length of the strip marked in thirds. Locate and label the points for $\frac{0}{3}$, $\frac{1}{3}$, $\frac{2}{3}$, and $\frac{3}{3}$. Be sure the points that correspond to 0 line up directly beneath one another. Continue marking the line to $\frac{9}{3}$.

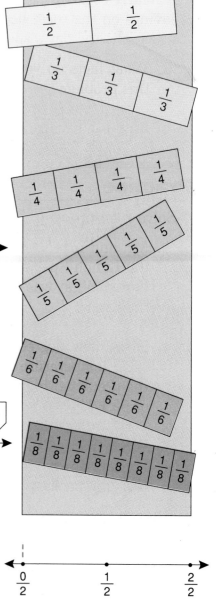

d. Use the rest of your fraction strips to draw number lines below and parallel to your halves and thirds number lines. Mark and label the corresponding fractions on each number line.

B. The number lines shown at the right can be used to compare $\frac{1}{2}$ and $\frac{2}{4}$.

The points labeled $\frac{1}{2}$ and $\frac{2}{4}$ are the same distance from 0. So $\frac{1}{2} = \frac{2}{4}$.

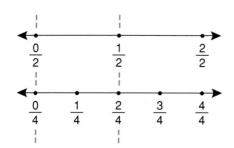

c. The number lines shown at the right can be used to compare $\frac{1}{2}$ and $\frac{2}{3}$.

Since the distance from the point $\frac{0}{2}$ to the point $\frac{1}{2}$ is less than the distance from the point $\frac{0}{3}$ to the point $\frac{2}{3}$, $\frac{1}{2} < \frac{2}{3}$.

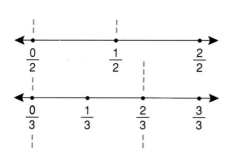

■**Talk About Math** Tell which of the fractions on your number lines can be written as a whole number and which can be written as a mixed number.

Check Understanding

For another example, see Set G, pages 382–383.

Choose the correct answer to each question.

1. Which fraction is equal to $\frac{2}{4}$?

   a. $\frac{6}{10}$ **b.** $\frac{1}{3}$ **c.** $\frac{4}{8}$ **d.** $\frac{2}{6}$

2. Which fraction is less than $\frac{3}{5}$?

   a. $\frac{3}{4}$ **b.** $\frac{5}{10}$ **c.** $\frac{6}{8}$ **d.** $\frac{2}{3}$

Tell if the sentence is *true* or *false*.

3. $\frac{5}{8} > \frac{1}{2}$ **4.** $\frac{4}{6} < \frac{2}{3}$ **5.** $1\frac{1}{10} > 1\frac{1}{8}$ **6.** $\frac{8}{3} = \frac{16}{6}$

Practice

For More Practice, see Set G, pages 384–385.

Use the number lines that you have drawn to compare the fractions. Write <, >, or =.

7. $\frac{3}{4} \diamond \frac{2}{5}$　　　**8.** $\frac{3}{9} \diamond \frac{2}{6}$　　　**9.** $\frac{0}{3} \diamond \frac{1}{8}$　　　**10.** $\frac{5}{9} \diamond \frac{1}{2}$

11. $\frac{5}{6} \diamond \frac{2}{2}$　　　**12.** $\frac{4}{5} \diamond \frac{6}{10}$　　　**13.** $\frac{6}{9} \diamond \frac{2}{3}$　　　**14.** $\frac{7}{8} \diamond \frac{3}{4}$

15. $\frac{2}{4} \diamond \frac{4}{6}$　　　**16.** $\frac{3}{3} \diamond \frac{8}{9}$　　　**17.** $\frac{0}{4} \diamond \frac{0}{5}$　　　**18.** $\frac{1}{2} \diamond \frac{7}{10}$

19. $\frac{7}{6} \diamond \frac{8}{8}$　　　**20.** $\frac{8}{4} \diamond \frac{6}{3}$　　　**21.** $\frac{4}{3} \diamond \frac{3}{2}$　　　**22.** $\frac{14}{5} \diamond \frac{20}{9}$

23. $1\frac{5}{9} \diamond 1\frac{1}{3}$　　　**24.** $\frac{18}{6} \diamond 3$　　　**25.** $2\frac{3}{8} \diamond \frac{5}{2}$　　　**26.** $2\frac{2}{5} \diamond 1\frac{3}{4}$

Problem Solving

Answer each question.

27. Katie said that fractions in which the numerator is twice as great as the denominator are all equal to the whole number 2. Do you agree with Katie? Explain your answer.

28. **Critical Thinking** Look for a pattern in the numerators and denominators of fractions equal to $\frac{1}{2}$. Describe the pattern.

29. **Use Data** Use the chart on page 306 to solve this problem. Horseshoe Falls is 8 feet higher than Big Manitou Falls. How high is Horseshoe Falls?

TIPS FOR PROBLEM SOLVERS

Compare problems to help you relate new problems to ones you've solved before.

The Canadian Horseshoe Falls are in Niagara Falls, Ontario.

The whole numbers that are described in a sentence can be graphed on a number line.

A. On a number line, graph all whole numbers greater than 2 *and* less than 8.

This is the graph of all whole numbers greater than 2.

The shaded arrow means that all of the whole numbers greater than 10 are shaded on the number line.

This is the graph of all whole numbers less than 8.

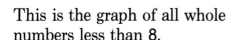

The whole numbers 3, 4, 5, 6, and 7 are graphed on *both* number lines. This is the graph of all whole numbers greater than 2 and less than 8.

B. On a number line, graph all whole numbers less than 3 *or* greater than 6.

This is the graph of all whole numbers less than 3.

This is the graph of all whole numbers greater than 6.

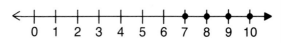

The whole numbers 0, 1, 2, 7, 8, 9, 10, and so on are on *at least one* of the number lines. This is the graph of all whole numbers less than 3 or greater than 6.

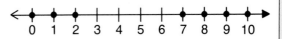

On a number line, graph all whole numbers

30. less than 9 and greater than 4.

31. greater than 2 and less than 6.

32. less than 5 or greater than 7.

33. greater than 3 or less than 1.

Fractional Parts

Build Understanding

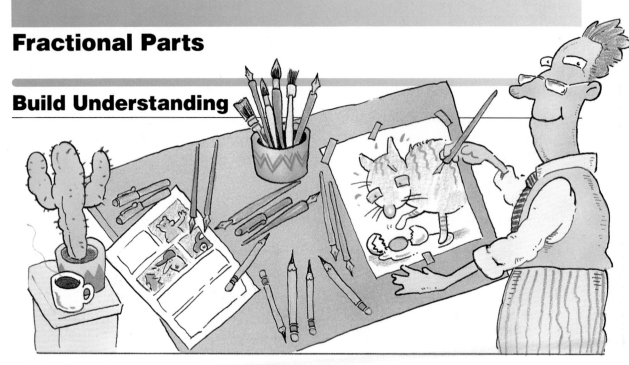

A. Mr. Spangler is a cartoonist. Of the 20 writing instruments on his desk, one fourth of them are pencils. How many pencils are on his desk?

Find $\frac{1}{4}$ of 20.

Use an X to represent each writing instrument. Draw 20 Xs and divide them into 4 equal groups.

XXXXX   XXXXX

XXXXX   XXXXX

There are 5 Xs in each group. So $\frac{1}{4}$ of 20 is 5.

Mr. Spangler has 5 pencils on his desk.

B. Of Mr. Spangler's 12 cartoon characters, $\frac{2}{3}$ of them are animals. How many cartoon characters are animals?

Find $\frac{2}{3}$ of 12.

Use 12 Xs for the 12 cartoon characters. Divide the Xs into 3 equal groups.

XXXX   XXXX   XXXX

One group is $\frac{1}{3}$ of the characters. Two groups are $\frac{2}{3}$ of the characters.

Therefore, $\frac{2}{3}$ of 12 is 8.

There are 8 animal characters.

■ **Talk About Math** In Example A, what fraction of Mr. Spangler's writing instruments are not pencils? How many writing instruments is this?

Check Understanding

For another example, see Set H, pages 382–383.

Complete each sentence.

1. To find $\frac{1}{5}$ of a number of Xs, divide the Xs into ▒ groups and count the number of Xs in one group.

2. To find $\frac{3}{5}$ of a number of Xs, divide the Xs into ▒ groups and count the number of Xs in ▒ of the groups.

Practice

For More Practice, see Set H, pages 384–385.

In each exercise, find the fractional part. Use pictures or letters of the alphabet if necessary.

3. $\frac{1}{3}$ of 18   4. $\frac{1}{4}$ of 36   5. $\frac{2}{5}$ of 25   6. $\frac{3}{10}$ of 40

7. $\frac{5}{8}$ of 40   8. $\frac{4}{5}$ of 20   9. $\frac{3}{4}$ of 4   10. $\frac{1}{8}$ of 80

11. $\frac{5}{6}$ of 48   12. $\frac{1}{2}$ of 42   13. $\frac{9}{10}$ of 50   14. $\frac{7}{8}$ of 56

Problem Solving

Solve the problem.

15. In one of Mr. Spangler's cartoons, a cat broke $\frac{3}{4}$ of a dozen eggs. How many eggs did she break?

Explore ———— Math

Calculator Find $\frac{3}{4}$ of 12 with paper and pencil. Then use a calculator. **Press:** 12 ÷ 4 × 3 = . Is the answer the same using either method?

Use your calculator to find each answer.

16. $\frac{3}{8}$ of 64   17. $\frac{2}{3}$ of 48   18. $\frac{5}{6}$ of 54   19. $\frac{7}{9}$ of 72

20. $\frac{5}{7}$ of 49   21. $\frac{3}{5}$ of 45   22. $\frac{8}{15}$ of 90   23. $\frac{5}{8}$ of 480

Work Backward

Build Understanding

Sam Wong bought some apples at the store. He gave Amy Lee half of them. Then he ate one apple. He had 8 apples left to take home. How many apples did Sam buy?

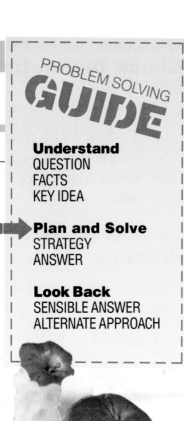

Understand   Sam Wong bought some apples. He gave half of the apples away and kept the other half. Of these, he ate one. He took 8 apples home.

► **Plan and Solve**   STRATEGY   Work backward to find the number of apples Sam bought.

Sam had 8 apples to take home. Before this he ate 1 apple. So before eating the apple, he had 9 apples. These 9 apples are the half not given to Amy. The half he gave to Amy also had 9 apples, so he left the store with 18 apples.

ANSWER   Sam bought 18 apples.

Look Back   Work through the problem to see whether 18 apples makes sense.

Sam gave Amy $\frac{1}{2}$ of 18 or 9 apples. He had 9 apples left. He then ate 1 apple and had 8 apples to take home. This checks, so 18 apples is a sensible answer.

■ **Talk About Math**   Can you use the Try-and-Check strategy to solve this problem? Explain your answer.

Check Understanding

Judy Wong spent one half of her money at the bookstore. Then she went to the fruit stand and spent one half of what was left. She had $3 left.

1. How much money did Judy spend at the fruit stand?

2. How much money did Judy have before she bought the fruit?

3. How much money did Judy spend at the bookstore?

4. How much money did Judy have at the start?

Practice

Solve each problem.

5. Sam took a bus ride that cost him 75¢. He bought a present for $9.45 and spent $3.87 for lunch. It cost him another 75¢ for the bus ride home. He had $5.63 left. How much money did he have when he left to go shopping?

6. Sam took all the change out of his piggy bank. On the way to the store, he lost a nickel and a penny. He spent $1.18, which was $\frac{1}{5}$ of what he had left. How much change did Sam take out of his bank?

7. Judy went to the post office to mail a letter. It cost her 85¢ in postage. The postal rate was 25¢ for the first ounce and 20¢ for each additional ounce. How much did the letter weigh?

8. Judy also bought some stamps at the post office. She gave 10 of the stamps to her father. She then gave her mother $\frac{1}{3}$ of the remaining stamps plus 1 more. How many stamps did she buy if she had 19 stamps left?

Reading —————— Math

Numbers and Symbols State whether the sentence is true or false.

1. Three fourths is greater than three halves.

2. Two thirds is equal to four sixths.

3. One and one sixth is greater than one and one fifth.

Problem Solving REVIEW

Solve each problem.

1. Mara gave half of her dinosaur cards to Carla. Then she gave 8 cards to Juan and 5 cards to Jill. Mara had 6 cards left. How many dinosaur cards did she have originally?

2. Write the fraction that shows how many days of the week begin with the letter T.

3. Elizabeth has $4.75. Does she have enough money to buy 2 styracosauri and 4 triceratops?

Mini dinosaurs!
Triceratops
$0.98 each
Styracosaurus
$1.49 each

4. Michael lives $\frac{4}{10}$ mile from school. Bart lives $\frac{1}{2}$ mile from school. Who lives farther from school?

5. Five of Mr. Perry's 25 dinosaur stamps show a stegosaurus. What fraction of the stamps shows a stegosaurus?

USA 25 *Stegosaurus*

6. Andrew spent 52¢ for airplane and boat stickers. Sam spent 55¢ for dinosaur and airplane stickers. How many of each kind of sticker did each boy buy?

Stickers

Dinosaurs 5¢	Airplanes 8¢	Boats 7¢

7. **Data File** Use data from pages 388-389. On the shepherds' pipe, how far apart should holes G and E be drilled?

8. **Make a Data File** Find the lengths and widths of 3 U.S. stamps to the nearest quarter inch. Make a display showing the differences in size among the stamps.

Explore with a Calculator

Estimating Quotients

A big green gator
Chewed my calculator.
Now the division key
Does not work for me!

You cannot use the division key to find the missing
number in this key sequence.

$$\underline{\quad ? \quad} \quad \boxed{\times} \quad 15 \quad \boxed{=} \quad \boxed{900}$$

Use estimation to make a guess. Check your guess by
pressing the key sequence. Keep guessing until you get
the answer.

| 50 | $\boxed{\times}$ | 15 | $\boxed{=}$ | $\boxed{750}$ | Try again. |
| 60 | $\boxed{\times}$ | 15 | $\boxed{=}$ | $\boxed{900}$ | Correct. |

1. Find the beginning number for each key sequence.
Look for patterns in pairs of consecutive exercises.

a. $\underline{\quad ? \quad} \quad \boxed{\times} \quad 24 \quad \boxed{=} \quad \boxed{408}$

b. $\underline{\quad ? \quad} \quad \boxed{\times} \quad 24 \quad \boxed{=} \quad \boxed{4080}$

c. $\underline{\quad ? \quad} \quad \boxed{\times} \quad 95 \quad \boxed{=} \quad \boxed{380}$

d. $\underline{\quad ? \quad} \quad \boxed{\times} \quad 950 \quad \boxed{=} \quad \boxed{3800}$

e. $\underline{\quad ? \quad} \quad \boxed{\times} \quad 3 \quad \boxed{=} \quad \boxed{1530}$

f. $\underline{\quad ? \quad} \quad \boxed{\times} \quad 30 \quad \boxed{=} \quad \boxed{1530}$

g. $\underline{\quad ? \quad} \quad \boxed{+} \quad 423 \quad \boxed{=} \quad \boxed{970}$

h. $\underline{\quad ? \quad} \quad \boxed{+} \quad 4,230 \quad \boxed{=} \quad \boxed{9700}$

i. $\underline{\quad ? \quad} \quad \boxed{+} \quad 99 \quad \boxed{=} \quad \boxed{349}$

j. $\underline{\quad ? \quad} \quad \boxed{+} \quad 199 \quad \boxed{=} \quad \boxed{349}$

Reteaching

Set A   pages 354–355

This figure has 8 equal parts. Four of the parts are red. This relationship can be written as a fraction.

Number of red parts → $\frac{4}{8}$ ← numerator
Number of equal parts → ← denominator

Remember that a fraction cannot be used to name a part of a whole unless the whole is divided into equal parts.

Write a fraction to show how much of the figure is shaded.

1. 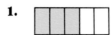   **2.**

Set B   pages 356–357

In the picture below, $\frac{3}{8}$ of the coins are dimes.

$\frac{3}{8}$ ← number of dimes
← total number of coins

Remember that the denominator tells the total number of objects in the set. What fraction of the

1. balloons are red?   **2.** candles are lit?

Set C   pages 358–359

Three parts of each circle are shaded, but sixths are smaller than fifths.

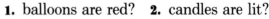

So, $\frac{3}{5} > \frac{3}{6}$.

Remember that if two fractions have the same numerator, the one with the smaller denominator is greater.

1. Compare the fractions. Use < or >.

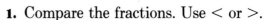 $\frac{3}{4} \vdots \frac{3}{8}$

Set D   pages 360–361

Use fraction strips to find the equal fractions.

$\frac{2}{5} = \frac{\ }{10}$
$\frac{2}{5} = \frac{4}{10}$

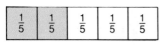

Remember that the denominator tells the number of equal parts in a fraction strip.

Use fraction strips to find the equal fractions.

1. $\frac{3}{4} = \frac{\ }{8}$ **2.** $\frac{1}{5} = \frac{\ }{10}$ **3.** $\frac{2}{3} = \frac{\ }{9}$

Set E   pages 362–363

This picture shows $2\frac{2}{5}$. Two wholes and 2 of 5 parts of another whole are shaded. There are 12 parts shaded in all.

$$2\frac{2}{5} = \frac{12}{5}$$

Remember that a mixed number is made up of a whole number and a fraction.

Write a fraction and a mixed number to describe this picture.

1.

Set F   pages 364–365

This bolt is $2\frac{1}{4}$ inches long.

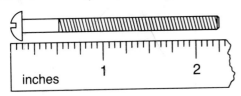

Remember to line up the end of the ruler with one end of the object to be measured.

Use a ruler to measure this object.

1.

Set G   pages 372–375

Compare: $\frac{1}{3} \;\square\; \frac{1}{4}$

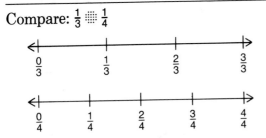

The distance from $\frac{0}{3}$ to $\frac{1}{3}$ is greater than the distance from $\frac{0}{4}$ to $\frac{1}{4}$. So, $\frac{1}{3} > \frac{1}{4}$.

Remember that $>$ means greater than and $<$ means less than.

Use the number lines that you have drawn to compare the fractions. Use $<$, $>$, or $=$.

1. $\frac{3}{4} \;\square\; \frac{4}{6}$ **2.** $\frac{3}{5} \;\square\; \frac{3}{8}$ **3.** $\frac{2}{3} \;\square\; \frac{3}{5}$

4. $\frac{7}{8} \;\square\; \frac{3}{3}$ **5.** $\frac{12}{4} \;\square\; 3$ **6.** $2 \;\square\; \frac{5}{2}$

Set H   pages 376–377

Find $\frac{3}{5}$ of 15.

Draw 15 Xs. Divide the Xs into 5 equal groups.

XXX   XXX   XXX   XXX   XXX

One group is $\frac{1}{5}$ of 15. So, the number of Xs in 3 groups is $\frac{3}{5}$ of 15. Thus $\frac{3}{5}$ of 15 is 9.

Remember that the denominator of the fraction tells you how many groups of equal size to make.

Find the fractional part. Use pictures or letters if necessary.

1. $\frac{2}{5}$ of 15   **2.** $\frac{3}{4}$ of 12   **3.** $\frac{2}{3}$ of 9

4. $\frac{1}{6}$ of 18   **5.** $\frac{3}{10}$ of 20   **6.** $\frac{5}{8}$ of 24

More Practice

Set A pages 354–355

Write a fraction to show how much of the figure is shaded.

1.

2.

3.

Write the numeral for each fraction phrase.

4. five ninths

5. four eighths

6. three sixths

Set B pages 356–357

What fraction of the

1. shapes are circles?

2. balls are footballs?

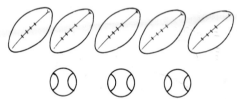

Mixed Practice For Exercises 3–5, tell if the fraction is a fraction of a set or a fraction of a whole.

3. three eighths of a pizza

4. one sixth of the eggs in a box

5. two fifths of the socks in a drawer

Set C pages 358–359

Compare the fractions. Use < or >.

1. $\frac{1}{7} \ \blacksquare\ \frac{2}{7}$

2. $\frac{4}{9} \ \blacksquare\ \frac{3}{9}$

3. $\frac{4}{5} \ \blacksquare\ \frac{4}{7}$

4. $\frac{6}{10} \ \blacksquare\ \frac{8}{10}$

5. $\frac{4}{6} \ \blacksquare\ \frac{4}{7}$

6. $\frac{5}{9} \ \blacksquare\ \frac{5}{8}$

7. $\frac{9}{12} \ \blacksquare\ \frac{7}{12}$

8. $\frac{3}{4} \ \blacksquare\ \frac{3}{6}$

Set D pages 360–361

Use fraction strips to find the equal fractions.

1. $\frac{1}{4} = \frac{\blacksquare}{8}$

2. $\frac{\blacksquare}{5} = \frac{6}{10}$

3. $\frac{1}{2} = \frac{\blacksquare}{8}$

4. $\frac{\blacksquare}{4} = \frac{7}{7}$

5. $\frac{2}{3} = \frac{\blacksquare}{6}$

6. $\frac{\blacksquare}{5} = \frac{4}{10}$

7. $\frac{8}{8} = \frac{\blacksquare}{5}$

8. $\frac{0}{6} = \frac{\blacksquare}{10}$

Set E pages 362–363

Write the mixed number.

1. four and two fifths

2. three and three eighths

3. one and four sevenths

4. two and one tenth

5. For Exercises 1–4, sketch figures to show the mixed numbers.

Write a fraction and a mixed number to describe each group of pictures.

6.

7.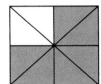

Set F pages 364–365

Use a ruler to measure each object.

1.

2.

3.

4.

Set G pages 372–375

Use the number lines that you have drawn to compare the fractions. Write <, >, or =.

1. $\frac{3}{4} \,\square\, \frac{5}{8}$

2. $\frac{3}{5} \,\square\, \frac{7}{10}$

3. $\frac{5}{6} \,\square\, \frac{7}{8}$

4. $\frac{0}{4} \,\square\, \frac{1}{8}$

5. $\frac{3}{6} \,\square\, \frac{4}{8}$

6. $\frac{9}{8} \,\square\, \frac{6}{6}$

7. $2\frac{1}{4} \,\square\, \frac{17}{8}$

8. $1\frac{4}{9} \,\square\, 1\frac{2}{3}$

Set H pages 376–377

In each exercise, find the fractional part. Use pictures or letters of the alphabet if necessary.

1. $\frac{2}{5}$ of 20

2. $\frac{1}{2}$ of 36

3. $\frac{2}{3}$ of 27

4. $\frac{7}{10}$ of 30

5. $\frac{7}{8}$ of 64

6. $\frac{5}{6}$ of 42

7. $\frac{3}{4}$ of 16

8. $\frac{3}{8}$ of 32

Enrichment

Finding Fractional Parts of Figures

Allen said that he could not find what fraction of this figure was shaded because it was not divided into equal parts.

Ellen drew a line in the figure so that it was divided into 4 equal parts. One part, or $\frac{1}{4}$, of the figure is shaded.

Trace each of these figures. Then draw the lines you need to find the fraction of the figure that is shaded. Write the fraction.

1.

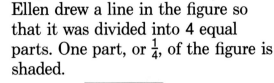

2.

3.

4.

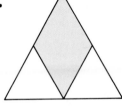

5.

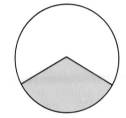

6.

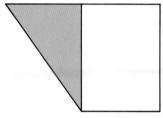

7.

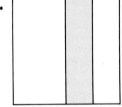

8.

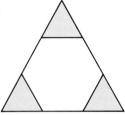

9.

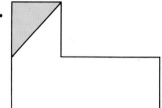

10.

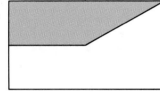

11.

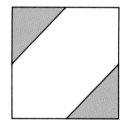

12.

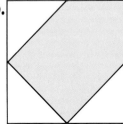

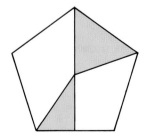

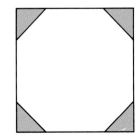

Chapter 11 Review/Test

1. Write a fraction to show how much of the figure is shaded.

2. What fraction of the letters in the word MISSISSIPPI are I's?

Compare the fractions. Use < or >.

3. $\frac{7}{12}$ ⬚ $\frac{11}{12}$ 4. $\frac{3}{5}$ ⬚ $\frac{3}{8}$

5. Use the fraction strips to find the equal fractions.

$\frac{2}{3} = \frac{⬚}{12}$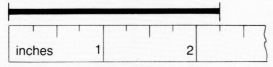

6. Write a fraction and a mixed number to describe the picture.

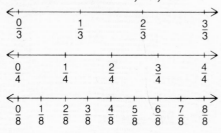

7. Give the length of the segment.

Use the number lines to compare the fractions. Write <, >, or =.

8. $\frac{2}{4}$ ⬚ $\frac{4}{8}$ 9. $\frac{3}{4}$ ⬚ $\frac{7}{8}$ 10. $\frac{2}{3}$ ⬚ $\frac{3}{8}$

11. Find $\frac{2}{3}$ of 9. Use pictures or letters if necessary.

Use the data from the picture to answer Item 12.

12. Suzanne bought 2 dozen eggs. How much did the eggs cost?

Read the following problem. Then answer Items 13 and 14.

Mrs. Jones spent $1.85 on train fare, $3.25 for lunch, and $2.00 on a card for her uncle. At the end of the day <u>she had $15.25 in her purse.</u> How much money did she start with?

13. Which statement best gives the meaning of the underlined words?

   a. The total amount she spent all day was $15.25.
   b. The amount she had before spending any money was $15.25.
   c. After spending $1.85, $3.25, and $2.00, she had $15.25.

14. Solve the problem.

15. **Write About Math** Explain the meanings of the numerator and the denominator for the fraction you wrote in Item 1.

1. Pasta

THIN SPAGHETTI

HIGH PROTEIN PASTA

SPAGHETTI

HIGH PROTEIN PASTA

NET WT. 8 OZ (227g)

NUTRITION INFORMATION	
(PER SERVING)	
SERVING SIZE	2 OZ-DRY
SERVINGS PER PACKAGE	8
CALORIES	210
PROTEIN	7 GRAMS
CARBOHYDRATES	41 GRAMS
FAT	1 GRAM

1. Product Label
Most products list nutritional information as well as ingredients.

2. Table of Measures
These measures are for capacity not weight.

3. Floor Plans
Dimensions are given in feet and inches.

4. Diagram
To make a pipe, use a section of bamboo or plastic pipe about $11\frac{1}{2}$ inches long and $\frac{7}{8}$ inch diameter.

5. Advertisement
8 ounces equal one cup.

2. Table of Measures

Liquid Measure
2 cups (c) = 1 pint (pt)
2 pints = 1 quart (qt)
4 quarts = 1 gallon (gal)

Dry Measure
2 pints (pt) = 1 quart (qt)
8 quarts = 1 peck (pk)
4 pecks = 1 bushel (bu)

3. **Parkside Model Home**

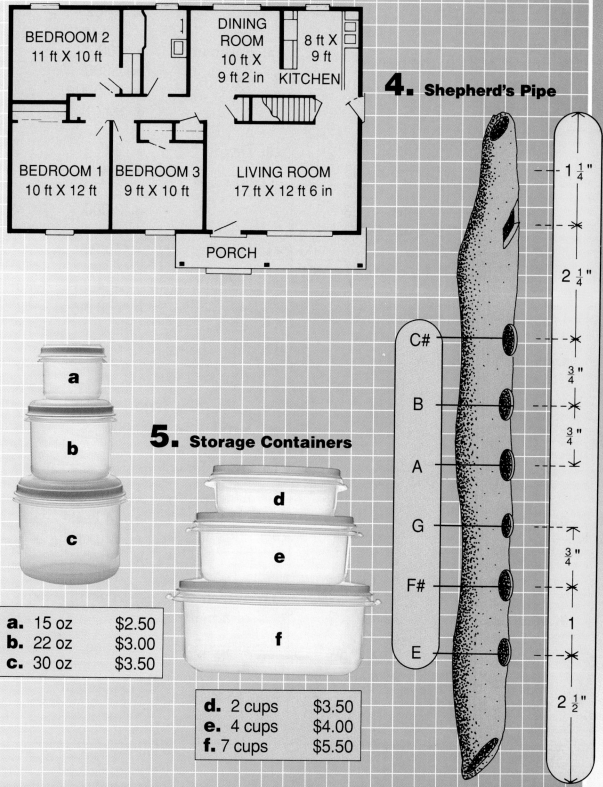

BEDROOM 2
11 ft X 10 ft

DINING ROOM
10 ft X 9 ft 2 in

8 ft X 9 ft
KITCHEN

BEDROOM 1
10 ft X 12 ft

BEDROOM 3
9 ft X 10 ft

LIVING ROOM
17 ft X 12 ft 6 in

PORCH

4. **Shepherd's Pipe**

1 $\frac{1}{4}$ "

2 $\frac{1}{4}$ "

C#

B

$\frac{3}{4}$ "

$\frac{3}{4}$ "

A

G

$\frac{3}{4}$ "

F#

1

E

2 $\frac{1}{2}$ "

5. **Storage Containers**

a.

b.

c.

a.	15 oz	$2.50
b.	22 oz	$3.00
c.	30 oz	$3.50

d.

e.

f.

d.	2 cups	$3.50
e.	4 cups	$4.00
f.	7 cups	$5.50

1. Which digit in 1,379 is in the hundreds place?

a. 1   c. 7
b. 3   d. 9

2. Round 7,681 to the nearest thousand.

a. 7,000   c. 7,600
b. 8,000   d. 7,700

3. Add.

1,799
+ 3,684

a. 5,483
b. 4,373
c. 4,383
d. 5,373

4. Which number is a multiple of 3?

a. 107   c. 162
b. 146   d. 181

5. Find the perimeter.

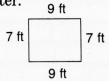

a. 25 ft   c. 32 ft
b. 16 ft   d. 63 ft

6. Divide.

72 ÷ 8

a. 8
b. 9
c. 7
d. 10

7. Multiply.

600 × 7

a. 42
b. 420
c. 4,200
d. 42,000

8. Multiply.

$0.08
×   9

a. $0.72
b. $7.20
c. $72
d. $7.02

9. Estimate.

49 × 39

a. 200
b. 2,000
c. 20,000
d. 90

10. Divide.

800 ÷ 4

a. 20
b. 200
c. 2
d. 2,000

11. Divide.

6)245

a. 40 R5
b. 4 R5
c. 405
d. 400 R5

12. Find the missing factor.

100 × ▦ = 6,000

a. 6   c. 600
b. 60   d. 600,000

13. Find the volume.

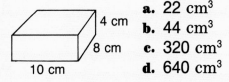

a. 22 cm³
b. 44 cm³
c. 320 cm³
d. 640 cm³

14. Which word describes the shape of a mattress?

a. cylinder   c. cube
b. cone   d. rectangular prism

15. Which fraction shows how much of the figure is shaded?

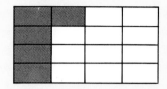

a. $\frac{5}{11}$ **b.** $\frac{16}{5}$ **c.** $\frac{5}{16}$ **d.** $\frac{11}{5}$

16. Which fraction or mixed number describes the shaded part?

a. $3\frac{1}{4}$ **b.** $\frac{13}{3}$ **c.** $\frac{16}{3}$ **d.** $4\frac{1}{4}$

17. Find the missing number.

4 lb = ▓ oz

a. 48   **b.** 40   **c.** 64   **d.** 400

18. Which is a true sentence?

a. $\frac{11}{12} < \frac{10}{12}$ **c.** $\frac{6}{8} > \frac{7}{8}$

b. $\frac{3}{4} < \frac{3}{8}$ **d.** $\frac{1}{2} > \frac{1}{4}$

19. Jim bought a cassette for $5.98 and a notebook for $1.75. He gave the clerk $10.00. How much change did he receive?

a. $2.73   **c.** $3.27
b. $7.73   **d.** $2.27

20. How many teams of 8 can be formed from a group of 50 boys?

a. 5 teams   **c.** 7 teams
b. 6 teams   **d.** 8 teams

21. What fraction of the letters in the word MATHEMATICS are Ms?

a. $\frac{2}{11}$ **c.** $\frac{2}{9}$

b. $\frac{11}{2}$ **d.** $\frac{9}{2}$

22. An airplane holds 246 passengers. How many passengers can the plane carry in 6 trips?

a. 1,476 passengers
b. 1,276 passengers
c. 252 passengers
d. 41 passengers

Read the table and the problem below it. Then answer Item 23.

MOVIE TICKETS

	Afternoon	Evening
Adult	$5	$6
Student	$2	$3

At 2:30 P.M. a group of 5 adults will attend a movie. What will be the total cost of the tickets?

23. Which data from the table must be used to solve this problem?

a. The cost of afternoon tickets for adults
b. The cost of evening tickets for adults
c. The cost of afternoon tickets for students
d. The cost of evening tickets for students

Decimals

12

5.00
4.75
4.50
4.25
4.00
3.75
3.50
3.25
3.00
2.75
2.50
2.25
2.00
1.75
1.50
1.25
1.00
.75
.50
.25

Number-Sense Project

Estimate

How many inches of rain do you think you get in your area each year? Do you think adults would give a higher or lower estimate than you did?

Gather Data

Make your own estimate of the number of inches of rain per year and then ask two or more adults to do the same.

Analyze and Report

Compare your estimate with the adults' estimates. Write a sentence describing how the estimates varied.

Tenths

Build Understanding

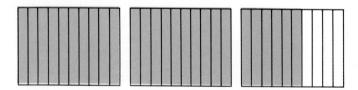

A. Designs with Tenths
Materials: Grid paper, crayons or colored pencils, scissors

a. Draw a rectangle that is 10 units long. Choose any number for the width. Draw lines to show 10 equal parts.

b. Use one or more colors to shade some of the parts.

c. Tell how many **tenths** of the rectangle are shaded in each color.

B. For this rectangle, 5 of 10 equal parts are shaded. You can say 5 tenths are shaded.

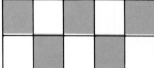

Write: $\frac{5}{10}$ or 0.5

↑   ↑
fraction   *decimal*

c. The model shows two and six tenths. You can write a mixed number or a decimal.

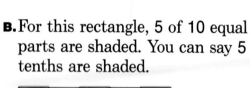

Write: $2\frac{6}{10}$ or 2.6

■ **Talk About Math** How many tenths make a whole? How many tenths make a half? How many tenths make one and a half?

394

For another example, see Set A, pages 422–423.

Check Understanding

Answer each question.

1. Which model shows 0.4?

a. 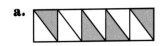 b.

2. Which model shows 1.3?

a. b.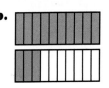

3. Draw a model for 7 tenths. Then write a fraction and a decimal.

4. Write a mixed number and a decimal for the shaded part.

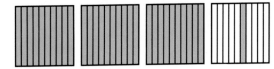

Practice

For More Practice, see Set A, pages 424–425.

For each exercise, draw a model. Then write a fraction and a decimal.

5. 1 tenth **6.** 9 tenths **7.** three tenths **8.** 5 tenths

9. two tenths **10.** 6 tenths **11.** 8 tenths **12.** ten tenths

For each exercise, write a mixed number and a decimal.

13. four and 2 tenths **14.** one and 3 tenths **15.** six and 8 tenths

16. 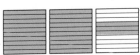 **17.**  **18.**

Reading ———— Math

Numbers and Symbols Write each decimal in words.

1. 0.3 **2.** 5.7 **3.** 6.3 **4.** 0.9 **5.** 3.5 **6.** 31.4

The Number Line and Measurement

Build Understanding

A. The blue strip is 1 unit long. Each section is one tenth of a unit. How long is the yellow strip? How long is the grasshopper?

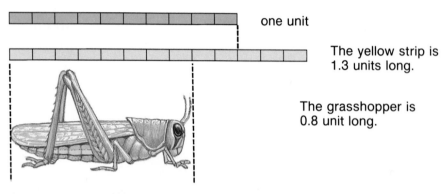

one unit

The yellow strip is 1.3 units long.

The grasshopper is 0.8 unit long.

B. A decimal number line is like a ruler. The unit of measure is the distance from 0 to 1. What decimal tells the position of the letter E on this number line? How long is segment OE?

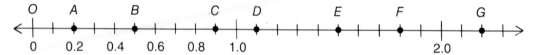

The position of letter E is 1.5. Segment OE is 1.5 units long.

■ **Talk About Math** How could you find the length of segment AB?

Check Understanding

For another example, see Set B, pages 422–423.

Answer each question.

1. How long is the insect shown at the right?

2. On the number line above, what is the length of line segment OD?

one unit

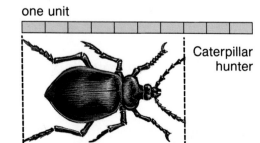

Caterpillar hunter

Practice

For More Practice, see Set B, pages 424–425.

3. Use the blue strip to find the wingspan of the butterfly.

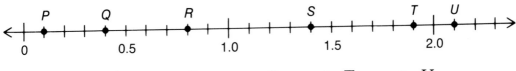

1 unit

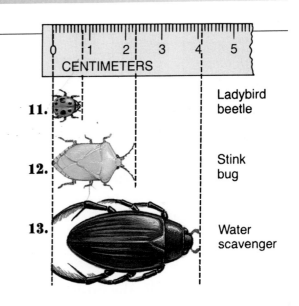

Common sulphur

What decimal tells the position of each letter on the number line?

P   Q   R   S   T   U

0   0.5   1.0   1.5   2.0

4. P **5.** Q **6.** R **7.** S **8.** T **9.** U

10. What is the length of line segment QT?

Problem Solving

Most centimeter rulers have markings to show tenths. Write a decimal for the length of each insect in centimeters.

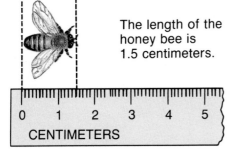

The length of the honey bee is 1.5 centimeters.

0   1   2   3   4   5
CENTIMETERS

0   1   2   3   4   5
CENTIMETERS

11. Ladybird beetle

12. Stink bug

13. Water scavenger

Explore ——— Math

This ruler is marked in **millimeters**.

0   10   20   30   40   50   60   70
MILLIMETERS

14. Find five small objects to measure in millimeters and centimeters. Record the lengths in a chart. What do you notice?

397

Hundredths

Build Understanding

A. When a whole unit or object is divided into 100 equal parts, each part is one **hundredth**. The small shaded square is $\frac{1}{100}$ or 0.01 of the large square.

Ones	Tenths	Hundredths
0	0	1

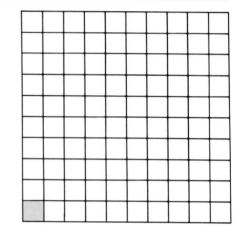

B. Write a decimal for the shaded part.

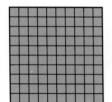

Each ☐ is 1 hundredth, so the shaded part of the second square is 26 hundredths. One and 26 hundredths is written as $1\frac{26}{100}$ or 1.26.

Ones	Tenths	Hundredths
1	2	6

C. What decimal tells the position of the letter C on this number line?

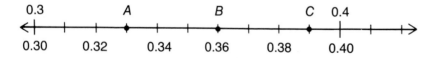

This number line has 10 parts between 0.30 and 0.40. Each part is 1 hundredth.

The position of letter C is 0.39.

■ **Talk About Math** How many hundredths make a tenth? How many hundredths make a half?

398

Check Understanding

For another example, see Set C, pages 422–423.

1. Which model shows 0.60?

a. **b.**

2. On the number line in Example C, what decimal gives the position of the letter A?

3. Draw a model for 2 and 8 hundredths. Then write a mixed number and a decimal.

4. Write four and twelve hundredths as a decimal.

Practice

For More Practice, see Set C, pages 424–425.

Write a decimal and a fraction or mixed number for the shaded part.

5.   **6.**   **7.**   **8.**   **9.**

10.   **11.**

12.

13.

Write a mixed number for the shaded part.

14.
15.

Write each number as a decimal.

16. five and twenty hundredths

17. sixty-eight hundredths

18. seven and three hundredths

19. ten and fourteen hundredths

20. 125 hundredths

21. 350 hundredths

On grid paper, draw a model for each decimal. Then write each decimal in words.

22. 0.21   **23.** 0.70   **24.** 1.85   **25.** 2.57   **26.** 1.04

What decimal gives the position of each letter on the number line?

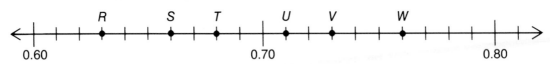

27. *R*   **28.** *S*   **29.** *T*   **30.** *U*   **31.** *V*   **32.** *W*

Problem Solving

Copy and use the number line below to answer Problems 33–34.

33. Rita uses a pedometer when she walks. One day she walked fifty-four hundredths mile to the park. Write the decimal. Mark the distance on the number line.

34. At the park, Rita met a friend and together they walked sixty-six hundredths mile. What did Rita's pedometer read then? Mark the decimal on the number line.

0 miles   1 mile

400

Estimation Estimate the answer to each question.

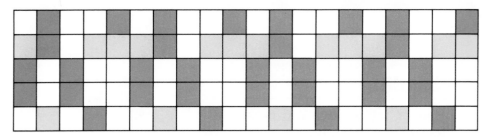

35. What part of this design is blue? Write the answer as a decimal.

36. What part of the design is yellow?

Skills **Review**

pages 124–129, 220–221, 224–225, 230–233, 328–329

1. Find the perimeter of the star.

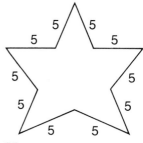

2. What is the area of *ABCD*?

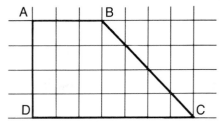

3. How many lines of symmetry does this figure have?

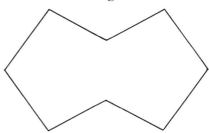

4. Are these shapes congruent?

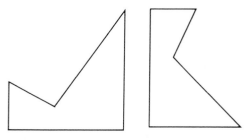

5. Is line *HI* perpendicular to line *JK*? Is ∠*KGI* a right angle?

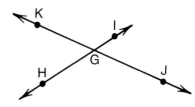

6. Find the volume.

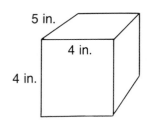

5 in. 4 in. 4 in.

Make a Table

Build Understanding

The bus fare in Scott City is 50¢. You must pay
with the exact change in half dollars, quarters,
dimes, or nickels. In how many different ways
can you pay the fare?

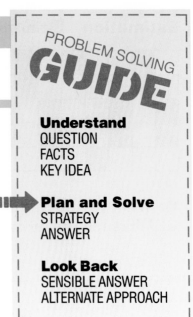

Understand You need to count all the ways
to pay the fare. You can use coins
worth 50¢, 25¢, 10¢, or 5¢.

**Plan
and Solve**   STRATEGY   Make a table. Each row
of the table shows a combination
of coins worth 50¢. Start with the
coins that have the greatest value.

Combination	Half Dollar	Quarter	Dime	Nickel	Value
1	1				50¢
2		2			25¢ + 25¢
3		1	2	1	25¢ + 20¢ + 5¢
4		1	1	3	25¢ + 10¢ + 15¢
5		1		5	.
6			5		.
7			4	2	.
8			3	4	
9			2	6	
10			1	8	
11				10	

ANSWER   There are 11 ways to pay the bus fare.

Look Back   You could also solve the problem by making a
list. For example, you could list Q D N N N
to represent combination 4 in the table above.

■ **Talk About Math**   Why is it important to
organize a table or list?

Check Understanding

1. Write a number sentence to show the value of the coins listed as combination 8 in the table.

2. If the coin boxes on the buses could not accept half dollars, how many ways could you pay the fare in Scott City?

3. Ria has 1 quarter and 4 dimes. Can she ride the Scott City bus? What must she do?

4. When you pay a bus fare, does the order in which you give out the coins matter? Explain.

Practice

In Glen City the bus fare is 60¢. You must have the exact fare, and you may not use pennies.

5. In how many ways can you pay the bus fare in Glen City? Make a table or a list to help you find the answer.

6. Bob has 2 half dollars. How many ways can he change one of his coins so that he can ride the Glen City bus?

7. Rosa has 3 quarters. In which city could she ride the bus, Scott City or Glen City?

8. The bus fare in Dobie is 75¢ using exact change. How many different ways can you pay it without using pennies?

Choose a ——— Strategy

Sparky's Spending Spree
Sparky spent $1.50 on bus fares, $2.75 on a new baseball, and $6.20 each for two shirts. After these purchases Sparky had $2.85 left.

9. How much money did he have before his purchases?

PROBLEM SOLVING STRATEGIES

Choose an Operation
Try and Check
Draw a Diagram
Solve a Simpler Problem
Write a Number Sentence
Make a Table
Use Logical Reasoning
Find a Pattern
Draw a Picture
Work Backward

Place Value and Equal Decimals

Build Understanding

A. In physical education class, Laura ran 100 yards in 15.23 seconds. You can write the decimal 15.23 on a place-value chart.

Tens	Ones	Tenths	Hundredths
1	5	2	3

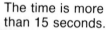

Read this as 15 and 23 hundredths.

The time is more than 15 seconds.

B. What part of the square is red?

Jamie thinks:
One column is 0.1 and
4 columns are 0.4.
So 0.4 of the square is red.

Suki thinks:
The square has 100 parts
and 40 are red.
So 0.40 of the square is red.

They are both correct. The decimals 0.4 and 0.40 are called *equal decimals*.

■ **Talk About Math** Which of these pairs of numbers are equal?

2.3 and 2.30   5.2 and 5.02   16 and 16.00

Check Understanding

For another example, see Set D, pages 422–423.

For Exercises 1–2, write two decimals for each model.

1.

2.

For Exercises 3–5, copy the place-value chart. Write each decimal in the chart.

Tens	Ones	Tenths	Hundredths

3. 17.05 **4.** 0.8 **5.** 56

Practice

For More Practice, see Set D, pages 424–425.

Write each decimal in a place-value chart.

6. 57.2 **7.** 0.29 **8.** 70.04 **9.** 8.01 **10.** 83.29

Write as a decimal.

11. 9 and 34 hundredths **12.** fourteen and two tenths

13. 2 tens, 6 tenths, 3 hundredths **14.** 8 tens, 2 tenths, 9 hundredths

Tell which decimal in the list is not equal to the others.

15. 0.50	**16.** 1.3	**17.** 6.00	**18.** 2.7	**19.** 8.88
0.05	1.30	6.60	2.77	88.80
0.5	1.03	6.6	2.70	8.880

Midchapter ——— Checkup

Draw a model for each number. Then write the number as a decimal.

1. nine tenths **2.** sixty-one hundredths **3.** two and six tenths

4. Make a table to show all the combinations of pennies, nickels, and dimes that have a value of 15¢.

Problem-Solving Workshop

Expore as a Team

1. Make a card or paper strip divided into 10 equal parts. You may copy this one if you like. Each team member's strip should be the same length.

2. Work with other students to measure six objects with the strips. Record the length of each object to the nearest tenth of a strip. To record a measurement of 7 strips and 8 tenths, write 7.8 strips. If the team members do not agree on the length, measure again.

TIPS FOR **WORKING TOGETHER**

Don't decide by voting. Try to understand which might be the best solution and why.

Object	Length to nearest tenth of a strip
desk (width)	7.8 strips
book (length)	2.3 strips

Real-Life Decision Making

Suppose you need to buy peanut butter. You have these two coupons for Yummy Peanut Butter.

PEANUT BUTTER

$1.19

1. Find the cost per jar if you use the Free coupon. Use play money to help you.

2. Find the cost for one jar if you use the 20¢-off coupon.

3. Which coupon would you use? Why?

FREE
YUMMY PEANUT BUTTER
Buy two 20-oz jars of Yummy and get a third jar free.

20¢ OFF
YUMMY PEANUT BUTTER
Buy any size jar of Yummy Peanut Butter and get 20¢ off.

Number-Sense Project

Look back at pages 392-393.
The "ruler" on the rain gauge is marked in units of 5 hundredths of an inch.

1. What is the amount of rain shown in the gauge on page 392?

2. What is the amount of rain shown in the gauge on this page?

3. Write a number sentence to show which is greater.

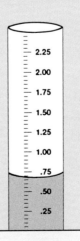

2.25
2.00
1.75
1.50
1.25
1.00
.75
.50
.25

Critical-Thinking Activity

When you count by tenths from 0.5 to 2.1, how many numbers do you say?

0.5 ?→ 2.1

Comparing and Ordering Decimals

Build Understanding

A. Compare 0.64 and 0.9 by using square decimal models.

0.64 is 6 tenths 4 hundredths.   0.9 is 9 tenths.

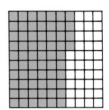 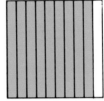

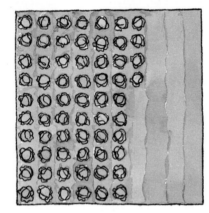

The model for 0.64 has less shaded. You can write two number sentences.

0.64 is less than 0.9.   0.9 is greater than 0.64.

$$0.64 < 0.9 \qquad\qquad 0.9 > 0.64$$

B. Show 0.7, 2, 0.25, and 1.3 on a number line. Then write the numbers in order from least to greatest.

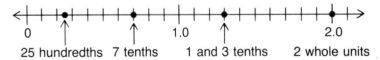

0   25 hundredths   7 tenths   1.0   1 and 3 tenths   2.0   2 whole units

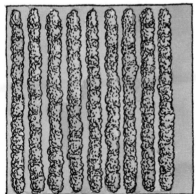

In order from least to greatest, the numbers are 0.25, 0.7, 1.3, and 2.

■ **Write About Math** Draw two line segments on your paper. Measure both to the nearest tenth of a centimeter. Which segment is longer? Write a number sentence to compare the lengths.

Check Understanding

For another example, see Set E, pages 422–423.

1. Write two number sentences to compare the decimals.

 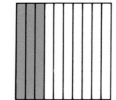

2. Copy the number line. Show 0.8 and 0.55. Then write two number sentences to compare the decimals.

0   1.0

Practice

For More Practice, see Set E, pages 424–425.

Compare the decimals. Use <, >, or =. Draw models if necessary.

3. 0.5 ▦ 0.3

4. 0.72 ▦ 0.67

5. 1.4 ▦ 1.7

6. 4.3 ▦ 4.5

7. 0.8 ▦ 0.80

8. 0.45 ▦ 0.19

9. 0.32 ▦ 0.23

10. 1.6 ▦ 1.60

11. 3.41 ▦ 3.25

12. 0.10 ▦ 0.01

13. 4.2 ▦ 0.59

14. 1.02 ▦ 1.2

Write the numbers in order from least to greatest. Use a number line if necessary.

15. 0.7   0.9   0.4

16. 1.7   1.5   1.8

17. 0.3   0.75   1.1

18. 0.32   0.73   0.6

19. 10.7   8.4   9

20. 29   29.9   29.99

Problem Solving

Solve each problem.

21. Chico rides his bicycle 3.8 miles to school. Is this greater or less than 4 miles?

22. Maryanne rides her bicycle 0.4 miles from her home to the library. Is the round-trip distance more or less than a mile?

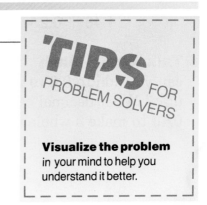

TIPS FOR PROBLEM SOLVERS

Visualize the problem in your mind to help you understand it better.

Using Models to Add Decimals

Build Understanding

A. An electrician needed two pieces of wire, one 0.6 m long and another 0.7 m long. How much wire did he need?

Locate 0.7 on the number line. Then move 6 tenths to the right.

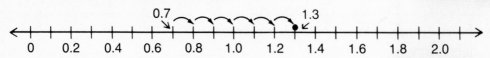

$$0.7 + 0.6 = 1.3$$

He needed 1.3 m of wire.

B. Add 1.48 + 0.2. Use square decimal models.

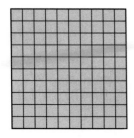 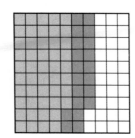

To show 1.48, shade a whole, 4 tenths, and 8 hundredths.

To show 0.2, shade 2 tenths or 20 hundredths.

The total amount shaded is 1.68.

$$1.48 + 0.2 = 1.68$$

■ **Talk About Math** What decimal can you add to 0.6 to make 1 whole unit? What decimal can you add to 0.48 to make a whole unit?

Electric power wires are made of copper, one of the best conductors of electricity.

Check Understanding

For another example, see Set F, pages 422–423.

1. Write an addition sentence to show the sum of the red part and the blue part.

 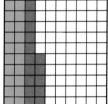

2. What number is 0.8 more than 0.2? Use the number line to add.

0   1.0

Practice

For More Practice, see Set F, pages 424–425.

Add. Use models if necessary.

| **3.** 0.7
+ 0.9 | **4.** 0.8
+ 0.7 | **5.** 1.2
+ 0.9 | **6.** 0.25
+ 0.46 | **7.** 1.96
+ 1.06 |

8. 0.83 + 0.17   **9.** 0.3 + 0.9 + 0.7   **10.** 0.64 + 2.13   **11.** 1.7 + 0.64

12. 0.4 + 0.37 + 1   **13.** 0.11 + 0.4 + 2.6

Mental Math   Add.

14. 2 + 0.6   **15.** 0.4 + 0.08   **16.** 1.2 + 9

17. 15 + 5.6   **18.** 2.2 + 3.3   **19.** 3 + 0.41

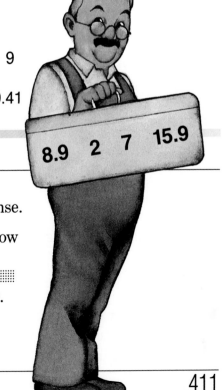

8.9   2   7   15.9

Problem Solving

Number Sense   Use numbers from the toolbox so that the paragraph below makes sense.

20. Mr. Pulaski has ▦ pieces of wire. The yellow piece is longer than the red piece. The red piece is ▦ cm long and the yellow piece is ▦ cm long. The total length is ▦ centimeters.

Using Models to Subtract Decimals

Build Understanding

A. Find 1.8 − 0.7. Use the number line.

Locate 1.8. Then move 7 tenths to the left.

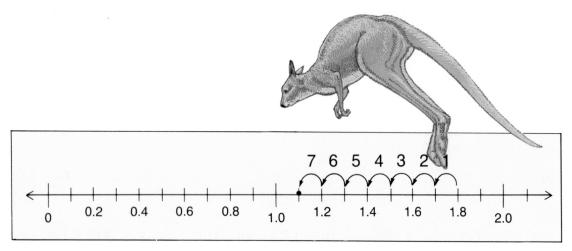

The difference is 1.1.
1.8 − 0.7 = 1.1

B. Subtract 0.45 from 1.3. Use square decimal models.

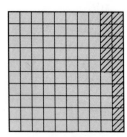 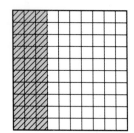

To show **1.3**, shade a whole and 3 tenths or 30 hundredths.

To subtract 0.45, mark off 4 tenths and 5 hundredths.

The unmarked part is 0.85.

1.3 − 0.45 = 0.85

■ **Talk About Math**   If you have whole units, how can you subtract tenths? If you have tenths, how can you subtract hundredths?

412

Check Understanding

For another example, see Set G, pages 422–423.

1. Copy the model and mark off 0.4. Write a subtraction sentence to show how much is left.

2. What number is 0.2 less than 0.65? Use the number line to subtract.

Practice

For More Practice, see Set G, pages 424–425.

Subtract. Use models if necessary.

3. 0.9 $-\,0.7$	**4.** 1.5 $-\,1.3$	**5.** 1.2 $-\,0.4$	**6.** 0.25 $-\,0.11$	**7.** 1.59 $-\,0.60$	**8.** 0.11 $-\,0.06$

9. $0.58 - 0.1$ **10.** $1 - 0.73$ **11.** $2.39 - 0.30$ **12.** $5 - 0.05$

13. $0.64 - 0.6$ **14.** $5.3 - 2.1$ **15.** $6 - 4.9$ **16.** $3.9 - 0.05$

Mental Math   Subtract.

17. $8.5 - 8$ **18.** $2.5 - 0.3$ **19.** $3 - 0.3$ **20.** $6.66 - 0.06$

21. $5.6 - 0.6$ **22.** $22.2 - 2.2$ **23.** $1.78 - 0.78$ **24.** $2 - 2.0$

Problem Solving

Use Data   Solve. Use data from pages 396–397.

25. Measure the grasshopper in centimeters. Which is longer, the grasshopper or the honey bee? How much longer?

26. Which is longer, the ladybird beetle or the honey bee? How much longer?

Rounding and Estimation

Build Understanding

A. Mrs. Yates, a bus driver, made a list of distances from the bus station to other places. When people ask her for a distance, she usually rounds decimals to whole numbers.

Look at the chart. To the nearest mile, how far is the zoo?

On the number line, 2.8 is between 2 and 3 but closer to 3. The zoo is about 3 miles away.

Distances from Station	
Post Office	0.7 mi
Zoo	2.8 mi
County Offices	1.4 mi
Library	0.3 mi
Airport	7.2 mi
Train Station	4.9 mi

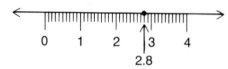

B. Mrs. Yates drove 8.6 miles on her first route and then 17.8 miles on the next route. About how many miles did she drive in all? About how much shorter was the first route?

One way to estimate the sum or difference of two decimals is to use the whole number part of each number. Use 8 instead of 8.6. Use 17 instead of 17.8.

8 + 17 = 25   She drove about 25 miles.
17 − 8 = 9   The first route was about 9 miles shorter.

Buses carry more passengers than any other form of public transportation in the United States.

■ **Talk About Math** In Example B, if you estimated the sum and difference by using rounded numbers, would your estimates be the same? Which method is easier for you?

Check Understanding

For another example, see Set H, pages 422–423.

Answer each question.

1. On a number line, what whole number is closest to 3.4?

2. Estimate the sum of 10.7 and 5.2 by rounding.

3. Since 2.5 is halfway between 2 and 3, you round up to 3. How would you round the decimal 6.5?

4. Estimate the difference between 23.0 and 9.3 by using the whole-number part of each number.

Practice

For More Practice, see Set H, pages 424–425.

Round each decimal to the nearest whole number. Use a number line if necessary.

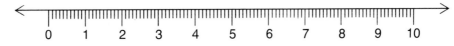

5. 1.7 **6.** 5.9 **7.** 8.1 **8.** 6.3 **9.** 9.8 **10.** 4.4

11. 0.4 **12.** 7.5 **13.** 9.05 **14.** 2.82 **15.** 6.94 **16.** 4.53

Estimate each answer.

17. 1.4 + 3.8 **18.** 9.6 − 4.5 **19.** 7.2 − 3.9 **20.** 9.3 + 4.8

21. 18.6 − 7.8 **22.** 42.7 − 21.2 **23.** 24.3 + 16.5 **24.** 41.3 + 6.7

25. 2.91 + 0.78 **26.** 4.09 − 1.8 **27.** 9.58 + 8.91 **28.** 5.6 + 10.21

Problem Solving

29. **Calculator** The lengths of five bus routes are given at the right. Which three routes have a total length of 100 miles?

Bus Routes

43.2 mi	27.2 mi
29.3 mi	38.5 mi
43.5 mi	

Adding and Subtracting Decimals

Build Understanding

Have you ever measured the lengths of hallways in your school? Mr. Roth's class made these measurements.

Front Hall	29 m
Back Hall	24.8 m

A. What is the total length of the two hallways? Think of place value to help you add. Remember to write a decimal point in the sum.

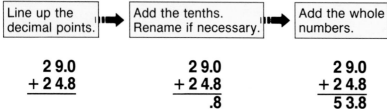

Line up the decimal points.	→	Add the tenths. Rename if necessary.	→	Add the whole numbers.

$$\begin{array}{r} 2\,9.0 \\ +\,2\,4.8 \\ \hline \end{array}$$
$$\begin{array}{r} 2\,9.0 \\ +\,2\,4.8 \\ \hline .8 \end{array}$$
$$\begin{array}{r} 2\,9.0 \\ +\,2\,4.8 \\ \hline 5\,3.8 \end{array}$$

The total length of the two hallways is 53.8 meters.

Calculator

29 ⊕ 24 ⊡ 8 ⊜ *53.8*

B. How much longer is the front hallway than the back hallway?

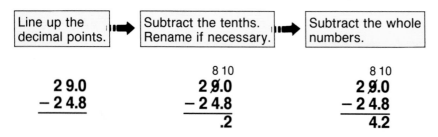

Line up the decimal points.	→	Subtract the tenths. Rename if necessary.	→	Subtract the whole numbers.

$$\begin{array}{r} 2\,9.0 \\ -\,2\,4.8 \\ \hline \end{array}$$
$$\begin{array}{r} \overset{8\ 10}{2\,\cancel{9}.0} \\ -\,2\,4.8 \\ \hline .2 \end{array}$$
$$\begin{array}{r} \overset{8\ 10}{2\,\cancel{9}.0} \\ -\,2\,4.8 \\ \hline 4.2 \end{array}$$

The front hallway is 4.2 meters longer.

■ **Talk About Math** Why is 29 written as 29.0?

416

Check Understanding

For another example, see Set I, pages 422–423.

1. Add 52.7 and 8.3. Remember to line up the decimal points.

2. Subtract 7.58 from 9. Explain why you would write 9 as 9.00 before you subtract.

Practice

For More Practice, see Set I, pages 424–425.

Add or subtract. **Remember** to line up the decimal points.

3. 0.73
      + 0.08

4. 18.3
      + 2.5

5. 17.1
      − 2.8

6. 2.57
      − 0.81

7. 0.67
      + 5.24

8. 16.3
      + 19.4

9. 3.24
      − 1.99

10. 27.05
       − 19.61

11. 21.09
       + 16.03

12. 38.7
       + 49.1

13. 0.40 + 6 + 1.92

14. 4.25 + 3 + 0.72

15. 1.78 + 4 + 3.95

Mixed Practice   Use paper and pencil, mental math, or a calculator to find each answer. Tell which method you used.

16. 0.06 − 0.02

17. 15.6 − 13

18. 10 + 7.43

19. 9.03 + 1.97

20. 4.35 + 2.09

21. 4.7 − 3.8

22. 25.7 + 3.5

23. 38.15 − 29.68

24. 2 + 3.6

25. 9 + 8.74

26. 6 − 2.92

27. 5.03 − 4.7

28. 12.9 + 29.4

29. 43.9 − 21

30. 4.01 − 2.09

31. 5.92 + 17.83

Problem Solving

Read for the facts. Then solve each problem.

32. The ceiling in Mr. Roth's classroom is 3.5 m high. Mr. Roth is 1.85 m tall. How far is the ceiling from the top of his head?

33. Critical Thinking   Use + and − to make this number sentence correct.
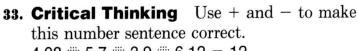
4.08 ░ 5.7 ░ 3.9 ░ 6.12 = 12

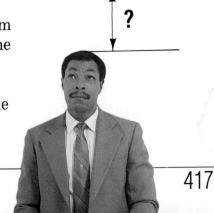

417

Choose an Operation

PROBLEM SOLVING
GUIDE

Understand
QUESTION
FACTS
KEY IDEA

▮▮▶ **Plan and Solve**
STRATEGY
ANSWER

Look Back
SENSIBLE ANSWER
ALTERNATE APPROACH

Build Understanding

Marla and Brian attended the 4th Annual Model Airplane Competition. In the longest flight competition, Marla's plane flew a distance of 52.4 meters. Brian's plane flew 38.2 meters. How much farther did Marla's plane fly?

Understand   You know how far each plane flew. You need to find out how much farther Marla's plane flew.

▮▮▶ **Plan and Solve**   STRATEGY   Use subtraction to compare the two distances. First, estimate: 52 − 38 = 14.

Paper and Pencil

$$\begin{array}{r} 5\,2.4 \\ -\,3\,8.2 \\ \hline 1\,4.2 \end{array}$$

Calculator

52 ⬚ . 4 ⬚ − 38 ⬚ . 2 ⬚ = *14.2*

ANSWER   Marla's plane flew 14.2 meters farther.

Look Back   Add 14.2 meters to the distance that Brian's plane flew. The sum should be 52.4 meters.

■ **Talk About Math**   Suppose Marla's plane flew 35.2 meters and Brian's plane flew 45.2 meters. How would you estimate the difference?

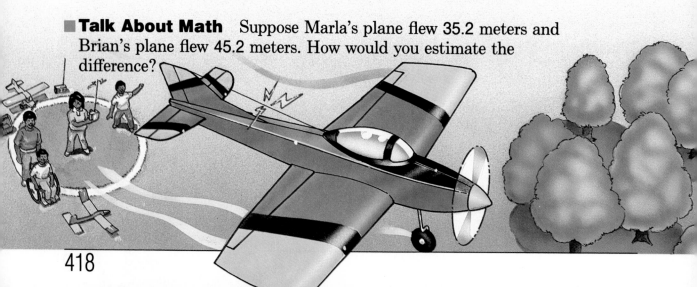

Check Understanding

Tell whether you would add or subtract. Then choose numbers that are reasonable and find the answers.

1. Simon's plane flew ▦ meters on the first flight and ▦ meters on the second flight. How far did his plane fly on both flights?

2. Deborah had two planes. One had a wingspan of ▦ meters. The other had a wingspan of ▦ meters. How much longer is the wingspan on the larger plane?

Practice

Tell whether you would add or subtract. Then find each answer.

3. To build his model airplane, Pedro spent $5.26 for wood, $2.73 for paint, and $1.40 for glue. How much did he spend in all?

4. John spent $11.00 for materials to build his model airplane. He then sold the plane for $16.85. How much money did he make on the sale?

5. During the first flight, Diane's glider stayed in the air for 20.14 seconds. On the second flight, it stayed up for 18.53 seconds. What was the total time Diane's glider stayed in the air?

6. Adam bought two stickers for his plane. One sticker cost $0.55. The other sticker cost $1.29. How much did the stickers cost together?

7. During two flights, Raul's glider stayed in the air for a total of 68.10 seconds. During the first flight, it stayed up for 29.63 seconds. How long did it stay up during the second flight?

8. Luisa's plane won first place for flying a distance of 63.8 meters. Kelly's plane flew a distance of 5.9 meters less than Luisa's. How many meters did Kelly's plane fly?

Solve each problem.

1. Three members of the Gainsville Track Team each ran 50 meters. Their times were 8.12 seconds, 8.54 seconds, and 8.01 seconds. List the times in order from least to greatest.

2. Phil spent $25.16 for a rosebush and some bulbs. The rosebush cost $8.29. How much did the bulbs cost?

3. Four people ran in a relay race. Their times were 32.41 seconds, 33.08 seconds 35.11 seconds, and 29.80 seconds. What was the total time?

4. Angela's time for 400 meters was 59.59 seconds. Cornelia's time was 56.07 seconds. How much faster was Cornelia's time?

5. Thomas has $8. Can he buy 2 cans of paint that cost $1.98 each and a $3.59 brush?

6. **Data File** Use data from pages 524-525. One third of the communities on the map had rainfall of more than 3.4 inches. How many communities was this? List the communities and rainfall as part of your answer.

7. **Make a Data File** Use a catalog. Find three or more items that cost a total of about $50. Find three or more items that cost about $100. Find three or more items that cost about $500. Make a display of your data.

Problem Solving REVIEW

Explore with a Calculator

Missing the Point

1. The decimal point on the right side of each number sentence is in the correct place. There is one decimal point missing from the left side of each number sentence. Use estimation to guess where the missing decimal point should go. Then check your guess with your calculator.

a. 243 ⊞ 32 ⊟ 56.3

b. 17.2 ⊟ 152 ⊟ 2

c. 6.8 ⊞ 74 ⊞ 9.3 ⊟ 23.5

d. 116 ⊞ 125 ⊟ 128.5

e. 12 ⊞ 15 ⊟ 13.5

f. 247 ⊟ 147 ⊟ 232.3

2. The report said that 45 inches of rain fell on Monday, 26 inches fell on Tuesday, and 1 inch fell on Wednesday for a total of 7.2 inches. Tell how many inches actually fell each day to make the total correct.

3. On a vacation trip, Mr. Kelton filled his gas tank 3 times. He recorded the number of gallons as 126, 134, and 97. How many gallons in all did he actually get if his tank holds no more than 16 gallons?

4. In an ad for a grocery store, the printers made some errors. Tell where the decimal points should go in this ad. Then tell how much a bag of apples and a head of cauliflower would cost.

CAULIFLOWER $179 a head

APPLES $199 for a 3 pound bag

ONIONS 3 pound for $119

PINEAPPLES $243 each

PEANUTS 24 ounce bag for $185

Reteaching

Set A   pages 394–395

The model shows one and nine tenths. Write a mixed number or a decimal.

Write $1\frac{9}{10}$ or 1.9.

Remember that ten tenths make a whole.

1. Write a mixed number and a decimal for this model.

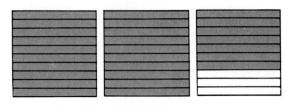

Set B   pages 396–397

This decimal number line shows tenths. The position of letter A is 0.8.

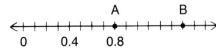

What decimal tells the position of B? The position of letter B is 1.4, which is greater than 1.

Remember that decimals get larger as you move to the right of 0. What decimal tells the position of each letter on the number line?

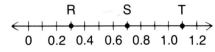

1. R   **2.** S   **3.** T

Set C   pages 398–401

Each ☐ is 1 hundredth. The first large square shows 1 because all the parts are shaded. In the second large square, 35 parts are shaded.

One and 35 hundredths is written as $1\frac{35}{100}$, or 1.35.

Remember that 100 hundredths is a whole; 100 hundredths is 1.

1. Write a decimal and a mixed number for the shaded part.

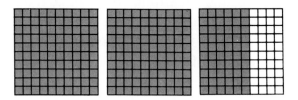

Set D   pages 404–405

This place-value chart shows the decimal 26.38.

tens	ones	tenths	hundredths
2	6	3	8

Read this as 26 and 38 hundredths.

Remember to read the decimal point as "and."

Write each decimal in a place-value chart.

1. 41.6   **2.** 0.58   **3.** 8.03   **4.** 86.29

Set E pages 408–409

Compare 0.52 and 0.25.

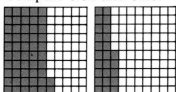

The model for 0.52 has more shaded.
So, 0.52 > 0.25 and 0.25 < 0.52.

Remember that > means is greater than and < means is less than.

Compare the decimals. Use <, >, or =. Draw models if necessary.

1. 0.7 ▦ 0.6   **2.** 0.82 ▦ 0.73

3. 0.36 ▦ 0.52   **4.** 0.19 ▦ 0.91

Set F pages 410–411

Add 1.25 + 0.3.

To show 1.25, shade a whole, 2 tenths, and 5 hundredths.

To show 0.3, shade 3 tenths or 30 hundredths.

The total amount shaded is 1.55.

Remember that 1 tenth is 10 hundredths, 2 tenths is 20 hundredths, and so on.

Add. Use models if necessary.

1. 0.6 + 0.8   **2.** 1.4 + 0.7

3. 1.35 + 0.41   **4.** 1.46 + 0.43

Set G pages 412–413

Subtract 0.38 from 1.2.

To show 1.2, shade a whole and 2 tenths or 20 hundredths.

To subtract 0.38, mark off 3 tenths and 8 hundredths.

The unmarked shaded part is 0.82.

Remember that you can also use a number line to subtract decimals.

Subtract. Use models if necessary.

1. 0.8 − 0.4   **2.** 1.4 − 0.5

3. 1.8 − 0.84   **4.** 2.0 − 1.6

Set H pages 414–415

Estimate each answer.

a. 15.3 + 9.8   **b.** 18.6 − 12.9
   ↓   ↓   ↓   ↓
   15 + 10 = 25   19 − 13 = 6

Remember that you can estimate the sum or difference of two decimals by rounding each decimal to the nearest whole number. Estimate each answer.
1. 4.7 + 9.2   **2.** 36.2 − 15.8

Set I pages 416–417

Add 16.5 + 11.6.

```
    1          1          1
  16.5       16.5       16.5
+ 11.6      + 11.6     + 11.6
   .1         8.1       28.1
```

Remember to line up the decimal points vertically. Add or subtract.

1. 16.8 + 6.6   **2.** 12.4 − 8.5

More Practice

Set A   pages 394–395

For each exercise, draw a model. Then write a fraction and a decimal.

1. 5 tenths   **2.** 4 tenths   **3.** 9 tenths

For each exercise, write a mixed number and a decimal.

4. five and 3 tenths   **5.** one and 8 tenths   **6.** six and 5 tenths

Set B   pages 396–397

What decimal tells the position of each letter on the number line?

1. A   **2.** B   **3.** C   **4.** D   **5.** E   **6.** F

Set C   pages 398–401

Write a decimal and a fraction or mixed number for the shaded part.

1. 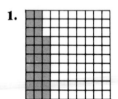   **2.**   **3.**

4.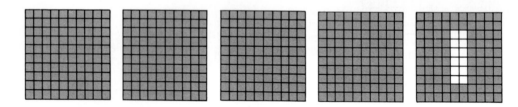

Set D   pages 404–405

Write each decimal in a place-value chart.

1. 62.9   **2.** 0.38   **3.** 6.02   **4.** 90.07   **5.** 74.53

Write as a decimal.

6. 3 tens, 7 tenths, 4 hundredths   **7.** six and 18 hundredths

8. 5 ones, 9 hundredths   **9.** thirty and 23 hundredths

Set E pages 408–409

Compare the decimals. Use <, >, or =.
Draw models if necessary.

1. 0.8 ▦ 0.5 **2.** 2.12 ▦ 2.21 **3.** 2.8 ▦ 2.80

Write the numbers in order from least to greatest.
Use a number line if necessary.

4. 0.4   0.2   0.7 **5.** 2.1   2.9   2.3 **6.** 0.52   0.41   0.8

Set F pages 410–411

Add. Use models if necessary.

1.	0.5	**2.**	1.5	**3.**	0.36	**4.**	0.87
	+ 0.6		+ 0.8		+ 0.58		+ 0.34

5. 1.8 + 0.75 **6.** 0.3 + 0.46 + 2 **7.** 0.8 + 0.5 + 0.2

Set G pages 412–413

Subtract. Use models if necessary.

1.	0.6	**2.**	1.7	**3.**	0.49	**4.**	0.54
	− 0.5		− 0.8		− 0.32		− 0.2

5. 2 − 0.34 **6.** 3.47 − 0.40 **7.** 6.5 − 4.2

Set H pages 414–415

Round each decimal to the nearest whole number.
Use a number line if necessary.

1. 1.9 **2.** 4.6 **3.** 5.4 **4.** 18.3 **5.** 4.03 **6.** 7.52

Estimate each answer.

7. 1.6 + 4.3 **8.** 8.7 − 3.2 **9.** 6.3 − 4.5 **10.** 7.2 + 5.9

Set I pages 416–417

Add or subtract.

1.	0.84	**2.**	19.4	**3.**	15.3	**4.**	23.06	**5.**	4.36
	+ 0.07		+ 3.5		− 4.7		+ 12.08		− 2.78

6. 0.20 + 4 + 2.83 **7.** 5.45 + 2 + 0.44 **8.** 2.63 + 5 + 6.79

Enrichment

Decimals and Money

A. Lamar uses his calculator to find how much one pair of shoelaces will cost. He presses 5 ÷ 10 =. He looks at the display and thinks:

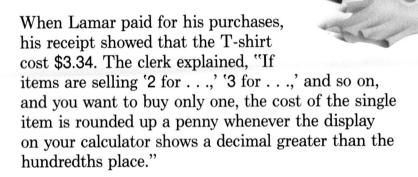

                  Dollars   Cents
                       ↘   ↙

0.5 is 0.50.   **$0.50**

Each pair of shoelaces will cost $0.50.

B. Lamar wants to buy one T-shirt. He presses 10 ÷ 3 = and thinks:

   Dollars Cents
      ↓↓
    3.3333333

When Lamar paid for his purchases, his receipt showed that the T-shirt cost $3.34. The clerk explained, "If items are selling '2 for . . .,' '3 for . . .,' and so on, and you want to buy only one, the cost of the single item is rounded up a penny whenever the display on your calculator shows a decimal greater than the hundredths place."

Write each amount as dollars and cents.

1. *0.1*   **2.** *4.*   **3.** *19.3*   **4.** *42.088888*

5. *0.0833333*   **6.** *4.502*   **7.** *2.7272727*   **8.** *5.0601*

About how much will one of the following cost?

9. Cassette tapes: 6 for $15   **10.** Socks: 5 for $5.99

11. Paperback books: 4 for $11.95   **12.** Compact disks: 3 for $17

Chapter 12 Review/Test

1. Which model shows 0.3?

   a.   **b.**

What decimal tells the position of each letter on the number line?

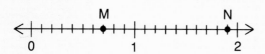

2. M   3. N

4. Write a decimal and a fraction for the shaded part.

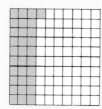

Write each number as a decimal.

5. four and twelve hundredths

6. 3 tens, 5 tenths, 7 hundredths

7. Tell which decimal in the list is not equal to the others.

   0.70   0.07   0.7

Compare the decimals.
Use <, >, or =.

8. 0.7 ⬚ 0.63   9. 1.20 ⬚ 1.2

10. Write the numbers from least to greatest.

   0.5   0.63   0.32

Add or subtract. Use the number line in Items 2 and 3 if necessary.

11. 0.9 + 0.4   12. 2.0 − 0.3

Use rounding to estimate each answer.

13. 12.8 + 4.1   14. 9.91 − 3.22

15. Use the whole-number parts to estimate the sum in Item 13.

Add or subtract.

16.   0.62
     + 0.09   17. 0.6 + 7 + 2.93

18.   4.16
    − 2.99   19. 14.2 − 12

20. The bus fare in Robinson is 40¢. You may not use pennies. You need exact change. In how many ways can you pay the fare?

Read the following problem. Then answer Items 21 and 22.

Alex bought flowers for $14.79. He gave the clerk $20. How much change did he receive?

21. One student got an answer of $6.31 for this problem. Is this answer reasonable? Explain.

22. Solve the problem.

23. **Write About Math** Explain how to use the number line to subtract in Item 12.

Statistics, Graphing and Probability 13

Did You Know: The screen of a color television or video monitor has more than 300,000 phosphor dots, arranged in groups of three. Each phosphor dot glows as red, blue, or green. Other colors seem to appear on the screen because dots blend together in the viewer's mind.

Number-Sense Project

Estimate
Estimate how much time you spend each week watching television and how much time you spend using a computer.

Gather Data
Record the number of hours and minutes spent doing each activity each day for one week.

Analyze and Report
For each activity, add to find the total amount of time. Make a bar graph to display your data. Compare your results with other students.

Collecting Data

Build Understanding

Ms. Kinney's class must choose which color T-shirt to order for Sports Day. T-shirts come in all colors. How can they decide?

Understand How will the class be able to choose a color? The class must collect data that tell which color is the favorite.

Plan and Solve STRATEGY Take a ***survey*** of the class. First think of a question to ask. Then collect data. Julia and John asked class members these questions.

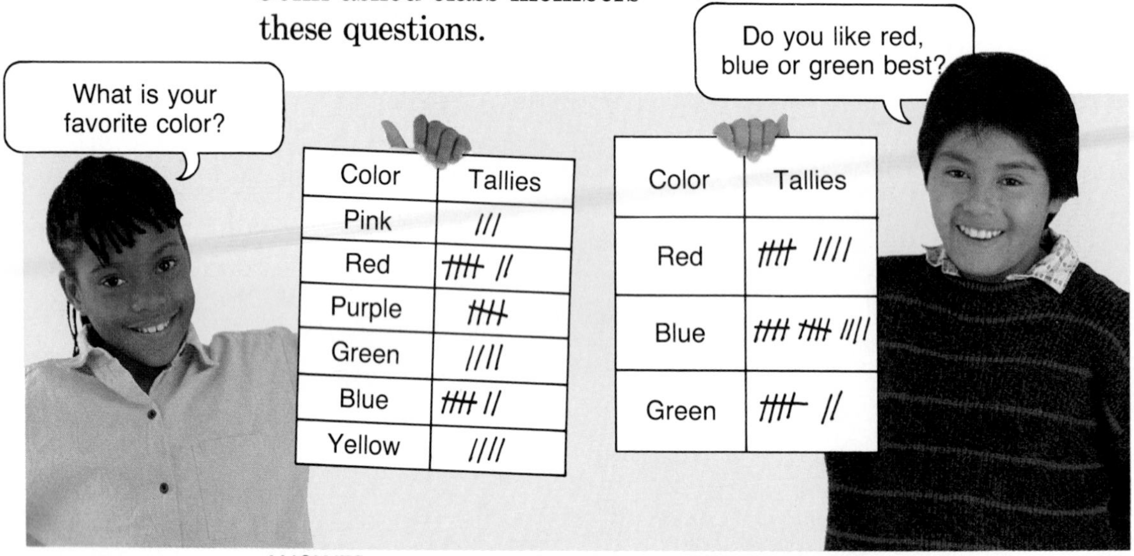
What is your favorite color?
Do you like red, blue or green best?
Color | Tallies
Pink | ///
Red | 卌 //
Purple | 卌
Green | ////
Blue | 卌 //
Yellow | ////
Color | Tallies
Red | 卌 ////
Blue | 卌 卌 ////
Green | 卌 //

ANSWER Look at the rows with the most tallies. The class should probably order blue T-shirts, since blue seems most popular.

Look Back Can you think of other ways to collect data about favorite colors?

PROBLEM SOLVING GUIDE

Understand
QUESTION
FACTS
KEY IDEA

Plan and Solve
STRATEGY
ANSWER

Look Back
SENSIBLE ANSWER
ALTERNATE APPROACH

■ **Talk About Math** Why is it better to ask a question with only a few answers?

Check Understanding

Which question would you ask? Why?

1. You need to decide what time Sports Day activities will begin.

    a. When should Sports Day start?

    b. Should Sports Day start at 8:00, 8:30, 9:00, or 9:30?

2. You need to decide how many small, how many medium, and how many large T-shirts to order.

    a. What size T-shirt do you wear?

    b. Do you want a small, medium, or large T-shirt?

Practice

Write a survey question for each situation.

3. You need to decide what games to play on Sports Day.

4. There will be apple, grape, grapefruit, and orange juice available. Decide how many bottles of each to order.

5. The students have to decide whether first prize winners will receive medals, statues, or sweatshirts with "Sports Day Winner" printed on the front.

6. Sports Day is usually on a Tuesday. This year some students want it to be Monday or Friday. The students need to decide on the day.

Choose a ——— Strategy

Monster Maze

7. Sam made up a computer maze. As you go through the maze, you meet 5 monsters. Plog is the second monster. Zan is between Rif and Yim. Thox is before Plog. Yim is not last. In what order do you meet the monsters in Sam's maze?

PROBLEM SOLVING
STRATEGIES
Choose an Operation
Try and Check
Draw a Diagram
Solve a Simpler Problem
Write a Number Sentence
Make a Table
Use Logical Reasoning
Find a Pattern
Draw a Picture
Work Backward

Organizing Data

Build Understanding

Ms. Fuentes, the school nurse, made this table for the students in Mrs. Jenson's class.

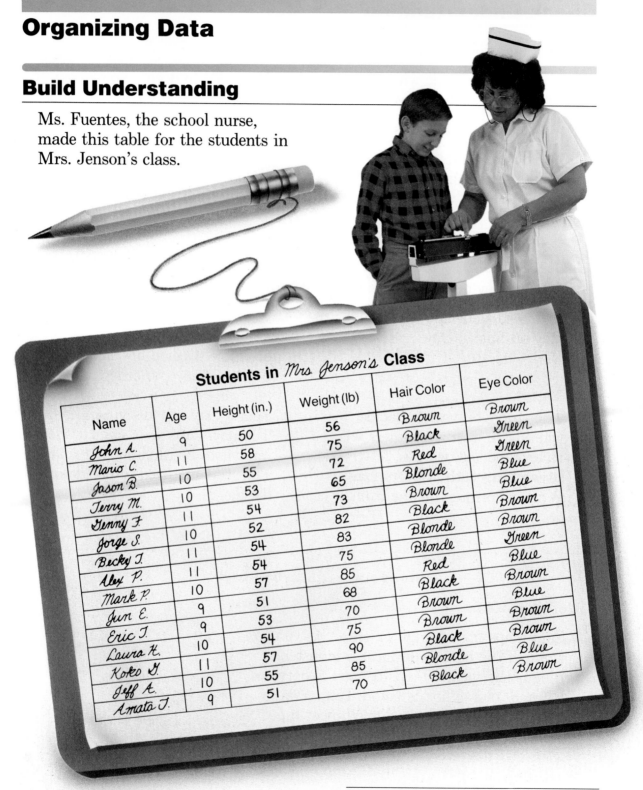

Students in *Mrs. Jenson's* Class

Name	Age	Height (in.)	Weight (lb)	Hair Color	Eye Color
John A.	9	50	56	Brown	Brown
Mario C.	11	58	75	Black	Green
Jason B.	10	55	72	Red	Green
Terry M.	10	53	65	Blonde	Blue
Genny F.	11	54	73	Brown	Blue
Jorge S.	10	52	82	Black	Brown
Becky T.	11	54	83	Blonde	Brown
Alex P.	11	54	75	Blonde	Green
Mark P.	10	57	85	Red	Blue
Jun E.	9	51	68	Black	Brown
Eric T.	9	53	70	Brown	Brown
Laura H.	10	54	75	Brown	Brown
Koko G.	11	57	90	Black	Blue
Jeff A.	10	55	85	Blonde	Brown
Amata T.	9	51	70	Black	Brown

If you could add your name to the list of students, could you complete the table?

Ms. Fuentes then made tally marks to organize the data in her table. Look at the tallies Ms. Fuentes made for the students' heights.

What is the height of the shortest student? What is the height of the tallest student?

How did Ms. Fuentes list the heights in the table?

Ms. Fuentes also listed the *frequency* of each height, or how often each height occurs.

The *mode* of the heights is the height that occurs most frequently.

What is the mode of the heights in the table?

■**Talk About Math** How can you make sure that all of the data from the table were included?

Height	Tallies	Frequency
50	/	1
51	//	2
52	/	1
53	//	2
54	////	4
55	//	2
56	—	0
57	//	2
58	/	1

Check Understanding

For another example, see Set A, pages 458–459.

Use the data from the table on page 432.

1. Copy and complete this tally chart using eye colors. Does the list need to be in a certain order?

Eye Color	Tallies	Frequency

2. Make a tally mark in your chart for each student's eye color.

3. What is the mode of the eye colors in Mrs. Jenson's class?

Practice

For More Practice, see Set A, pages 460–461.

Use data from the table on page 432.
Copy and complete each tally chart.

4.

Age	Tallies	Frequency

5.

Hair Color	Tallies	Frequency

6. Ms. Fuentes wanted to group data for the weights of the students in Mrs. Jenson's class. Copy and complete her tally chart.

Weight	Tallies	Frequency
50-59		
60-69		

In Mrs. Jenson's class, what is the mode for each set of data?

7. Age

8. Weight

9. Hair Color

Mixed Practice   Complete the following exercises.

10. Write a survey question to find the time that some of your classmates got up this morning.

11. Take the survey of at least 10 classmates and make a tally chart. What is the mode?

434

Problem Solving

Use the data in the table on page 432.
Explain each of your answers.

12. Do you think that students who are the same height would be about the same weight?

13. Do you think that students with the same eye color would be about the same height?

14. Do you think that older students would be shorter or taller than younger students?

15. Do you think that students with the same color eyes would have the same color hair?

16. **Calculator** A large elevator holds 1,300 pounds. Can all the children in Mrs. Jenson's class ride at the same time?

17. In Problem 16, about how many more children can still get on the elevator?

Explore ——— Math

Ask five to eight friends to tell you how much time they spent doing household chores yesterday. Then ask how much time they spent watching television.

18. For each activity complete a tally chart like the one shown.

19. What is the mode for each activity?

20. Write another survey question that you could use with this tally chart.

Activity: _____

Time Spent	Tally	Frequency
Up to $\frac{1}{2}$ hour		
$\frac{1}{2}$ to 1 hour		
1 to $1\frac{1}{2}$ hours		
$1\frac{1}{2}$ hours or more		

Bar Graphs

Build Understanding

A principal's assistant sometimes prepares graphs. A bar graph shows comparisons between data. Which graph do you think the assistant gave the principal?

The scale on Graph A shows multiples of 3.

The scale on Graph B shows every number from 16 to 24, but does not show 1 to 15.

How many more students were absent on Tuesday than on Wednesday? Which graph did you use?

Numbering a scale in ones makes it easier to compare numbers that are close to each other on a graph.

■ **Talk About Math** When would numbering a graph in multiples be a good idea?

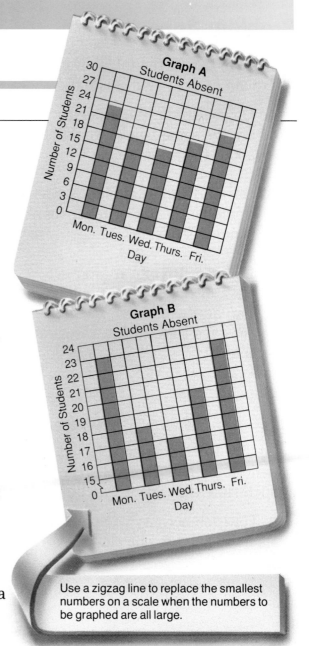

Use a zigzag line to replace the smallest numbers on a scale when the numbers to be graphed are all large.

Check Understanding

For another example, see Set B, pages 458–459.

1. On which day were the fewest students absent?

2. On which days were the most students absent?

3. Explain why it was not necessary for the assistant to show the numbers 1 to 15 on the scale of Graph B.

4. In one school, the numbers of students absent ranged from 8 to 97. How would you number the scale of a graph for the data?

Practice

For More Practice, see Set B, pages 460–461.

5. Copy and complete the bar graph that one principal's assistant began. The bars on this graph go from left to right.

Students Attending After-School Clubs

Monday	12
Tuesday	20
Wednesday	36
Thursday	26
Friday	16

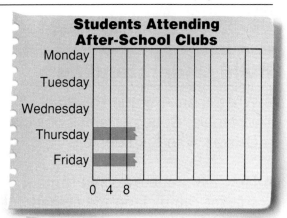

Students Attending After-School Clubs

Use the data in the table at the right for Exercises 6–8.

6. What is the greatest number of points scored?

7. What is the least number of points scored?

8. Make a bar graph to show the data.

Points Scored by Basketball Team Members

Tomás	9
Lynn	17
Tony	12
Lien	6
Anoki	14

Problem Solving

9. Use Data Assistants to principals also prepare graphs to show the ages of students in school. Use the table on page 432. Choose a scale and make a bar graph to show the ages of the students in Mrs. Jenson's class.

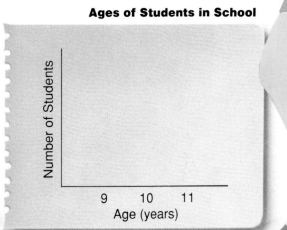

Ages of Students in School

Finding Averages

Build Understanding

What Is an Average Handful?
Materials: Cubes or small objects
Groups: 4 to 6 students

A. How many cubes do you think a student can pick up in one handful?

   a. Take as many cubes in one hand as you can and place them in a row. Put your row next to the rows that the other group members make.

   b. Make all the rows the same length by moving cubes from row to row. Put any leftover cubes to the side.

   c. How many cubes are in each row? The number of cubes in each row is the **average** number of cubes a student can pick up in one handful.

B. You can also compute to find an average. Suppose 4 students picked up 22 cubes.

Divide 22 by 4.

$$\begin{array}{r} 5 \text{ R2} \\ 4\overline{)2\,2} \end{array}$$

The average is about 5 cubes.

■ **Talk About Math**   If each student has a different number of cubes in a handful, what does "average number of cubes" mean?

438

Check Understanding

For another example, see Set C, pages 458–459.

1. Can the average of a group of numbers be greater than the greatest number? Explain.

2. Can the average of a group of numbers be less than the least number? Explain.

Practice

For More Practice, see Set C pages 460–461.

Use rows of cubes to find the average. Then compute the average.

3. 5, 9, 6, 10

4. 3, 2, 5, 8, 4

5. 4, 3, 9, 7, 6

6. 5, 8, 10, 3, 6

7. 5, 7, 9, 2, 4

8. 1, 12, 11, 9, 2

Estimation Tell whether the average is greater than or less than 10. How do you know?

9. 7, 11, 10, 9, 6

10. 5, 20, 4, 18, 15

11. 3, 7, 8, 13, 4

Problem Solving

Read for the facts. Then answer the question.

12. Mental Math One student earns $40 a week. Four others earn $20 a week. Is the average pay closer to $20 or $40? Why?

Reading ——— Math

Looking for Main Ideas Read the Build Understanding and Talk About Math on page 436. Then answer the questions.

1. What are the two main ideas about making the scale for a bar graph?

2. What is a bar graph used for?

Graphing Number Pairs

Build Understanding

A *number pair* can be used to graph a point on a grid.

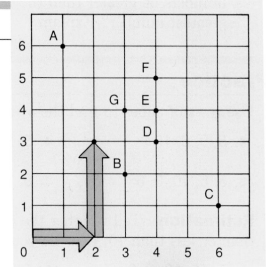

A. To graph the point (2,3), start at 0. Move 2 units to the right. Then, move 3 units up.

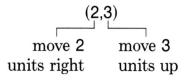

(2,3)

move 2 units right   move 3 units up

B. To find the number pair for the point B on the graph, start at 0. B is 3 units to the right of 0 and 2 units up. The number pair for point B is (3,2).

■ **Talk About Math** Is the number pair (2,3) the same as the number pair (3,2)? Explain.

Check Understanding

For another example, see Set D, pages 458–459.

Use the grid above for Exercises 1–6.
Write the letter for each point.

1. (4,5)   **2.** (1,6)   **3.** (6,1)

Copy and complete the number pair for each point.

4. D (4, ▦)   **5.** G (▦, 4)   **6.** E (▦,▦)

Practice

For More Practice, see Set D, pages 460–461.

Write the letter located at each point.

7. (2,5)   **8.** (4,1)   **9.** (7,6)

10. (3,8)   **11.** (7,2)   **12.** (1,10)

13. (10,0)   **14.** (3,10)   **15.** (2, 2)

Give the number pair for each point.

16. T **17.** C **18.** H **19.** U **20.** I **21.** K

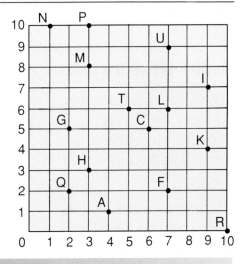

Problem Solving

Graph these points on grid paper.
Connect them in order. Name the shape.

22. (1,8)   (2,9)   (3,8)   (1,8)

23. (2,7)   (2,5)   (4,5)   (4,7)   (2,7)

24. (8,7)   (5,7)   (5,9)   (8,9)   (8,7)

25. Graph three shapes of your own and list
the number pairs for each vertex. Ask a
classmate to locate the points and name
the shape formed.

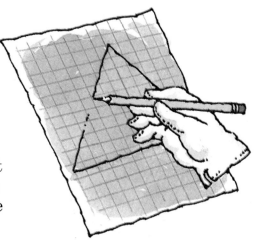

Skills ____ **Review**   pages 362–363

Write a fraction and a mixed number for the shaded area.

1.   **2.**   **3.**

4.   **5.**   **6.**

Using Number Pairs

Build Understanding

Anne is designing her poster for Safety Week. She drew a small sketch of a stop sign.

To enlarge her sketch, she made a larger grid by numbering every other line on her grid paper.

What number pairs did Anne connect to make the outline of the stop sign in her sketch?

How did she make her enlargement?

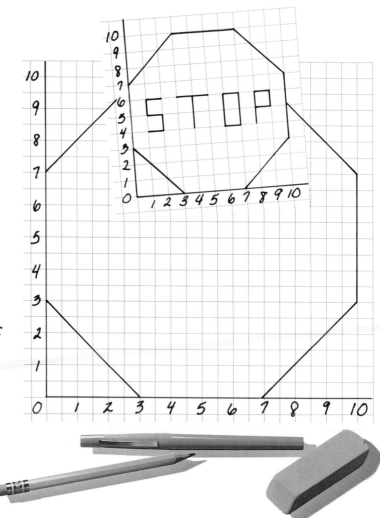

■Talk About Math
What other method could Anne have used to enlarge her outline?

Check Understanding

For another example, see Set E, pages 458–459.

Find the number pairs for each of these letters on the sign. Use grid paper to enlarge the letters.

1. S   **2.** T   **3.** O   **4.** P

442

Practice

For More Practice, see Set E, pages 460–461.

Use grid paper. Connect the number pairs in order.
Draw each figure in at least two sizes. **Remember** to
start at 0, move right, and then move up.

5. (5,9) (3,6) (5,3) (7,6) (5,9)   **6.** (3,1) (4,3) (7,3) (6,1) (3,1)

7. (2,7) (2,3) (9,3) (9,7) (5,3)   **8.** (5,4) (5,6) (3,6) (3,4) (5,4)
   (2,7)   (5,2) (7,2) (7,4) (5,4)

9. (2,2) (3,2) (3,5) (5,5) (5,2) (6,2) (4,0) (2,2)

10. (13,3) (13,5) (12,5) (11,4) (9,4) (11,6) (7,4) (3,4) (1,3)
   (7,3) (10,0) (9,3) (13,3)

Problem Solving

11. Sketch the shapes of two road signs on grid paper. Enlarge your sketches.

12. **Visual Thinking** Explain how you would reduce the size of your sketches.

Midchapter Checkup

At a dog show, a collie owner took a survey to find the
weights of all the collies. One collie weighed 55 lb, 2
weighed 60 lb, 4 weighed 63 lb, 2 weighed 65 lb, and 1
weighed 70 lb. Use these data for Items 1–4.

1. Write a survey question that would give the data.

2. Make a tally chart showing the results of the survey.

3. Draw a graph to show the data.

4. Find the average and the mode.

Use the grid at the right.

5. Write the number pair for each point.

6. Enlarge the figure.

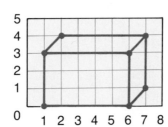

Problem-Solving Workshop

Explore as a Team

1. Find your pulse in your wrist or neck.

2. Do these exercises with your team for 1 minute. Immediately take your pulse for 10 seconds. Record the results in a table like the one shown.

Activity	Pulse for 10 sec		Pulse for 1 minute
Sitting quietly		x 6	
Walking in place		x 6	
Running in place		x 6	

TIPS FOR **WORKING TOGETHER**

Help keep your group on task.

3. Compare your results with those of other students on your team. When sitting quietly, what is your team's average pulse for 1 minute?

4. What is your team's average pulse for walking in place and running in place?

Math-at-Home Activity

Take a survey of 8 people who live near you. Ask them to identify each of these close-up photographs. Make a bar graph showing how many people identified each photograph correctly.

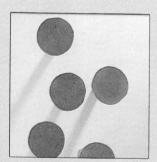

Explore with a Computer

Use the *Graphing and Probability Workshop Project* for this activity.

1. At the computer, spin the spinner 100 times. How many times did it land on blue? on white?

2. What do you think would happen if you have the computer spin the spinner 200 times? Try it.

3. Change the spinner so that three of the eight sections are colored blue. Repeat steps 1 and 2.

```
File Edit Table Graph Data Extras Help
10 spins
Pattern  Frequency
A            8
C            2




Press Return to spin again.
Press Esc for menus.
```

Number-Sense Project

Look back at pages 428-429.
Here is a table showing the time spent by four students during one week.

1. Which student spent the same amount of time on each activity?

2. What is the average number of hours that a student watched TV during the week?

3. What is the average number of hours that a student used a computer during the week? (Round the answer to a whole number.)

4. Which student's data was closest to the average?

HOURS SPENT IN A WEEK		
Student's Name	**Watching TV**	**Using a Computer**
Alan	12	3
Bonita	7	13
Carl	5	5
Debra	8	6

445

Broken-Line Graphs

Build Understanding

Each noon, Norma Lee reports the weather on radio station WSJN. The table shows the noontime temperatures for this week.

Each day Norma also graphs the temperature. She then connects the points to make a *broken-line graph*.

Day	Temperature
Monday	35° F
Tuesday	42° F
Wednesday	45° F
Thursday	39° F
Friday	39° F

■ **Talk About Math** Suppose the temperature on Tuesday was 32°F. Explain how you would locate that point on the graph.

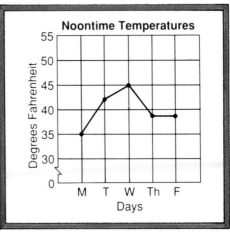

There is at least one radio station in every country of the world, and altogether there are more than 25,000 stations.

Check Understanding

For another example, see Set F, pages 458–459.

1. Which day was warmer at noon, Wednesday or Thursday?

2. Did the noontime temperature rise or fall from Monday to Tuesday?

3. For what two days was the temperature the same at noon?

4. Describe how the temperatures changed through the week.

Practice

For More Practice, see Set F, pages 460–461.

For Exercises 5–9, use the data given in the table and the grid below it.

5. What number will you count by to label the temperature scale?

6. Why is it important that the distances between marks on the scales be equal?

7. Why is it important that the months be in order?

8. Locate and connect the points.

9. Describe the change in the lowest temperatures through the months.

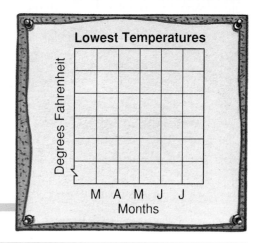

Lowest Temperatures

Month	Temperature
March	34° F
April	47° F
May	58° F
June	67° F
July	71° F

Lowest Temperatures

Degrees Fahrenheit

M A M J J
Months

Problem Solving

Critical Thinking   Norma Lee wrote a riddle for her listeners. Answer the questions about her riddle.

10. What was the hottest day?

11. What was the coolest day?

RIDDLE

Friday's high was 5° cooler than Thursday's. Monday's high was 10° cooler than Friday's. Tuesday's high was 78°. Thursday's high was 10° hotter than Wednesday's. Wednesday's high was 2° warmer than Tuesday's.

What was the hottest day?

Make a Graph

Build Understanding

Dan did some record keeping at his mother's office. Dot did some at her father's office.

Dot's Data

Dr. Jordan's Patient, Chen Wong	
Age	Height
1 month	21 in.
3 months	23 in.
4 months	24 in.
6 months	26 in.

Dan's Data

Dr. Jordan's Patients	
dogs	ЖЖ |||
cats	ЖЖ ЖЖ
birds	|||
turtles		

PROBLEM SOLVING
GUIDE

Understand
QUESTION
FACTS
KEY IDEA

Plan and Solve
STRATEGY
ANSWER

Look Back
SENSIBLE ANSWER
ALTERNATE APPROACH

Dot and Dan want to make graphs to show each set of data. What kinds of graphs should Dot and Dan use?

Understand   QUESTION   What kinds of graphs should they use?

FACTS   Dot's data show one patient's height at different dates. Dan's data tell the number of each animal.

KEY IDEA   Dot's graph should show changes in numbers over time and Dan's graph should compare different amounts.

Plan and Solve   ANSWER   Dot's graph is a *line graph*. Dan made a bar graph.

Look Back   Do the graph choices seem sensible?

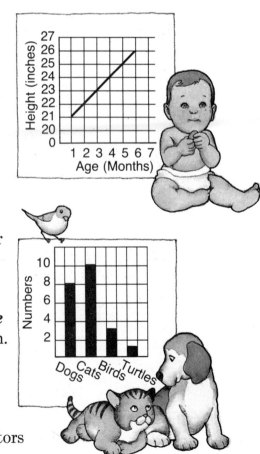

■ **Talk About Math**   How else might the doctors use graphs in their work?

448

Check Understanding

Which type of graph would best show the following?

1. Heights of all 3-month-old babies Dr. Jordan has seen.

2. Number of dogs Dr. Jordan saw each month last year.

Practice

Which type of graph would best show the following?

3. The number of dogs given rabies shots in January and in July.

4. The number of babies treated for colds each month of the year.

5. Make a graph for the egg-hatching times.

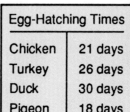

Egg-Hatching Times	
Chicken	21 days
Turkey	26 days
Duck	30 days
Pigeon	18 days

6. Two packages of yarn cost $1.20, 4 packages cost $2.40, and 6 packages cost $3.60. Make a line graph to find how much 18 packages of yarn cost.

7. In Exercise 6, how many packages of yarn can be bought for $9.60?

Choose a ⬛ Strategy

Visual Thinking Rosa cuts a piece of paper to line a small trunk. Look at the drawings of the trunk and the piece of paper. Then answer the questions.

8. How many inches are there from A to B?

9. How many inches are there from C to D?

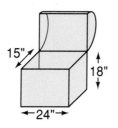

15"

18"

←24"→

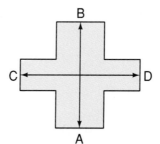

B

C — D

A

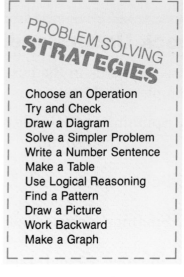

PROBLEM SOLVING
STRATEGIES

Choose an Operation
Try and Check
Draw a Diagram
Solve a Simpler Problem
Write a Number Sentence
Make a Table
Use Logical Reasoning
Find a Pattern
Draw a Picture
Work Backward
Make a Graph

Outcomes

Build Understanding

If you spin this spinner, what are the possible outcomes?

Tell why spinning a 2 and spinning a 3 are equally likely.

Is spinning an even number more likely or less likely than spinning an odd number?

■ **Write About Math** Explain why these statements about the spinner are true.

You are certain to spin a number from 1 to 7.

It is possible that you will spin a 5.

It is impossible for you to spin a 10.

Check Understanding

For another example, see Set G, pages 458–459.

Use the words in the box to complete each statement.

1. Spinning a number less than 6 is ____?____ than spinning a 6.

2. Spinning a 0 is ____?____.

3. Spinning a single digit is ____?____.

4. Spinning a 1 and spinning a 6 at the same time is ____?____.

> equally likely
> less likely
> more likely
> certain
> possible
> impossible

Practice

For More Practice, see Set G, pages 460–461.

Write whether you think each outcome is *certain,*
possible, or *impossible.*

5. This week will have 8 days.

6. Saturday will follow Friday.

7. Your next math test score will
be over 90.

8. You will wear a raincoat
tomorrow.

Suppose you put these cards face down and mix them up.

9. List the possible outcomes if you
draw one card.

10. Are you more likely to pick a
red card or a green card?

11. Which outcomes are equally likely?

12. Which two cards would you remove
to make all outcomes equally likely?

Problem Solving

Number Sense   Choose a number to tell how many dogs
were in the Golden Dog Show. Then solve Problems 13 and 14.

13. The Silver Dog Show had twice
as many dogs as the Golden Dog
Show. How many dogs were in
the Silver show?

14. The Grand Woof Show had
about half as many dogs as the
Golden Dog Show. How many
dogs were in that show?

	Skills	Review	pages 182–197

Divide.

1. 49 ÷ 7   **2.** 16 ÷ 4   **3.** 27 ÷ 3   **4.** 63 ÷ 7   **5.** 35 ÷ 5

6. 48 ÷ 6   **7.** 81 ÷ 9   **8.** 16 ÷ 2   **9.** 42 ÷ 6   **10.** 72 ÷ 8

Experiments

Build Understanding

Tally Ho!
Materials: Two number cubes
with digits 1–6 on them
Groups: 3 to 4 students

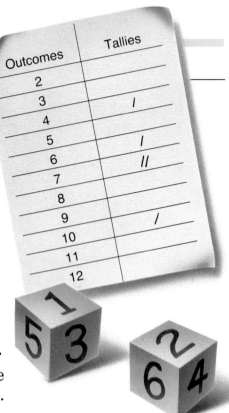

Outcomes	Tallies
2	
3	/
4	
5	/
6	//
7	
8	
9	/
10	
11	
12	

a. List all possible outcomes for the sum of the numbers on two number cubes.

b. One student tosses the cubes. Another puts a tally next to the sum rolled. Toss the cubes until you have ten tally marks for one sum.

■ **Talk About Math**   For which sum did you first get ten tally marks? Compare your results with other groups. Explain why some sums are more likely to be tossed than others.

Check Understanding

For Exercises 1–9, you have a red cube and a blue cube. Both have digits 1 through 6 on them.

1. Is   the same as ? Explain.

List the ways you can roll each sum.

2. 3   **3.** 9   **4.** 7   **5.** 12

Tell if the sums in the following pairs are equally likely.

6. 3 and 12   **7.** 10 and 5   **8.** 6 and 8

9. Predict which sum will be first to get 20 tallies. Check your prediction.

Practice

Experiment A
Draw a card. Return it.
Draw again.

Experiment B
Spin.

Experiment C
Toss at the same time.
Record heads and tails.

Complete Exercises 10–12 for each experiment.

10. List the possible outcomes.

11. Predict which outcome will get 10 tallies first.

12. Experiment and compare your results with your predictions.

13. List the possible outcomes for spinning the spinner and drawing a card.

Problem Solving

Explore ———— Math

Experiment Put every letter in each of these words on a card: TEMPERATURE, ABOUT, GLASSES. Put the letters into 3 bags, one bag for each word. For each bag, draw a card and tally the result. Return the card to the bag and draw again.

Organize your work
to help you think clearly.

14. If you tally vowels and consonants, for which word do you think a vowel will receive 10 tallies before a consonant?

15. If you tally the letters in the word GLASSES, which letter do you think will receive 10 tallies first?

16. Try the experiments. Compare the results to the predictions.

Probabilities

Build Understanding

A. There are ten marbles in a box as shown at the right. Suppose you draw one marble without looking. What is the probability of drawing blue? of drawing red?

Out of 10 marbles, 7 are blue. The rest are red. The **probability**, or chance, of drawing a blue marble is 7 out of 10. The probability of drawing red is 3 out of 10.

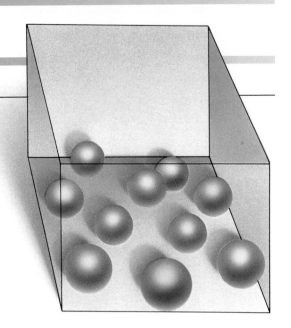

B. If you spin the spinner, what is the probability of not landing on red?

Out of 5 equal parts, two parts are red and 3 are not red. The probability is 3 out of 5.

■ **Talk About Math** If you spin the spinner five times, would you get red exactly two times? What is the probability of spinning purple?

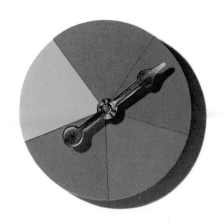

Check Understanding

For another example, see Set H, pages 458–459.

Copy and complete each statement.

1. The probability of tossing tails is _____?_____ out of _____?_____.

2. If the numbers 1 through 6 are on this number cube, the probability of not rolling a 4 is _____?_____ out of _____?_____.

Practice

For More Practice, see Set H, pages 460–461.

Write the probability of each outcome when the number cube is tossed.

3. the number 5

4. an even number

5. a number less than 3

6. not a 4

Write the probability of each outcome when you spin the spinner.

7. yellow

8. green

9. yellow or green

10. not blue

11. blue or white

12. brown

Problem Solving

Leon took these pictures of his family. When he went home to show them the pictures, he put them in a large envelope.

Sister   Father   Mother   Grandmother

If Leon pulls one picture out of the envelope without looking, what is the probability that the picture will

13. be of his grandmother?

14. be of his mother?

15. be of his dog?

16. not be of his father?

17. be of his sister?

18. be of his mother or father?

Problem-Solving Review

Solve each problem.

1. Louise visited five friends. She visited John last. Alex was between Sergei and Fran. Bev was after Fran. In what order did Louise visit her friends?

2. Who lives farther from school, Tyrone or Skip? How much farther?

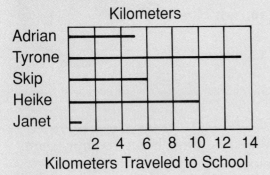

Kilometers

	Kilometers Traveled to School
Adrian	
Tyrone	
Skip	
Heike	
Janet	

2 4 6 8 10 12 14
Kilometers Traveled to School

3. What is the average number of kilometers the five students in Problem 2 live from school?

4. Mr. Swahn's heart beats 18 times in 15 seconds. How many times does it beat per minute?

5. At noon, Darlene began walking at 2 miles per hour. At 1:00 P.M. Cornelia followed Darlene, walking at 3 miles per hour. At what time will Cornelia catch up with Darlene?

6. **Data File** Use data from pages 524-525. For their favorite dinner, how many more children named pizza than hamburger? Make a bar graph with the information on Dinner Favorites.

7. **Make a Data File**
In newspapers and magazines, find examples of at least 1 pictograph, bar graph, and broken-line graph. Make a display with them, separating the different types.

Problem Solving REVIEW

Explore with a Calculator

Patterns in Ordered Pairs

1. The chart shows that if you buy 2 packages of socks you get 6 pairs. If you buy 10 packages, you get 30 pairs. Following the pattern, how many pairs of socks are in 7 packages? in 2,581 packages?

Number of Packages	Number of Pairs of Socks
2	6
10	30
7	■
2,581	■

2. The numbers in the chart above make number pairs that follow a rule. The rule is *multiply by 3*. For each list below, write the rule for finding the second number in each number pair. Then copy and complete each list.

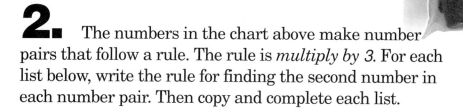

a. (1, 100)
(10, 109)
(44, 143)
(3, ___)
(98, ___)

b. (9, 3)
(33, 11)
(60, 20)
(24, ___)
(261, ___)

c. (24, 8)
(32, 16)
(50, 34)
(17, ___)
(205, ___)

d. (3, 36)
(5, 60)
(10, 120)
(2, ___)
(49, ___)

3. If Charlotte buys 3 packages, she will get 12 headbands. A carton of headbands holds 48 packages. How many headbands are in each package? How many are in a full carton?

Reteaching

Set A   pages 432–435

This table shows the ages of the students at Central Elementary School who play field hockey.

Age	Frequency	Tallies
8	12	卌 卌 ‖
9	16	卌 卌 卌 ‖
10	14	卌 卌 ‖‖
11	10	卌 卌

Remember that the mode of the ages is the age that has the greatest frequency.

1. How many players are 8 years old?

2. Which age has the fewest players?

3. What is the mode of the ages?

Set B   pages 436–437

A bar graph can be drawn for the table in Set A. A bar graph makes it easy to compare data.

Remember that each bar shows the number of players for that age.

1. Make a bar graph for the table in Set A.

2. Which bar shows the mode?

3. Which bar is the shortest?

Set C   pages 438–439

There are 60 cubes arranged in 7 rows. You divide to find the average number of cubes in a row.

$$\frac{8 \text{ R4}}{7)\overline{60}}$$ The average is about 8 cubes.

Remember that to find the average, first find the total. Then divide by the number of addends. Use cubes to find the average. Then compute the average.

1. 4, 5, 3, 2, 7   2. 5, 4, 5, 6

Set D   pages 440–441

On the graph, D is 4 units to the right of 0 and 3 units up. The number pair for D is (4, 3).

Remember to start at 0, move right, and then move up.

Write the letter located at each point.

1. (2, 5)   2. (5, 2)

3. (3, 4)   4. (0, 4)

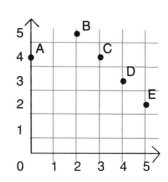

Set E pages 442–443

Figures can be formed by joining points on graph paper. In the graph in Set D, a triangle is formed by using points A, B, and E as vertices.

Remember that points should be connected in order.
Connect these numbers pairs.

1. (2, 5), (3, 4), (0, 0), (2, 5)

2. (1, 1), (3, 1), (3, 3), (1, 3), (1, 1)

Set F pages 446–447

This table and this graph show the temperature for every two hours beginning at 6:00 A.M. and ending at 2:00 P.M.

Time	Temperature
6:00 A.M.	5°F
8:00 A.M.	10°F
10:00 A.M.	25°F
Noon	35°F
2:00 P.M.	35°F

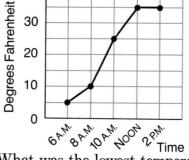

Temperature Changes

1. What was the lowest temperature?

2. For what two times was the temperature the same?

Remember that each point gives the temperature for that time.

Set G pages 450–451

If you spin this spinner, the four possible outcomes are A, B, C, and D.

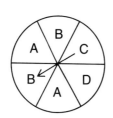

Remember that outcomes are not always equally likely.

1. Are you more likely to spin an A or a C?

2. Which outcome is equally likely to spinning a B?

3. Which outcomes are less likely than spinning a B?

Set H pages 454–455

If you spin the spinner in Set G, the probability of spinning an A is 2 out of 6.

Remember that there are 6 possible places for the spinner to stop.

Refer to the spinner in Set G.

1. The probability of not spinning a B is ____?____ out of ____?____.

2. The probability of spinning a C is ____?____ out of ____?____.

More Practice

Set A pages 432–435

This table gives the ages and weights of the gymnastics team members. Copy and complete each tally chart.

Name	Age	Weight (lb)
Joey D.	12	56
Donna K.	10	54
Suzie G.	12	54
Vince L.	12	58
Fran B.	11	51

1.

Age	Tallies	Frequency

2.

Weight	Tallies	Frequency

3. Find the mode of the ages.

4. Find the mode of the weights.

Set B pages 436–437

For Exercises 1–4, refer to the table in Set A.

1. What is the oldest age of the members?

2. Make a bar graph to show the members' names and their ages.

3. What is the least weight given?

4. Make a bar graph to show the members' names and weights.

Set C pages 438–439

Use rows of cubes to find the average. Then compute the average.

1. 8, 5, 4, 5, 8   **2.** 8, 4, 7   **3.** 2, 3, 6, 6   **4.** 3, 3, 8, 7, 4

Estimation Tell whether the average is more or less than 10. How do you know?

5. 8, 12, 9, 14, 12   **6.** 4, 13, 6   **7.** 17, 4, 6, 22, 18

Set D pages 440–441

Write the letter located at each point.

1. (3, 1)   **2.** (2, 5)

3. (4, 2)   **4.** (2, 2)

Give the number pair for each point.

5. D   **6.** B   **7.** A   **8.** F

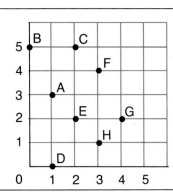

Set E   pages 442–443

Use graph paper. Connect the number pairs in order.
Draw each figure in at least two sizes.

1. (3, 1), (3, 4), (1, 4), (2, 7), (5, 7), (6, 4), (4, 4), (4, 1), (3, 1)

2. (7, 2), (9, 1), (9, 7), (7, 6), (4, 6), (2, 7), (2, 1), (4, 2), (7, 2)

3. (1, 1), (2, 3), (2, 7), (1, 7), (3, 9), (5, 7), (4, 7), (4, 3), (5, 1), (1, 1)

4. (2, 4), (4, 7), (6, 4), (5, 4), (7, 1), (5, 1), (5, 0), (3, 0), (3, 1), (1, 1), (3, 4), (2, 4)

Set F   pages 446–447

Copy and complete a broken-line graph
for the data in the table.

1. By what number will you count on
   the temperature scale?

2. Locate and connect the points.

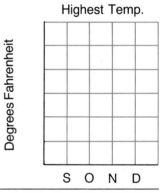

Month	Temp.
Sept.	88°F
Oct.	81°F
Nov.	76°F
Dec.	78°F

Set G   pages 450–451

Suppose you spin this spinner.

1. Is it certain, possible, or impossible to spin the
   number 5?

2. List the possible outcomes.

3. Are you more likely to spin a 3 or a 4?

4. Which outcomes are equally likely?

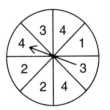

Set H   pages 454–455

Write the probability of each outcome when a
number cube is tossed.

1. The number 3   2. A number more than 2   3. *Not* a 1

Write the probability of each outcome when the
spinner in set G is spun.

4. 1   5. 4   6. An odd number   7. Not a 3   8. 3 or 4   9. 2 or 3

Enrichment

Four Coin Toss

Toss four coins. What is the probability of tossing *exactly* two heads?

Make an organized list of possible outcomes. Each coin can fall heads (H) or tails (T). How can two coins fall? They can fall HH, HT, TH, or TT.

Copy and complete the list for four coins.

Outcome

1	H	H	H	H
2	H	H	H	T
3	H	H	T	H
4	H	H	T	T

Begin with HH for the first two coins. List the four ways that the second two coins can fall.

5	H	T	H	H
6	H	T	H	T
7	H	T	T	H
8	H	T	T	T

Next, use HT for the first two coins. Again list the four ways that the second two coins can fall.

9	T	H	?	?
10	T	H	?	?
11	T	H	?	?
12	T	H	?	?

Now use TH for the first two coins. What are the possible outcomes for the second two coins?

13	?	?	?	?
14	?	?	?	?
15	?	?	?	?
16	?	?	?	?

What outcome is left for the first two coins?

There are **16** possible outcomes for tossing four coins.

1. Which of the possible outcomes have exactly two heads?

2. How many possible outcomes have exactly two heads?

3. The probability of tossing four coins and having exactly two heads turn up is ▒ out of ▒.

Chapter 13 Review/Test

Jordan took a survey to find out which colors the students in his class liked best. Three people chose pink, 4 liked yellow, 7 chose blue, 1 named lilac, and 3 liked green.

1. Write a survey question that might give the data above.

2. Make a tally chart showing the results of Jordan's survey.

3. Draw a bar graph to show Jordan's data.

4. Six students took the following numbers of marbles: 10, 7, 10, 11, 14, 8. What was the average number of marbles taken? Draw pictures of marbles to show how you found your answer.

Use the grid for Items 5 and 6.

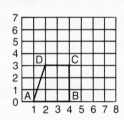

5. Write the number pairs for points A, B, C, and D.

6. Copy the grid and enlarge figure ABCD.

7. A storekeeper wants to show that sales of whole wheat bread have increased each month this year. What type of graph would best show this?

Use the graph at the right for Items 8–10.

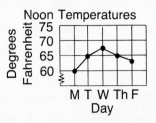

8. Which day had the highest noon temperature?

9. For which two days was the noon temperature the same?

10. Anna said that the average noon temperature for the 5 days was 60°F. Is this reasonable? Explain your answer.

Suppose you put these cards face down and mixed them up.

| 1 | 2 | 1 | 3 | 2 | 2 |

11. List the possible outcomes if you pick one card.

12. Predict which outcome would happen most often if you picked a card 100 times, replacing the card after each pick.

13. What is the probability of picking a card with 1?

14. Write About Math Sketch and label a spinner so that the probability of getting red will be 2 out of 8 and so that getting green will be more likely than getting red. Let white be the third color on the spinner.

Exploring Addition and Subtraction of Fractions

14

Did You Know:

In one minute:
- the human heart beats about 70 times.
- the heart of a shrew beats about 1,000 times.

In two minutes:
- a giraffe can run a mile.
- a blue shark can swim a mile.

In three minutes:
- after receiving an alarm, a fire or rescue unit can be on the road.

Number-Sense Project

Estimate
Estimate the average playing time of music selections you hear on the radio.

Gather Data
Select one kind of music you like. Time 5 or 6 selections played on the radio. Record these data in a chart.

Analyze and Report
Make a graph showing the playing times of the selections. Compare your results with those of other students. What generalizations can you make about the playing times?

Fractions and Mixed Numbers

Build Understanding

ACTIVITY

A. Coloring More Than 1
Materials: Crayons

a. Draw three equal circles like those at the right.

b. Color the circles to show the mixed number $2\frac{1}{4}$.

c. Into how many parts is each circle separated? How many of those parts did you color?

d. Write a fraction for the number of colored parts.

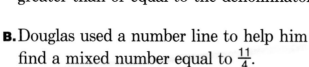

Numbers like $\frac{9}{4}$ are *improper fractions*. The numerator of an improper fraction is greater than or equal to the denominator.

B. Douglas used a number line to help him find a mixed number equal to $\frac{11}{4}$.

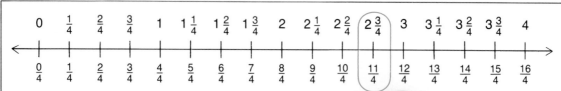

Douglas circled $2\frac{3}{4}$ and wrote $\frac{11}{4} = 2\frac{3}{4}$.

Talk About Math Which fraction shown on the number line above equals 1? 2?

Check Understanding

Answer each question.

1. Is $\frac{2}{3}$ an improper fraction? Why or why not?

2. Draw two circles and divide them into sixths. Shade $\frac{11}{6}$. What mixed number equals $\frac{11}{6}$?

Practice

For More Practice, see Set A, pages 492–493.

Write a whole number or a mixed number for each improper fraction. Use the pictures or number lines.

3. $\frac{10}{4}$ 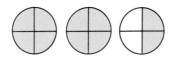 **4.** $\frac{10}{6}$ **5.** $\frac{6}{2}$

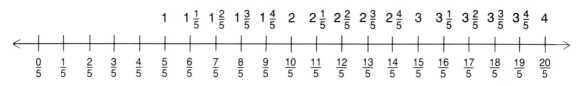

6. $\frac{5}{5}$ **7.** $\frac{7}{5}$ **8.** $\frac{12}{5}$ **9.** $\frac{20}{5}$

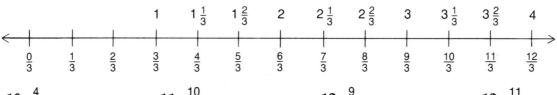

10. $\frac{4}{3}$ **11.** $\frac{10}{3}$ **12.** $\frac{9}{3}$ **13.** $\frac{11}{3}$

Skills ——— **Review** pages 90–91, 266–267, 310–311

Add, subtract, multiply, or divide.

1. $\$4.08 - \$1.49$ **2.** $\$9.27 \times 5$ **3.** $\$9.12 \div 3$ **4.** $\$2.94 + \$8.11$

Addition: Same Denominator

Build Understanding

A. Add It Up!
Materials: Crayons

a. Trace the circle at the left.

b. Color 2 parts yellow. What fraction of the circle did you color yellow?

c. Color 3 parts blue. What fraction of the circle did you color blue?

d. What fraction of the circle did you color blue or yellow?

Here are two ways to record your work.

$$\frac{2}{6} + \frac{3}{6} = \frac{5}{6} \quad \text{or} \quad \begin{array}{r} \frac{2}{6} \\ + \frac{3}{6} \\ \hline \frac{5}{6} \end{array}$$

What do you notice about the denominator of the sum? What can you say about the numerator of the sum?

For another example, see Set A, pages 490–491.

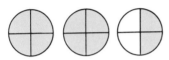   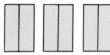

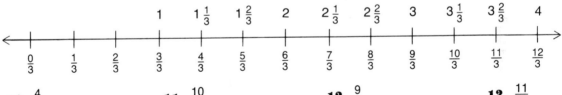

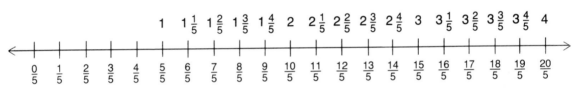

B. Find $1\frac{2}{4} + 1\frac{1}{4}$.

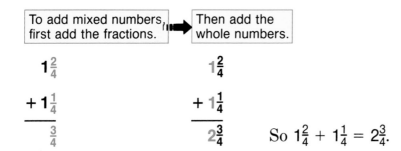

| To add mixed numbers, first add the fractions. | ➡ | Then add the whole numbers. |

$$1\frac{2}{4}$$
$$\underline{+\,1\frac{1}{4}}$$
$$\frac{3}{4}$$

$$1\frac{2}{4}$$
$$\underline{+\,1\frac{1}{4}}$$
$$2\frac{3}{4}$$

So $1\frac{2}{4} + 1\frac{1}{4} = 2\frac{3}{4}$.

■ **Write About Math** Write a rule for adding fractions that have the same denominators.

Check Understanding

For another example, see Set B, pages 490–491.

Use your circle from the Activity. Color 1 part red.

1. What fraction of the circle is red?

2. What fraction of the circle is red or blue?

3. What fraction of the circle is red or yellow?

4. What fraction of the circle is colored?

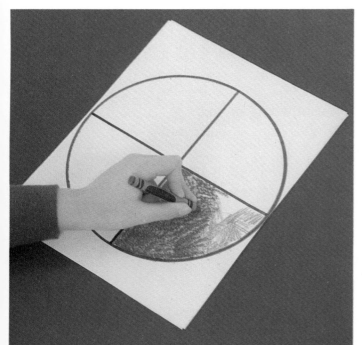

5. Use the circle at the left. One part is red. Write a fraction sentence that shows the sum of the red and white parts.

Add the mixed numbers.

6.

$$1\frac{1}{3} \quad + \quad 1\frac{1}{3}$$

7.

$$1\frac{1}{4} \quad + \quad 2\frac{2}{4}$$

Practice

For More Practice, see Set B, pages 492–493.

Find each sum.

8.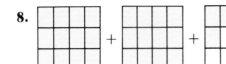

9.

10. $1\frac{3}{5} + 2\frac{1}{5}$ **11.** $3\frac{3}{8} + 1\frac{2}{8}$ **12.** $5\frac{6}{10} + 4\frac{3}{10}$ **13.** $2\frac{1}{9} + 4\frac{3}{9}$

14. + **15.**

16. $\frac{5}{8}$ **17.** $\frac{4}{12}$ **18.** $2\frac{3}{14}$ **19.** $1\frac{1}{2}$

$\quad +\frac{1}{8}$ $\quad +\frac{3}{12}$ $\quad +1\frac{7}{14}$ $\quad +\frac{1}{2}$

20. $\frac{7}{50} + \frac{17}{50}$ **21.** $\frac{2}{20} + \frac{15}{20}$ **22.** $\frac{19}{100} + \frac{38}{100} + \frac{2}{100}$

23. $8\frac{1}{10} + 7\frac{4}{10}$ **24.** $4\frac{3}{8} + 6\frac{4}{8}$ **25.** $10\frac{1}{9} + 4\frac{6}{9} + \frac{2}{9}$

26. $2\frac{1}{8} + 4\frac{2}{8}$ **27.** $9\frac{3}{25} + 6\frac{4}{25}$ **28.** $17\frac{20}{30} + 5\frac{2}{30} + 1\frac{5}{30}$

Mixed Practice Write each fraction as a whole number
or a mixed number. Draw pictures or number lines to help you.

29. $\frac{6}{4}$ **30.** $\frac{4}{4}$ **31.** $\frac{7}{4}$ **32.** $\frac{10}{4}$ **33.** $\frac{12}{3}$

34. $\frac{7}{3}$ **35.** $\frac{9}{3}$ **36.** $\frac{13}{5}$ **37.** $\frac{17}{5}$ **38.** $\frac{10}{5}$

Problem Solving

Solve each problem.

39. Marta Flores is making up bouquets of 12 roses in her flower shop. In each bouquet she puts 3 yellow roses, 4 white roses, and 5 red roses. What part of each bouquet is made up of yellow roses? White roses? Red roses?

40. Suppose Mrs. Flores adds 2 pink roses to each bouquet described in Problem 39. What fraction of the bouquet will be pink roses?

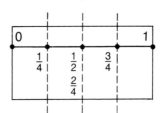

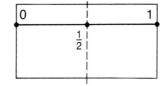

Explore ———— **Math**

Fractions Between 0 and 1 On a sheet of paper, draw a segment lengthwise from one edge to the opposite edge as shown at the right. Label its endpoints 0 and 1. Then follow these directions.

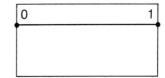

a. Fold the paper in half. Then open it. Label the point where the segment and the fold meet as $\frac{1}{2}$.

b. Refold the paper. Then fold it in half again. Open it and label the points on the segment as $\frac{1}{4}$, $\frac{2}{4}$, and $\frac{3}{4}$.

c. Continue folding in halves and labeling the points on the segment until the paper becomes too thick to fold.

41. If you were able to continue making folds, how many fractions could you find?

Subtraction: Same Denominator

Build Understanding

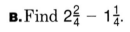

A. What's the Difference?
Materials: Crayons, scissors

a. Trace the circle at the right.

b. Color 7 of the parts red. What fraction of the circle did you color red?

c. Cut out 2 of the red parts. What fraction of the circle did you cut out?

d. How many eighths that are colored red are left?

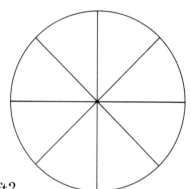

You can record your work as shown below.

$$\frac{7}{8} - \frac{2}{8} = \frac{5}{8} \quad \text{or} \quad \begin{array}{r} \frac{7}{8} \\ -\frac{2}{8} \\ \hline \frac{5}{8} \end{array}$$

What is the denominator of the difference? How could you find the numerator of the difference?

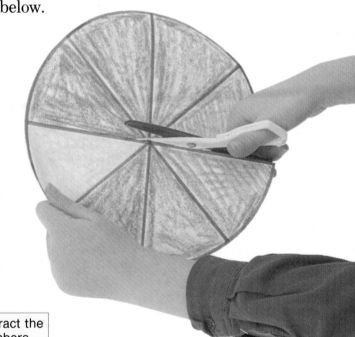

B. Find $2\frac{2}{4} - 1\frac{1}{4}$.

To subtract mixed numbers, first subtract the fractions.	➡	Then subtract the whole numbers.

$$\begin{array}{r} 2\frac{2}{4} \\ -1\frac{1}{4} \\ \hline \frac{1}{4} \end{array} \qquad \begin{array}{r} 2\frac{2}{4} \\ -1\frac{1}{4} \\ \hline 1\frac{1}{4} \end{array} \qquad \text{So } 2\frac{2}{4} - 1\frac{1}{4} = 1\frac{1}{4}.$$

■ Write About Math Write a rule for subtracting
fractions that have the same denominator.

Check Understanding

For another example, see Set C, pages 490–491.

Use your circle from the Activity. Cut out 1
more red part.

1. What fraction of the circle is cut
out?

2. What fraction of the circle is
left?

3. Write two number sentences to
show your work for Exercises 1
and 2 in two different ways.

4. How could you use a circle to
find $\frac{5}{8} - \frac{5}{8}$?   What is $\frac{5}{8} - \frac{5}{8}$?

Practice

For More Practice, see Set C, pages 492–493.

Find each difference.

5. $\frac{7}{8} - \frac{5}{8}$

6. $\frac{9}{10} - \frac{3}{10}$

7. $\frac{14}{15} - \frac{8}{15}$

8. $\frac{5}{25} - \frac{4}{25}$

9. $4\frac{2}{5} - 1\frac{1}{5}$

10. $3\frac{13}{28} - 1\frac{9}{28}$

11. $4\frac{15}{33} - 2\frac{7}{33}$

12. $6\frac{5}{6} - \frac{4}{6}$

13. $\frac{8}{14}$
$-\frac{6}{14}$

14. $\frac{20}{25}$
$-\frac{13}{25}$

15. $2\frac{7}{8}$
$-1\frac{4}{8}$

16. $3\frac{3}{12}$
$-1\frac{1}{12}$

Problem Solving

Solve each problem.

17. Jorge made $6\frac{5}{8}$ gallons of fruit punch for his party.
His guests drank $4\frac{3}{8}$ gallons. How much fruit
punch did Jorge have left at the end of the party?

18. Jorge divided pasta into 20 equal portions.
Each of his 12 guests ate a portion. Half of them
took second helpings. What fraction of the pasta
was left?

Draw a Picture

Build Understanding

Tammy trains horses. The distance that horses run is measured in furlongs. A furlong is one eighth of a mile. How many fourths of a mile equal 6 furlongs?

Understand You know that a furlong is one eighth of a mile. So you know that 6 furlongs is $\frac{6}{8}$ of a mile. This information can help you find how many fourths of a mile equal 6 furlongs.

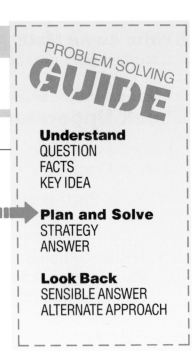

PROBLEM SOLVING
GUIDE

Understand
QUESTION
FACTS
KEY IDEA

▮▮▶ **Plan and Solve**
STRATEGY
ANSWER

Look Back
SENSIBLE ANSWER
ALTERNATE APPROACH

▮▮▶ **Plan and Solve** STRATEGY Draw a picture showing $\frac{8}{8}$. Then draw a picture showing $\frac{4}{4}$.

Next, shade 6 of the eighths. Then compare it to the picture showing fourths. Shade the parts of the fourths that match 6 parts of the eighths.

ANSWER Three fourths of a mile equals 6 furlongs.

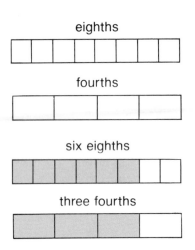

eighths

fourths

six eighths

three fourths

Look Back The pictures show that $\frac{3}{4}$ is equal to $\frac{6}{8}$. The answer is sensible.

▮**Talk About Math** How could you have used circles to help you solve the problem?

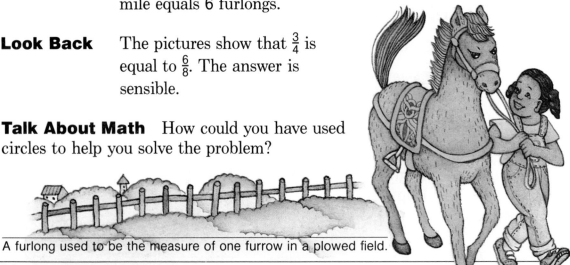

A furlong used to be the measure of one furrow in a plowed field.

474

Check Understanding

Follow the directions given for each picture. Answer each question.

1. Copy the pictures for *a* and *b*. Divide each picture into 3 equal parts.

   a.

   b.

2. Divide each of the 3 equal parts of picture *b* into 4 equal parts. How many parts are now in *b*?

3. Shade $\frac{2}{3}$ of picture *a*. Shade $\frac{2}{3}$ of picture *b*.

4. How many parts of picture *a* did you shade? How many parts of picture *b* did you shade?

5. How many twelfths equal $\frac{2}{3}$?

6. How many inches equal $\frac{2}{3}$ of a foot? **Remember** that 12 inches are in a foot.

Practice

Draw pictures to answer each question.

7. The height of a horse is measured in hands. One hand is 4 inches. How many hands are there in 12 inches?

8. A horse drinks at least 10 gallons of water each day. One gallon is 4 quarts. How many quarts are there in 5 gallons?

9. A horse eats about 14 pounds of hay each day. About how many pounds does it eat in $2\frac{1}{2}$ days?

10. A horse eats from 4 to 12 quarts of oats each day. You know that 2 pints equal one quart. How many pints are there in 12 quarts?

475

Estimation with Fractions and Mixed Numbers

Build Understanding

A. Jennifer Mason designs tiles to fit walls and floors. She often needs to add and subtract fractions and mixed numbers. Before she adds or subtracts, she often estimates a sum or a difference. Today she needs to estimate the sum of $\frac{7}{8}$ and $2\frac{3}{4}$.

She thinks: $\frac{7}{8}$ is close to 1, and $2\frac{3}{4}$ is close to 3. You can use pictures to show this.

$\frac{7}{8}$

$2\frac{3}{4}$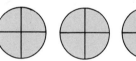

Since $1 + 3 = 4$, she knows before she adds the actual numbers that $\frac{7}{8} + 2\frac{3}{4}$ is about 4.

B. For one of her designs, Ms. Mason needs to estimate $5\frac{1}{4} - 2\frac{5}{8}$.

She thinks: $5\frac{1}{4}$ is close to 5, and $2\frac{5}{8}$ is close to 3. Since $5 - 3 = 2$, she knows before she subtracts the actual numbers that $5\frac{1}{4} - 2\frac{5}{8}$ is about 2.

■ **Talk About Math** Do you think that the actual sum in Example A is less than 4, equal to 4, or greater than 4? Explain.

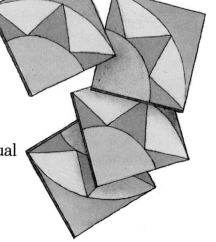

Check Understanding

For another example, see Set D, pages 490–491.

Find each answer.

1. Draw pictures for Example B to show that the difference is closer to 2 than it is to 3.

2. Is the actual difference in Example B less than 2, equal to 2, or greater than 2? Explain.

Practice

For More Practice, see Set D, pages 492–493.

Round to the nearest whole number.

3. $1\frac{2}{3}$ **4.** $\frac{3}{4}$ **5.** $4\frac{1}{5}$ **6.** $2\frac{5}{6}$ **7.** $\frac{2}{9}$ **8.** $3\frac{1}{8}$

Estimate each sum or difference.

9. $1\frac{5}{6} + \frac{2}{3}$ **10.** $3\frac{4}{5} - 1\frac{1}{10}$ **11.** $2\frac{9}{10} + 1\frac{1}{5}$ **12.** $1\frac{11}{12} + \frac{5}{6}$

13. $4\frac{7}{8} - 1\frac{1}{4}$ **14.** $\frac{1}{6} + 1\frac{2}{3}$ **15.** $1\frac{11}{12} - \frac{1}{3}$ **16.** $3\frac{7}{16} + 4\frac{1}{4}$

17. $4 - 1\frac{7}{10}$ **18.** $\frac{6}{7} + \frac{1}{3}$ **19.** $\frac{2}{5} + 1\frac{1}{12}$ **20.** $2\frac{1}{8} - 1\frac{7}{9}$

21. $\frac{1}{8} + 1\frac{5}{8} + 6\frac{2}{3} + 1\frac{1}{3}$ **22.** $7\frac{2}{5} + 3\frac{1}{4} + \frac{8}{9} + \frac{1}{3}$

Mixed Practice   Tell whether you would use mental math or paper and pencil. Then add or subtract.

23. $\frac{12}{17} + \frac{4}{17}$ **24.** $\frac{45}{47} - \frac{20}{47}$ **25.** $2\frac{4}{8} - \frac{1}{8}$ **26.** $5\frac{3}{4} + 1$

Write a whole number or a mixed number for each improper fraction. Draw pictures or number lines to help you.

27. $\frac{18}{17}$ **28.** $\frac{25}{5}$ **29.** $\frac{20}{4}$ **30.** $\frac{16}{12}$ **31.** $\frac{19}{6}$

Tell whether the sum or difference will be greater than 1, equal to 1, or less than 1.

32. $\frac{2}{3} + \frac{5}{8}$ **33.** $1\frac{1}{5} - \frac{4}{5}$ **34.** $\frac{15}{8} - \frac{7}{8}$ **35.** $\frac{1}{8} + \frac{2}{5}$

Problem Solving

Solve each problem.

36. Ms. Mason needs $2\frac{5}{8}$ pints of blue paint and $1\frac{1}{2}$ pints of purple paint to apply to some tiles. About how many pints of blue paint and purple paint does she need?

37. To lighten the blue paint, Ms. Mason takes half a pint of white paint from a gallon can and mixes it with blue paint. About how many gallons of white paint are left?

38. Critical Thinking
Ms. Mason needs to know the sum of the widths of 2 tiles. The tiles are $3\frac{5}{8}$ inches and $2\frac{1}{4}$ inches wide. Estimate the sum by rounding.

39. Number Sense A fraction that is less than 1 is called a *proper fraction*. What is true about the sum of any 2 proper fractions? About the sum of any 3 proper fractions?

40. An art student is helping Ms. Mason. He tells her that the sum of the widths in Problem 38 is $6\frac{7}{8}$ inches. Do you think that he is correct? Explain. Use paper and pencil to find the exact sum. Is the student's work correct?

Draw a number line and label
it from 0 to 6. Then mark it
in thirds. Use the number
line to answer each question.

1. What is the mixed number for $\frac{11}{3}$?

2. What is the mixed number for $\frac{17}{3}$?

3. What is the whole number for $\frac{12}{3}$?

4. What is the whole number for $\frac{18}{3}$?

5. What is the whole number for $\frac{3}{3}$?

6. What is the improper fraction for $3\frac{1}{3}$?

Find each sum or difference.

7. $\frac{5}{32} + \frac{2}{32}$

8. $\frac{10}{17} + \frac{4}{17}$

9. $\frac{12}{19} - \frac{9}{19}$

10. $\frac{84}{100} - \frac{12}{100}$

11. $2\frac{1}{13} + 4\frac{6}{13}$

12. $5\frac{6}{21} + 3\frac{7}{21}$

13. $11\frac{4}{9} - 2\frac{2}{9}$

14. $15\frac{8}{9} - 12\frac{6}{9}$

Draw pictures to show each problem. Then answer
the question.

15. How many thirds are in $\frac{6}{9}$?

16. How many fourths are in $\frac{9}{12}$?

17. How many fourths are in $\frac{12}{16}$?

18. How many fifths are in $\frac{6}{15}$?

Estimation Estimate each sum or difference.

19. $6\frac{3}{4} + 2\frac{1}{8}$

20. $4\frac{1}{3} + 6\frac{2}{6}$

21. $10\frac{5}{8} - 4\frac{1}{4}$

22. $6\frac{8}{9} - 2\frac{1}{3}$

Sketch circles or rectangles and
shade them to show each number.

23. $\frac{8}{4}$

24. $\frac{1}{6}$

25. $2\frac{1}{3}$

Problem Solving WORKSHOP

Real-Life Decision Making

It is 2:00 P.M. You are making muffins to take next door for a party that begins at 3:00 P.M. The recipe calls for $\frac{1}{3}$ cup brown sugar. You have $\frac{1}{4}$ cup brown sugar. You can ride your bike and back to the store in $\frac{1}{4}$ hour. It will take you $\frac{3}{4}$ hour to mix and bake the muffins.

1. Do you have enough brown sugar?

2. Do you have enough time to finish baking the muffins and still arrive at the party on time?

3. Decide what you are going to do.

Critical-Thinking Activity

My sister is half as old as I am. My brother is twice as old as I am. The sum of our ages is 28. How old am I?

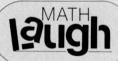

MATH **laugh**

There are twelve 1¢ stamps in a dozen. How many 2¢ stamps are there in a dozen?

ANSWER: Twelve stamps

Number-Sense Project

Look back at pages 464-465. Three students timed different kinds of music. The average times of their selections are listed below.

Student	Average Time
Pam	$2\frac{3}{4}$ minutes
Steve	$3\frac{1}{3}$ minutes
Wilt	3 minutes, 30 seconds

1. How many seconds longer was Steve's average selection than Pam's?

2. If Wilt's radio station played 2 songs between commercials, about how many minutes passed from one commercial to another?

Math-at-Home Activity

Do these probability experiments with someone at home.

1. Flip a quarter or another coin 50 times. Keep a tally of how many heads and tails you get.

2. Do you think you will get the same results when you spin the coin? Spin the coin on a table or floor 50 times. Keep another tally.

3. Did you get the results you expected?

4. How can you explain the results?

Result	Tally	Number
heads		
tails		
Total		50

Addition: Different Denominators

Build Understanding

A. Louise Sands is buying fabric. She needs $\frac{1}{4}$ yard of blue fabric and $\frac{5}{8}$ yard of red fabric. How many yards of fabric does she need?

Find $\frac{1}{4} + \frac{5}{8}$. Use number lines to rewrite $\frac{1}{4}$ with a denominator of 8. Then add the fractions.

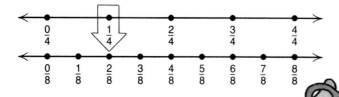

$$\frac{1}{4} + \frac{5}{8}$$
$$\downarrow \qquad \downarrow$$
$$\frac{2}{8} + \frac{5}{8} = \frac{7}{8}$$

Mrs. Sands needs $\frac{7}{8}$ yard of fabric.

B. Find $2\frac{6}{8} + 1\frac{1}{4}$.

Use the number lines to rewrite $\frac{6}{8}$ as $\frac{3}{4}$. Then use the pictures to find the sum.

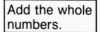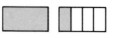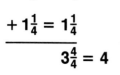

	Add the whole numbers.	Add the fractions.

$$2\frac{6}{8} = 2\frac{3}{4}$$
$$+\,1\frac{1}{4} = 1\frac{1}{4}$$
$$\overline{\qquad 3\frac{4}{4} = 4}$$

482

■ **Talk About Math** In Example A,
why do you rename $\frac{1}{4}$ instead of $\frac{5}{8}$?

Check Understanding

For another example, see Set E, pages 490–491.

Which fraction must be renamed in order to find
the sum? What will the new denominator be?

1. $\frac{3}{4} + \frac{1}{2}$ **2.** $\frac{1}{4} + \frac{5}{8}$ **3.** $\frac{1}{3} + \frac{5}{12}$ **4.** $3\frac{1}{12} + 1\frac{3}{4}$

Practice

For More Practice, see Set E, pages 492–493.

Find each sum. Use the number lines or pictures.

5. $\frac{1}{2} + \frac{1}{6}$ **6.** $\frac{1}{2} + \frac{1}{4}$ **7.** $\frac{1}{8} + \frac{1}{2}$

8. $\frac{1}{4} + \frac{1}{8}$ **9.** $\frac{1}{4} + \frac{3}{8}$ **10.** $\frac{1}{8} + \frac{3}{4}$

11. $\frac{1}{2} + \frac{5}{8}$ **12.** $\frac{7}{8} + \frac{1}{4}$ **13.** $\frac{1}{2} + \frac{3}{10}$

14. $\frac{1}{3} + \frac{1}{6}$ **15.** $\frac{1}{2} + \frac{7}{10}$ **16.** $\frac{5}{6} + \frac{2}{3}$

17. $1\frac{1}{2}$ **18.** $2\frac{1}{3}$ **19.** $1\frac{2}{5}$
$+2\frac{3}{8}$ $+1\frac{5}{6}$ $+1\frac{3}{10}$

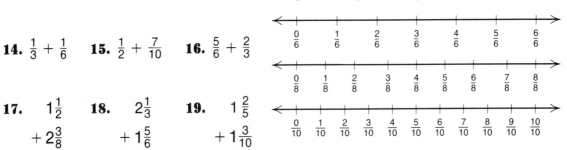

Reading ———— Math

Choose the words that make each sentence true.

1. Two is ▦ nine fourths.   **a.** greater than

2. Three is ▦ fifteen fifths.   **b.** less than

3. Four is ▦ ten sixths.   **c.** equal to

Subtraction: Different Denominators

Build Understanding

A. Sandi Sheppard jogs to keep healthy. Barth Park, where she jogs, is $\frac{9}{10}$ mile long and $\frac{2}{5}$ mile wide. How much greater is the park's length than its width?

Find $\frac{9}{10} - \frac{2}{5}$.

Use a number line to rewrite $\frac{2}{5}$ with a denominator of 10.

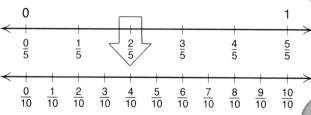

$$\frac{9}{10} - \frac{2}{5}$$
$$\downarrow \qquad \downarrow$$
$$\frac{9}{10} - \frac{4}{10} = \frac{5}{10}$$

Jogging builds and maintains physical fitness by improving the function of the circulatory and respiratory systems.

The length of Barth Park is $\frac{5}{10}$ of a mile greater than the width.

B. Find $2\frac{1}{2} - 1\frac{3}{10}$.

$$
\begin{array}{r}
2\frac{1}{2} = 2\frac{5}{10} \\
-1\frac{3}{10} = -1\frac{3}{10} \\
\hline
1\frac{2}{10}
\end{array}
$$

■ **Talk About Math** In Example B, why do you rename $\frac{1}{2}$ instead of $\frac{3}{10}$?

Check Understanding

For another example, see Set F, pages 490–491.

Which fraction must be renamed
in order to find the difference?
What will the new denominator be?

1. $4\frac{1}{5} - 3\frac{1}{10}$ **2.** $3\frac{6}{10} - 2\frac{3}{5}$ **3.** $8\frac{1}{2} - \frac{8}{10}$ **4.** $9\frac{1}{2} - 5\frac{9}{10}$

Practice

For More Practice, see Set F, pages 492–493.

Find each difference. Use the
number lines, or draw pictures.

5. $\frac{2}{5} - \frac{1}{10}$ **6.** $\frac{7}{10} - \frac{3}{5}$

7. $\frac{8}{10} - \frac{1}{2}$ **8.** $\frac{4}{5} - \frac{5}{10}$

9. $\frac{3}{4} - \frac{5}{8}$ **10.** $\frac{5}{6} - \frac{2}{3}$

11. $\frac{3}{4} - \frac{5}{12}$ **12.** $\frac{11}{12} - \frac{1}{3}$

13. $\quad 1\frac{5}{6}$ **14.** $\quad 3\frac{2}{3}$

$\quad\; -1\frac{1}{2}$ $\quad\; -1\frac{5}{12}$

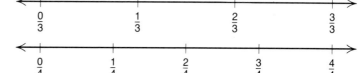
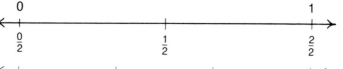
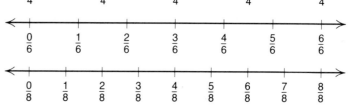
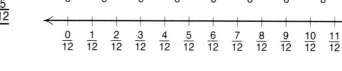

Problem Solving

Solve each problem.

15. Sandi also cycles to keep fit. Last weekend she rode her bike $5\frac{1}{5}$ miles on Saturday and $7\frac{1}{2}$ miles on Sunday. How many more miles did she ride on Sunday than on Saturday?

16. **Use Data** Sandi jogs and cycles a total of 40 miles a week. Use the data on page 474 to find how many furlongs this would be if a horse ran the same distance.

Write a Number Sentence

Build Understanding

Rosetta Randolph is buying blank tapes to record the band's rehearsals for the musical comedy she is directing for the school. She knows the band will rehearse 90 minutes a day for 20 days and that she will need 20 tapes that can record for 90 minutes.

The store is selling 90-minute tapes in packages of 4 tapes. How many packages should Mrs. Randolph buy?

Understand   Each package has 4 tapes. Mrs. Randolph needs 20 tapes. How many groups of 4 are in 20?

 **Plan and Solve**   STRATEGY   Write a number sentence to show how the parts of the problem are related.

▦ packages with 4 tapes in each is 20 tapes.

$$▦ \times 4 = 20$$

To find the missing number, think of a division fact.

$20 \div 4 = ▦$ $20 \div 4 = 5$

ANSWER   Mrs. Randolph should buy 5 packages of tapes.

Look Back   There are too many tapes in 6 packages ($6 \times 4 = 24$) and not enough in 4 packages ($4 \times 4 = 16$). The answer makes sense.

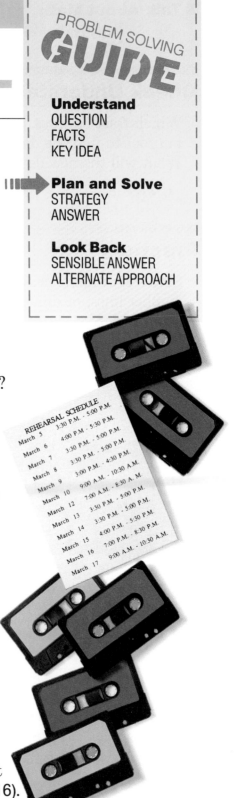

PROBLEM SOLVING GUIDE

Understand
QUESTION
FACTS
KEY IDEA

Plan and Solve
STRATEGY
ANSWER

Look Back
SENSIBLE ANSWER
ALTERNATE APPROACH

REHEARSAL SCHEDULE
March 5   3:30 P.M. - 5:00 P.M.
March 6   4:00 P.M. - 5:30 P.M.
March 7   3:30 P.M. - 5:00 P.M.
March 8   3:30 P.M. - 4:30 P.M.
March 9   3:00 P.M. - 4:30 P.M.
March 10   9:00 A.M. - 10:30 A.M.
March 12   7:00 A.M. - 8:30 A.M.
March 13   3:30 P.M. - 5:00 P.M.
March 14   3:30 P.M. - 5:30 P.M.
March 15   4:00 P.M. - 5:30 P.M.
March 16   7:00 P.M. - 8:30 P.M.
March 17   9:00 A.M. - 10:30 A.M.

Write About Math Explain how you could use objects to solve Mrs. Randolph's problem.

Check Understanding

Solve the problem.

Mrs. Randolph is holding rehearsals for 24 singers. She can rehearse only 3 singers at a time. How many rehearsals should she hold?

1. Which number sentence can you use to solve this problem?

    a. $24 - 3 = $ ▦   **b.** ▦ $+ 3 = 24$ **c.** ▦ $\times 3 = 24$

2. Write the answer to the problem in a complete sentence.

Practice

Write a number sentence for each problem. Then solve the problem.

3. The school sold 842 tickets for the first performance and 906 tickets for the second. How many tickets were sold altogether?

4. Ben bought a granola bar for himself and each of his 11 friends. There are 3 bars in a package. How many packages did he buy?

Choose a ▦ Strategy

Grace's Gifts Grace Gordon bought a bunch of grapes and gave her friends some of them. Arnold Abbott asked for 8 grapes. Sam Soong got half of what she had left plus 1 more. Then Carol Carter asked for 3 grapes. Pablo Perez ate half of what was left. Then Walter Wong asked for half of what was left plus 1 more. Finally, Grace ate the last 2 grapes.

5. How many grapes did Grace buy?

PROBLEM SOLVING STRATEGIES

Choose an Operation
Try and Check
Draw a Diagram
Solve a Simpler Problem
Write a Number Sentence
Make a Table
Use Logical Reasoning
Find a Pattern
Draw a Picture
Work Backward
Make a Graph

Solve each problem.

1. The letters A, E, I, O, and U are vowels. What fraction of the letters in the name Reggie Jackson is vowels? What fraction of the letters in your name is vowels?

2. A sheet of paper is $8\frac{1}{2}$ inches wide and 11 inches long. What is the difference between the length and the width?

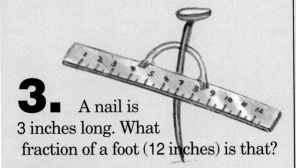

3. A nail is 3 inches long. What fraction of a foot (12 inches) is that?

4. Ron has $\frac{1}{2}$ pound of cheese. If he uses $\frac{1}{8}$ pound of cheese for a sandwich, how many sandwiches can he make?

5. Joan has $1\frac{3}{4}$ yards of material. If she uses $\frac{3}{8}$ yard for a stuffed toy, how much material will she have left?

6. **Data File** Use data from pages 524-525. Find the height of the abacus if the three slats are each $\frac{3}{8}$ inch thick.

7. **Make a Data File**
Stock prices are quoted as fractions. In a newspaper business section find the closing price of one stock. Do this for 5 days for the same stock. Make a broken-line graph to show how the price of the stock goes up or down.

Explore with a Calculator

One Step Leads to Another

Here is a puzzle to solve.

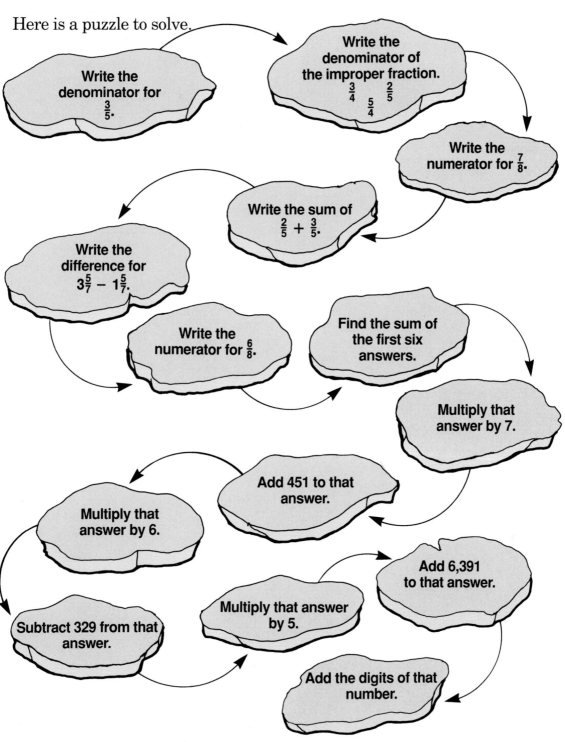

Write the denominator for $\frac{3}{5}$.

Write the denominator of the improper fraction. $\frac{3}{4}$ $\frac{2}{5}$ $\frac{5}{4}$

Write the numerator for $\frac{7}{8}$.

Write the sum of $\frac{2}{5} + \frac{3}{5}$.

Write the difference for $3\frac{5}{7} - 1\frac{5}{7}$.

Write the numerator for $\frac{6}{8}$.

Find the sum of the first six answers.

Multiply that answer by 7.

Add 451 to that answer.

Multiply that answer by 6.

Subtract 329 from that answer.

Multiply that answer by 5.

Add 6,391 to that answer.

Add the digits of that number.

Use those digits to make a fraction that will be one less than nine.

Reteaching

Set A   pages 466–467

Write a whole number or a mixed number for $\frac{7}{3}$.

You can use pictures to help you.

       $\frac{7}{3} = 2\frac{1}{3}$

Remember that the denominator of a fraction tells how many equal parts make up the whole.

Write a whole number or a mixed number for the improper fraction.

1. $\frac{11}{8}$

Set B   pages 468–471

Find $3\frac{4}{10} + 6\frac{3}{10}$.

To add mixed numbers, first add the fractions.

$$3\frac{4}{10}$$
$$+6\frac{3}{10}$$
$$\overline{\frac{7}{10}}$$

Then add the whole numbers.

$$3\frac{4}{10}$$
$$+6\frac{3}{10}$$
$$\overline{9\frac{7}{10}}$$

Remember that when you add fractions that have the same denominator, you add the numerators only and keep the same denominator.

Find each sum.

1. $4\frac{1}{5} + 5\frac{3}{5}$ **2.** $7\frac{1}{8} + 5\frac{4}{8}$

3. $8\frac{1}{10} + 3\frac{3}{10}$ **4.** $9\frac{3}{13} + 6\frac{2}{13}$

Set C   pages 472–473

Find $4\frac{6}{7} - 2\frac{3}{7}$.

To subtract mixed numbers, first subtract the fractions.

$$4\frac{6}{7}$$
$$-2\frac{3}{7}$$
$$\overline{\frac{3}{7}}$$

Then subtract the whole numbers.

$$4\frac{6}{7}$$
$$-2\frac{3}{7}$$
$$\overline{2\frac{3}{7}}$$

Remember when you subtract fractions that have the same denominator, subtract the numerators only and keep the same denominator.

Find each difference.

1. $5\frac{7}{10} - 2\frac{3}{10}$ **2.** $7\frac{5}{8} - 4\frac{3}{8}$

3. $6\frac{5}{6}$ **4.** $5\frac{7}{13}$
  $-3\frac{1}{6}$ $-2\frac{4}{13}$

5. $5\frac{2}{5}$ **6.** $6\frac{7}{8}$
  $-\frac{2}{5}$ $-6\frac{6}{8}$

Independent Study RETEACHING

Set D   pages 476–478

Estimate the sum of $\frac{5}{6}$ and $2\frac{1}{3}$.

Think: $\frac{5}{6}$ is close to 1 and
$\quad\quad 2\frac{1}{3}$ is close to 2.

So the estimated sum is $1 + 2$, or 3.
You know before you add the actual
numbers that $\frac{5}{6} + 2\frac{1}{3}$ is about 3.

Remember that the actual sum will be
less than the estimated sum if the
addends were rounded up.

Estimate each sum or difference.

1. $3\frac{7}{8} + 5\frac{3}{4}$ **2.** $4\frac{7}{10} + 4\frac{1}{5}$

3. $6\frac{9}{13} - 1\frac{11}{13}$ **4.** $5\frac{5}{6} - 2\frac{1}{3}$

Set E   pages 482–483

Find $\frac{2}{3} + \frac{1}{6}$.

Use a number line to rewrite $\frac{2}{3}$ with a
denominator of 6.

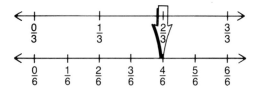

Then add.

$$\begin{array}{ccc} \frac{2}{3} & + & \frac{1}{6} \\ \downarrow & & \downarrow \\ \frac{4}{6} & + & \frac{1}{6} = \frac{5}{6} \end{array}$$

Remember that before you add two
fractions, both fractions must have the
same denominator.

Find each sum. Use the number lines
on page 483 or draw your own.

1. $\frac{1}{2} + \frac{2}{6}$ **2.** $\frac{2}{4} + \frac{3}{8}$

3. $\frac{1}{3} + \frac{1}{6}$ **4.** $\frac{5}{8} + \frac{1}{4}$

5. $3\frac{3}{5} + 4\frac{3}{10}$ **6.** $7\frac{3}{8} + 2\frac{1}{2}$

Set F   pages 484–485

Find $\frac{5}{6} - \frac{5}{12}$.

Use a number line to rewrite $\frac{5}{6}$ with a
denominator of 12.

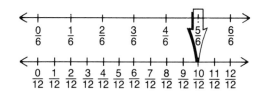

Then subtract.

$$\begin{array}{ccc} \frac{5}{6} & - & \frac{5}{12} \\ \downarrow & & \downarrow \\ \frac{10}{12} & - & \frac{5}{12} = \frac{5}{12} \end{array}$$

Remember that before you subtract
two fractions, both fractions must have
the same denominator.

Find each difference. Use the number
lines on pages 484 and 485.

1. $\frac{9}{10} - \frac{2}{5}$ **2.** $\frac{5}{8} - \frac{1}{4}$

3. $\frac{7}{12} - \frac{1}{4}$ **4.** $\frac{1}{3} - \frac{1}{12}$

5. $3\frac{7}{12} - 2\frac{2}{4}$ **6.** $4\frac{5}{6} - 2\frac{1}{2}$

More Practice

Set A pages 466–467

Write a whole number or mixed number for each
improper fraction. Use the pictures or number lines.

1. $\frac{13}{8}$ **2.** $\frac{9}{5}$

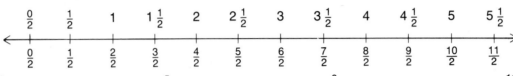

3. $\frac{2}{2}$ **4.** $\frac{5}{2}$ **5.** $\frac{8}{2}$ **6.** $\frac{11}{2}$

7. $\frac{7}{2}$ **8.** $\frac{0}{2}$ **9.** $\frac{4}{2}$ **10.** $\frac{9}{2}$

Set B pages 468–471

Find each sum.

1. $\begin{array}{r} \frac{2}{6} \\ +\frac{3}{6} \\ \hline \end{array}$ **2.** $\begin{array}{r} \frac{4}{11} \\ +\frac{3}{11} \\ \hline \end{array}$ **3.** $\begin{array}{r} 4\frac{1}{12} \\ +3\frac{8}{12} \\ \hline \end{array}$ **4.** $\begin{array}{r} 1\frac{1}{5} \\ +6\frac{2}{5} \\ \hline \end{array}$

5. $\frac{7}{25} + \frac{9}{25}$ **6.** $\frac{3}{20} + \frac{6}{20}$ **7.** $\frac{9}{17} + \frac{4}{17}$ **8.** $\frac{4}{9} + \frac{3}{9}$

9. $9\frac{4}{15} + 2\frac{3}{15}$ **10.** $1\frac{7}{30} + 4\frac{11}{30}$ **11.** $8\frac{2}{7} + 4\frac{2}{7}$ **12.** $5\frac{1}{8} + 7\frac{3}{8}$

Set C pages 472–473

Find each difference.

1. $\frac{5}{9} - \frac{2}{9}$ **2.** $\frac{7}{11} - \frac{2}{11}$ **3.** $\frac{6}{7} - \frac{3}{7}$ **4.** $\frac{11}{23} - \frac{7}{23}$

5. $5\frac{6}{8} - 2\frac{3}{8}$ **6.** $4\frac{12}{19} - 1\frac{7}{19}$ **7.** $6\frac{13}{23} - 3\frac{4}{23}$ **8.** $8\frac{4}{5} - 2\frac{1}{5}$

9. $\begin{array}{r} \frac{11}{15} \\ -\frac{4}{15} \\ \hline \end{array}$ **10.** $\begin{array}{r} \frac{14}{27} \\ -\frac{8}{27} \\ \hline \end{array}$ **11.** $\begin{array}{r} 5\frac{5}{7} \\ -2\frac{2}{7} \\ \hline \end{array}$ **12.** $\begin{array}{r} 6\frac{8}{9} \\ -4\frac{3}{9} \\ \hline \end{array}$

Set D   pages 476–478

Round to the nearest whole number.

1. $2\frac{3}{4}$ **2.** $5\frac{1}{8}$ **3.** $\frac{5}{6}$ **4.** $3\frac{7}{8}$ **5.** $\frac{3}{10}$ **6.** $6\frac{1}{5}$

Estimate each sum or difference.

7. $3\frac{1}{4} + \frac{5}{6}$ **8.** $2\frac{7}{8} - \frac{3}{4}$ **9.** $4\frac{10}{12} + 1\frac{1}{7}$ **10.** $2\frac{5}{7} + \frac{1}{3}$

11. $3\frac{13}{16} - 2\frac{1}{8}$ **12.** $4\frac{1}{6} + 2\frac{9}{10}$ **13.** $5\frac{2}{9} - 2\frac{1}{10}$ **14.** $3\frac{5}{17} + 3\frac{10}{11}$

Mixed Practice   Tell whether you would use mental math or paper and pencil. Then add or subtract.

15. $\frac{8}{13} + \frac{3}{13}$ **16.** $\frac{32}{37} - \frac{10}{37}$ **17.** $3\frac{5}{6} - 1\frac{1}{6}$ **18.** $7\frac{3}{5} + 2$

Write a whole number or a mixed number for each improper fraction. Draw pictures or number lines to help you.

19. $\frac{13}{10}$ **20.** $\frac{20}{4}$ **21.** $\frac{18}{6}$ **22.** $\frac{13}{8}$ **23.** $\frac{17}{5}$

Set E   pages 482–483

Find each sum. Use the number lines on page 483, or draw pictures.

1. $\frac{1}{4} + \frac{3}{8}$ **2.** $\frac{1}{2} + \frac{2}{6}$ **3.** $\frac{1}{2} + \frac{4}{10}$ **4.** $\frac{1}{6} + \frac{2}{3}$

5. $\frac{1}{2} + \frac{3}{8}$ **6.** $\frac{1}{2} + \frac{2}{10}$ **7.** $\frac{1}{3} + \frac{1}{6}$ **8.** $\frac{1}{4} + \frac{4}{8}$

9. $\frac{1}{10} + \frac{1}{2}$ **10.** $1\frac{1}{4} + 2\frac{3}{8}$ **11.** $\frac{4}{8} + \frac{1}{4}$ **12.** $2\frac{1}{2} + 3\frac{1}{10}$

Set F   pages 484–485

Find each difference. Use the number lines on pages 484–485, or draw pictures.

1. $\frac{3}{5} - \frac{3}{10}$ **2.** $\frac{7}{10} - \frac{3}{5}$ **3.** $\frac{3}{4} - \frac{5}{12}$ **4.** $\frac{5}{8} - \frac{2}{4}$

5. $\frac{3}{4} - \frac{1}{8}$ **6.** $1\frac{11}{12} - \frac{1}{2}$ **7.** $3\frac{3}{8} - 1\frac{1}{4}$ **8.** $4\frac{2}{3} - 2\frac{7}{12}$

Enrichment

Subtracting by Adding

In a proper fraction, the numerator is less than the denominator. Mr. Maladd likes to add proper fractions. So if you ask him to find $\frac{5}{6} - \frac{2}{3}$, he doesn't find the answer by subtracting two fractions. Instead, he finds the sum $\frac{5}{6} + \frac{1}{3}$ and then subtracts 1. (He likes to subtract a whole number, you see.) This gives him the right answer.

First, study Mr. Maladd's method. Then use it to subtract in Exercises 1–12.

One Method	Mr. Maladd's Method
$\frac{5}{6} = \frac{5}{6}$ $-\frac{2}{3} = \frac{4}{6}$ $\overline{\quad \frac{1}{6}}$	$\frac{5}{6} \rightarrow \frac{5}{6} + \frac{1}{3} = \frac{5}{6} + \frac{2}{6} = \frac{7}{6} = 1\frac{1}{6}$ $-\frac{2}{3} \rightarrow \frac{2}{3} + \frac{1}{3} = \quad \frac{3}{3} = 1 = 1$ $\overline{\hspace{6cm} \frac{1}{6}}$
$\frac{3}{4} = \frac{6}{8}$ $-\frac{1}{8} = \frac{1}{8}$ $\overline{\quad \frac{5}{8}}$	$\frac{3}{4} \rightarrow \frac{3}{4} + \frac{7}{8} = \frac{6}{8} + \frac{7}{8} = \frac{13}{8} = 1\frac{5}{8}$ $-\frac{1}{8} \rightarrow \frac{1}{8} + \frac{7}{8} = \quad \frac{8}{8} = 1 = 1$ $\overline{\hspace{6cm} \frac{5}{8}}$

1. $\frac{3}{4} - \frac{3}{8}$ **2.** $\frac{3}{4} - \frac{5}{12}$ **3.** $\frac{5}{12} - \frac{1}{6}$ **4.** $\frac{5}{9} - \frac{1}{3}$

5. $\frac{5}{6} - \frac{1}{3}$ **6.** $\frac{3}{8} - \frac{1}{4}$ **7.** $\frac{5}{9} - \frac{1}{3}$ **8.** $\frac{1}{6} - \frac{1}{12}$

9. $\frac{5}{8} - \frac{1}{2}$ **10.** $\frac{7}{12} - \frac{1}{3}$ **11.** $\frac{11}{15} - \frac{2}{5}$ **12.** $\frac{11}{20} - \frac{1}{2}$

13. Explain Mr. Maladd's method.

Chapter 14 Review/Test

Write a whole number or mixed number for each improper fraction. Use the pictures.

1. $\frac{5}{3}$

2. $\frac{9}{5}$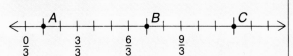

Which fraction must be renamed in order to find the sum or difference? What will the new denominator be?

3. $\frac{1}{6} + \frac{1}{12}$ **4.** $\frac{7}{8} - \frac{1}{2}$

Add or subtract.

5. $\frac{3}{8} + \frac{1}{8}$ **6.** $7\frac{11}{12} - 3\frac{1}{12}$

7. $\frac{1}{4} + \frac{3}{8}$ **8.** $2\frac{1}{10} + 5\frac{3}{10}$

9. $\frac{9}{10} - \frac{1}{10}$ **10.** $\frac{1}{2} + \frac{3}{10}$

11. $\frac{5}{6} - \frac{1}{12}$ **12.** $3\frac{1}{3} - 1\frac{1}{6}$

Use the number line to answer Items 13–15.

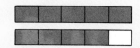

Give the mixed number, whole number, or fraction for each point.

13. A **14.** B **15.** C

Estimate each sum or difference.

16. $5\frac{7}{8} + 2\frac{3}{4}$ **17.** $3\frac{11}{12} - 1\frac{1}{6}$

18. Mr. Pinelli has a board that is $4\frac{3}{4}$ feet long. He cuts off $1\frac{1}{4}$ feet from the board. How long is the remaining piece?

19. There are 3 feet in 1 yard. Draw two pictures to find the number of feet in 5 yards.

Read the following problem. Then answer Items 20 and 21.

Hector had 96 baseball cards. He gave 16 of them to a friend. How many does he have left?

20. Which number sentence could you use to solve this problem?

     a. $96 + 16 =$ ▦
     b. $96 - 16 =$ ▦
     c. $96 \times 16 =$ ▦
     d. $96 \div 16 =$ ▦

21. Solve the problem.

22. Write About Math Is your estimate in Item 16 greater than or less than the actual sum? Explain.

Division: 2-Digit Divisors

15

Did You Know:
Some roller coasters reach high speeds of 65 miles per hour.

Number-Sense Project

Estimate
Estimate how many trips the roller coaster will take to give everybody standing in line a ride.

Gather Data
How many people can the roller coaster in this picture carry in one trip? Estimate how many people are standing in the line at the bottom of pages 496-497.

Analyze and Report
Compute how many trips the roller coaster will take to give everyone standing in line a ride. Compare your answer with those of other students.

497

Dividing by Tens

Build Understanding

Have you ever heard of Luck, Wisconsin? It was called the "Yoyo Capital of the World." At one time, approximately 60 yoyos were made every minute at the Duncan plant in Luck.

Suppose yoyos were shipped in boxes of 20. How many boxes would be needed to ship 100 yoyos?

Divide to find how many groups of 20 there are in 100. Find $100 \div 20$.

Use ten-sticks to show 100.

Divide 100 into groups of 20.

$$100 \div 20 = 5 \text{ or } 20\overline{)100}^{\,5}$$

Donald F. Duncan is credited with starting the yoyo fad in the United States in the early 1930s.

There are 5 groups of 20. So 5 boxes would be needed to ship 100 yoyos.

■ **Talk About Math** What basic division fact can help you find $120 \div 40$?

Check Understanding

For another example, see Set A, pages 518–519.

Answer Exercises 1–4 to find $150 \div 30$.

1. How many ten-sticks would you draw to show 150?

2. How many ten-sticks would be in each group of 30?

3. How many groups of 30 would there be?

4. So $150 \div 30 = $ ▒▒▒.

Practice

For More Practice, see Set A, pages 520–521.

Find each quotient. Draw ten-sticks if necessary.

5. 70 ÷ 10   **6.** 90 ÷ 30   **7.** 80 ÷ 40   **8.** 200 ÷ 50

9. 320 ÷ 40   **10.** 160 ÷ 80   **11.** 240 ÷ 80   **12.** 350 ÷ 70

13. 210 ÷ 30   **14.** 450 ÷ 50   **15.** 300 ÷ 60   **16.** 810 ÷ 90

Mixed Practice   Find each answer. **Remember** to estimate each quotient to help you decide if your answer is reasonable.

17. 60 ÷ 3   **18.** 180 ÷ 90   **19.** 202 ÷ 2   **20.** 220 ÷ 2   **21.** 382 ÷ 3

22. 420 ÷ 7   **23.** 440 ÷ 20   **24.** 396 ÷ 3   **25.** 786 ÷ 8   **26.** 450 ÷ 9

Problem Solving

Solve each problem.

27. If 60 yoyos were packaged 20 to a box, how many boxes would be needed?

28. **Calculator**   If 60 yoyos are made a minute, can a million yoyos be made in 300 hours?

Explore ———— Math

Study the patterns shown below.

8 ÷ 4 = 2	80 ÷ 40 = 2	800 ÷ 400 = 2
80 ÷ 4 = 20	800 ÷ 40 = 20	8,000 ÷ 400 = 20
800 ÷ 4 = 200	8,000 ÷ 40 = 200	
8,000 ÷ 4 = 2,000		

Find each quotient. Use the patterns above to help you.

29. 3)9   **30.** 3)90   **31.** 3)900   **32.** 3)9,000   **33.** 30)90

34. 30)900   **35.** 30)9,000   **36.** 300)900   **37.** 300)9,000

Exploring Division: 2-Digit Divisors and 1-Digit Quotients

Build Understanding

Quotient Quest!
Materials: Ten-sticks and ones
Groups: 2 to 4 students

a. Choose a number between 29 and 129 to divide into groups of 13. Show this amount with ten-sticks and ones using as few ones as possible. How many ten-sticks and ones are there?

b. Form a group of 13. Did you have to trade a ten-stick for 10 ones?

c. Continue to form as many groups of 13 as you can. How many groups can you form?

d. Are there any ten-sticks left over? Are there any ones left over?

e. When Joan divided 99 by 13, she recorded her quotient of 7 and remainder of 8 as shown at the right. Write your division problem, recording the quotient and remainder.

$$\overset{7 \ R8}{13\overline{)99}}$$

■ **Talk About Math** Bryant divided a number by 13. He wrote a quotient of 5 and a remainder of 14. What did Bryant fail to realize?

Check Understanding

For another example, see Set B, pages 518–519.

Complete each division sentence.

1.

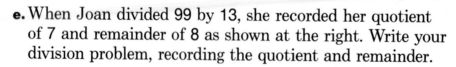

$$36 \div 12 = \text{\scriptsize▦▦}$$

2.

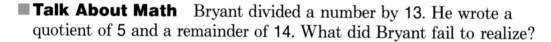

$$60 \div \text{\scriptsize▦▦} = \text{\scriptsize▦▦}$$

Practice

For More Practice, see Set B, pages 520–521.

Use ten-sticks and ones to divide.

3. $32 \div 16$ **4.** $68 \div 17$ **5.** $39 \div 13$ **6.** $75 \div 14$

7. $38\overline{)114}$ **8.** $21\overline{)147}$ **9.** $18\overline{)118}$ **10.** $44\overline{)176}$

Mixed Practice Choose paper and pencil or mental math to divide. Tell why you chose that method.

11. $4\overline{)240}$ **12.** $3\overline{)714}$ **13.** $6\overline{)780}$ **14.** $8\overline{)640}$ **15.** $9\overline{)550}$ **16.** $5\overline{)400}$

Problem Solving

Solve each problem. Use ten-sticks and ones if necessary.

17. Joan used 9 ten-sticks and 6 ones to show a number. How many groups of 16 could she make from this number? Write the division problem.

18. Joan found that 4 ten-sticks and 7 ones can be divided into 2 groups of 21 with some ones left over. How many ones will be left over?

19. Critical Thinking You can form 18 groups of 7 from a number. How many groups of 14 can you form from the same number?

20. Estimation With ten-sticks and ones the class made 21 groups with 38 in each group. About how many is this in all?

Skills	Review	pages 468–473

Add.

1. $\frac{1}{4} + \frac{1}{4}$ **2.** $\frac{2}{3} + \frac{1}{3}$ **3.** $\frac{7}{8} + \frac{5}{8}$ **4.** $1\frac{2}{5} + 3\frac{2}{5}$ **5.** $2\frac{3}{6} + 2\frac{4}{6}$

Subtract.

6. $\frac{1}{2} - \frac{0}{2}$ **7.** $\frac{3}{5} - \frac{1}{5}$ **8.** $\frac{4}{7} - \frac{3}{7}$ **9.** $5\frac{3}{4} - 2\frac{3}{4}$ **10.** $4\frac{7}{9} - 2\frac{1}{9}$

Using Multiplication to Divide

Build Understanding

The manager of a restaurant has to schedule different jobs. The chart at the right shows time estimates.

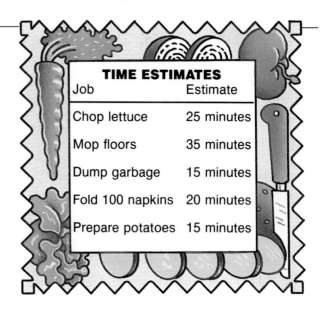

TIME ESTIMATES

Job	Estimate
Chop lettuce	25 minutes
Mop floors	35 minutes
Dump garbage	15 minutes
Fold 100 napkins	20 minutes
Prepare potatoes	15 minutes

A. It takes 15 minutes to prepare a sack of potatoes. How many 15-minute periods are in one hour?

Since there are 60 minutes in an hour, find $60 \div 15$.

You can count by 15s on a clock.

$$60 \div 15 = 4$$

There are four 15-minute periods in one hour.

B. Find $23\overline{)115}$.

Use multiples of 23 to help you find the quotient.

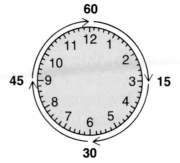

23	46	69	92	115
1×23	2×23	3×23	4×23	5×23

So $23\overline{)115}^{\,5}$.

■**Talk About Math** How can you use addition to list the multiples of a number? Give an advantage and a disadvantage of using this method.

502

Check Understanding

For another example, see Set C, pages 518–519.

Find the answers to Exercises 1–3.

1. List the multiples of 19 up to 95.

2. $95 \div 19 = $ ▦

3. Continue your list of multiples to find $171 \div 19$.

Practice

For More Practice, see Set C, pages 520–521.

List the numbers described below.

4. The multiples of 11 up to 99

5. The multiples of 14 up to 84

6. The multiples of 21 up to 147

7. The multiples of 25 up to 125

Use your lists of multiples from Exercises 4–7 to find each quotient.

8. $11 \overline{)88}$ **9.** $25 \overline{)75}$ **10.** $14 \overline{)56}$ **11.** $21 \overline{)42}$ **12.** $14 \overline{)84}$

13. $25 \overline{)100}$ **14.** $21 \overline{)105}$ **15.** $11 \overline{)99}$ **16.** $14 \overline{)70}$ **17.** $21 \overline{)147}$

Divide. Make a list of multiples to help you.

18. $12 \overline{)60}$ **19.** $17 \overline{)51}$ **20.** $26 \overline{)104}$ **21.** $21 \overline{)168}$ **22.** $52 \overline{)364}$

Problem Solving

For Problems 23–24, use the time estimates given in the chart on page 502.

23. A worker is scheduled to fold napkins for one hour. About how many napkins can he fold during this time?

24. A worker spent 125 minutes during one day chopping lettuce. How many times was she scheduled to chop lettuce?

TIPS FOR PROBLEM SOLVERS

Be confident so you can do your best.

503

Choose an Operation

PROBLEM SOLVING
GUIDE

Understand
QUESTION
FACTS
KEY IDEA

IIII▶ **Plan and Solve**
STRATEGY
ANSWER

Look Back
SENSIBLE ANSWER
ALTERNATE APPROACH

Build Understanding

The foods that you eat supply your body with energy. This energy is measured in Calories.

There were 640 Calories in the scrambled eggs that Mrs. LaRocco prepared. If there are 80 Calories in each egg, how many eggs did Mrs. LaRocco use?

Understand There are 80 Calories in each egg. There were 640 Calories in all the eggs used.

IIII▶ **Plan and Solve** STRATEGY Divide the total number of Calories by the number of Calories in each egg.

List multiples of 80 to help you divide.

$$\begin{array}{r} 8 \\ 80\overline{)640} \end{array}$$ 80, 160, 240, 320, 400, 480, 560, 640

ANSWER Mrs. LaRocco scrambled 8 eggs.

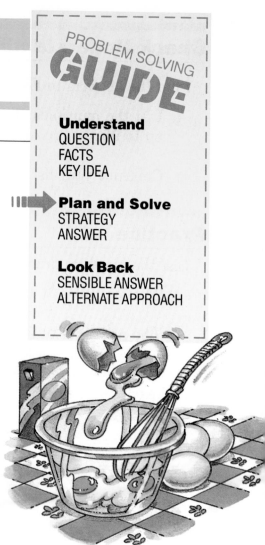

Look Back Since $80 \times 8 = 640$, an answer of 8 eggs is sensible.

■ **Talk About Math** Mrs. LaRocco divided the scrambled eggs that she prepared into 4 servings. How many eggs were in each serving? How many Calories were in each serving?

Check Understanding

Which operation is suggested by each situation?

1. Each of ▦ people drank ▦ ounces of juice. How many ounces of juice were drunk in all?

2. ▦ slices are in a loaf of bread. In making toast, ▦ slices are used. How many slices are left?

Practice

Use the data in the table for Problems 3–9. Tell whether you add, subtract, multiply, or divide. Then find the answer.

3. How many Calories are in the 4 cups of whole milk that Brian drinks each day?

4. Jodi made a salad with 4 cups of lettuce, a carrot, and a tomato. How many Calories did the salad have?

5. With salad dressing Jodi's salad contained 420 Calories. Jodi put the salad into 4 bowls. How many Calories were in each bowl of salad?

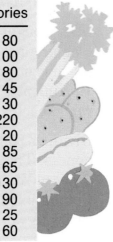

Food	Calories
apple, 1 medium	80
banana, 1 medium	100
bread, 1 slice	80
broccoli, 1 stalk	45
carrot, 1 medium	30
lamb chop, 3 oz	220
lettuce, 4 cups	20
milk, skim, 1 cup	85
milk, whole, 1 cup	165
oatmeal, 1 cup	130
potato, 1 medium	90
tomato, 1 medium	25
tuna, 2 oz	60

6. How many more Calories are in a banana than in an apple?

7. How many Calories are in 6 ounces of tuna?

8. Tim made a fruit salad with apples, celery, walnuts, and raisins. The apples provided 320 Calories. How many apples did Tim use in the salad?

9. Dean is having a lamb chop, a potato, and a stalk of broccoli. If he wants no more than 500 Calories, should he have a cup of whole milk?

Choose a ———— Strategy

Apple Addition   Solve this problem.
10. Pedro ate 21 apples in 3 weeks. Each week he ate one apple more than the week before. How many apples did Pedro eat each week?

PROBLEM SOLVING
STRATEGIES

Choose an Operation
Try and Check
Draw a Diagram
Solve a Simpler Problem
Write a Number Sentence
Make a Table
Use Logical Reasoning
Find a Pattern
Draw a Picture
Work Backward
Make a Graph

Estimation with Compatible Numbers

Build Understanding

Mrs. Gaughan's class is studying the four basic food groups. They want to divide 78 ounces of freshly squeezed orange juice equally among 19 students. About how many ounces of juice would each student receive?

Dividing 78 by 19 gives the exact number of ounces. The question does not require an exact answer. You can use **compatible numbers**. Compatible numbers are numbers that are easier to work with mentally.

Since 19 is about 20, think of a multiple of 20 that is close to 78.

$$78 \div 19$$
$$\downarrow \qquad \downarrow$$
$$80 \div 20 = 4$$

Each student will get about 4 ounces of juice.

■ **Talk About Math** How might you check that 4 ounces is a reasonable answer?

Oranges are a good source of vitamin C.

Check Understanding

For another example, see Set D, pages 518–519.

What compatible number would you use for each of these dividends if you were going to divide by 20?

1. 63   **2.** 91   **3.** 124   **4.** 86   **5.** 209   **6.** 175

What pairs of compatible numbers would you use to estimate each quotient?

7. 95 ÷ 31   **8.** 148 ÷ 24   **9.** 355 ÷ 42   **10.** 403 ÷ 49

Practice

For More Practice, see Set D, pages 520–521.

Estimate each quotient. Write the division problem
with the compatible numbers that you used.

11. 87 ÷ 29　　　**12.** 65 ÷ 32　　　**13.** 76 ÷ 25　　　**14.** 164 ÷ 41

15. 137 ÷ 22　　　**16.** 142 ÷ 71　　　**17.** 255 ÷ 53　　　**18.** 158 ÷ 19

19. 358 ÷ 64　　　**20.** 620 ÷ 88　　　**21.** 315 ÷ 57　　　**22.** 238 ÷ 39

23. 197 ÷ 49　　　**24.** 725 ÷ 82　　　**25.** 568 ÷ 71　　　**26.** 487 ÷ 77

Problem Solving

Solve each problem.

27. Use Data　Refer to the chart
on page 505. How many Calories
are in 2 slices of bread?

28. A 510-gram box of whole wheat
flakes contains 18 servings.
About how many grams of flakes
are in one serving?

Midchapter _____ Checkup

Divide. Draw ten-sticks and ones to help you.

1. 240 ÷ 60　　**2.** 180 ÷ 90　　**3.** $16\overline{)48}$　　**4.** $22\overline{)110}$

Divide. Make a list of multiples to help you.

5. $18\overline{)90}$　　**6.** $37\overline{)111}$　　**7.** $25\overline{)200}$　　**8.** $51\overline{)204}$

Estimate each quotient using compatible numbers.

9. 62 ÷ 28　　**10.** 460 ÷ 53　　**11.** 415 ÷ 62　　**12.** 485 ÷ 79

Solve each problem.

13. There are 480 Calories in a
quart of apple juice. How many
Calories are in each of the
4 cups of juice?

14. There are 145 Calories in a
slice of cheese pizza. How
many Calories are there in
3 slices of cheese pizza?

Problem Solving WORKSHOP

Real-Life Decision Making

You and your three friends made some pictures in class. Each of you will wrap one picture as a gift. You need one 48-inch strip of ribbon for each gift.

Spools of ribbon cost
4 feet 1.00
9 feet $1.20
15 feet $1.80

1. How many feet of ribbon do you need for each gift? (**Remember** that 12 inches equals 1 foot.)

2. How many feet of ribbon will you need for all four gifts?

3. List the combinations of spools of ribbon that will give you enough ribbon. (You may have extra ribbon left over.)

4. How much will it cost to buy 1 spool of ribbon 4 feet long and 1 spool of ribbon 15 feet long?

5. *Decide* which combination you will buy and why you will buy those spools.

Number-Sense Project

Look back at pages 496-497.

1. This roller coaster makes a trip, including loading and unloading, in 4 minutes. If you got at the end of the line at 2:00 P.M. and there were 240 people ahead of you, what time would it be when you got a ride? Sixteen people can ride at one time.

2. If everyone in your school were going to ride this roller coaster, how many trips would the roller coaster have to make?

3. At 4 minutes a trip, how long will it take for your whole school to have a ride?

Visual-Thinking Activity

The pattern at the left can be folded into a cube. Which of the cubes to the right can be formed from this pattern?

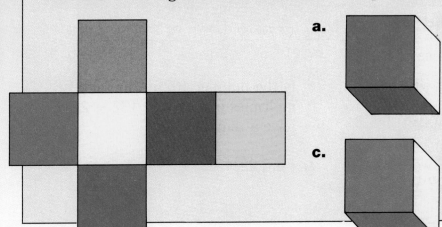

a.

b.

c.

d.

509

2-Digit Divisors and 1-Digit Quotients

Build Understanding

Mr. Klein's science class is studying plant growth. He has 180 bean seeds to share among his 22 students.

How many seeds will Mr. Klein give to each student? Will there be any seeds left over?

Find 180 ÷ 22.

Look at the table of multiples of 22. Find the largest multiple that is less than or equal to 180.

×	22
1	22
2	44
3	66
4	88
5	110
6	132
7	154
8	176	←
9	198

$$\begin{array}{r} 8\,\text{R}\,4 \\ 22\overline{)180} \\ -176 \\ \hline 4 \end{array}$$

8 seeds each with ← 4 seeds left over

Each student will receive 8 seeds. Mr. Klein will have 4 seeds left over.

Seeds need water, oxygen, and the proper temperature to germinate.

■ **Write About Math**   Show how you would check the answer.

Check Understanding

For another example, see Set E, pages 518–519.

Use the table of multiples of 22.

1. Why is the answer 8 written above the ones digit of the dividend in the example?

2. Is the number 132 in the table of multiples of 22? Will 132 ÷ 22 have a remainder?

3. What multiple of 22 would you use to find 150 ÷ 22? Why?

4. Find 22$\overline{)150}$.

Practice

For More Practice, see Set E, pages 520–521.

Use the tables of multiples to divide.

5. $60\overline{)70}$

×	60
1	60
2	120
3	180
4	240
5	300
6	360
7	420
8	480
9	540

6. $60\overline{)123}$

7. $60\overline{)500}$

8. $60\overline{)540}$

9. $60\overline{)185}$

10. $37\overline{)79}$

×	37
1	37
2	74
3	111
4	148
5	185
6	222
7	259
8	296
9	333

11. $37\overline{)190}$

12. $37\overline{)111}$

13. $37\overline{)306}$

14. $37\overline{)287}$

15. $84\overline{)90}$

×	84
1	84
2	168
3	252
4	336
5	420
6	504
7	588
8	672
9	756

16. $84\overline{)252}$

17. $84\overline{)675}$

18. $84\overline{)429}$

19. $84\overline{)645}$

Problem Solving

Use the table of multiples of 22 on page 510 when needed.

20. Mr. Klein evenly distributed 88 containers for growing bean seeds to his 22 students. How many containers did each student receive?

21. If Plant A was given 8 hours of light each day while Plant B was given 12 hours, how many more hours of light did Plant B have in a week?

22. Critical Thinking Explain why this statement is false: When you divide by a 2-digit number, the remainder is always a 1-digit number.

23. Number Sense Look at the division problem $180 \div 22$ on page 510. What would happen to the quotient if the dividend were made larger?

Reading ———— Math

Reading and Understanding Charts The foods in the chart on page 505 are listed in alphabetical order.

1. List the foods in the chart, arranging them from fewest to greatest Calories.

2. List the foods in the chart, arranging them into food groups.

3. Which is the more useful method of arranging the foods? Why?

2-Digit Divisors and 2-Digit Quotients

Build Understanding

A. You can use place-value materials to divide 195 by 12.

There are not enough hundreds to divide.

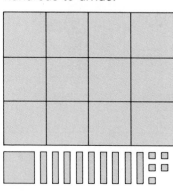

Hundreds	Tens	Ones
12) 1	9	5

Exchange 1 hundred for 10 tens. Divide 19 tens.

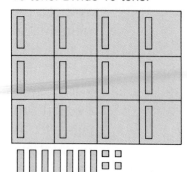

Hundreds	Tens	Ones
	1	
12) 1	9	5
− 1	2	
	7	

Exchange 7 tens for 70 ones. Divide 75 ones.

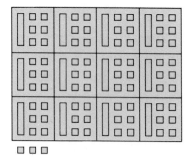

Hundreds	Tens	Ones	
	1	6	R3
12) 1	9	5	
− 1	2	↓	
	7	5	
	− 7	2	
		3	

B. You can use a table of multiples of 12 to divide 195 by 12.

$$\begin{array}{r} 16 \text{ R3} \\ 12\overline{)195} \\ -12 \\ \hline 75 \\ -72 \\ \hline 3 \end{array}$$

×	1	2	3	4	5	6	7	8	9
12	12	24	36	48	60	72	84	96	108

■ **Talk About Math**   How would you check your answer in Example B?

Check Understanding

For another example, see Set F, pages 518–519.

Copy and complete. Use the table of multiples of 12.

1.

	Hundreds	Tens	Ones
		3	▦
12)	4	2	0
	−3	6	
		▦	0
		−▦	▦
			▦

2.

	Hundreds	Tens	Ones
			▦ R▦
12)	1	1	9
	−▦	▦	▦
		▦	▦

3.

	Hundreds	Tens	Ones
			▦ R▦
12)	5	6	7
	−▦	▦	
		▦	▦
		−▦	▦
			▦

Practice

For More Practice, see Set F, pages 520–521.

Use tables of multiples to find each quotient.

4. $23\overline{)483}$ **5.** $45\overline{)765}$ **6.** $17\overline{)221}$ **7.** $30\overline{)720}$

8. $495 \div 14$ **9.** $464 \div 29$ **10.** $780 \div 25$ **11.** $868 \div 31$

Problem Solving

Solve the problem below.

12. The art teacher evenly distributed 600 strips of paper for making paper weavings among 25 students. How many strips did each student receive?

Multiple-Step Problems

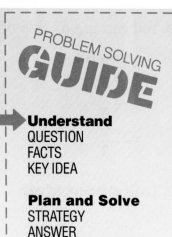

PROBLEM SOLVING
GUIDE

Understand
QUESTION
FACTS
KEY IDEA

Plan and Solve
STRATEGY
ANSWER

Look Back
SENSIBLE ANSWER
ALTERNATE APPROACH

Build Understanding

Felipa scored 45, 30, and 90 points playing 3 games of darts. What was her average score?

**Understand**   QUESTION   What is Felipa's average score per game?

FACTS   She scored 45, 30, and 90 points in 3 games.

KEY IDEA   Add the points scored. Then divide by the number of games to find the average.

Plan and Solve

Add the points.   Divide by 3.

$$
\begin{array}{r}
45 \\
30 \\
+\ 90 \\
\hline
165
\end{array}
$$

$$
\begin{array}{r}
55 \\
3\overline{)165} \\
-15 \\
\hline
15 \\
-15 \\
\hline
0
\end{array}
$$

Felipa's average score was 55 points.

Look Back   The average score is greater than the lowest score and less than the highest score, so it is a sensible answer.

■**Talk About Math**   Felipa says that if she scores 35 points in the fourth game, her average will increase. Do you agree with Felipa? Why?

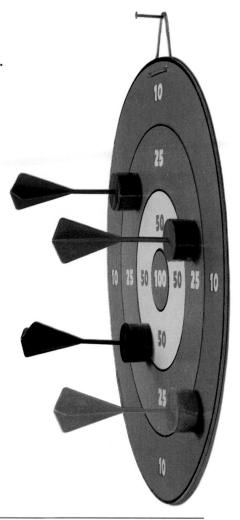

Check Understanding

There are 5 boys on each of 3 teams. If 4 boys go home, how many boys are left?

1. How many boys are on one team? How many boys are on 3 teams?

2. What happens to the total number of boys when 4 boys leave? How many boys are left?

Practice

Solve each problem.

3. Brad needs 250 points to win a video game. He captured 8 robots worth 30 points each. How many more points does Brad need to win?

4. Lisa scored 2 points for each of the 17 basketball shots she made and 6 points in free throws. How many points did she score in all?

5. While playing a ring toss game, Joe ringed four 30-point pegs and six 25-point pegs. What was his score?

6. Sandy scored 21, 34, 18, and 19 in 4 rounds of a memory game. What was her average score for a round?

7. Fred had 48 marbles. He gave 9 of them to his sister and then shared the remaining marbles equally with his two brothers. How many marbles do each of the 3 boys have?

8. A checkerboard has 8 rows with 8 squares in a row. There are as many red squares as black squares on the board. How many red squares are there?

Choose a ——— Strategy

Checkers, Anyone? Cindy organized a checker tournament for 8 players. Each player was to play one game against every other player.

9. How many games did Cindy need to schedule?

Problem Solving Review

Solve each problem.

1. Eddie read 51 books in 3 months. Each month he read 2 more books than he read the month before. How many books did Eddie read each month?

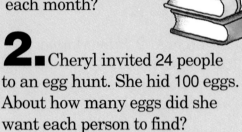

2. Cheryl invited 24 people to an egg hunt. She hid 100 eggs. About how many eggs did she want each person to find?

3. Mr. Koufax puts his homemade apple juice in 32-ounce bottles. How many bottles will he need for 224 ounces of apple juice?

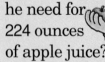

4. If Mr. Koufax wants to fill 12 bottles, how many ounces of apple juice should he make?

5. Jim scored 14, 20, 15, and 18 points in the past four basketball games. How many points must he score in the fifth game to average 17 points per game for the five games?

6. Cy Young won 511 of the 751 games he pitched. How many more wins than losses did he have?

7. **Data File** Use data from pages 524-525. Evelyn bought a pad of stationery. Find the approximate cost per sheet.

8. **Make a Data File** List 5 tall buildings and the number of stories in each building.

Explore with a Calculator

Amazing Division

1. Pick a path through each maze from the START to the END boxes. The sum of the quotients on each path must equal 100. You cannot go on a diagonal or retrace a path. Your path must go down and to the left or right.

a.

A. START	B.	C.
1,036÷37	261÷29	2,624÷64
D.	E.	F. END
3,976÷56	1,701÷63	612÷17

b.

A. START	B.	C.
378÷54	481÷13	817÷19
D.	E.	F.
700÷50	783÷87	1,020÷60
G.	H.	I. END
2,523÷87	451÷11	3,763÷71

2. This time, your path from START to END must follow a pattern. After you do some of the division problems, you will find a number pattern to follow. Once found, your path will follow the pattern to the END box. Your path will not cross itself or go on any diagonals.

A. START	B.	C.	D.	E.
294÷98	595÷85	345÷23	3,763÷71	612÷17
F.	G.	H.	I.	J.
336÷56	423÷47	924÷77	645÷43	561÷11
K.	L.	M.	N.	O.
486÷54	114÷19	399÷19	1,404÷78	1,045÷95
P.	Q.	R.	S.	T.
168÷14	782÷34	1,368÷57	343÷49	975÷25
U.	V.	W.	X.	Y. END
2,511÷81	2,684÷61	621÷23	2,520÷84	1,683÷51

Explain the pattern, and write the letters of the boxes that form your path.

Reteaching

Set A   pages 498–499

Find 120 ÷ 30.
Use ten-sticks to show 120.

Divide 120 into groups of 30.

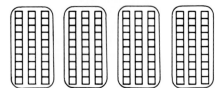

There are 4 groups of 30. So,

$$120 \div 30 = 4, \text{ or } 30\overline{)120}.$$

Remember that you can use basic division facts to help you divide.

Find each quotient. You may want to draw ten-sticks to help you divide.

1. 60 ÷ 10   **2.** 60 ÷ 20

3. 80 ÷ 20   **4.** 80 ÷ 40

5. 240 ÷ 40   **6.** 350 ÷ 50

7. 420 ÷ 60   **8.** 640 ÷ 80

Set B   pages 500–501

Use ten-sticks and ones to find
84 ÷ 16.
Form groups of 16.

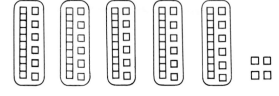

There are 4 ones left over.

$$16\overline{)84} \quad \text{5 R4}$$

Remember that the remainder must be smaller than the divisor.

Use ten-sticks and ones to find each quotient.

1. 48 ÷ 16   **2.** 64 ÷ 16

3. 92 ÷ 17   **4.** 105 ÷ 32

5. 112 ÷ 22   **6.** 154 ÷ 38

7. 106 ÷ 12   **8.** 120 ÷ 15

Set C   pages 502–503

Find 133 ÷ 19.
Use multiples of 19.

1 × 19	2 × 19	3 × 19	4 × 19
19	38	57	76

5 × 19	6 × 19	7 × 19
95	114	133

$$19\overline{)133} \quad 7$$

Remember that you can find multiples of a number by using repeated addition.

Divide. Make a list of multiples to help you.

1. 11)77   **2.** 14)70

3. 17)85   **4.** 21)126

5. 14)112   **6.** 19)152

Set D pages 506–507

Estimate 144 ÷ 18 using compatible numbers.

Since 18 is close to 20, think of a multiple of 20 that is close to 144. Multiples of 20:

20, 40, 60, 80, 100, 120, 140

144 ÷ 18

↓   ↓

140 ÷ 20 = 7

So, 144 ÷ 18 is about 7.

Remember that there may be more than one way to choose compatible numbers. Use compatible numbers to estimate each quotient.
Write the division problem with the compatible numbers that you used.

1. 78 ÷ 17   **2.** 87 ÷ 29

3. 82 ÷ 38   **4.** 145 ÷ 45

5. 172 ÷ 62   **6.** 96 ÷ 24

Set E pages 510–511

Find 262 ÷ 42.
Look at the table of multiples of 42 at the right.

Find the largest multiple of 42 that is less than or equal to 262. →

×	42
1	42
2	84
3	126
4	168
5	210
6	252
7	294
8	336
9	378

$$\begin{array}{r} 6 \text{ R}10 \\ 42\overline{)262} \\ -252 \\ \hline 10 \end{array}$$

Remember that the remainder must not be larger than the divisor.

Use the table of multiples of 42 to solve each problem.

1. $42\overline{)72}$ **2.** $42\overline{)127}$

3. $42\overline{)215}$ **4.** $42\overline{)95}$

5. $42\overline{)300}$ **6.** $42\overline{)180}$

Set F pages 512–513

Find $16\overline{)214}$.
There are not enough hundreds to divide.

Divide 21 tens. → $16\overline{)214}$
$$\begin{array}{r} 1 \\ 16\overline{)214} \\ -16 \\ \hline 5 \end{array}$$

Use the table of multiples of 16 to complete the division.

$$\begin{array}{r} 13 \text{ R}6 \\ 16\overline{)214} \\ -16 \\ \hline 54 \\ -48 \\ \hline 6 \end{array}$$

×	16
1	16
2	32
3	48
4	64
5	80
6	96
7	112
8	128
9	144

Remember to exchange hundreds for tens when there are not enough hundreds to divide.

Use the table of multiples of 16 to find each quotient.

1. $16\overline{)240}$ **2.** $16\overline{)268}$

3. $16\overline{)496}$ **4.** $16\overline{)352}$

5. $16\overline{)391}$ **6.** $16\overline{)307}$

Independent Study **RETEACHING**

More Practice

Find each quotient. You may want to draw ten-sticks to help you divide.

1. 90 ÷ 10   **2.** 80 ÷ 10   **3.** 60 ÷ 30   **4.** 100 ÷ 20

5. 120 ÷ 40   **6.** 280 ÷ 40   **7.** 400 ÷ 80   **8.** 350 ÷ 70

9. 360 ÷ 40   **10.** 360 ÷ 60   **11.** 420 ÷ 70   **12.** 630 ÷ 90

Mixed Practice   Mental Math   Find each answer.

13. 40 + 8   **14.** 60 − 6   **15.** 40 × 5   **16.** 90 ÷ 3   **17.** 80 × 4

18. 480 ÷ 8   **19.** 30 × 5   **20.** 420 − 7   **21.** 680 + 6   **22.** 540 ÷ 9

Use ten-sticks and ones to find each quotient.

1. 51 ÷ 17   **2.** 64 ÷ 16   **3.** 78 ÷ 13   **4.** 80 ÷ 14

5. $32\overline{)128}$ **6.** $28\overline{)112}$ **7.** $19\overline{)140}$ **8.** $23\overline{)184}$

Mixed Practice   Choose paper and pencil or mental math to find each quotient. Tell why you chose that method.

9. $6\overline{)240}$ **10.** $4\overline{)848}$ **11.** $5\overline{)625}$ **12.** $7\overline{)365}$ **13.** $8\overline{)560}$

List the numbers described below.

1. The multiples of 12 up to 108   **2.** The multiples of 16 up to 144.

3. The multiples of 23 up to 207   **4.** The multiples of 26 up to 156

Use your lists of multiples from Exercises 1–4 to find each quotient.

5. $12\overline{)60}$ **6.** $26\overline{)78}$ **7.** $23\overline{)92}$ **8.** $16\overline{)96}$ **9.** $23\overline{)138}$

10. $26\overline{)130}$ **11.** $16\overline{)112}$ **12.** $12\overline{)108}$ **13.** $23\overline{)184}$ **14.** $16\overline{)144}$

Divide. Make a list of multiples to help you.

15. $13\overline{)52}$ **16.** $18\overline{)72}$ **17.** $22\overline{)110}$ **18.** $27\overline{)108}$ **19.** $42\overline{)252}$

Set D   pages 506–507

Estimate each quotient. Write the division problem
with the compatible numbers that you used.

1. 37 ÷ 19   **2.** 91 ÷ 28   **3.** 78 ÷ 21   **4.** 119 ÷ 37

5. 122 ÷ 22   **6.** 304 ÷ 63   **7.** 176 ÷ 58   **8.** 291 ÷ 54

9. 284 ÷ 66   **10.** 241 ÷ 33   **11.** 403 ÷ 77   **12.** 342 ÷ 48

13. 417 ÷ 72   **14.** 483 ÷ 84   **15.** 267 ÷ 28   **16.** 635 ÷ 81

Set E   pages 510–511

Use the tables of multiples to solve each problem.

1. 40)60   **7.** 29)62   **13.** 73)91

2. 40)124   **8.** 29)101   **14.** 73)150

3. 40)330   **9.** 29)135   **15.** 73)222

4. 40)200   **10.** 29)221   **16.** 73)330

5. 40)255   **11.** 29)232   **17.** 73)547

6. 40)301   **12.** 29)164   **18.** 73)675

×	40
1	40
2	80
3	120
4	160
5	200
6	240
7	280
8	320
9	360

×	29
1	29
2	58
3	87
4	116
5	145
6	174
7	203
8	232
9	261

×	73
1	73
2	146
3	219
4	292
5	365
6	438
7	511
8	584
9	657

Set F   pages 512–513

Use tables of multiples to find each quotient.

1. 24)528   **2.** 43)774   **3.** 18)270   **4.** 20)380

5. 32)512   **6.** 37)481   **7.** 28)616   **8.** 14)364

9. 470 ÷ 15   **10.** 378 ÷ 27   **11.** 750 ÷ 31   **12.** 775 ÷ 25

13. 831 ÷ 46   **14.** 508 ÷ 21   **15.** 760 ÷ 33   **16.** 841 ÷ 29

17. 770 ÷ 15   **18.** 712 ÷ 32   **19.** 782 ÷ 46   **20.** 870 ÷ 58

Enrichment

Using a Formula

Use these formulas to find distance traveled (d), rate of speed (r), and time traveled (t).

$$d = r \times t$$
$$r = d \div t$$
$$t = d \div r$$

At a rate of speed of 75 miles per day, how far would a ship travel in 3 days?

$d = r \times t$
$d = 75 \times 3$
$d = 225$

225 miles

A ship traveled 774 miles in 18 days. What was its rate of speed?

$r = d \div t$
$r = 774 \div 18$
$r = 43$

43 miles per day

At a rate of 68 miles per day, how long would it take a ship to travel 272 miles?

$t = d \div r$
$t = 272 \div 68$
$t = 4$

4 days

Copy and complete the table. Make a table of multiples to help you divide.

	Distance traveled (d)	Rate of speed (r)	Time spent traveling (t)
1.	936 miles		24 hours
2.		95 yards per minute	6 minutes
3.	960 feet	30 feet per second	
4.	748 blocks		34 hours
5.	912 miles	48 miles per hour	

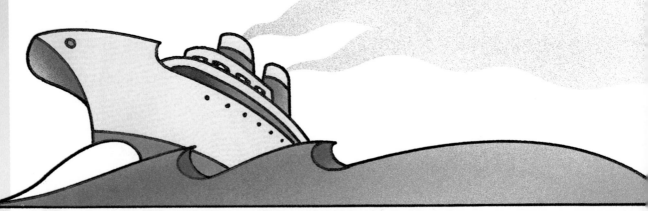

Chapter 15 Review/Test

Find each quotient. Draw ten-sticks to help you.

1. 50 ÷ 10   **2.** 160 ÷ 40

3. Complete the division sentence.

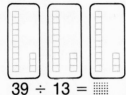

39 ÷ 13 = ▦

4. List 5 multiples of 16. Then use your list of multiples to find 64 ÷ 16.

Estimate each quotient. Write the division problem with the compatible numbers that you used.

5. 91 ÷ 29   **6.** 312 ÷ 51

Use the table of multiples to find each quotient.

7. 28)‾88‾

8. 28)‾255‾

×	28
0	0
1	28
2	56
3	84
4	112
5	140
6	168
7	196
8	224
9	252

9. Copy and complete. Use the table of multiples for 28 given with Items 7 and 8.

HUNDREDS	TENS	ONES
	3	▦
28) 8	6	9
− 8	4	
	▦	9
	− ▦	▦
		▦

10. There are 80 Calories in a slice of bread. If a loaf of the bread has 22 slices, how many Calories are in the loaf?

11. Alice got scores of 86, 89, and 95 on 3 tests. What was the average of her scores?

Read the following problem. Then answer Items 12 and 13.

A farmer planted 336 fruit trees. He planted 28 trees in each row. How many rows of trees did he plant?

12. Which sentence could be completed to answer this problem?

   a. Every row had ▦ trees.
   b. He planted ▦ trees in all.
   c. He planted ▦ rows of trees.

13. Solve the problem.

14. **Write About Math** When dividing, what do you look for in your list of multiples of the divisor?

DATA FILE

1. Map
These are rainfall amounts for some communities in Illinois. All measurements are in inches.

2. Advertisement
Prices for A, B, and C include envelopes.

3. Diagram
The abacus was invented thousands of years ago.

4. Line Graph
Students recorded the number of hours that each computer was used each month. The average usage per computer is shown in this broken line graph.

5. Chart
In a survey, 6,800 children ages 6–12 were asked to name their favorite dinner foods.

1. Rainfall Amounts

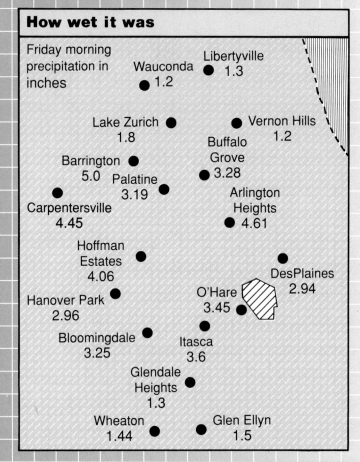

How wet it was

Friday morning precipitation in inches

Wauconda 1.2
Libertyville 1.3
Lake Zurich 1.8
Vernon Hills 1.2
Buffalo Grove 3.28
Barrington 5.0
Palatine 3.19
Arlington Heights 4.61
Carpentersville 4.45
Hoffman Estates 4.06
DesPlaines 2.94
Hanover Park 2.96
O'Hare 3.45
Bloomingdale 3.25
Itasca 3.6
Glendale Heights 1.3
Wheaton 1.44
Glen Ellyn 1.5

2. Stationery Supplies

C. Pad of Stationery

B. Thank-You Notes

A. Note Cards

Set of 12
$2.75

Set of 10
$3.00

50 Sheets
$4.10

3. The First Computer

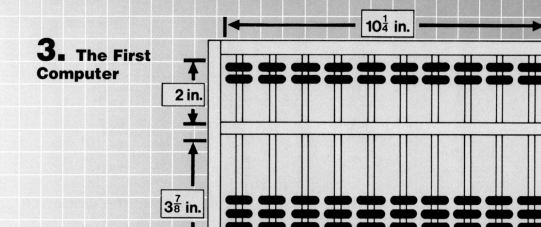

$10\frac{1}{4}$ in.

2 in.

$3\frac{7}{8}$ in.

4. Computer Use in Forest Hills Schools

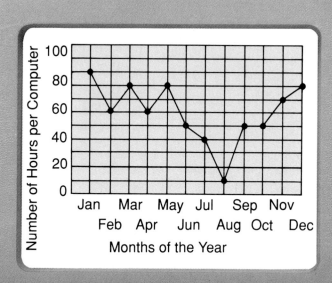

Number of Hours per Computer

100
80
60
40
20
0

Jan Feb Mar Apr May Jun Jul Aug Sep Oct Nov Dec

Months of the Year

5. Dinner Favorites

Dinner Favorites	
Pizza	2,900
Spaghetti	1,400
Chicken	1,000
Steak	800
Hamburger	700

D. All-Occasion Cards

FOR A WONDERFUL COUPLE

* Get Well *
SOON

It's your Day!

Set of 32
$7.75

Cumulative Review/Test Chapters 1–15

1. Subtract.

$$\begin{array}{r} 6,284 \\ -\,2,476 \\ \hline \end{array}$$

  a. 4,818
  b. 4,808
  c. 3,818
  d. 3,808

2. Multiply.

$$\begin{array}{r} 26 \\ \times\,53 \\ \hline \end{array}$$

  a. 910
  b. 1,310
  c. 1,378
  d. 978

3. Divide.

$7\overline{)32}$

  a. 5 R3
  b. 4 R4
  c. 3 R6
  d. 4 R5

4. Find the missing number.

7 kg = ▦ g

  a. 7,000 **c.** 700
  b. 70 **d.** 7

5. Which number sentence is true?

  a. $\frac{3}{5} < \frac{2}{5}$ **c.** $\frac{5}{8} > \frac{7}{16}$

  b. $\frac{1}{5} > \frac{1}{3}$ **d.** $\frac{7}{8} < \frac{7}{16}$

6. What is the probability of spinning an even number?

  a. 4 out of 5
  b. 5 out of 9
  c. 4 out of 9
  d. 3 out of 9

7. Estimate 761 + 132 by using front-end digits.

  a. 700 **c.** 900
  b. 800 **d.** 1,000

8. Divide.

$7\overline{)712}$

  a. 10 R12
  b. 11 R5
  c. 101 R5
  d. 110 R5

9. Which segment is a diameter?

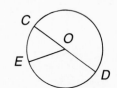

  a. *OC*
  b. *OD*
  c. *OE*
  d. *CD*

10. Which decimal represents the shaded part?

  a. 0.7
  b. 0.07
  c. 0.007
  d. 7

11. Subtract.

13.9 − 11

  a. 2.9
  b. 128
  c. 12.8
  d. 4.8

12. Find the average of the numbers.

12   18   20   22

  a. 72 **c.** 18
  b. 19 **d.** 4

13. Which number sentence is true?

  a. 0.8 = 0.08 **c.** 0.8 < 0.09
  b. 0.56 > 0.6 **d.** 1.80 = 1.8

14. Which ordered pair names point *A*?

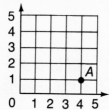

    a. (4, 1)   **c.** (4, 0)

    b. (1, 4)   **d.** (0, 4)

15. Add.

$$\frac{2}{7} + \frac{3}{7}$$

    a. $\frac{5}{7}$

    b. $\frac{5}{14}$

    c. $\frac{9}{10}$

    d. $\frac{4}{5}$

16. Estimate.

$$5\frac{11}{12} - 3\frac{1}{6}$$

    a. 4

    b. 3

    c. 8

    d. 1

17. Find the perimeter.

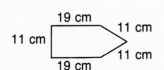

    a. 53 cm

    b. 60 cm

    c. 66 cm

    d. 71 cm

18. Estimate. Use compatible mumbers.

$$81 \div 19$$

    a. 4

    b. 40

    c. 3

    d. 30

19. Alonzo trimmed $1\frac{1}{4}$ inches from a table leg that was $28\frac{7}{8}$ inches long. How long was the leg after he trimmed it?

    a. $30\frac{1}{8}$ inches   **c.** $27\frac{6}{8}$ inches

    b. $27\frac{5}{8}$ inches   **d.** $29\frac{8}{12}$ inches

Use the graph to answer Item 20.

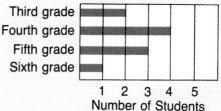

Students with Perfect Attendance

20. How many fifth-grade students had perfect attendance?

    a. 1 student   **c.** 3 students

    b. 2 students   **d.** 4 students

Read the problem below. Then answer Item 21.

Martha is packing books in boxes that hold 15 books each. How many boxes are needed if she has 75 books to pack?

21. Which number sentence can you use to solve this problem?

    a. $75 \div 15 = n$

    b. $75 - 15 = n$

    c. $75 + 15 = n$

    d. $75 \times 15 = n$

Whole Numbers Through Hundreds

Review

The number one hundred twenty-eight written in standard form is 128.
It has **3** digits. The 1 is the hundreds digit. The 2 is the tens digit. The 8
is the ones digit.

hundreds	tens	ones
1	**2**	**8**
1 hundred	**2 tens**	**8 ones**

Practice

Write each number in standard form.

1. three hundred forty

2. two hundred sixty-two

3. seven hundred ninety-six

4. four hundred ten

5. eight hundred sixteen

6. nine hundred thirty-one

7. five hundred twenty-three

8. six hundred five

Write each number in words.

9. 142   **10.** 356   **11.** 908   **12.** 715   **13.** 280

Tell what the digit 5 means in each number.

14. 538   **15.** 235   **16.** 156   **17.** 500   **18.** 850

Tell what the digit 2 means in each number.

19. 126   **20.** 200   **21.** 320   **22.** 296   **23.** 402

Tell what each digit means in each number.

24. 237   **25.** 148   **26.** 889   **27.** 502   **28.** 600

Addition Basic Facts

Review

How many bells are there in all?
This addition fact gives the answer.

$4 + 7 = 11$

There are 11 bells in all.

Practice

Find each sum.

1. $6 + 3$ **2.** $5 + 8$ **3.** $1 + 7$ **4.** $8 + 2$ **5.** $4 + 4$

6. $0 + 5$ **7.** $2 + 9$ **8.** $3 + 3$ **9.** $5 + 5$ **10.** $8 + 8$

11. $1 + 5$ **12.** $4 + 0$ **13.** $9 + 4$ **14.** $8 + 8$ **15.** $2 + 6$

16. $6 + 6$ **17.** $7 + 3$ **18.** $9 + 9$ **19.** $6 + 1$ **20.** $7 + 8$

21. $3 + 8$ **22.** $8 + 4$ **23.** $7 + 5$ **24.** $7 + 7$ **25.** $2 + 8$

26. $9 + 7$ **27.** $5 + 6$ **28.** $3 + 9$ **29.** $6 + 4$ **30.** $6 + 7$

Copy and complete each table.

31.

+	3
9	12
4	
2	
5	
8	

32.

+	5
2	
8	
4	
9	
3	

33.

+	9
1	
4	
6	
0	
8	

34.

+	8
6	
4	
9	
1	
0	

Subtraction Basic Facts

Review

How many balls would be left if you took 5 away? This subtraction fact gives the answer.

12 − 5 = 7

There would be 7 balls left.

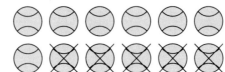

Practice

Find each difference.

1. 8 − 2	**2.** 5 − 3	**3.** 10 − 7	**4.** 3 − 1	**5.** 15 − 6
6. 9 − 2	**7.** 12 − 8	**8.** 11 − 5	**9.** 14 − 9	**10.** 6 − 2
11. 18 − 9	**12.** 13 − 7	**13.** 9 − 6	**14.** 7 − 2	**15.** 14 − 6
16. 8 − 6	**17.** 9 − 5	**18.** 10 − 6	**19.** 11 − 7	**20.** 12 − 9
21. 7 − 3	**22.** 8 − 7	**23.** 6 − 0	**24.** 8 − 4	**25.** 5 − 5
26. 14 − 8	**27.** 17 − 8	**28.** 9 − 4	**29.** 13 − 7	**30.** 15 − 9

Copy and complete each table.

31.

−	4
7	
11	
6	
13	
10	

32.

−	2
5	
4	
9	
11	
10	

33.

−	8
16	
15	
9	
11	
10	

34.

−	9
17	
11	
16	
10	
13	

Easy Multiplication Facts

Review

An arrangement of objects in rows and columns is an **array**. Every array has a matching multiplication fact.

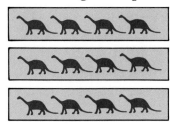 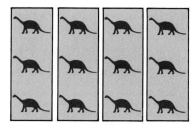

3 × 4 = 12
↑_____ Number in each group
↑_____ Number of groups

3 ← Number in each group
× 4 ← Number of groups
——
12

Remember that any number times one is that number.

Practice

Find each product. You may draw an array to help.

1. 2 ×5	**2.** 3 ×6	**3.** 3 ×1	**4.** 7 ×3	**5.** 8 ×0	**6.** 6 ×4
7. 1 ×8	**8.** 3 ×3	**9.** 9 ×2	**10.** 7 ×4	**11.** 2 ×2	**12.** 4 ×8
13. 0 ×6	**14.** 8 ×2	**15.** 5 ×3	**16.** 8 ×3	**17.** 5 ×8	**18.** 2 ×6

19. 5 × 5   **20.** 4 × 3   **21.** 0 × 4   **22.** 2 × 7   **23.** 9 × 5

24. 9 × 3   **25.** 2 × 4   **26.** 4 × 4   **27.** 7 × 5   **28.** 4 × 9

29. 4 × 5   **30.** 1 × 1   **31.** 6 × 5   **32.** 2 × 1   **33.** 0 × 9

Comparing Numbers

Review

A. Compare 24 and 58. Use < or >.

24 ⠿ 58	Compare the tens digits. 2 is less than 5.
24 < 58	24 is less than 58.

B. Compare 128 and 126. Use < or >.

128 ⠿ 126	Compare the hundreds digits. They are the same.
128 ⠿ 126	Compare the tens digits. They are the same.
128 ⠿ 126	Compare the ones digits. 8 is greater than 6.
128 > 126	128 is greater than 126.

Practice

Compare these numbers. Use > or <.

1. 9 ⠿ 3   **2.** 5 ⠿ 16   **3.** 8 ⠿ 29   **4.** 24 ⠿ 16

5. 96 ⠿ 84   **6.** 72 ⠿ 70   **7.** 38 ⠿ 46   **8.** 47 ⠿ 94

9. 13 ⠿ 17   **10.** 68 ⠿ 55   **11.** 85 ⠿ 58   **12.** 63 ⠿ 82

13. 38 ⠿ 149   **14.** 207 ⠿ 110   **15.** 381 ⠿ 211   **16.** 492 ⠿ 491

17. 806 ⠿ 608   **18.** 362 ⠿ 38   **19.** 782 ⠿ 389   **20.** 587 ⠿ 593

21. 235 ⠿ 229   **22.** 972 ⠿ 875   **23.** 41 ⠿ 417   **24.** 207 ⠿ 605

25. 773 ⠿ 792   **26.** 964 ⠿ 96   **27.** 318 ⠿ 308   **28.** 341 ⠿ 349

Ordering Numbers

Review

Write the numbers 135, 238, 26, and 42 in order from least to greatest.

Put the numbers in order by first looking at the hundreds digits.

0 hundreds	1 hundreds	2 hundreds
26	135	238
42		

Since there are no hundreds in 26 and 42, compare the tens.

2 tens < 4 tens
26   <   42

The numbers in order from least to greatest are 26, 42, 135, and 238.

Practice

Write the numbers in order from least to greatest.

1. 64   89   28   68

2. 79   97   82   43   34

3. 17   23   15   38   42

4. 26   85   19   76   55

5. 892   963   404   766

6. 143   206   630   499

7. 723   614   520   665

8. 551   515   106   240

9. 315   210   163   94

10. 18   24   124   16

11. 83   109   43   106

12. 262   342   76   142

13. 332   449   216   283

14. 206   712   217   194

15. 645   465   546   456   564

16. 787   720   802   782   847

Addition

Review

Find 238 + 76.

Add the ones.

```
  1
  2 3 8
+   7 6
───────
      4
```

Rename 14 ones
as 1 ten 4 ones.

Add the tens.

```
  1 1
  2 3 8
+   7 6
───────
    1 4
```

Rename 11 tens
as 1 hundred 1 ten.

Add the hundreds.

```
  1 1
  2 3 8
+   7 6
───────
  3 1 4
```

Practice

Add.

1. 26 + 34	**2.** 78 + 48	**3.** 49 + 34	**4.** 54 + 24	**5.** 84 + 58
6. 124 + 38	**7.** 376 + 63	**8.** 207 + 39	**9.** 614 + 93	**10.** 148 + 81
11. 368 + 46	**12.** 835 + 64	**13.** 716 + 90	**14.** 344 + 59	**15.** 645 + 86
16. 437 + 256	**17.** 745 + 245	**18.** 578 + 333	**19.** 470 + 369	**20.** 546 + 126

21. 41 + 49

22. 63 + 26

23. 35 + 46

24. 206 + 34

25. 682 + 79

26. 143 + 99

27. 603 + 129

28. 448 + 78

29. 576 + 232

30. 16 + 498

31. 47 + 853

32. 86 + 673

33. 99 + 327

34. 145 + 73

35. 57 + 783

Three or More Addends

Review

Find 326 + 43 + 138

Add the ones.	Add the tens.	Add the hundreds.

Add the ones.

```
  1
 326      6 + 3 = 9
  43
+138      9 + 8 = 17
────
   7
```

Add the tens.

```
 11
 326      1 + 2 = 3
  43      3 + 4 = 7
+138      7 + 3 = 10
────
  07
```

Add the hundreds.

```
 11
 326      1 + 3 = 4
  43
+138      4 + 1 = 5
────
 507
```

Practice

Add.

```
 1.    12      2.    37      3.    24      4.    46      5.    37
        6            15            37            17            28
      +37          + 9          + 6          +65          +15
```

```
 6.    79      7.   432      8.   140      9.   105     10.   630
      127            71           361            62            79
      +18          +54          +33          +347          +235
```

```
11.   192     12.   322     13.   306     14.   492     15.   721
      647           174           245           647           646
     +141          +429          +124          +323          +747
```

```
16.    63     17.    97     18.   532     19.   777     20.   235
       24            52            48           121           529
       43           113            36           344           716
      +36          +228          +119          +678          +543
```

21. 76 + 52 + 62 + 13   22. 46 + 56 + 65 + 71

23. 460 + 56 + 65 + 107   24. 418 + 66 + 902 + 271

25. 234 + 567 + 45 + 780   26. 432 + 524 + 791 + 142

Subtraction

Review

Find 734 − 65.

Rename to show 10 more ones.
Subtract the ones.

```
  2 14
7 3 4      3 tens and 4 ones is
−  6 5     2 tens and 14 ones.
      9
```

Rename to show 10 more tens.
Subtract the tens and hundreds.

```
6 12 14
7 3 4      7 hundreds and 2 tens is
−   6 5    6 hundreds and 12 tens.
6 6 9
```

Practice

Subtract.

1. 54 − 27	**2.** 97 − 59	**3.** 80 − 64	**4.** 34 − 23	**5.** 76 − 38
6. 364 − 81	**7.** 723 − 16	**8.** 462 − 25	**9.** 368 − 93	**10.** 226 − 48
11. 927 − 681	**12.** 635 − 250	**13.** 763 − 427	**14.** 453 − 124	**15.** 347 − 168
16. 739 − 560	**17.** 308 − 136	**18.** 830 − 619	**19.** 763 − 239	**20.** 614 − 155

21. 92 − 45   **22.** 73 − 29   **23.** 550 − 31   **24.** 137 − 29

25. 700 − 31   **26.** 417 − 37   **27.** 458 − 99   **28.** 736 − 87

29. 348 − 69   **30.** 312 − 49   **31.** 502 − 23   **32.** 225 − 58

33. 453 − 139   **34.** 625 − 486   **35.** 900 − 123   **36.** 329 − 147

37. 816 − 367   **38.** 937 − 744   **39.** 475 − 296   **40.** 533 − 377

Identifying and Counting Money

Review

A. Tell the name and value of each coin and bill.

penny
1¢ or $0.01

nickel
5¢ or $0.05

dime
10¢ or $0.10

quarter
25¢ or $0.25

half-dollar
50¢ or $0.50

dollar
100¢ or $1.00

B. Use $ and . to write the value of 2 quarters and 3 dimes. Count to find the value.

2 quarters
25, 50,

3 dimes
60, 70, 80

The amount of money is $0.80.

Practice

Write the amount of money.

1.

2.

3. 4 dimes, 3 nickels

4. 1 half-dollar, 5 pennies

5. 1 dollar, 1 quarter, 1 dime

6. 3 quarters, 4 nickels, 2 pennies

7. 3 dollars, 6 dimes, 7 nickels, 1 penny

8. 2 half-dollars, 1 quarter, 2 dimes, 3 nickels

Customary Units of Length: Inches and Feet

Review

Inches and **feet** are customary units for measuring length.
There are 12 inches in a foot.

A. Choose the most sensible answer.

Length of a notebook
1 inch   1 foot

The most sensible answer is 1 foot.

B. Measure the line segment to the nearest $\frac{1}{2}$ inch.

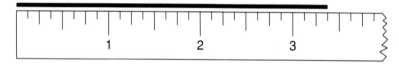

The end of the line segment is closer to $3\frac{1}{2}$ inches than 3 inches.

The length to the nearest $\frac{1}{2}$ inch is $3\frac{1}{2}$ inches.

Practice

Choose the most sensible answer.

1. Length of a paper clip
   2 inches   2 feet

2. Length of a classroom
   14 inches   25 feet

Measure each line segment to the nearest $\frac{1}{2}$ inch.

3. ─────────────────

4. ───────────

5. ──────────────────────

6. ────────────────────────────

7. ──────────────────────────────────────

Metric Units of Length: Centimeters and Meters

Review

Centimeters and meters are metric units for measuring length. There are 100 centimeters in 1 meter.

A. Choose the most sensible answer.

Height of a bicycle
1 centimeter   1 meter

The most sensible answer is 1 meter.

B. Measure the line segment to the nearest centimeter.

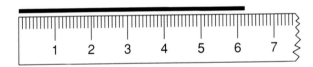

The end of the line segment is closer to 6 centimeters than 7 centimeters. The length to the nearest centimeter is 6 centimeters.

Practice

Choose the most sensible answer.

1. Length of a jump rope
2 centimeters   2 meters

2. Height of a trophy
30 centimeters   30 meters

Measure each line segment to the nearest centimeter.

3. ⎯⎯⎯

4. ⎯⎯⎯⎯⎯

5. ⎯⎯

6. ⎯⎯⎯⎯⎯⎯

7. ⎯⎯⎯⎯⎯⎯

8. ⎯⎯⎯⎯⎯⎯⎯

Geometry Terms

Review

Several geometric figures are shown below.

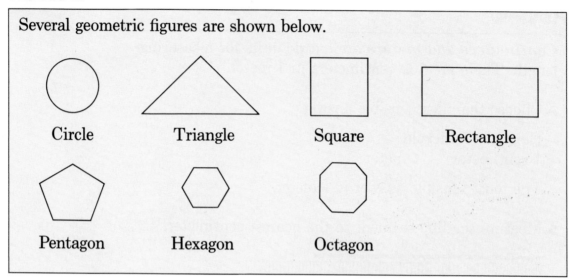

Circle   Triangle   Square   Rectangle

Pentagon   Hexagon   Octagon

Practice

Give the name of each figure. Then give the number of sides and corners that each figure has.

1.

2.

3.

4.

5.

6.

7.

8.

9.

Bar Graphs and Pictographs

Review

A. The bar graph shows the number of pets sold in Luann's Pet Shop last week. How many cats were sold last week?

The bar for cats stops at 4. So 4 cats were sold.

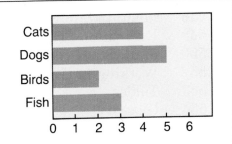

B. The pictograph shows favorite sports of students in Mr. Fischer's class. How many students like soccer best?

There are 6 pictures. Since each picture represents 2 students, 2 × 6 or 12 students like soccer best.

Favorite Sports

Basketball	☺☺☺☺
Baseball	☺☺☺
Football	☺☺☺☺☺☺
Soccer	☺☺☺☺☺☺
Tennis	☺☺

Each ☺ stands for 2 students.

Practice

Use the bar graph above to answer questions 1 and 2.

1. How many birds were sold?

2. How many more dogs than fish were sold?

Use the pictograph above to answer questions 3 and 4.

3. How many students like baseball best?

4. Do more students like soccer or baseball best?

5. Make a bar graph and a pictograph to show the data below.

Members of Ski Club	
Third graders	8
Fourth graders	10
Fifth graders	6

Independent Study Handbook

Contents

How to Use a Calculator

Calculators are used in everyday life at home and at work. They save time when solving problems with large numbers or problems with many numbers. *Remember*:

▶ **Do** estimate to check whether you pushed the correct buttons.

▶ **Don't** use a calculator when paper and pencil or mental math is faster.

Calculator displays

▶ **Number of digits** How many digits will your calculator display? If you press 99,999 × 99,999 to generate a number with more digits than the display can show, most calculators will show some kind of "error" message.

▶ **Unnecessary zeros** If you add 2.10 and 3.20, does your display show 5.3 or 5.30? Calculators usually drop unnecessary zeros.

▶ **Rounding** If you divide 2 by 3, do you see 0.6666666 or 0.6666667? Many calculators drop any digits after 8 digits, rather than round.

Calculator keys

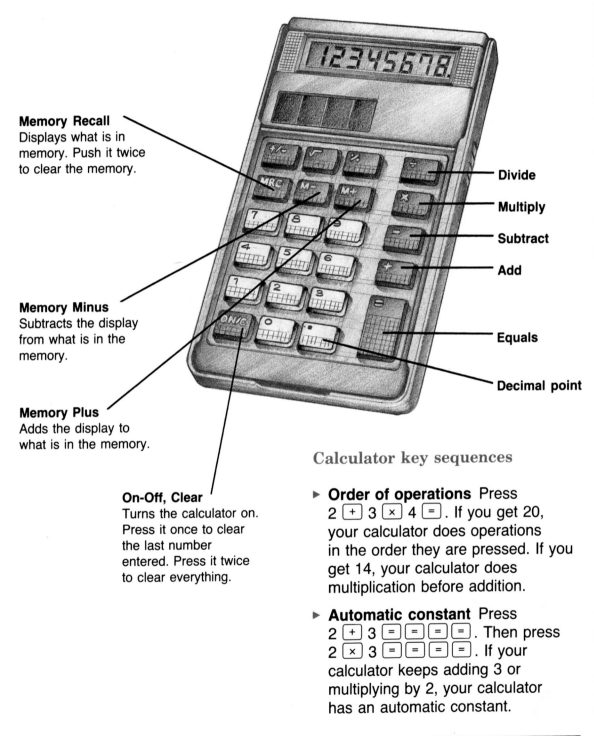

Memory Recall
Displays what is in memory. Push it twice to clear the memory.

Memory Minus
Subtracts the display from what is in the memory.

Memory Plus
Adds the display to what is in the memory.

On-Off, Clear
Turns the calculator on. Press it once to clear the last number entered. Press it twice to clear everything.

Divide

Multiply

Subtract

Add

Equals

Decimal point

Calculator key sequences

▶ **Order of operations** Press 2 ⊞ 3 ⊠ 4 ⊟ . If you get 20, your calculator does operations in the order they are pressed. If you get 14, your calculator does multiplication before addition.

▶ **Automatic constant** Press 2 ⊞ 3 ⊟ ⊟ ⊟ ⊟ . Then press 2 ⊠ 3 ⊟ ⊟ ⊟ ⊟ . If your calculator keeps adding 3 or multiplying by 2, your calculator has an automatic constant.

Problem-Solving Help File

Use these pages when you need help with problem solving.

Problem-Solving Guide

There is no recipe or magic formula for solving problems. But keeping a problem-solving guide in mind can help you become a better problem solver.

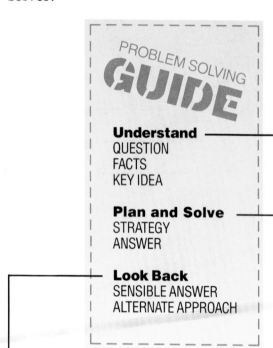

PROBLEM SOLVING GUIDE

Understand
QUESTION
FACTS
KEY IDEA

Plan and Solve
STRATEGY
ANSWER

Look Back
SENSIBLE ANSWER
ALTERNATE APPROACH

Understand
QUESTION
- ▶ What are you asked to find?
- ▶ Try to state the question in your own words.
- ▶ Is an exact answer needed?

FACTS
- ▶ What facts are given?
- ▶ Is there too much or too little information?
- ▶ Is data needed from a picture, table, graph?
- ▶ Do you need to collect some data?

KEY IDEA
- ▶ How are the facts and the question related?
- ▶ Are there groups that are part of a whole?
- ▶ Are two groups being compared?
- ▶ Are there groups that are joining or separating?
- ▶ Are there groups of the same size?

Plan and Solve
STRATEGY
- ▶ What can you do to solve the problem?
- ▶ Can the problem be solved by computing?
- ▶ Estimate the answer.
- ▶ Choose a strategy. Try another, if needed.

ANSWER
- ▶ Give the answer in a sentence.
- ▶ Do you need to interpret a remainder?
- ▶ Is rounding needed?

Look Back
SENSIBLE ANSWER
- ▶ Did you check your work?
- ▶ Did you use all the needed data?
- ▶ Does your answer have the correct units?
- ▶ Is your answer close to the estimate?
- ▶ Is your answer reasonable for the situation?

ALTERNATE APPROACH
- ▶ Is there another way to get the same answer?
- ▶ Could you use the same strategy differently?
- ▶ Would another strategy be faster or simpler?

Problem-Solving Strategies

You might think of problem-solving strategies as problem-solving tools that you own and use when needed. One or more strategies might be used for a problem. And if one strategy doesn't work, try another one.

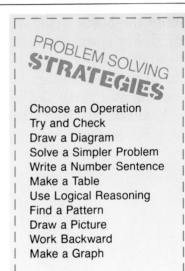

PROBLEM SOLVING **STRATEGIES**

Choose an Operation
Try and Check
Draw a Diagram
Solve a Simpler Problem
Write a Number Sentence
Make a Table
Use Logical Reasoning
Find a Pattern
Draw a Picture
Work Backward
Make a Graph

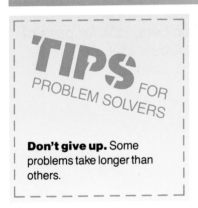

TIPS FOR PROBLEM SOLVERS

Don't give up. Some problems take longer than others.

Problem-Solving Behaviors and Attitudes

When you solve problems, do you give up quickly or lack confidence? Behaviors and attitudes can affect your work. So, remember these tips. They can help you become a better problem solver.

Tips for Problem Solvers

▶ **Don't give up.** Some problems take longer than others.

▶ **Be flexible.** If you get stuck, try another idea.

▶ **Be confident** so you can do your best.

▶ **Take risks.** Try your hunches. They often work.

▶ **Brainstorm to get started**—one idea will lead to another.

▶ **Visualize the problem** in your mind to help you understand it better.

▶ **Compare problems** to help you relate new problems to ones you've solved before.

▶ **Think about your thinking.** Pause to ask, "How is this going to help me solve the problem?"

▶ **Share your thinking with others.** Explaining your ideas helps you think better.

▶ **Organize your work** to help you think clearly.

545

Mental Math Strategies

Often the best calculator is your own mind. For simple calculations, mental math can be better than paper and pencil or a calculator. To sharpen your mental math skills, use the mental computation strategies shown on these pages.

Breaking Apart Numbers

Break apart one or more numbers to get numbers that are easier to use.

54 + 23
54 + 20 + 3   Break apart 23.
74 + 3
77

87 × 2
(80 + 7) × 2   Break apart 87.
(80 × 2) + (7 × 2)   Use the distributive
160 + 14   property.
174

35 + 48
(30 + 5) + (40 + 8)   Break apart 35 and 48.
(30 + 40) + (5 + 8)   Regroup the numbers.
70 + 13
83

Compatible Numbers

Compatible numbers are pairs of numbers that are easy to use. Look for numbers like 1, 10, 100 or 3, 30, 300 that are easy to use.

40 + 30   **28 × 10**
70   280

180 ÷ 60
3

When there are 3 or more numbers, look for pairs of numbers that are compatible.

3 + 48 + 7
3 + 7 + 48
10 + 48
58

$\frac{1}{3}$ **× 7 × 12**
$\frac{1}{3}$ × 12 × 7
4 × 7
28

Using Equivalent Forms

Divide to find "fraction of."

$$\frac{1}{3} \times 180$$
$$180 \div 3$$
$$60$$

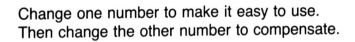

Compensation

Change one number to make it easy to use. Then change the answer to compensate.

57 + 29

$57 + 30 = 87$	Add 1 to 29 to get 30.
$87 - 1 = 86$	Subtract 1 from the answer.

165 − 97

$165 - 100 = 65$	Add 3 to 97 to get 100.
$65 + 3 = 68$	Add 3 to the answer.

Change one number to make it easy to use. Then change the other number to compensate.

66 + 19

$65 + 20$	Add 1 to 19 and subtract
85	1 from 66.

157 − 98

$159 - 100$	Add 2 to 98 and to 157.
59	

Estimation Strategies

In everyday life, an exact answer is often unnecessary. For example, you can estimate while shopping to see if you have enough money.

When you do need an exact answer, estimation helps you find possible errors. Estimation is especially important for checking whether you pushed a wrong button on a calculator.

To help you make good estimates, use the estimation strategies shown on these pages.

Front-End Digits

Use just the first digit in each number to help you make an estimate.

$$
\begin{array}{rr}
173 & 100 \\
421 & 400 \\
+348 & +300 \\
\hline
& 800
\end{array}
$$

You can also adjust the estimate by adding 100 to get 900.

$$4\tfrac{1}{2} + 6\tfrac{5}{8} + 2\tfrac{1}{3}$$
$$4 + 6 + 2$$
$$12$$

Rounding

Round to one nonzero digit.

$$
\begin{array}{rr}
425 & 400 \\
\times\ 28 & \times 30 \\
\hline
& 12{,}000
\end{array}
$$

Round to the same place.

$$
\begin{array}{rr}
28.45 & 28 \\
-\ 3.79 & -\ 4 \\
\hline
& 24
\end{array}
$$

$$13\tfrac{1}{4} + 8\tfrac{7}{8}$$
$$13 + 9$$
$$22$$

Round to the nearest half.

$$\tfrac{3}{8} + 2\tfrac{5}{8} + \tfrac{1}{4}$$
$$\tfrac{1}{2} + 2\tfrac{1}{2} + \tfrac{1}{2}$$
$$3\tfrac{1}{2}$$

Round both numbers up and both numbers down to get a range.

$$57 \times 84 \qquad \begin{array}{l} 60 \times 90 = 5{,}400 \\ 50 \times 80 = 4{,}000 \end{array}$$

57×84 is between 4,000 and 5,400.

Substituting Compatible Numbers

Use numbers that are close to the original numbers.

$23)\overline{476}$

$24)\overline{480}$ or $23)\overline{460}$ or $25)\overline{500}$

$23)\overline{476}$ is about 20.

24 × 78 × 4

25 × 78 × 4

100 × 78

24 × 78 × 4 is about 7,800.

$\frac{1}{3} \times 187$

$\frac{1}{3} \times 180$

$\frac{1}{3} \times 187$ is about 60.

26% of 32

25% of 32

$\frac{1}{4} \times 32$

26% of 32 is about 8.

Clustering

Look for groups of numbers that are close to the same number.

6,278	Each number
6,589	is about 6,000,
5,893	so the sum is
+6,134	about
	4 × 6,000 or
	24,000.

$4\frac{7}{8} + 5\frac{1}{5} + 4\frac{2}{3}$

Each number is about 5, so the sum is about 3 × 5 or 15.

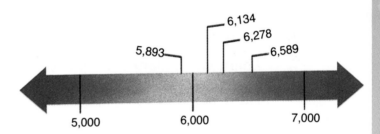

Comparing to a Reference Point

Compare the numbers to numbers you can work with easily.

346	Both numbers are less than 500, so the
+438	sum is less than 1,000.

$\frac{5}{8} + \frac{3}{5}$ Both numbers are greater than $\frac{1}{2}$, so the sum is greater than 1.

Math Study Skills

Try these math study skills to help you do your best.

Before a Lesson

▶ **Preview the lesson.** Look over the lesson to see what it's about.

▶ **Set a purpose.** Are you about to learn a new topic or revisit a familiar one?

▶ **Recall what you know.** What have you learned about this topic previously?

Build Understanding

Reading the lesson

▶ **Read slowly.** Don't try to read a math book as fast as a story book.

▶ **Learn vocabulary and symbols.** Note new math terms and symbols. Use the glossary and index. Watch for words like "product" that have other meanings outside of math.

▶ **Read diagrams, tables, graphs.** Use a ruler to help you read rows and columns.

▶ **Do the examples.** Work the examples yourself as you go through them.

Doing Activities

▶ **Use materials.** Keep the materials organized. Use them to explore new ideas.

▶ **Work with others.** When you work with others, use the tips for working together given on page 552.

Build Understanding

A. A market gets boxes of 24 heads in each box. H heads of lettuce are in

Since each box contai same number of he

Check Understanding

Trying on your own

▶ **Note what you don't understand.** When you try some exercises, be aware of what you don't understand.

▶ **Reread the lesson.** When you don't understand, reread the "Build Understanding" section.

Preventing errors

▶ **Find another example.** When you need another example, turn to the "Reteaching" set at the back of the chapter.

▶ **Try again.** Keep trying until you feel you understand.

Practice and Problem Solving

Reading the exercises

▶ **Read directions.** Read carefully.

▶ **Read word problems.** Read slowly and reread, if needed.

Doing written work

▶ **Show your work.** Record what you did. Make your paper easy to follow and the answer easy to find.

▶ **Check your work.** Read what you write.

▶ **Find more practice.** Use the "More Practice" at the back of the chapter when needed.

After a Lesson

▶ **Look back.** Summarize the lesson. Would you be able to teach it to another student?

▶ **Connect to other lessons.** Think about how this lesson is related to other lessons.

Working in Groups

When you do math working with others, you'll learn more math, you'll learn how to work as a team, and you'll enjoy math more.

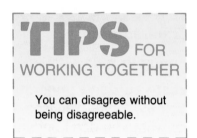

Roles for Group Members

When you work in a group, it can be helpful for each person to have a role. Some roles are:

▶ **Reporter**—This person summarizes the group's thinking.

▶ **Encourager**—This person encourages group members to take part and to work together well.

▶ **Recorder**—This person records the group's work.

▶ **Checker**—This person asks group members to explain their thinking or may ask others if they agree.

▶ **Materials Manager**—This person gets any materials that are needed and returns them at the end of class.

Tips for Working Together

Here are some tips for working well with others in a group.

▶ Involve your whole group. Help everyone to participate.

▶ Help keep your group on task.

▶ To make sure your group understands the task or solution, have each group member say it in his or her own words, summarize the steps, or give an example.

▶ Work as a group. If you understand, help another group member. Don't work ahead of the others.

▶ Be a good tutor. Make up similar problems or easier ones to help someone understand.

▶ When you are unsure, ask someone in your group for help or say you don't understand.

▶ Tell someone when he or she does or says something that helps you.

▶ Don't decide by voting. Try to understand which might be the best solution and why.

▶ Remember, you can disagree without being disagreeable.

Tables

Metric System

Length

10 millimeters (mm)	= 1 centimeter (cm)
10 centimeters 100 millimeters	= 1 decimeter (dm)
10 decimeters 100 centimeters	= 1 meter (m)
1,000 meters	= 1 kilometer (km)

Area

100 square millimeters (mm^2)	= 1 square centimeter (cm^2)
10,000 square centimeters	= 1 square meter (m^2)
100 square meters	= 1 are (a)
10,000 square meters	= 1 hectare (ha)

Volume

1,000 cubic millimeters (mm^3)	= 1 cubic centimeter (cm^3)
1,000 cubic centimeters	= 1 cubic decimeter (dm^3)
1,000,000 cubic centimeters	= 1 cubic meter (m^3)

Mass (weight)

1,000 milligrams (mg)	= 1 gram (g)
1,000 grams	= 1 kilogram (kg)
1,000 kilograms	= 1 metric ton (t)

Capacity

1,000 milliliters (mL)	= 1 liter (L)

Time

60 seconds	= 1 minute
60 minutes	= 1 hour
24 hours	= 1 day
7 days	= 1 week
365 days 52 weeks 12 months	= 1 year
366 days	= 1 leap year

Addition-Subtraction Table

+	0	1	2	3	4	5	6	7	8	9
0	0	1	2	3	4	5	6	7	8	9
1	1	2	3	4	5	6	7	8	9	10
2	2	3	4	5	6	7	8	9	10	11
3	3	4	5	6	7	8	9	10	11	12
4	4	5	6	7	8	9	10	11	12	13
5	5	6	7	8	9	10	11	12	13	14
6	6	7	8	9	10	11	12	13	14	15
7	7	8	9	10	11	12	13	14	15	16
8	8	9	10	11	12	13	14	15	16	17
9	9	10	11	12	13	14	15	16	17	18

Multiplication-Division Table

×	1	2	3	4	5	6	7	8	9
1	1	2	3	4	5	6	7	8	9
2	2	4	6	8	10	12	14	16	18
3	3	6	9	12	15	18	21	24	27
4	4	8	12	16	20	24	28	32	36
5	5	10	15	20	25	30	35	40	45
6	6	12	18	24	30	36	42	48	54
7	7	14	21	28	35	42	49	56	63
8	8	16	24	32	40	48	56	64	72
9	9	18	27	36	45	54	63	72	81

Customary System

Length

12 inches (in.)	= 1 foot (ft)
3 feet 36 inches	= 1 yard (yd)
1,760 yards 5,280 feet	= 1 mile (mi)
6,076 feet	= 1 nautical mile

Area

144 square inches (sq in.)	= 1 square foot (sq ft)
9 square feet	= 1 square yard (sq yd)
4,840 square yards	= 1 acre (A)

Volume

1,728 cubic inches (cu in.)	= 1 cubic foot (cu ft)
27 cubic feet	= 1 cubic yard (cu yd)

Weight

16 ounces (oz)	= 1 pound (lb)
2,000 pounds	= 1 ton (T)

Capacity

8 fluid ounces (fl oz)	= 1 cup (c)
2 cups	= 1 pint (pt)
2 pints	= 1 quart (qt)
4 quarts	= 1 gallon (gal)

Glossary

Add To find the total when putting together two or more quantities.

Addend A number that is added. In 8 + 4 = 12, the addends are 8 and 4.

Angle (∠) The figure formed by two rays with the same endpoint.

Area A number given in square units that indicates the size of the inside of a plane figure.

Array An arrangement of objects or numbers in rows and columns.

Associative property (Grouping property) The way in which addends (or factors) are grouped does not affect the sum (or product).
(7 + 2) + 5 = 7 + (2 + 5)
(7 × 2) × 5 = 7 × (2 × 5)

Average A number obtained by dividing the sum of two or more addends by the number of addends.

Basic fact A number sentence that has at least two one-digit numbers. The sentences below are examples of basic facts.
7 + 2 = 9   16 − 7 = 9
5 × 3 = 15   8 ÷ 4 = 2

Billion The word name for 1,000,000,000.

Broken-line graph A drawing that shows how quantities change over time.

Centimeter A unit of length in the metric system. Your little finger is about 1 centimeter wide.

Circle A plane figure with all points the same distance from a given point called the *center*.

Circumference The distance around a circle.

Closed figure A figure with an inside and an outside.

Clustering An estimation method used when all the numbers are close to the same number.

Common denominator A common multiple of two or more denominators. A common denominator for $\frac{1}{6}$ and $\frac{3}{8}$ is 48.

Common factor A number that is a factor of two or more numbers. A common factor of 6 and 12 is 3.

Common multiple A number that is a multiple of two or more numbers.

Commutative property (Order property) The order in which numbers are added (or multiplied) does not affect the sum (or product).
4 + 6 = 6 + 4
4 × 6 = 6 × 4

Compass An instrument used for drawing circles.

Compatible number A number close to the number in the problem being solved that is used for mental computation.

Composite number A whole number, greater than 0, that has more than two factors.

Cone A solid figure formed by connecting a circle to a point not in the plane of the circle.

Congruent figures Two figures with the same size and shape.

Coordinates Integers in an ordered pair giving the location of a point in a coordinate plane.

Count A number of particular things.

Cube A prism with all square faces.

Cup A unit for measuring capacity in the customary system. 2 cups equals 1 pint.

Cylinder A space figure with two circular bases that are parallel and congruent.

Data A collection of gathered information that has not been organized.

Decimal A number used to name a whole quantity and/or a fractional part. It is written in standard form with a point to separate the whole number and fraction parts.

Decimeter A metric unit for measuring length. 10 decimeters equal 1 meter.

Degree (of an angle) A unit for measuring angles.

degree Celsius A unit for measuring temperature in the metric system.

degree Fahrenheit A unit for measuring temperature in the customary system.

Denominator The number below the line in a fraction. It names the number of equal parts or objects. In $\frac{3}{4}$, the denominator is 4.

Diagonal In a polygon, a line segment that connects corners not next to each other.

Diameter In a circle, a segment that passes through the center and that has both endpoints on the circle.

Difference The number found by subtracting one number from another. In 95 − 68 = 27, the difference is 27.

Digit One of the symbols used for writing numbers: 0, 1, 2, 3, 4, 5, 6, 7, 8, and 9.

Distributive property If a factor is a sum, multiplying each addend before adding does not change the product.

Divide To find how a total amount can be separated into an equal number of groups, or into groups of equal size.

Dividend A number that is divided by another number.

Divisible One number is divisible by another if the remainder is zero after dividing.

Divisor The number by which another number is divided.

Edge Segment where two faces of a polyhedron meet.

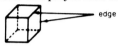

Endpoint The point at the end of a line segment or a ray.

Equal decimals Decimals that name the same number. 1.8 and 1.80 are equal decimals.

Equal fractions Fractions that name the same number. $\frac{2}{3}$ and $\frac{8}{12}$ are equal fractions.

Equally likely Outcomes that will happen about as often as each other.

Equation A number sentence used to show how the parts of a problem are related.

Estimate A number that is close to another number. A name used for a calculation not requiring an exact answer.

Even number A whole number that has 0, 2, 4, 6, or 8 in the ones place.

Expanded form A way to write a number to show the value of each digit.

Face Flat surface that is part of a polyhedron.

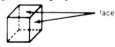

Factor (1) A number to be multiplied. (2) A number that divides evenly into a given second number is a factor of that number.

Family of facts The related number sentences for addition and subtraction (or multiplication and division) that contain all the same numbers.

$$5 + 3 = 8 \qquad 8 - 3 = 5$$
$$3 + 5 = 8 \qquad 8 - 5 = 3$$

Flip A change in location of a figure by flipping it over a line, creating a mirror image (reflection) of the figure.

Foot A unit for measuring length in the customary system. 1 foot equals 12 inches.

Fraction A number that names a part of a whole or of a set. It is written in the form $\frac{a}{b}$.

Frequency The number of times a certain item occurs in a set of data.

Front-end digit The digit in a number that has the greatest place value.

Gallon A unit for measuring capacity in the customary system. 1 gallon equals 4 quarts.

Geometric figure A closed shape made with line segments or curves in a plane.

Gram A unit for measuring weight in the metric system. A raisin weighs about 1 gram.

Graph A drawing used to show information in an organized way. Some types of graphs are *bar graphs* and *pictographs*.

Greater than (>) A relation between two numbers with the greater number given first. 8 > 5   9 > 1.4

Grouping Putting a known number of objects into each group and making as many groups as you can.

Hexagon A six-sided polygon.

Hundredth The name for one of 100 equal parts.

Improper fraction A fraction whose numerator is greater than or equal to its denominator.

Inch A unit for measuring length in the customary system. A paperclip is about 1 inch long.

Integers The whole numbers and their opposites. Some integers are +3, -3, 0, +16, -16.

Intersecting lines Lines that meet at a point.

Kilogram A unit for measuring weight in the metric system. 1 kilogram equals 1,000 grams.

Kilometer A unit for measuring length in the metric system. 1 kilometer equals 1,000 meters.

Label To use letters, numbers, or words to name, or identify something

Less than (<) A relation between two numbers with the lesser number given first. 5 < 8   1.4 < 9

Line A set of points continuing without end in both directions.

Line graph A drawing that shows the rate at which something happens.

Line plot A graph that uses Xs to show information and compare quantities.

Line of symmetry A line on which a figure can be folded into two congruent parts.

Liter A unit for measuring capacity in the metric system. 1 liter equals 1,000 milliliters.

Lowest terms A fraction for which 1 is the greatest common factor of both the numerator and the denominator.

Measure A number found by comparing the length, capacity, or weight of something with a unit.

Meter A unit for measuring length in the metric system. 1 meter equals 100 centimeters.

Mile A unit for measuring length in the customary system. 1 mile equals 5,280 feet.

Milliliter A unit for measuring capacity in the metric system. An eyedropper holds about 1 milliliter.

Million The word name for 1,000,000.

Mixed number A number that has a whole number part and a fraction part.

Multiple A multiple of a number is the product of that number and a whole number.

Multiply To find the total when putting together groups of equal size, or to find the number that is "times as many" as another number.

Number pair See Ordered pair.

Number sentence A way to write a relationship between numbers.
18 + 27 = 45   9 > 6

Numerator The number above the line in a fraction. It names the number of parts or objects being thought about. In $\frac{3}{4}$, the numerator is 3.

Octagon An eight-sided polygon.

Odd number A whole number that has 1, 3, 5, 7, or 9 in the ones place.

Ordered pair A pair of numbers arranged so there is a first number and a second number, used to locate a point on a grid.

Ordinal number A number, such as *third,* used to tell *order* or position of things in a group.

Organized list All the possibilities for a situation written in a certain order.

Ounce A unit for measuring weight in the customary system. A slice of bread weighs about 1 ounce.

Outcome A possible result of an action.

Parallel lines Lines in a plane that never meet.

Parallelogram A quadrilateral with opposite sides parallel and congruent.

Pattern A general idea by which things or numbers can be arranged or events can happen in an organized way.

Pentagon A five-sided polygon.

Percent (%) A word meaning "hundredths" or "out of 100." 45 percent (45%) equals 0.45 or $\frac{45}{100}$.

Perimeter The sum of the lengths of the sides of a polygon.

Perpendicular lines Lines that intersect to form right angles.

Pint A unit for measuring capacity in the customary system. 1 pint equals 2 cups.

Place value The number each digit represents is determined by the position the digit occupies.

Plane A flat surface that extends without end in all directions.

Point An exact location in space.

Polygon A plane figure made by line segments called *sides,* each side meeting two other sides, one at each of its endpoints.

Polyhedron A solid figure made up of flat surfaces called *faces.* Each face is a polygon.

Polyomino A figure made of squares that are the same size. Each square shares at least one of its sides with another square.

Pound A unit for measuring weight in the customary system.

Prime factor A factor that is a prime number. The prime factors of 10 are 2 and 5.

Prime number A whole number, greater than 1, that has exactly two factors: itself and 1.

Prism A polyhedron with two parallel, congruent faces, called bases. All other faces are parallelograms.

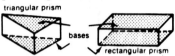

Probability A number from 0 to 1 that tells how likely it is that a given outcome will occur. The closer to 1, the *more likely* the outcome is to occur. The closer to 0, the *less likely* it is to occur.

Product The number found by multiplying numbers. In 27 × 3 = 81, the product is 81.

Proper fraction A fraction that is less than 1.

Property of one The product of one and a number is that number.

Property of zero The sum of zero and a number is that number. The product of zero and a number is zero.

Protractor An instrument used to measure angles.

Pyramid A polyhedron formed by connecting points of a polygon to a point not in the plane of the polygon. The polygon and its interior is the *base.*

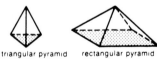

triangular pyramid   rectangular pyramid

Quadrilateral A four-sided polygon.

Quart A unit for measuring capacity in the customary system. 2 pints equals 1 quart.

Quotient The answer after dividing one number by another.

Radius   In a circle, a segment that connects the center of the circle with a point on the circle.

Range   The difference between the greatest and the least numbers in a set of data.

Ratio   A pair of numbers that names a rate or a comparison.

Ray   A set of points that has one endpoint and that extends without end in one direction.

Rectangle   A parallelogram with four right angles.

Regular polygon   A polygon with all sides congruent and all angles congruent.

Remainder   The number that is left over after dividing. When 20 is divided by 6, the remainder is 2.

Repeating decimal   A decimal in which one or more digits keep repeating, such as 0.518181818...

Rhombus   A parallelogram with four congruent sides.

Right angle   An angle with a measure of 90°.

Right triangle   Triangle with one right angle.

Rounded number   A number expressed to the *nearest 10, 100, 1,000,* and so on. 368 rounded to the nearest 10 is 370; rounded to the nearest 100 is 400.

Sample   Part of a group upon which an experiment or survey is conducted.

Segment   Two points and the part of a line between them.

Sequence   A set of numbers formed by a pattern.

Sharing   Putting the same number of objects into each group when you know the number of groups.

Side   (1) A segment used to form a polygon. (2) A ray used to form an angle.

Similar figures   Figures with the same shape but not necessarily the same size.

Slide   A change in location of a figure by moving it without turning it.

Solid figure   A figure that has three dimensions, length, width, and height.

Sphere   A solid figure with all points the same distance from a given point called the *center*.

Square   (Geometry) A rectangle with four congruent sides. (Numeration) To multiply a number by itself.

Square products   A sequence of numbers that can be shown by dots arranged in the shape of a square.

Standard form   The notation for writing numbers using the digits 0–9 and each place represents a power of ten.

Statistics   Numerical facts that are collected, organized and analyzed.

Subtract   To find how many are left when some are taken away, or to compare two quantities.

Sum   The number found by adding numbers. In 8 + 4 = 12, the sum is 12.

Surface   The faces of a solid figure.

Survey   To get an overview by gathering data.

Symmetric figure   A plane figure that can be folded in half so the two halves match.

Tally chart   A table to help with counting when collecting data.

Terminating decimal   A decimal with an exact number of nonzero digits, such as 0.375.

Tenth   The name for one of 10 equal parts.

Thousand   The word name for 1,000.

Triangle   A three-sided polygon.

Triangular numbers   A sequence of numbers that can be shown by dots arranged in the shape of a triangle.

Turn   A change in location of a figure by moving it around a given point.

Unit fraction   A fraction with a numerator of one

Vertex   (1) The point where the 2 sides of an angle meet. (2) The point where 2 sides of a polygon meet. (3) The point where edges of a polyhedron meet.

Volume   A number given in cubic units that indicates the size of the inside of a solid figure.

Watt   A measure of electric power.

Whole number   One of the numbers 0, 1, 2, 3, and so on.

Yard   A unit for measuring length in the customary system. 1 yard equals 3 feet.

Index

INDEX

The Stock Market: Tom
Bean 496–497; Peter Beck
428–429; Robert Garvey 70;
Brownie Harris 176–177,
428–429; Kalish/Dimaggio
176–177; Roy Morsch 2–3; Kunio
Owaki 64; Ben Simmons
176–177; Christopher Springman
509; Richard Steadman
176–177; Wes Thompson
212–213 Harald Sund: 50

Illustrations
Jacque Auger, Ron Becker, Eliot
Bergman, Randall Birkey, Lloyd
Birmingham, Alex Bloch, Lee Lee
Brazeal, Dan Bridy, David Cain,
Susan Johnston Carlson, Pat
Chapin, Chi Chung, Jim Deigan,
Jim Delapine, Nancy Didion, Mac
Evans, David Febland, Mark
Fisher, Robert Frank, Janice
Fried, Toni Goffe, Renee Graef,
Susan Gray, Fred Harsh, Steve
Henry, Mark Herman, Lionel
Kalish, Mark Kaplan, Andy
Levine, Ron Lieberman, Peter
McMahon, Kimble Mead, James
Needham, Earl Parker, Charles
Peale, Bob Pepper, Brenda
Pepper, Magdalen Pierrakos,
Sandra Shap, Deborah Sims,
Susan Skoorka, Kirsten
Soderlind, Randy South, Barton
Stabler, Susan Swan, Phyllis
Tarlow, Rhonda Voo

Data
p. 248. From Amtrak Train
Schedule, "S.F. Bay
Area–Sacramento Valley."
Reprinted by permission of
National Railroad Passenger
Corporation